Power and Wealth in Rural China

The Political Economy of Institutional Change

Boasting one of the fastest growing economies in the world at the turn of the twenty-first century, China is simultaneously making the transition from agriculture to industry and from socialism to capitalism. China's rural industrial sector (also known as township and village enterprises) has been the engine driving much of the Chinese economy's dynamism since the initiation of economic reform in 1978. Thus, rural industry provides a uniquely valuable window on the issue of institutional change.

This book examines changes in the institutions governing rural industry. Susan Whiting explains not only the striking regional variation in the form of property rights in rural industry during the first decade and a half of China's post-Mao reform, but also the dramatic move toward privatization that has occurred throughout China since the mid-1990s. She further relates the evolution of property rights to changes in state extractive institutions. Property rights in rural industry shaped the development of local state extractive institutions during the first fifteen years of reform, and political conflicts created by these same institutions were an impetus for major national fiscal reforms in 1994. As dramatic as these changes in both property rights and fiscal institutions are, they can be readily understood in the context of the theoretical framework developed in the study.

Whiting develops a dynamic approach to the study of institutional change by theorizing across three levels of analysis. She argues that institutional change can best be explained by examining the complex interactions of individuals, institutions, and the broader political economy. Analysis at the individual level provides careful, empirical grounding for assumptions about individual behavior; analysis at the institutional level examines the ways in which local institutions create incentives for and constraints on individual actions; and analysis at the level of the national political economy focuses on how changes in the broader environment can transform the incentives and constraints imposed by local institutions. The analysis draws on research in political economy, cognitive psychology, and evolutionary economics to advance our understanding of institutional change in comparative politics.

Employing comparative case-study and quantitative evidence gathered during twenty-one months of field and archival research, Whiting also challenges two dominant interpretations of rural industrial development in China: the view that all rural industry was self-reliant from its inception, operating completely outside of state plans, and the claim that all rural industry was effectively disciplined by market forces even in the early years of reform.

Susan H. Whiting is Assistant Professor of Political Science at the University of Washington.

Cambridge Modern China Series

Edited by William Kirby, Harvard University

Other books in the series:

Warren I. Cohen and Li Zhao, eds., *Hong Kong under Chinese Rule: The Economic and Political Implications of Reversion*

Tamara Jacka, *Women's Work in Rural China: Change and Continuity in an Era of Reform*

Shiping Zheng, *Party vs. State in Post-1949 China: The Institutional Dilemma*

Michael Dutton, *Streetlife China*

Edward Steinfeld, *Forging Reform in China: The Fate of State-Owned Industry*

Jing Huang, *Factionalism in Chinese Communist Politics*

Edmund Fung, *In Search of Chinese Democracy: Civil Opposition in Nationalist China, 1929–1949*

Yung-Chen Chiang, *Social Engineering and the Social Sciences in China*

Xin Zhang, *Social Transformation in Modern China: The State and Local Elites in Henan, 1900–1937*

David Shambaugh, ed., *The Modern Chinese State*

Power and Wealth in Rural China

The Political Economy of Institutional Change

SUSAN H. WHITING

University of Washington

CAMBRIDGE
UNIVERSITY PRESS

PUBLISHED BY THE PRESS SYNDICATE OF THE UNIVERSITY OF CAMBRIDGE
The Pitt Building, Trumpington Street, Cambridge, United Kingdom

CAMBRIDGE UNIVERSITY PRESS
The Edinburgh Building, Cambridge CB2 2RU, UK
40 West 20th Street, New York, NY 10011-4211, USA
10 Stamford Road, Oakleigh, VIC 3166, Australia
Ruiz de Alarcón 13, 28014 Madrid, Spain
Dock House, The Waterfront, Cape Town 8001, South Africa

http://www.cambridge.org

First published 2001

Printed in the United States of America

Typeface Times New Roman 10/13 pt.   *System* QuarkXPress™ [BTS]

A catalog record for this book is available from the British Library.

Library of Congress Cataloging in Publication Data

Whiting, Susan H., 1964–
Power and wealth in rural China: the political economy of institutional change / Susan
H. Whiting.
p.   cm. – (Cambridge modern China series)
Includes bibliographical references and index.
ISBN 0-521-62322-7 (hbk.)
1. Rural industries – China   I. Title.   II. Series.

HC427.92.W52 2000
338.951′0091734 – dc21   99-054879

ISBN   0 521 62322 7   hardback

For my family

Contents

List of Maps, Figures, and Tables   *page* xi
Preface   xv

1 Explaining Institutional Change   1
    Institutional Change in State and Market   5
    Institutional Variation and Change in
        Rural Industry   20
    Design of the Study   29
    Structure of the Book   37

2 The Maoist Legacy in Rural Industry   40
    Historical Accounts of Rural Industrialization   44
    Central State Policy toward Rural Industry   46
    Local State Policy toward Rural Industry   53
    Conclusion: The Legacies of the Maoist Era   70

3 Incentive Structures and Local Cadre Behavior   72
    The Township Fiscal System   74
    The Cadre Evaluation System   100
    Conclusion: Reevaluating the "Township as
        Corporation" Model   118

4 Incentives, Constraints, and the Evolution of
    Property Rights   121
    The Spatial Pattern of Property Rights   123
    The Quest for Credible Commitment:
        Aggressive Policy Innovation and Private
        Investor Choice in Wenzhou   151
    Conclusion: The Evolution of Property Rights   173

ix

5   Stasis and Change in Extractive Institutions   176
     The Institutional Legacy of the Centrally
       Planned Economy   178
     The Evolution of Local Institutions for Revenue
       Extraction from the Newly Emerging Private Sector   182
     Resistance to Institutional Change in
       the Collective Sector   197
     Subnational Regulatory Frameworks   213
     A Test of the Hypotheses   219
     Conclusion: Property Rights, Regulatory
       Environments, and Revenue Mobilization   224

6   Credit Allocation and Collective Organizational
     Structures   226
     Banking System Reforms: System Structure and
       Policy Goals   227
     Implementation of Credit Policy in the
       Collective Sector   234
     Implementation of Credit Policy in the Private Sector   258
     Conclusion: State Building and Financial Reform   263

7   The Political Economy of Institutional Change   265
     Change in Local Institutions before 1994   267
     Reform at the National Level: "Endogenizing"
       Central State Institutions   277
     Change in Local Institutions after 1994   289
     Conclusion: The Politics of Market Transition   293

Appendix   300
Bibliography   315
Index   343

Maps, Figures, and Tables

MAPS

1.1 Map of China Showing Jiangsu, Shanghai, and
Zhejiang   *page* 33
1.2 Map of Jiangsu, Shanghai, and Zhejiang Research
Sites   34

FIGURES

1.1 Explaining Institutional Change at the Local Level   26
1.2 Administrative Hierarchy Governing Townships in
the Research Sites   31
2.1 Gross Value of Industrial Output (GVIO), Township
(Commune) and Village (Brigade) Level and Below,
1949–78   41
2.2 GVIO Per Capita, Township (Commune) and Village
(Brigade) Level and Below, 1949–78   42
3.1 Newspaper Cartoon Illustrating Lack of Attention to
Efficiency   112
3.2 Newspaper Cartoon Illustrating Lack of Attention to
Salability of Products   113
4.1 Total Value of Fixed Assets of Private Shareholding
Cooperatives, Yueqing County, Wenzhou, 1986–94   172
4.2 Gross Value of Industrial Output by Ownership, 1994   174
7.1 Central Government Share of Total Budgetary
Revenue and Expenditure, 1978–97   282
7.2 Gross Value of Industrial Output by Ownership, 1997   291
7.3 Explaining Local and National Institutional Change   294

TABLES

1.1	Explaining Institutional Change at the Local Level	27
1.2	Regional Variation in Industrial Output by Ownership at Mid-Reform, 1990	32
1.3	Regional Variation in Economic Structure at Mid-Reform, 1990	35
2.1	Gross Value of Industrial Output, 1949–78	43
2.2	Gross Value of Agricultural and Industrial Output Per Capita, 1949–78	54
3.1	Nantang Township Fiscal Accounts, 1990–91	81
3.2	Total Revenues in Nantang Township, Jiading County, Shanghai, 1988–91	87
3.3	Total Revenues in Songyang Town, Songjiang County, Shanghai, 1989–95	88
3.4	Sources of Township Revenue, 1991	88
3.5	Township Government Funds Derived from Collective and Private Firms	97
3.6	National Guidelines for Performance Criteria of Local Party and Government Leaders	103
3.7	Performance Criteria for Township Government Executives and Party Secretaries, Jiading County, Shanghai, 1989	106
3.8	Taxes Owed by Township- and Village-run Enterprises, 1978–97	114
4.1	Gross Value of Industrial Output, by Ownership Type, Township Level and Below, 1978–97	128
4.2	Original Value of Fixed Assets in Industry	130
4.3	Ownership Breakdown of Large-scale Rural Industry, Hualing Town, Wenzhou, 1991	169
4.4	Growth of Shareholding Cooperatives, Township Level and Below, Yueqing County, Wenzhou, 1985–94	170
5.1	Sample Composition of the "Simultaneous Taxation" Rate for Private Enterprises in the Electronics Industry, Hualing Town, Wenzhou	186
5.2	Taxation of Township- and Village-run Collectives, 1978–97	206
5.3	The Impact of Ownership Form and Provincial Environment on the Tax Ratio	224
6.1	Agriculture Bank and Rural Credit Cooperative Assets and Liabilities, 1987–95	230

6.2   Loans to Township- and Village-run Enterprises and
      Rural Household Savings Deposits, 1978–95   232
6.3   Losses of Township- and Village-run Enterprises,
      1985–97   248
6.4   Sources of Fixed-asset Investment for Township- and
      Village-run Enterprises, 1987–97   252

Preface

THIS book represents an effort to make the concerns of those engaged in the study of Chinese politics relevant to students of comparative politics, to extend the boundaries of comparative theory, and to shed new light – both empirically and theoretically – on the issue of institutional variation and change in China.

Empirically, the book focuses on the development of China's rural industrial sector since 1949. In theoretical terms, it develops a dynamic approach to the study of institutional variation and change by engaging in theorizing across three levels of analysis. Analysis at the individual level provides careful, empirical grounding for assumptions about individual behavior; analysis at the institutional level examines the ways in which local institutions create incentives for and constraints on individual actions; and finally, analysis at the level of the national political economy focuses on the ways in which changes in the broader environment can transform the incentives and constraints imposed by local institutions.

This approach allows me to explain in a systematic manner not only the striking regional variation in the form of property rights in rural industry during the first decade and a half of China's post-Mao reform, but also the dramatic move toward privatization that has occurred throughout China since the mid-1990s. Moreover, I show that the evolution of property rights and state extractive institutions are integrally related. Property rights in rural industry shaped the evolution of local state extractive institutions during the first fifteen years of reform, and political conflicts created by these same institutions were an impetus for major national fiscal reforms in 1994. As stark a departure from the previous policy environment as the post-1994 fiscal reforms appear to be, and as dramatic a repudiation of the past as the privatization of public enterprises appears to be, these developments can be readily understood in the context of the theoretical framework developed in the study.

Much of the recent research in the statist tradition in comparative politics has focused exclusively on the institutional level of analysis, thus overlooking many of the motive forces for institutional change. Research in the rational choice tradition has brought individual motivations into the calculus, but assumptions about individual motivations often lack adequate empirical foundation. Findings in cognitive psychology regarding the limited cognitive processing capabilities of human decision makers and the pervasiveness of imperfect information highlight the need for richer contextualization of individual decision processes. Research in the rational choice tradition has also focused on predicting unique, "first-best" outcomes. However, not only are individuals not perfectly rational, but also selection pressures in the environments in which individuals and enterprises exist are themselves imperfect and do not always lead to "first-best" outcomes. Nevertheless, when selection pressures in the environments change, outcomes are likely to change as well. In order to explain institutional change, therefore, we must take into account forces for change that come from both individual actions and the broader environment.

This study addresses both variation and change in institutions, and the research on which it is based spans both space and time. It is the culmination of twenty-one months of field and archival research conducted in China and Hong Kong between 1991 and 1999. The research was designed as a comparative case study of three locales, and it addresses developments over four decades, from the 1950s to the present, with a focus on the period of reform from 1978 to the late 1990s.

Although the conditions for fieldwork in China have improved dramatically since 1978, the fieldwork for this project posed many challenges. The original research design called for sites to be selected for variation in the concentration of property rights forms in rural industry, including public, private, and foreign ownership. Research sites in Songjiang County of Shanghai Municipality and Yueqing County of Zhejiang Province met the criteria for concentration of public and private ownership, respectively. However, gaining approval for the third site, the one in which foreign ownership predominated – a site originally intended to be in Guangdong Province – proved to be bureaucratically infeasible at the time fieldwork began in 1991 to 1992. As a result, I selected another site in which public ownership predominated – Wuxi County in Jiangsu Province. This unavoidable consequence of the research environment, by generating two sites in two different provinces in which public ownership predominated, ultimately enabled me to develop and test a new hypothesis about the effect of the provincial regulatory environment on revenue extraction from rural industry. Thus, the research environment not only threw up roadblocks but also created opportunities.

A second challenge involved the nature of the research itself. During the early 1990s, the very concept of private property rights was controversial in China – particularly among local government officials. As a result, probing questions – in interviews either with local officials or with enterprise owners and managers – about how an investor's claims on assets were enforced (or not) were perceived as politically sensitive by my informants. Similarly, questions about revenue extraction – particularly those involving tax evasion, not surprisingly – could be sensitive as well. What was surprising was the wide range of response styles to these questions among my informants. Informants were selected both through official introductions and through informal encounters, but response styles did not vary on this basis. Some informants were open and forthcoming in interviews – regardless of the nature of our introduction. By the same token, some informants stuck to the official line – again regardless of the nature of our introduction.

As this discussion suggests, protecting the identity of informants is of utmost importance. Therefore, the names of townships and villages where research was conducted have been changed, and informants are identified only by interview number in the text. An appendix links the interview number with the informant's position and institutional affiliation and the date of the interview.

Like the financial debts of many of the enterprises I investigated for this project, the personal debts I have incurred in the course of research and writing are too numerous to repay. While many of the people who helped me with this project must remain anonymous, I am happy to be able to thank some of the most important people by name. Official support in China was critical to coordinating with local cadres in each of the research sites, to setting up interviews with a complete set of local government bureaus, and to attaining as representative a sample of enterprises in each site as was possible. The Shanghai Academy of Social Sciences (SASS) provided an excellent institutional base. Zhang Zhongli, SASS president and a University of Washington alumnus, was gracious, enthusiastic, and most supportive. Xie Zifen, director of the

SASS Institute of the National Economy, was a warm and welcoming host. Ling Yaochu, director of the SASS Center for Research on Rural Enterprises, was a wonderful colleague and friend. This project could not have been completed without their support. Ling Yaochu's fellow researchers at the center made it a home away from home for me. I am honored to know them. The representatives of the foreign office at SASS were always ready to help. Finally, I thank the faculty and staff of the Department of International Politics at Fudan University who provided early institutional support.

In Hong Kong, Jean Hung, vice director of the Universities Service Centre of the Chinese University of Hong Kong, made my time there both productive and enjoyable.

This book began as my doctoral dissertation at the University of Michigan, and many thanks are due to the members of my committee: Michel Oksenberg, Kenneth Lieberthal, Robert Dernberger, Yasheng Huang, and Matthew Evangelista all provided invaluable advice throughout the project. I have also been privileged to have stimulating colleagues both at the University of Washington and beyond who have influenced this manuscript in innumerable ways, large and small. In particular, I would like to thank David Bachman, Tani Barlow, Yoram Barzel, Loren Brandt, Kiren Chaudhry, Madeleine Yue Dong, Gary Hamilton, Stephen Hanson, Stevan Harrell, Kent Guy, Nicholas Lardy, Margaret Levi, Jamie Mayerfeld, Joel Migdal, Barry Naughton, Victor Nee, Kevin O'Brien, Jean Oi, Albert Park, Elizabeth Perry, Kazimierz Poznanski, Scott Rozelle, Dorothy Solinger, Andrew Walder, Christine Wong, and Glennys Young. Naturally, responsibility for any remaining errors of evidence or interpretation is my own.

The research for this book was completed in part with financial support from the Committee on Scholarly Communications with the People's Republic of China and the American Council of Learned Societies with funds from the Chiang Ching-kuo Foundation. Additional support was provided through the University of Washington by a Boeing Faculty Assistance Grant and a China Studies Faculty Research Grant. I wish to thank these sponsors for their support.

Some material in the book appeared previously, in different forms, in three publications: *Property Rights and Economic Reform in China*, edited by Jean C. Oi and Andrew G. Walder, published by Stanford University Press, 1999; *Trust and Governance*, edited by Valerie Braithwaite and Margaret Levi, published by Russell Sage Foundation, 1998; and

Reforming Asian Socialism: The Growth of Market Institutions, edited by John McMillan and Barry Naughton, published by University of Michigan Press, 1996. I am grateful to the publishers for permission to use the material here. I am also grateful to Cai Yong of the University of Washington for assistance with the maps that appear in the book.

Mary Child and Helen Wheeler of Cambridge University Press shepherded the book through the production process with great care and good cheer. Nancy Hearst, the librarian at the Fairbank Center for East Asian Research of Harvard University, brought her expertise to bear in proofreading. I offer my thanks to them for the roles they played in the publication of the book.

"Unofficial" support was also critical to this project. My brother, Van Whiting Jr., gave me my theoretical ambitions, and my parents, Sara and Van Whiting, supported me in all my endeavors to pursue them. To my family I express my love and appreciation in dedicating this book to them.

1

Explaining Institutional Change

A MID predictions that the opening years of the new millennium will
usher in a "Chinese century," we are confronted daily with conflicting images of the Chinese state – at once predatory and developmental, weak and strong. Indeed, the "reach of the state"[1] is an issue of
vigorous debate not only among students of Chinese politics but also
among students of comparative politics. The debate centers on the capacity of the state to promote the generation of wealth and to command
some portion of that wealth for state purposes.[2] While arguments about
state strength or weakness pervade the literature, they are, by their very
nature, inconclusive. What the debate fails to capture fully is the extent
to which state capacity changes over time and varies across policy arenas
and geographic settings. Rather, the "reach of the state" ultimately
depends on the nature of the institutions that govern the economy and
society. This study moves beyond formulations of state strength or
weakness and focuses the analysis on issues of institutional variation and
change.

Institutional change is at the heart of the rapid socioeconomic transformation in China since 1978. With one of the fastest growing economies
in the world at the beginning of the twenty-first century, China is simultaneously making the transition from agriculture to industry and from

---

[1] This term is borrowed from the title of Vivienne Shue's (1988) book, *The Reach of the State: Sketches of the Chinese Body Politic*.

[2] A note on my use of the term "state" is necessary at the outset. While a convenient shorthand, the term is in no way intended to imply that "the state" can act in any meaningful
way apart from the individuals who populate its offices. I adopt the Weberian definition
of the state as a complex organization, staffed by individuals and composed of numerous agencies across various levels of administration, that has a monopoly on the legitimate use of coercion and the authority to establish binding rules in a given territory
(Gerth and Mills 1946:78).

socialism to capitalism.[3] This study examines changes in the institutions governing one of the most dynamic sectors of China's economy – the rural industrial sector.[4] Rural industrial output has grown at an average annual rate of nearly 25 percent in real terms since the initiation of economic reform in 1978. As of the late 1990s, it accounted for fully 45 percent of total industrial output, although it generated a much smaller share of total state tax revenue (*Zhongguo tongji nianjian* 1998).

While the remarkable expansion of rural industry is undisputed, theoretical puzzles about how rural industrial wealth is generated and who commands that wealth remain unresolved. The first puzzle concerns the striking regional variation in property rights that has characterized China's rural industrial sector.[5] This study focuses on rural industrial development in three locales: Wuxi, Shanghai, and Wenzhou – home to some of the wealthiest and most industrialized counties and townships in China.[6] However, the wealth of these locales was based on very different forms of property rights. Through the mid-1990s, publicly owned firms dominated rural industry to varying degrees in Wuxi and Shanghai, while privately owned firms dominated in Wenzhou. Such variation is surprising in light of the claims of neoliberal economic theory about the strict necessity of private property rights for economic growth. Such variation might also seem surprising because it arose out of the Maoist era, which some scholars (e.g., Kelliher 1992) have portrayed as characterized by uniformity in the rural economic structure.[7] In fact, as this study shows, regional variation stems in part from patterns of state intervention in the economy that prevailed during the Maoist period.

I argue that central state institutions in place at the beginning of the

---

[3] The agricultural sector accounted for half of total employment in 1997. Private ownership of productive assets and market allocation of factors and products occupy growing proportions of the Chinese economy. These transformations play central roles in this study.

[4] "Rural industry" refers to all industrial enterprises at the levels of the township (formerly the commune), village (formerly the brigade), and below – hence the common usage of township and village enterprises (TVEs) to refer to the sector as a whole.

[5] The rural industrial sector encompasses a wide array of ownership forms ranging from collective firms (*jiti qiye*) that are owned and run by community governments to private firms (*siying qiye*) that are owned and run by individuals. The terms "ownership" and "property rights" are used interchangeably; a formal definition of property rights is introduced in the next section.

[6] These locales are introduced in greater detail later in this chapter.

[7] By contrast, other scholars (e.g., Perry 1980) have highlighted the ecological and institutional diversity of the Chinese countryside. This study builds on this tradition of scholarship.

reform era created strong positive incentives for local state officials to promote rural industry. However, the choices of local officials concerning what forms of property rights to support were constrained by distinct local resource endowments inherited from the Maoist period as well as by incompleteness in national market and legal institutions in the post-Mao era. Dependence on local resource endowments on the one hand, and complementarities between the nature of market and legal institutions and the form of property rights on the other, combined to create apparent path dependence in the trajectories of rural industrial development in each region.[8]

As the incentives and constraints created by the national institutional environment changed, however, so did the property rights forms that local officials were likely to support. This framework explains both the apparent path dependence of property rights forms during the first decade and a half of reform and the dramatic move toward privatization of publicly owned firms and widespread support for new entry of private firms that began to occur during the mid-1990s in areas where public ownership had previously dominated. The core of this study focuses on the apparently path-dependent development of distinct regional patterns of property rights through the mid-1990s. The concluding chapter of this book shows how and why movement off the path is now taking place.

The second puzzle concerns the ability of the Chinese state to extract revenue from and control the allocation of credit to the rural industrial sector in ways consistent with central state priorities. This ability is subject to dispute and differing interpretation. Some scholars (e.g., Pei 1997; Walder 1995) find pervasive bureaucratic decay undermining state capacity, while others (e.g., Blecher and Shue 1996; Shue 1988) find growing bureaucratic competence and strength. However, assessments of China as either a weak or a strong state fail to adequately capture the nature of institutional change.

As this study will show, the form and effectiveness of extractive institutions and allocative practices were integrally related to the forms of property rights in each locale. The constellation of property rights determined to a large extent the level of information costs and the distribution

---

[8] Complementarities arise when the presence of one institution or policy increases the utility of or benefits from another institution or policy. Path dependence occurs when the outcome of a dynamic process is highly sensitive to a seemingly insignificant feature of initial conditions. Its importance in economic analysis derives from the claim that it can lead to inefficient outcomes not predicted by standard neoclassical economic models (Arthur 1989; Liebowitz and Margolis 1995).

of bargaining power confronting local officials within each community. In communities where private ownership dominated, political and economic power were quite distinct. As a result, local officials faced high information costs in governing private firms. At the same time, the bargaining power of private capital constrained the ways in which local state officials innovated in the design of extractive institutions to cope with high information costs. Surprisingly, however, where institutional innovations were employed to extract revenue from private firms for local coffers, these innovations also revealed new fiscal capacity to the central state.

By contrast, in communities where public ownership dominated, the fusion of political and economic power in the hands of local state officials allowed these local leaders to harness the resources of the community to their own political purposes. Although one might expect the central state to exercise relatively effective control over all public enterprises, even those located at the local level, local officials were able to manipulate revenue extraction to hide fiscal capacity from higher levels and to channel credit on concessional terms from the state-run banking system to local public firms. Ultimately, such strategic maneuvering on the part of local state officials helped to precipitate the initiation of major national reforms in fiscal, banking, and legal institutions beginning in November 1993.[9] As the concluding chapter of this book shows, these reforms have begun to transform the institutional landscape of the Chinese countryside, fundamentally altering the incentives that shape how local officials intervene in the local economy.

This book represents an effort to develop a dynamic approach to the study of institutional variation and change. The approach explores the complex interactions of individuals, institutions, and their broader environment to explain the process of change. In so doing, the book integrates theories located at three distinct levels of analysis. At the individual level, it develops empirically grounded assumptions about the goals pursued by the individuals embedded in local state and market institutions. At the institutional level, it provides an analysis of the incentives and constraints created by local institutions and how those incentives and constraints influence the ways in which individuals pursue their goals. At the level of the national political-economic system, it derives insights from evolutionary theories of economic change to analyze how shifts in the national institutional environment transform the incentives

---

[9] Zhonggong zhongyang, "Guanyu jianli shehui zhuyi shichang jingji tizhi ruogan wenti de jueding (Decision regarding Several Questions on the Establishment of a Socialist Market Economic System)," *Guowuyuan gongbao* No. 28 (1993), pp. 1286–302.

and constraints created by local institutions. Viewed from an evolutionary perspective, even dramatic changes have clear origins that can be identified in the interactions of individuals, institutions, and the broader environment in which those institutions exist. This framework helps to explain the dominance of public ownership in Wuxi and Shanghai from the Maoist period through the first decade and a half of reform, as well as the dramatic move toward privatization of public enterprises in these locales beginning in the mid-1990s. It also helps to explain the expanding presence of private capital in the Chinese economy more generally and the challenges for state revenue mobilization that accompany the transition to a private, market economy.

This chapter explicates the theoretical and methodological underpinnings of the study. The opening section examines how social scientists exploring the role of the state in development have come to focus on the evolution of institutions linking the state and the economy. It also presents an overview of the core concepts derived from institutional economics that inform the approach to institutions taken in this study. The next section illustrates how these concepts can be used to explain the evolution of property rights, extractive institutions, and allocative practices in rural industry. The penultimate section describes the research design. The last section provides an outline of the book as a whole.

INSTITUTIONAL CHANGE IN STATE AND MARKET

"The state" has been at the center of scholarly inquiry in the fields of comparative politics and political economy for more than two decades.[10] Reacting against the claims of modernization and dependency theorists on the one hand,[11] and neoliberal theorists on the other,[12] statist theo-

---

[10] The publication of the volume *Bringing the State Back In* self-consciously marked the reemergence of statism as an important perspective (Evans, Rueschemeyer, and Skocpol 1985). It hearkened back to the classic insights of Weber as well as more recent work by economic historians such as Polanyi and Gerschenkron. Path-breaking works consistent with the statist perspective include Evans (1979), Katzenstein (1978), Krasner (1978), Stepan (1978), Trimberger (1978), and Zysman (1977).

[11] Modernization theory suggests that the nature of the development process is determined mainly by the characteristics and values of the domestic economy and society. Dependency theory explains developmental outcomes based primarily on a country's position in the global political-economic structure and on the interaction between that global structure and the domestic class structure. These theories have been extensively reviewed elsewhere. See, for example, Huntington (1971), Migdal (1983), Smith (1979; 1985), and Valenzuela and Valenzuela (1978).

[12] Neoliberal theory is addressed in subsequent paragraphs.

rists hold that the state has an important, independent impact on social, political, and economic development within its borders. A central preoccupation of those working in the statist tradition has been to understand the determinants of state capacity – broadly defined as the state's ability "to penetrate society, regulate social relationships, extract resources, and appropriate or use resources in determined ways" (Migdal 1988:4). However, this quest has been hindered by the lack of theoretical tools necessary to build a dynamic theory that can adequately account for institutional change. Such an account is crucial because institutions are themselves the building blocks of state capacity.

The approach to institutional change that I develop in this study weds insights from institutional economics to the concerns of comparative politics. Explaining institutional change requires bridging three distinct levels of analysis encompassing theories regarding the motivations of individuals, the nature of institutions in which individuals are embedded, and the dynamics of the broader environment in which institutions function. As I demonstrate here, much of the recent research in the statist tradition has focused on the institutional level of analysis to the neglect of cross-level theorizing.[13]

Statism and Its Critics

In contrast to statist theory, neoliberal theory regards the interventionist state as a serious impediment to development (Buchanan, Tollison, and Tullock 1980). This view reflects the dual conviction that efficient allocation of resources is the key to development and that efficient resource allocation is best achieved through the unfettered functioning of the market.[14] Neoliberals, therefore, concede only a minimal role for the state – a role limited to protecting individual rights to both person and property and enforcing voluntarily negotiated private contracts (Buchanan 1980:9).

Statist theorists, on the other hand, regard the accumulation of capital for productive investment and the direction of investment capital to particular uses, rather than efficient resource allocation per se, as the keys

---

[13] Cortell and Peterson (1999) and Remmer (1997) also make this point.

[14] However, the very notion of a free market that functions in the absence of effective regulation by the state has been questioned by political economists and economic historians as diverse as Adam Smith (1965 [1776]) and Karl Polanyi (1957 [1944]). The point has been driven home forcefully by Russia's painful experience with the transition to capitalism. See also Chaudhry (1993).

to economic development (Amsden 1989; Gerschenkron 1962). Moreover, as Alexander Gerschenkron's fundamental insight reveals, the later the timing of industrialization, the greater the role of the state in facilitating this process. Thus, analysis of the state as an agent of economic development is a central concern of the statist perspective.

Much of the early "state-centered" research equates state autonomy with state strength (Evans, Rueschemeyer, and Skocpol 1985). State autonomy implies that decision makers are capable of pursuing economic goals distinct from those of any particular group in society. The sources of autonomous state interests have a diverse genealogy: they reflect both the realist emphasis on the state's unique position at the boundary between domestic society and the international state system, and the neo-Marxist emphasis on the state's position as ultimate guarantor of hegemony by the putative ruling class (Skocpol 1979; Stepan 1978).

Work in a more empirical vein identifies as sources of state autonomy the degree of insulation of state institutions and political elites from societal pressures and the degree of ideological coherence among those who staff state institutions (Evans 1995; Haggard 1990).[15] In particular, studies of East Asian developmental states have focused on the ability of highly autonomous state agencies to use tax, credit, and trade policies to promote the rapid development of particular industries (Wade 1990).[16] Such ability has enabled the newly industrialized countries of East Asia to demonstrate considerable "virtuosity in moving through the product cycle" in the decades since the end of Japanese colonialism in the region (Cumings 1981:2). In contrast, studies of post-colonial Africa have emphasized the predatory nature of the state, in which state power is used to benefit a narrow segment of the elite, thus undermining rather than enhancing the potential for economic development (Bates 1981).

Elaboration of a typology of "developmental" and "predatory" states, however, fails to capture the complexities of institutional stasis and change. In Peter Evans' (1995) formulation, developmental states such as Korea and predatory states such as Zaire both enjoy significant autonomy vis-à-vis society, but they differ in terms of their societal

---

[15] This type of research also represents an effort to disaggregate excessively reified notions of "the state" by examining the interests and capabilities of particular agencies.

[16] The best of these studies identify the social, political, and historical roots of autonomy exercised by state agencies. In addition to Wade (1990), see Winckler and Greenhalgh (1988).

embeddedness. For Evans, embeddedness, or the density of connections between public agencies and private citizens, is essential to the developmental state's ability to formulate collective goals and promote social welfare. "Embedded autonomy" is desirable because embeddedness provides information channels that link state and society and facilitate policy implementation while autonomy prevents state power from being captured by narrow societal interests. This account of embedded autonomy is too static, however. Because Evans (1995:44) defines regime types in terms of the developmental outcomes they produce, his analysis becomes tautological, foreclosing the possibility of analyzing dynamic interaction between state and societal forces. Thus, his analysis fails to explain how state capabilities are enhanced or dissipated over time.

Indeed, examined temporally, the notion of state autonomy and the relationship of state autonomy to state capacity are highly problematic. State governance of capital and the market is continuously subordinated to the political imperatives of maintaining power (Boone 1992; Geddes 1994; Moore 1997:339).[17] The political contingency of state autonomy is apparent, even in paradigmatic cases of the developmental state, such as Korea. The military-authoritarian Korean state was successful in creating a new industrial base through the state's control over a credit-based system of industrial finance (Woo 1991). "State control over finance not only made the implementation of industrial policy possible but had the added benefit of bolstering the power base of the state by creating a whole entrepreneurial class as beneficiaries of the political leadership" (Woo-Cumings 1998:9). Ultimately, however, the autonomy of the Korean state was attenuated by its dependence on the very firms – the *chaebol* – that it had helped to build. Subsequent attempts by the state to regulate the *chaebol* have been blunted and deflected because the financial structure links the fate of the state itself to the fate of big capital.[18] Indeed, the very nature of the business–state relationship in

---

[17] Writing about Senegal, Boone makes the argument that because of the class origins of the state, the political imperatives of rule in fact led the state to undermine rather than promote the accumulation of capital for industrialization.

[18] See Woo (1991) for a discussion of early attempts at financial reform. This is not to suggest that structural reform is impossible but rather to suggest that it is difficult, requiring the realignment of major interests behind change. The combination of the shock caused by the Asian financial crisis, resultant pressures from the international community, and the election of a new president by fledgling democratic institutions may bring about such a realignment.

Korea made it vulnerable to threats such as that posed by the Asian financial crisis of 1997. Thus, to the extent that particular interests can colonize the state apparatus, they can undermine both its autonomy and its ability and willingness to implement state policy. As Atul Kohli (1990) points out with respect to India, this phenomenon is particularly common in late modernizers in which the state is a primary agent of development.[19] In these cases, the state controls a substantial share of society's resources; as a result, competition and conflict over access to these resources become focused on the state itself.

The nature and origins of capital have a particularly important impact on the design and effectiveness of state extractive institutions (Tilly 1990). Kiren Aziz Chaudhry (1989; 1997) cites the case of Saudi Arabia to demonstrate that the fiscal autonomy provided by oil revenue actually hindered the ability of the Saudi state to regulate the economy. The state's fiscal autonomy allowed its extractive and information-gathering institutions to atrophy, and, as a result, state policy came to be "informed by primordial ties and political considerations rather than by economic rationality" (Chaudhry 1989:114). In contrast, Chaudhry demonstrates that, although the Yemeni state was dependent for fiscal revenue on the financially independent private sector – financed primarily through labor remittances – the state's capacity to regulate the economy was much greater than in its Saudi neighbor. Indeed, where business interests had developed without state support, they lacked mediating ties with the local state and were therefore less able to block unfavorable policy implementation at the local level. Thus, there is no simple formula equating state autonomy and state strength. The ways in which business interests emerge dramatically shape the subsequent development of the state institutions tasked with regulating them.

Furthermore, Chaudhry (1997), drawing on a venerable tradition of dependency and international political economy theorizing, reminds us that state institutions do not exist in isolation: they function in a broader – in this case, international – environment.[20] For example, the collapse of oil prices on the world market in the 1980s changed the incentives for how the Saudi state would intervene in the domestic economy. Yet, the Saudi state's actions were hindered by the atrophy that had beset its

---

[19] See also Rueschemeyer and Evans (1985:60).

[20] Chaudhry (1997:18) characterizes contemporary development studies as suffering from "an under-theorized sense of structural junctures in the international economy." See also Stallings (1995).

domestic institutions. The more general point in this instance is that any theoretical approach must be able to account for two distinct sources of change in the institutions that govern society and economy: the dynamic pressures that come from state–society interactions and those that come from the broader environment in which state–society interactions occur.

Sympathetic critiques of statist theory from the emerging perspective of state–society relations suggest that any assessment of state capacity must examine not only the nature of the state itself but also the nature of society (Migdal, Kohli, and Shue 1994).[21] These critiques stem in part from the tendency of research in the statist tradition to focus on policy making at the central level rather than policy implementation at the grass roots. As Joel Migdal (1988:xvii) indicates, "There is a need constantly to look back and forth between the top reaches of the state and local society. One must see how the organization of society, even in remote areas, may dictate the character and capabilities of politics at the center, as well as how the state (often in unintended ways) changes society." Migdal employs the notion of a "triangle of accommodation" to describe the "disjuncture" between state policy as articulated at the center and what is actually implemented at the grass roots. The "triangle of accommodation" refers to collusion between the local state apparatus and powerful local interests in opposition to "the declared intentions of state leaders and the formal language of laws and regulations" (Ibid:265). This point is crucial in focusing attention on tensions within the state itself. Societal interests are not the only – or even necessarily the most critical – obstacles to effective policy implementation at the grass roots.

In sum, there are potential pressures for institutional change emanating from the dynamics of state–society interactions and the tensions within the state apparatus, as well as from the broader environment in which state–society interactions occur. Institutional economic approaches offer key insights into these sources of institutional change. Before turning to the contributions of new institutional approaches, however, it is necessary to draw out the connections between the comparative political theory discussed thus far and analyses of the Chinese case.

---

[21] The distinction here is, in part, one of emphasis. As Skocpol (1985:20) points out, even early studies of state capacity demonstrate that states must be viewed "in relation to socioeconomic and sociocultural contexts."

Chinese Politics Meets Comparative Politics

Scholarly debates about the role of the state in development have parallels in the field of Chinese politics. Debate in the field focuses on neoliberal versus statist interpretations of economic development, on differing assessments of central state capacity, and on the predatory versus developmental nature of the state apparatus.

With respect to rural industry, one of the most prominent debates pits neoliberal against developmental-state conceptualizations of rural industrialization. Minxin Pei (1994:43) characterizes China's rural reforms in both agriculture and industry as "carried out by societal forces through the market and not by the state."[22] Similarly, Edward Steinfeld (1998:254–5) explains the growth of township and village enterprises (TVEs) in China by pointing to what he sees as the essentially free-market conditions in which they exist. He supports his view by appealing to the historical conditions under which rural enterprises first emerged during the pre-reform period: TVEs "behave far more like textbook market-oriented producers than do their counterparts in the traditional state[-owned enterprise] sector. . . . Even prior to reform, these firms were manifestations of local self-sufficiency, operating on the marketized fringes of the command economy" (Steinfeld 1998:12–13). However, as I show in Chapter 2, beginning in the Maoist era, state intervention provided rural enterprises with crucial access to capital, technology, and other inputs, as well as access to distribution channels through state plans. Thus, state intervention has long been a core characteristic of rural industrial development.

A competing explanation for the growth of TVEs during the reform period is the notion of "local state corporatism," which grows out of the statist tradition (Oi 1992).[23] This explanation likens rural community governments to profit-seeking corporations that face fairly hard budget constraints and therefore bear the risks of their investments in industry (Oi 1995:1137–42; 1998; 1999; Walder 1998:17). In this view, local governments are themselves entrepreneurs who are constructing "a qualitatively new variety of developmental state" in order to bring about the industrialization of rural China (Oi 1995:1133). However, as Catherine

---

[22] I provide a comprehensive review of this work in Whiting (1996b).

[23] Jean Oi's use of the term corporatism in this context departs from the familiar use of the term denoting a system of interest representation. The *locus classicus* for the latter usage is Schmitter (1979).

11

Boone reminds us in her analysis of the subordination of capital and markets to political imperatives in the developing world, local state officials are first and foremost political, not economic, actors.[24] Local state officials in China do intervene actively in local economies, but they do so in highly politicized ways. As a result, publicly owned township and village enterprises, while experiencing dramatic growth, share many of the same pathologies of state-owned enterprises (SOEs) throughout the developing world (Waterbury 1993).[25] Thus, we should think of local Chinese officials more as "politicos" – individuals who make their careers in the political system – than as risk-bearing entrepreneurs. As I show in subsequent chapters, publicly owned TVEs have been buttressed by access to soft bank credits and cushioned by softness in their tax obligations – precisely the factors that Janos Kornai (1980; 1992) identifies as perpetuating soft budget constraints.[26] Thus, both the managers of these firms and the township and village officials who oversee them have, in fact, avoided bearing the risks associated with their investments. However, as this study will also demonstrate, TVEs exist in evolving political and economic environments; as constraints change, both the nature of corporate governance and the performance of TVEs change as well.

Debates in the field of Chinese politics extend beyond the role of the state in promoting economic growth. Scholars disagree about the ability of the central state to penetrate, regulate, and extract resources from townships and villages at different points in time. Reflecting the concerns of state–society theorists, Vivienne Shue (1988) portrays the late Maoist era as characterized by pervasive localism: local cadres aggressively pursued the development of commune and brigade enterprises to increase their own control over financial and material resources, often in contravention of plan priorities. However, Shue hypothesizes that in the reform era the expansion of market forces and the separation of politi-

---

[24] Contrast this with the view of local state officials first and foremost as economic actors "just as surely as are . . . households and . . . enterprises" (Walder 1998:19). See also Oi (1995; 1998). As the next section demonstrates, local officials respond to economic incentives such as those contained in the fiscal system, but their behavior cannot be equated with households and enterprises, since local officials simultaneously exercise political authority within their jurisdictions.

[25] Recognizing that SOEs and TVEs share many of the same pathologies is not to equate them in all respects. Those who supervise and manage SOEs and TVEs are embedded in the state apparatus in distinct ways; thus, the incentives and constraints they face are not exactly the same.

[26] See also Huang (1996:43). Oi (1995:1146) discusses these factors in her empirical accounts of rural industry, but they are not adequately theorized in the concept of local state corporatism.

12

cal, economic, and social authority will allow the state more effectively to penetrate local society and to tap its resources. In contrast, Helen Siu (1989a) portrays communes and brigades in the late Maoist era as effectively controlled by the central state. Not only does she view the Maoist era differently than Shue does, but she sees the impact of reform as having very different consequences. Siu uses the notion of "state involution" to describe changes at the local level during the reform era. This notion suggests that local cadres, who served as agents of the state in the pre-reform era, will now use their entrenched positions in the political structure to maintain their power, contravening the liberalizing goals of the state (Siu 1989b). Thus, a debate exists over the ability of the state to elicit compliance and support in the face of an increasingly entrepreneurial local society oriented toward production for the market.

Scholars also disagree over whether the contemporary Chinese state is best characterized as developmental or predatory. The debate turns on conflicting evidence of institutional adaptability versus decay as China's economic reforms progress. Recent research by Marc Blecher and Vivienne Shue (1996) offers some support for Shue's earlier hypothesis of increasing state capacity in the post-Mao period. Although the fact of state intervention in the economy has changed little, according to Blecher and Shue, the nature of state intervention is changing from direct ownership and participation in the economy to indirect regulation. Barry Naughton's analysis of China's gradual approach to socialist transition similarly highlights the importance of institutional adaptability in guiding the reforms. "For better and for worse, government kept trying throughout the reform era to develop investment policy, restructure enterprise incentives, and devise new and appropriate institutions" (Naughton 1995:95). Indeed, Blecher and Shue (1996:205) suggest that the work of the "developmental state" at the local level is becoming "more detailed, intense, specialized, and technically sophisticated and demanding."[27] At the same time, they find that the local state remains closely integrated into the larger state apparatus. Yasheng Huang concurs. He argues that central administrative control over local cadres has, if anything, increased, even though economic reform has created new incentives for local leaders to pursue economic goals distinct from those

---

[27] Moreover, early reform measures in the economic realm were accompanied by political reforms that led to the retirement of a large portion of the revolutionary generation of party-state bureaucrats and the advancement of cadres with greater education and skills more relevant to economic reform (Lee 1991; Manion 1993).

of the center (Huang 1996:113). He cautions that ignoring mechanisms of *political* control may lead analysts to underestimate the continued power of the central party-state (Ibid:305–25).

By contrast, other scholars associate economic reform with institutional decay. Andrew Walder (1995) suggests that the reduction in bureaucratic allocation of goods and the end of state monopoly ownership of industry – both hallmarks of a planned economy – have reduced the economic dependence of local cadres on the state, thereby eroding the ability of the center to elicit compliance with state policies. Others (Pei 1997; Wang 1995) point to the decline in budgetary revenue and the concomitant rise in nonbudgetary revenue[28] during the reform period as indicative of an increasingly predatory state "in which the government preys upon society to extract economic resources which are used more to support the privileged lifestyle of the elite than to benefit the nation as a whole" (Pei 1997:20–1). Indeed, TVEs contribute significantly to nonbudgetary revenues at the local level. What this position overlooks, however, are the historical roots and legitimate uses of nonbudgetary revenue (Whiting 1999a; Wong 1997). Nonbudgetary revenues were an integral part of Soviet-style planning that injected some flexibility into the rigidity of the planned economy. Moreover, as I demonstrate in Chapter 3, a sizable portion of nonbudgetary revenue has gone toward financing legitimate government functions and providing public goods and services that were underfunded in the formal budgets of local governments. While local officials exercise significant discretion over the use of nonbudgetary funds, the central state indirectly influences the use of these funds by monitoring the performance of local cadres in providing public goods. Furthermore, as I show in Chapter 7, the central government has launched a major reform initiative to unify the budget in response to the diversion by local cadres of budgetary revenue into off-budget channels. This reform is indicative of the fundamental transformation of regulatory institutions that is accompanying China's transition from the plan to the market, and it highlights the need for a theoretical approach that can account for substantial institutional change. Therefore, this study moves decisively beyond competing conceptualizations of state strength or weakness and places the focus on the process of institutional change itself.

---

[28] I use the term nonbudgetary revenue to encompass both officially sanctioned and unsanctioned levies beyond the narrowly defined, formal budget. "Off-budget revenue" refers to the unsanctioned, nontax revenues that are handled outside the formal budget. See Chapter 3 and Whiting (1999a).

State and Society: A Reprise

The notion of a predatory or developmental state – in Chinese politics as in comparative politics more broadly – fails to explain the dynamics of institutional change. Simply contrasting developmental and predatory states provides little insight into the dynamics of how regimes reach or move away from these stationary states. Furthermore, the lack of scholarly agreement over whether to characterize the Chinese state as developmental or predatory highlights not only the complexity of empirical reality on the ground but also the underlying multidimensionality and ambiguity of the concepts themselves. Similarly, assessments of state capacity are often too diffuse to capture state–society interactions in a meaningful way. Capabilities are not constant across policy arenas, and policy arenas are sufficiently diverse to make aggregation difficult.

By contrast, the state–society approach, which holds that any assessment of state capacity must examine not only different elements and levels of the state but also the nature of interactions between state and society, incorporates some of the key elements necessary to explain institutional change. However, a drawback of the state–society approach, like the statist approach more generally, is that it provides little explicit theoretical guidance as to what motivates individuals in either the state or society. For example, Migdal (1988) implies that individuals act rationally to pursue their interests. He suggests that individuals in society seek "strategies of survival" that provide for their basic material needs and desires; political elites seek strategies to stay in power; and local strong men seek to maximize their control over resources. Nevertheless, Migdal fails to formalize this notion or incorporate it into his theoretical treatment of state capacity. Indeed, he rejects the possibility of making an explicit theoretical statement about individual motivations.[29] However,

---

[29] This rejection becomes clear in his characterization of one of the major debates on peasant behavior. According to Migdal (1988:26–7), "attempting to distinguish whether peasants act according to a 'moral economy,' emphasizing symbolic configurations, or are 'rational actors' driven only by material needs is a futile exercise; it loses sight of the integration of the material and the moral." However, Douglass North's (1981) approach to institutional economics shows how ideology, or "symbolic configurations," can be integrated into a rational choice framework – without sacrificing an explicit theory of individual motivation. North's pioneering research on the role of ideology in overcoming the free-rider problem clearly demonstrates how "symbolic configurations" can be manipulated for rational ends. According to North (1981:19), "compliance is so costly that the enforcement of any body of rules in the absence of some degree of individual restraint from maximizing behavior would render the political or economic institution nonviable – hence the enormous investment that is made [in ideology] to convince indi-

social and political change require human agency. Without an explicit theory of individual motivation, it is impossible to develop a dynamic theory of state–society relations.

Rational Choice and the New Institutionalism

Scholars seeking to understand the role of the state in development and the nature of state–society interaction have increasingly turned to the study of institutions.[30]

Institutionalists working in the rational choice tradition combine an explicit theory of individual motivation (the intention of acting with rational self-interest) with detailed analysis of the ways in which institutions shape the specific content and expression of self-interest. The institutions of the state and the incentives and constraints they create are not assumed to be the same for all states at all times; rather they are historically contingent. Once political institutions are in place, however, they lead political elites to intervene in the society or economy in particular ways. As social and economic interests coalesce in response to state actions, they, in turn, influence subsequent state institutions and policies. As Robert Bates (1989:154) concludes in his study of agrarian development in Kenya,

> [Institutions] create incentives; and these incentives influence the way in which economic interests are defined and the manner in which they receive organized political expression. When political actors intervene in the economy and seek to restructure economic relations, the policies they choose depend upon the incentives generated by the institutional context within which they are made. Economic forces thus generate institutions and the structure of these institutions in turn shapes the way in which governments transform

viduals of the legitimacy of these institutions." Furthermore, new research combining the insights of institutional economics and cognitive psychology may ultimately form the basis for a fully integrated theory of individual decision making, ideology, culture, and institutional change. Cognitive psychological approaches examine the cognitive limitations on intentionally rational behavior. They highlight the role of uncertainty and the impact of limited cognitive processing abilities on human decision making. For Denzau and North (1994), culture and ideology represent different types of shared beliefs about how the world works and what the outcomes of one's actions are likely to be, according to that particular set of beliefs. Thus, they simplify the cognitive process of making "rational" choices in a complex and uncertain environment.

[30] Institutions, as defined by North (1990:3), are "the rules of the game in a society or, more formally, the humanly devised constraints that shape human interaction."

their economies. Economy and polity thus interact, generating a process of change.

Moreover, this model of human behavior is inherently probabilistic, not deterministic (Huang 1996:8). The claim is that, given a particular structure of incentives and constraints, individuals are more likely to act in ways predicted by the model.[31]

The study of institutions is by no means the exclusive domain of rational choice theorists, however. Kathleen Thelen and Sven Steinmo (1992), for example, adopt an "historical institutionalist" approach. While advocating a focus on institutions in general, they seek to distinguish their work from rational choice treatments of institutions by emphasizing their inductive approach to preferences. In fact, however, historical institutionalism shares with some of the best work in the rational choice tradition an inductive approach to preferences. Moreover, the ability of historical institutionalists to produce a dynamic theory of institutional change is hindered by an unwillingness to make explicit their underlying assumptions. As Herbert Simon (1995:53) indicates with respect to rational choice research, "At every step in our analysis we encounter the need to make auxiliary assumptions about the content of peoples' goals, and we find that our power to explain and predict depends almost wholly on these assumptions." In other words, while assumptions are necessary, the analyst cannot simply assume that individuals seek to "maximize expected utility." Rather, one of the major tasks of research is to identify "under what particular circumstances and at what particular points of time people will hold and act upon particular goals and values" (Ibid).

The empirical requirements of research in the rational choice tradition have increased further as a result of findings in cognitive psychology regarding the limited cognitive processing capabilities of human decision makers and the problem of imperfect information (Jones 1999). Since both cognitive capacity and information are limited, it is important to understand which among an individual's goals are likely to receive attention, what information an individual can bring to bear in pursuing those goals, what heuristic devices an individual is likely to use in processing available information, and how the individual defines an acceptable level of performance (Nee and Ingram 1998; Simon 1995; Tversky and Kahneman 1974; 1981). These empirical features of the decision-

---

[31] The model can be tested. It is falsified if the distribution of repeated representative samples of behavior does not accord with predictions.

making process serve to simplify the cognitive challenges that individuals face in making "rational" choices in a complex and uncertain reality, but they simultaneously complicate scholarly efforts to explain the decision-making process. These characteristics of decision making must be incorporated into our understanding of institutional change.

In sum, the new institutionalism, like the more sophisticated statist literature, allows the analyst to disaggregate the state and examine how incentives for individuals embedded in the state apparatus vary, depending on the particular institutional context and level of administration. Like the state–society literature, the new institutionalism captures the "mutually transforming" and "mutually constitutive" nature of state–society relations (Evans 1995:35; Kohli and Shue 1994:294). But proponents of new institutionalism go further: employing an empirically grounded theory of bounded rational choice allows them to explain the dynamics of institutional change that are addressed in only an ad hoc manner by other approaches.

The Institutional Economic Framework

Institutional economics offers a systematic theoretical framework in which to understand changing institutional arrangements – particularly those that undergird the generation and extraction of revenue (Eggertsson 1990; Levi 1988; North 1981; 1984). At the center of the institutional economic model of the state is the assumption that state officials seek to maximize revenue, subject to certain constraints. In light of the preceding discussion, however, I modify this assumption for the local state officials who are of particular interest in this study. I assume that local officials pursue career success, keeping in mind that "political institutions determine which strategies for staying in office are likely to work" (Geddes 1994:8).[32] Indeed, the political institutions in rural China in which local officials are embedded have created an imperative for them to generate and extract revenue from the local economy – as I demonstrate on empirical grounds in the next section and in detail in Chapter 3.

In the general institutional economic model, the state faces a revenue imperative created by the need to finance state functions. According to

---

[32] Detailed empirical support for the assumptions that local officials seek career success and that career success is linked to an official's ability to promote the generation and extraction of revenue is presented in Chapter 3. See also P. Huang (1990:322), Rozelle (1994:115), and Wong (1992).

this model, state officials meet their revenue imperative by specifying property rights that generate revenue as efficiently as possible. Property rights encompass four sets of rights; these rights govern the use or sale of an asset and the disposition of income derived from the use or sale of an asset.[33] The state's goal in specifying property rights is to maximize the size of the economic base from which it can extract revenue. However, the state is constrained by three factors in extracting revenue.

First, the state is constrained by the transaction costs it faces. Transaction costs characterize contracts between parties who have conflicting interests and for whom acquiring information is costly; they include the costs of gathering information, negotiating agreements, measuring resources, monitoring behavior, and enforcing performance. The most important transaction cost in this context is the cost of measuring the tax base. According to Douglass North (1981:28), "Efficient property rights may lead to higher income in the [society] but lower revenues for the ruler because of the transaction costs ([of] monitoring, metering, and collecting such [revenues]). . . ." Thus, there is a trade-off between property rights that generate the most revenue in society and those from which the state can most easily extract the revenue. Private enterprises, for example, may produce revenue very efficiently, but the state may not be able to tap into that revenue if it cannot readily measure and collect it.

Second, the state is constrained in extracting revenue by its ability to control the opportunistic behavior of its agents – the tax collectors. Agency costs stem from the conflicting interests of principals and agents and from the information asymmetry that characterizes principal–agent relations (Moe 1984:757). Because the interests of the state and its agents do not correspond completely and because monitoring the behavior of agents is costly, agents often act in ways contrary to the interests of the

---

[33] Property rights can usefully be thought of as a bundle that can be divided in different ways among different actors, including among different agencies of the state itself (Alchian and Demsetz 1973:18; Granick 1990). This definition does not assume any particular division of rights; nor does it assume that the existing division of property rights is secure. Some analysts, e.g., Steinfeld (1998), equate the concept of property rights with the particular assignment of the property rights bundle commonly found in Western capitalist democracies. By contrast, in the analytical approach adopted here, a "right" refers to de facto control over some part of the bundle. Thus, my use of the term is to be distinguished from its use in the sense of constitutionally protected or inalienable rights. The approach employed here is particularly useful in analyzing property rights across space and time.

state. For example, agents may collect revenue but fail to turn it over to state coffers.

Third, the state is constrained from pursuing policies that alienate key constituents. The relative bargaining power of the state vis-à-vis its constituents is determined by the extent to which one party controls resources on which the other party depends – be they coercive, political, or economic in nature. For instance, the state may confer special benefits on constituents who control significant economic resources. Bargaining power is a relative concept: a constituent who supplies a small share of a needed resource holds less bargaining power than a constituent who provides proportionally more. Thus, according to the institutional economic model, the state's specification of property rights and, relatedly, its ability to extract revenue are constrained in predictable ways.

At the same time, as institutional economics has begun to address the problem of uncertainty, it has increasingly moved away from the deterministic assumptions of neoliberal economic theory that predict unique, "first-best" outcomes and toward more evolutionary theorizing. Thus, individuals in both firms and state agencies alike are portrayed as searching for the best action rather than having found it (Nelson 1995). In this way, institutional economics examines the logic of both individual actions and contractual arrangements (Eggertsson 1990:53). It predicts that individual strategies and contractual forms that minimize costs tend to survive and spread. Under conditions of incomplete and costly information, rational parties to a contract may rely on various modes of behavior such as custom, experimentation, or imitation to determine a satisfactory course of action or an adequate contractual form (March 1978; Simon 1957). Thus, a variety of individual strategies and contractual forms may coexist at any given time. However, because individuals and organizations are themselves in competitive environments in which selection pressures operate, they will choose, from among the options of which they are aware, the one which gives them the highest return at the lowest cost (Nelson and Winter 1982). When selection pressures in the environment change, outcomes are likely to change as well.

INSTITUTIONAL VARIATION AND CHANGE
IN RURAL INDUSTRY

The approach to institutional change developed here begins by examining how the incentives and constraints contained in the institutional frameworks in place at the beginning of the reform era led to the emergence of distinct models of property rights in rural industry. These models, in turn, had implications both for the evolution of local institutions for revenue extraction and for the ability of the central state to enforce its claim on a share of those revenues for central state purposes.

This argument takes as its starting point the incentive structure created by the public institutions in which local cadres functioned during the first decade and a half of the reform era. It focuses on cadres at the township level, the lowest level of government in the state administrative hierarchy.[34] Township cadres, who were appointed by their superiors at the next highest level, responded to two powerful sets of incentives. First, township cadres responded to the revenue imperative intensified by fiscal reforms initiated in 1980, which made local levels of the state essentially self-financing at the same time as they increased local responsibility for financing public goods and perpetuated local obligations to remit some revenue to the central government.[35] Second, township cadres responded to the evaluation criteria by which their level of remuneration, tenure of office, and opportunities for advancement were determined.[36] These criteria focused overwhelmingly on rapid industrial expansion but also included targets for provision of public goods, such as education, infrastructure, and public order.[37] Both sets of incentives

---

[34] Below the township are villages and villagers' small groups, which replaced commune-era production brigades and production teams, respectively. Although villages are not formal governmental units, they still perform certain governmental functions. (In some of the communities investigated for this study, the term "team" was still used when referring to villagers' small groups.)

[35] During the period under the study, the Chinese government operated a unified tax system: the central government had the exclusive right to determine tax policy for all levels (although lower levels could influence effective tax rates through their approach to implementation), while each lower level of government was responsible for collecting taxes from the enterprises under its jurisdiction. Tax revenues were shared with higher levels under a revenue-sharing fiscal system. This issue is addressed in detail in Chapter 3.

[36] The extent to which local officials were willing to pursue public over private interests depended in part on these payoffs. As Geddes (1994:193) notes, "Convergence between individual interests and regime goals ... occurs when organizations offer benefits to individuals – whether in the form of power, status, wealth, or promotions – for expending their energies to pursue regime goals (and, of course, impose costs for failing to do so) that outweigh the benefits associated with the various behaviors that undermine the pursuit of these goals."

[37] Susan Shirk (1993:189–90) identifies similar incentives for provincial-level officials in China.

created great demand for revenue on the part of township cadres. These local officials, therefore, had powerful incentives to develop the local revenue base and extract from it as much revenue as possible. Moreover, capital was still relatively immobile; thus, investors were often unable to relocate in order to avoid what they considered to be excessively high levels of extraction.

As suggested by the institutional economic model, property rights evolved in response to the incentives for local cadres to develop local sources of revenue. The differing dispositions of cadres in various locales toward private property rights in particular were shaped by the historical legacies of enterprise development in each area.[38] In areas with a legacy of weak collective enterprise development, such as Wenzhou in southeastern Zhejiang Province, local cadres moved aggressively to support private property rights. These cadres, when first faced with the imperative of self-financing in the early 1980s, had a poor revenue base and little revenue to invest in collectively owned enterprises. They responded to the revenue imperative by acting to guarantee the property rights of private investors in order to encourage investment and develop the tax base. Local officials were constrained in their efforts by national ideological and legal environments hostile to private ownership of industry, by the incomplete nature of markets for capital, land, and other scarce inputs, and by restrictions on domestic markets for many final products. These conditions made it more difficult to promote private investment in industry.

In areas with a legacy of strong collective enterprise development, such as Wuxi in southeastern Jiangsu Province or suburban Shanghai, local cadres favored collective property rights. At the time of fiscal reform, these cadres already had a strong revenue base and were able to further invest in collective enterprise development. Local officials in Shanghai and Wuxi resisted the development of private enterprise to varying degrees and opted instead to protect and nurture collective ownership, greatly facilitating the rapid growth of these firms. Official support for the collective economy played a crucial role in light of restrictions on factor and product markets throughout the 1980s and into the 1990s. At the same time, the absence of guaranteed private property rights or support for private economic activity stifled investment on the part of private entrepreneurs in these areas.

The institutional economic model also holds that different levels of

---

[38] These historical legacies are the subject of Chapter 2.

transaction costs are associated with the governance of different forms of property rights. Local governments faced lower transaction costs in governing collective enterprises than in governing private enterprises. As Margaret Levi (1988:29) notes, "The better the quality of rulers' information about the actual wealth, income, and property produced in the polity [and] about the behavior of those from whom they extract revenue, . . . the more they are able to extract in revenue from the population."[39] The cost to the local government of acquiring information on collective enterprises was relatively low. According to Athar Hussain and Nicholas Stern (1991), "much of the information and many of the devices for monitoring enterprise income which are available to the government in transitional economies are based on the structures of the command economy."[40] Collective enterprises were closely integrated into the existing collective organizational structure of the township. Local officials, as de facto owners and superiors in an administrative hierarchy over collective enterprises, had ready access to firm-level information and decision making. In addition to extracting revenue, local officials could also allocate responsibility for provision of certain public goods to the firm itself, and collective firms played a special role in maintaining public order and social welfare by providing employment to community residents.

Therefore, local officials had little incentive to change existing institutions for public goods provision or revenue extraction from collective firms. Indeed, they could readily manipulate these institutional arrangements for local community goals. Township officials were simultaneously de facto owners of collective enterprises and agents of the central state, acting as both tax collectors and overseers of the state banking system. Given their position in the collective organizational structure, township officials could divert funds out of the budgetary tax category (on which the central government also had a claim) into the "off-budget" category (which they effectively controlled) in order to increase the revenues of the township government. Similarly, they could manipulate the allocation of bank loans to the benefit of collective firms. Thus, there was an institutionally defined conflict of interest between central and local offi-

---

[39] The relevant population in China during the period under study were firms and not individuals. The taxation of individual income provided only a small share of state revenue at any level.

[40] Although collective enterprise managers might have had personal incentives to hide income from local officials, the existence of these structures made this more difficult for collective managers than for private manager-owners. Hussain and Stern (1991:35).

cials with respect to the taxation of and allocation of credit to collective enterprises.

By contrast, local cadres had relatively poor information about the resources of private firms. While local officials could rely on the collective organizational structure in extracting revenue from collective firms, no such structure existed for private firms.[41] Given the absence of a comparable administrative structure to govern the private sector, many Chinese observers saw it as beyond the reach of the state.[42] The difficulty of acquiring information on the actual amount of revenue generated by private firms did make the costs of revenue extraction significantly higher. High transaction costs reflected the comparatively high degree of autonomy enjoyed by private firms vis-à-vis the local state apparatus.

In this situation township officials had clear incentives to innovate in order to reduce the high transaction costs. In Wenzhou, where local officials were heavily dependent on private enterprises to meet their revenue imperative, local tax officials established a simple procedure for estimating and collecting enterprise taxes simultaneously (*daizhengshui*), which allowed them to extract revenue at lower cost to both the government and the firm. In Shanghai, where private enterprises comprised only a small proportion of the tax base, local officials also developed new institutional arrangements to extract revenue from newly emerging private firms. In this case, the firms themselves were made to bear the high cost of extraction. Consistent with the institutional economic model, extractive institutions reflected the degree of bargaining power exercised by constituents. The institutional arrangements devised in Wenzhou, where private firms controlled many of the economic resources of the community, reflected an accommodation with private capital. Institutional arrangements in Shanghai, by contrast, reflected an adversarial approach to the taxation of private firms. Consistent with boundedly rational approaches to problem solving, local officials in both communities who were tasked with taxing private firms

[41] As Barry Naughton (1992a:15) points out, "[T]he tax code and the government's administrative capabilities to collect taxes from the remainder of the economy [the non-state sector] are underdeveloped."

[42] See, for example, Li Bingkun (1990:188–226) and Luo, Quan, and Gao (1989:371–85). The Chinese state has tried to compensate for lack of bureaucratic control over the private sector by creating corporatist controls over private entrepreneurs through the compulsory Individual and Private Entrepreneurs' Associations. However, this corporatist structure is comparatively weak as either a means of control or a source of information. This issue is addressed in detail in Chapter 5.

adapted historical practices that had been used in governing the private sector in the 1950s and earlier as they designed new institutional arrangements for revenue extraction from the private sector during the reform period.

The hypothesized process of institutional change at the local level is summarized in Figure 1.1. The incentives contained in the fiscal system and the cadre evaluation system, interacting with the legacy of local public enterprise development, influenced the degree of political support for private as opposed to collective property rights. The effectiveness of local political support was constrained by the broader national political-legal environment and the nature of markets for factors and products. Together these factors affected the proportion of private enterprise in the local economy. The proportion of private enterprise, in turn, influenced both the total transaction costs of revenue extraction and the bargaining power of private capital. These two factors shaped the nature of institutional arrangements for revenue extraction. Table 1.1 shows in simple form the values of these key variables for each of the three research sites during the first decade and a half of reform.

Looking beyond the strictly local level, township officials were both principals and agents in the extraction of revenue. They were principals with respect to the extraction of revenue for local coffers and agents of the central government (albeit not necessarily good ones) in a nested hierarchy of subnational governments with respect to extraction of revenue for central coffers. The issue of monitoring clearly came into play in this agency relationship. Where monitoring was lax, local officials succeeded in diverting more revenue (particularly revenue from collective firms) from centrally controlled to locally controlled channels. The intensity of monitoring of township-level behavior was influenced by the incentives contained in central–provincial fiscal agreements several steps up the administrative ladder. Heavy fiscal burdens created incentives for provincial-level officials to intensify their monitoring of revenue extraction at lower levels. During the period under study, officials at the provincial level in Shanghai, for example, perceived their fiscal contract with the center to be particularly burdensome, leading them to intensify their monitoring of tax collection at lower levels.[43]

Both the intensity of monitoring of township behavior by higher levels and the nature of township-level institutional arrangements had

---

[43] Shanghai is a "provincial-level city," indicating that it is overseen directly by the central government.

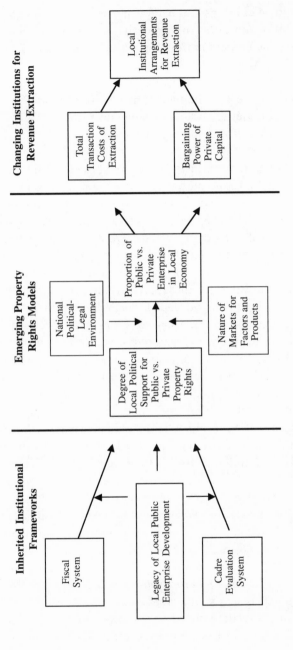

Figure 1.1. Explaining institutional change at the local level.

Table 1.1. *Explaining Institutional Change at the Local Level*

Locale	Legacy of Public Enterprise Development	Degree of Political Support for Private Property Rights	Proportion of Private Enterprise in Local Economy	Property Rights Model	Total Transaction Costs of Extraction	Bargaining Power of Private Capital	Institutional Arrangements for Revenue Extraction
Wuxi	very strong	low	low	collective	low	low	status quo for collective enterprises
Shanghai	strong	low–moderate	low–moderate	mixed	low–moderate	low–moderate	status quo for collective enterprises/ adversarial approach to private enterprises
Wenzhou	weak	high	high	private	high	high	accommodational approach to private enterprises

implications for the ability of the central state to extract revenue at the grass roots. All township officials had incentives to try to retain as much revenue as possible at the township level. Lax monitoring of local collection efforts by provincial-level officials contributed to poor implementation of central tax policy. Similarly, the continued existence of collective organizational structures at the township level hindered the mobilization of revenue from collective enterprises into channels controlled by the central government. However, the development of new institutional arrangements designed to overcome the difficulties of taxing newly emerging private firms at the local level also facilitated the mobilization of revenue into centrally controlled channels to the extent that it exposed the fiscal capacity of these firms.

The necessity of designing new institutional arrangements capable of taxing private firms highlights the challenges involved in making the transition from a command to a market economy. Despite the dominant role of the state in the pre-reform economy, the institutions of tax administration were relatively underdeveloped. Under reform, as the World Bank (1990b:7) notes, "the emphasis has moved towards the use of 'indirect levers' and tax policy to regulate the behavior of increasingly autonomous economic agents." However, this effort has been handicapped at the local level, on the one hand, by the absence of established practices in governing the private sector and, on the other, by the interference of local governments in policy implementation, particularly with respect to the collective enterprises under their jurisdiction. This interference distorts the effects of centrally determined industrial and stabilization policies (World Bank 1990a; 1990b). The central government has, for example, been unable to prevent over-investment by local governments in collectively owned processing industries and, even more importantly, has been unable to employ fiscal and monetary policy effectively to prevent overheating of the economy. The inability of the central government to wield the indirect levers of tax and credit policy effectively forced it to resort repeatedly to campaign-style application of administrative controls, exacerbating boom–bust cycles in the economy.[44]

The new reform agenda articulated at the Third Plenum of the Fourteenth Central Committee in November 1993 represents an effort by the central state to put in place new national institutions more capable of

---

[44] See, for example, Y. Huang (1990) and Naughton (1990:109–40; 1991:50–82; 1992b:135–59).

governing a market economy. Most dramatically, the central leadership used its remaining administrative control to push through aggressive fiscal reforms in 1994 intended to centralize control over revenue. Banking and legal reforms intended to reduce political influence over these regulatory institutions followed, albeit more slowly, while marketization of domestic trade continued apace. Together, fiscal and banking reforms and increasingly competitive product markets are beginning to truly harden the budget constraints of local state officials. As constraints in the institutional environment for local officials change, we can expect to see concomitant changes in the forms of property rights supported by local officials. Thus, as market and legal institutions become more complete, and as the budget constraints of local communities harden, support for private ownership is likely to increase, even in areas where public ownership has predominated. In light of the higher transactions costs in taxing private firms, increasing privatization only heightens the importance of innovations in grass roots extractive institutions. Mobilization of revenue remains one of the greatest challenges facing transition economies.

DESIGN OF THE STUDY

The research reported here was conducted as a comparative case study based on interviews and archival research. The goal of this study is to identify and explain the particular patterns that emerged in the evolution of property rights and extractive institutions. This study was designed to gain theoretical leverage by taking advantage of variation in empirical relationships among the variables of interest. Two types of cases were selected. Counties and subordinate townships were selected for variation in the concentration of private and collective ownership forms, and enterprises were selected to represent the full range of ownership forms found within the township.[45] The small sample of counties

---

[45] At the enterprise level, interviews were conducted with enterprise managers and, whenever possible, with enterprise accountants. Interviews were open-ended and generally lasted between two and three hours. In conducting interviews, I allowed managers to respond freely to questions but attempted to cover the same content in each interview based on a standard format. The standard format included questions on the manager's personal background; the terms of his or her contract; the circumstances surrounding the founding of the firm; the sources for inputs, including materials, land, labor, and capital; the extent of the manager's decision-making authority with respect to major operational issues; the nature of the product market and market access; the nature of taxes, fees, and profit remittances paid by the firm in the past fiscal year; and the per-

and townships investigated for this study is not intended to be representative of rural China as a whole.[46] Rather, this research is intended
to generate hypotheses about the evolution of property rights and
extractive institutions in the context of rural China. Analysis of quantitative data collected for all 138 counties in the three provinces where
research was conducted provides a preliminary test of the hypotheses,
but the generalizability of the findings must be established through
further research.

Research was conducted in three locales in the southeastern coastal
region of China. The study focuses primarily on the three counties of
Songjiang, Wuxi, and Yueqing.[47] Their location in the administrative hierarchy is shown in Figure 1.2, and their geographic location is shown in
Maps 1.1 and 1.2. The counties and townships governed by the munici-
palities of Wenzhou, Wuxi, and Shanghai exhibited distinct patterns of
property rights forms in industry as of the early 1990s.[48] As Table 1.2

formance record of the firm over the past several years. At the township level, interviews
were conducted with representatives of the party apparatus, government apparatus,
finance bureau, tax bureau, industrial-commercial bureau, Agriculture Bank and rural
credit cooperative, industrial corporation, and economic management office. Additional
interviews were conducted with representatives of bureaucratic organs involved in rural
industrial development especially at the county level, but also at the provincial and
national levels.

[46] As Alexander George (1979:60) notes in his discussion of case studies as structured,
focused, comparisons, "The small *n* in a controlled comparison is not necessarily representative of the universe of instances belonging to that class of events; what is more, it
need not be representative in the statistical sampling sense in order to contribute to
theory development. The desideratum that guides selection of cases in the controlled
comparison approach is not numbers but variety, that is, cases belonging to the same
class that differ from each other."

[47] In Shanghai I conducted the bulk of the research in Songyang Town of Songjiang County.
However, because of bureaucratic restrictions on the amount of time I was allowed to
spend in any single township, I conducted supplementary research in two additional
townships in Shanghai: Luhang Town in Shanghai County and Nantang Township in
Jiading County. Short research visits were also made to several other townships, including Meilin Town in Shanghai County and Chenjiaqiao Town in Chuansha County. In
Wuxi I conducted research in Dongtan Town of Wuxi County, and in Wenzhou I conducted research in Hualing Town of Yueqing County. The township names employed in
the study are pseudonyms in order to protect the identities of informants.

[48] A note on administrative hierarchies is in order here: The Chinese state has five levels
of formal state administration: center, province, prefecture, county, and township. The
term city or municipality (*shi*) designates a more urbanized jurisdiction and is used to
refer to units existing at the provincial, prefectural, and county levels. In recognition of
increasing urbanization, the designation of "prefecture (*diqu*)" is gradually being phased
out altogether to be replaced entirely with the term "city." The sites chosen for this
research project have undergone some changes to reflect increasing urbanization. Shanghai Municipality is a provincial-level unit that directly governs the counties in its sub-

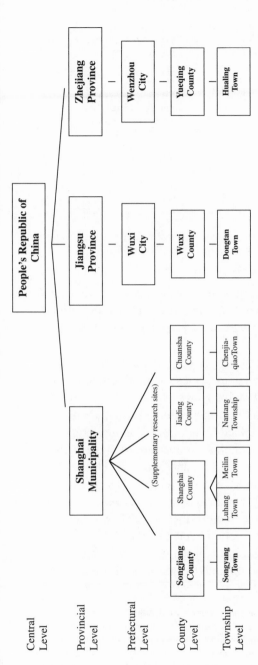

Figure 1.2. Administrative hierarchy governing townships in the research sites.

Notes: (1) Shanghai Municipality has the administrative status of a province; it deals directly with the central government and directly governs the counties within its jurisdiction.

(2) Recent administrative reforms have resulted in the following changes: Shanghai County has been incorporated into the city proper and renamed Minhang District of Shanghai Municipality; Jiading and Chuansha counties have been similarly incorporated as districts of Shanghai Municipality. Wuxi County has been renamed Xishan City and has been placed directly under the jurisdiction of Jiangsu Province. Yueqing County has been reclassified as Yueqing City.

(3) With respect to fiscal contracts, some county-level units deal directly with the provincial government, bypassing the city level. In Zhejiang Province, for example, although Yueqing is administratively subordinate to Wenzhou City, it negotiates its fiscal contract directly with the province.

(4) The township administrative level includes both townships (*xiang*) and towns (*zhen*). Put simply, the distinction is based on the criteria that towns are more urbanized than townships and have a higher percentage of residents employed in nonagricultural pursuits. For a more detailed discussion, see Chan (1994) and Martin (1992).

(5) The township-level names employed in this study are pseudonyms to protect the identities of informants.

Table 1.2. *Regional Variation in Industrial Output by Ownership at Mid-Reform, 1990 (percentage)*

		Wenzhou	Wuxi	Shanghai		
	National	Yueqing County	Wuxi County	Songjiang County	Shanghai County	Jiading County
Township-run collective	40	10	49	61	51	55
Village-run collective	34	14	49	22	41	35
Private[a]	26	75	2	17	8	9

[a] Residual, includes team-run collectives.

Sources: Zhongguo tongji nianjian. Yueqing tongji nianjian. Wuxi xian tongji nianjian. Shanghai xian guomin jingji tongji xiliao. Jiading xian tongji ziliao huibian.

shows, private ownership predominated in Wenzhou, while collective ownership predominated in Wuxi. Collective ownership also predominated in Shanghai, but private ownership was better represented there than in Wuxi.

In terms of the concentration of property rights forms, the Wenzhou and Wuxi sites represent particular extremes in the Chinese context, stemming in part from their distinctive geographical locations and historical legacies.[49] Wenzhou, located on the mainland coast across from the northern tip of Taiwan, is bounded by mountains and coastline. The area has little arable land, and residents traditionally supported themselves through petty commerce and long-distance trade. As Philip Huang (1990:263) notes, "The area has a special history: opened as a treaty port in 1876, and pressed by its very low land–man ratio, Wenzhou had a strong tradition of petty commerce and production. . . . Few other areas enjoy this kind of tradition and commercial network." Residents of Wenzhou resisted collectivization during the mid-1950s, and collective organizational structures continued to be weak throughout the

urban areas. During the mid-1990s, Shanghai County was absorbed into the city proper and became Minhang District; Jiading and Chuansha Counties were similarly incorporated as districts of the city of Shanghai. Among the Shanghai sites addressed in this study, Songjiang County receives primary emphasis. In Jiangsu Province, Wuxi County was administratively subordinate to the larger Wuxi City. As Wuxi County grew, its official designation was changed to Xishan City, and it was put directly under the jurisdiction of Jiangsu Province. Yueqing County has been reclassified as Yueqing City.

[49] I will return to this issue in Chapter 2.

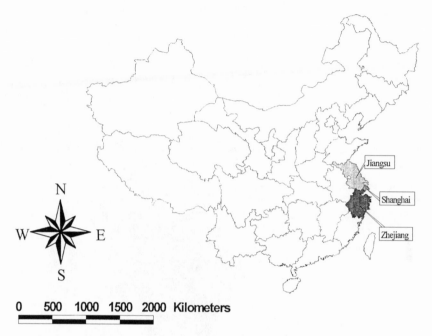

N

W —✶— E

S

0   500   1000   1500   2000   Kilometers

Map 1.1. Map of China Showing Jiangsu, Shanghai, and Zhejiang.

commune era, which spanned the years 1958–83.[50] Private petty commerce and handicraft production continued to exist underground during the Maoist era and were quick to emerge "above ground" in the more permissive atmosphere of the reform era.

In Wuxi and Shanghai the collective organizational structures of the commune and brigade (now the township and village) were more prominent features in the lives of rural residents than elsewhere in China. This prominence was a result of the scale of resources controlled at the commune and brigade levels. Even before 1949, the Yangzi River Delta, where Wuxi and Shanghai are located, was "one of the most advanced areas of China" both in terms of agricultural and industrial development (P. Huang 1990:323). Commune and brigade industries received early and sustained support, and they generated significant revenues. As of the mid-1970s, communes in Wuxi County already derived about 40 percent of their income from these enterprises. As Dwight Perkins (1977:224–5)

[50] "An Alarming Case of Counterrevolutionary Restoration in Wenzhou," *Renmin ribao*, March 22, 1977, cited in A. Liu (1992).

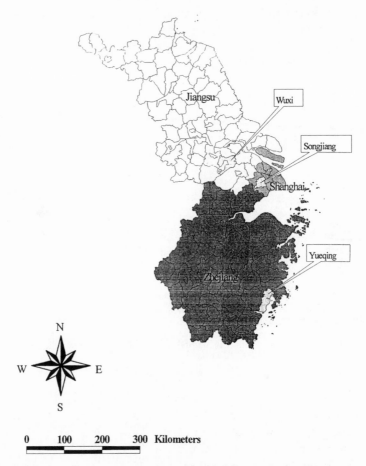

Map 1.2. Map of Jiangsu, Shanghai, and Zhejiang research sites.

observed at the time, "This growth of commune income gives the commune administrators much more influence over the life of the countryside. In the most developed places, they are using their new-found income not only to reinvest in more sophisticated industry, but also to stimulate new programs in the units below the commune. This sort of development was particularly stressed in Wuxi County." In addition to industrial expansion, communes in Wuxi also invested substantially in agricultural infrastructure, education, and health care. These factors gave collective organizational structures in Wuxi particular strength and vitality. They also contributed to higher levels of industrialization in the rural

Table 1.3. *Regional Variation in Economic Structure at Mid-Reform,*
1990 (Percentage Share of GNP)

| | National | Wenzhou | Wuxi | Shanghai | | |
		Yueqing County	Wuxi County	Songjiang County	Shanghai County	Jiading County
Agriculture	28	34	14	24	20	14
Industry	44	44	71	55	64	63
Commerce	28	22	15	22	16	23

Sources: See Table 1.2.

areas surrounding Wuxi and Shanghai than in other rural areas, as Table 1.3 demonstrates.

Townships in all three regions shared certain characteristics that also set them apart from the average. The success of rural industry in the three regions was related in part to the traditionally high degree of marketization of the local economies. Entrepreneurs in Wenzhou reactivated commercial contacts and marketing networks: by the mid-1980s, hundreds of thousands of marketing agents from Wenzhou could be found throughout the country (Yuan 1987). For the townships in suburban Wuxi and Shanghai, proximity to the major cities of the Yangzi Delta and subcontracting arrangements with nearby, urban state-run industries provided markets for the output of rural industry (Tao 1988). Along with their success in rural industry, all three regions generated substantial tax revenues. Yueqing, Wuxi, and Songjiang counties all ranked among the top 5 percent of counties in terms of tax revenue during the late 1980s and early 1990s.[51]

At the enterprise level, the range of property rights forms found in the research sites fell mainly within the broad categories of collective and private, but the official statistics reported in Table 1.2 mask the full range of variation. In the collective category were township- (*xiangban*), village- (*cunban*), and team-run (*duiban*) enterprises (*qiye*); domestic

---

[51] The supplementary research sites of Shanghai and Jiading counties in Shanghai Municipality also ranked among the top 5 percent. The rankings are prominently advertised in *Zhongguo baiming caizheng da xian* (1991). A note on the citation of Chinese sources is in order here. In many cases, the official author of an edited volume is an editorial committee with an extremely long and unwieldy name. In order to avoid excessively long author-date citations in the text, the title of such sources is used instead. In these cases, the source is also listed by title in the bibliography.

state–collective joint ventures (*lianying qiye*); the government-run variant of shareholding cooperatives (*gufen hezuo qiye*); and individually contracted collectives (*geren chengbao jiti qiye*) (found mainly at the level of the team) – the assets of which were originally financed by the collective. In the private category were private enterprises (*siying qiye*), the private variant of shareholding cooperatives, and individually contracted (fake) collectives (*jia jiti*) – the assets of which were originally financed by private individuals. Individual household firms (*getihu*), which employ fewer than eight people, are sometimes included in the category of private ownership; however, *getihu* are governed by a separate regulatory framework and do not fall within the scope of this study.[52] Individual household firms are addressed only to the extent that the governance practices for such firms impinge on those of other privately invested firms. Falling outside the collective and private categories are Chinese–foreign joint ventures (*Zhongwai hezi qiye*), which are also beyond the scope of this study. A complete list of interviews with enterprises and government agencies can be found in Appendix 1. Interviews are identified in the text by "Informant" followed by interview number.

This study focuses exclusively on industrial enterprises. While commercial and industrial firms accounted for roughly equal shares (about 40 percent each) of the total number of rural enterprises nationwide as of the early 1990s, industrial enterprises accounted for the lion's share of output value (about 75 percent). Given the close link between output value and taxation in the Chinese system and in light of the analytic focus on extractive institutions, the exclusive focus on industry was a theoretically justified way to limit the scope of the study. The distinction between industry and commerce does affect the analysis of property rights, however. The most blatant protectionism against private firms occurred in the industrial sector. Where local officials sought to protect the collective sector, they appeared resigned to allow private firms in commerce, while they excluded the private firms from industry. Secure property rights were arguably even more important to encouraging

---

[52] The distinction between *getihu* and other private firms is based on the notion that owners of *getihu* are themselves directly involved in labor, while owners of larger private firms, who employ eight or more workers, are engaged in the exploitation of labor. The cutoff of eight employees is derived from Marx. In theory, a firm of this size generates sufficient surplus value to support an owner who does not directly engage in labor. For a discussion of the ideological justification for distinguishing between *getihu* and other privately invested firms, see Yu-shan Wu (1994:189).

private investment in industry, because industrial assets tended to be less mobile and because less mobile assets entailed greater risks for investors.

STRUCTURE OF THE BOOK

The argument is presented in seven chapters. Chapter 2 focuses on the Maoist period, 1949 to 1978.[53] It examines the historical legacies of enterprise development in Wenzhou, Shanghai, and Wuxi, and demonstrates that the assets acquired by rural communities during the Maoist period created the foundation for their further industrialization efforts during the reform period. Chapter 2 challenges the conventional wisdom regarding the "self-reliant" development of commune and brigade enterprises by providing evidence of substantial state support for these firms in Shanghai and Wuxi.

Chapters 3 to 6 focus on the first decade and a half of reform, spanning the years 1978–93. Chapter 3 builds the foundation for the analysis presented in subsequent chapters by illuminating the incentives that shaped local cadre behavior. Specifically, it examines the incentives contained in the cadre evaluation system and the revenue-sharing fiscal system and shows that local cadres had political as well as economic incentives to promote rural industry in order to further expand the industrial base, generate revenue for local government coffers, finance the provision of public goods, and create jobs.

Chapter 4 focuses on property rights in rural industry and explains the emergence of distinct spatial patterns of property rights in the three research sites. It shows how collective forms of property rights continued to dominate in Wuxi, and, to a lesser extent, in Shanghai and how private forms of property rights came to dominate in Wenzhou. It documents the political and legislative efforts of Wenzhou cadres to make a credible commitment to the property rights of private investors as a means of encouraging sizable, long-term investments. By contrast, it shows how cadres in Shanghai and Wuxi channeled administrative and material resources into the development of collective enterprises, while inhibiting the development of private firms. Chapter 4 also highlights the challenges that weak markets and legal institutions posed

---

[53] For purposes of this study, the Maoist period extends two years beyond Mao's death, until the Third Plenum of the Eleventh Central Committee in December 1978; this meeting marks the beginning of the reform period.

for the development of rural industry in general and private industry in particular.

Chapter 5 examines the evolution of local institutions for revenue extraction from both private and collective firms. It shows how local cadres in Wenzhou and Shanghai responded to incentives to innovate in the extraction of revenue from private firms. Specifically, it demonstrates that the particular institutional arrangements established in the two locales reflected not only the transaction costs involved in revenue extraction but also the bargaining power of private firms. At the same time, innovative arrangements in both communities had the effect of revealing greater fiscal capacity to higher levels. By contrast, the chapter highlights the collusion between local officials and collective enterprise managers seeking to evade central taxes and to resist institutional change vis-à-vis the collective sector. Moreover, Chapter 5 illustrates the differential impact of provincial regulatory environments on revenue extraction at the grass roots. Finally, the chapter presents the results of a statistical model of revenue extraction as a means of testing the implications of the hypotheses developed through case studies.

Chapter 6 examines the implementation of credit policy in collective and private firms. It demonstrates that the rapid development of collective firms and their ability to undertake direct and indirect provision of public and welfare goods was supported by privileged access to credit from the state-run banking system. In other words, it shows that the allocation of credit to, like the extraction of revenue from, collective enterprises operated as part of the larger collective organizational structure at the township and village levels. Chapter 6 highlights the ways in which access to soft credit from the state-run banking system contributed to soft budget constraints well into the 1990s for townships, villages, and the collective firms they governed. By contrast, it shows that private firms were largely shut out by the state-run banking system during the period under study.

Chapter 7 focuses on the post-1993 period. It demonstrates how the new reform agenda articulated by the center in late 1993 is fundamentally reshaping the incentives and constraints of local officials with critical implications for the nature of both property rights and extractive institutions. It shows how the strategic manipulation of revenue extraction and credit allocation by local officials over the course of the first decade and a half of reform, particularly with respect to collective firms, created pressure for change in central state institutions. It highlights the far-reaching changes in central fiscal, banking, and legal institutions that were initiated by the Third Plenum of the Fourteenth Central Committee in November 1993. These changes have begun to transform the incentives and constraints facing local officials, most notably by hardening the budget constraints of local governments and the firms they supervise. As the concluding chapter demonstrates, it is only in the context of these changes in the environment for local officials that we have begun to see a dramatic move toward privatization of collective firms in the years since 1994. Indeed, within a given arrangement of national institutions, the evolution of property rights appears to be path dependent. However, when substantial change occurs in the broader institutional environment, dramatic change can occur at the local level as well. As this study demonstrates, institutional change can best be explained by examining the complex interaction of individuals, institutions, and the larger environment in which they exist.

2

The Maoist Legacy in Rural Industry

R URAL industry has expanded dramatically since 1978; indeed, Deng Xiaoping described it as one of the great, unanticipated successes of the post-Mao economic reforms (Ma, Wang, and Liu 1994:2). However, it would be historically inaccurate to characterize rural industrial growth simply as a product of reform. While key changes in the institutional environment of local officials at the outset of the reform period contributed in important ways to the takeoff of rural industry, its development in the 1980s and 1990s also had deeper historical roots.[1] The legacy of rural industrial development during the Maoist period has had profound implications for the subsequent development of rural industry during the reform period.

Rural industrialization was in part a legacy of the Great Leap Forward from 1958 to 1961, as epitomized by the slogans of "self-reliance" and "walking on two legs."[2] However, contrary to the commonly accepted official rhetoric of "self-reliance," the areas in which rural industries were most successful under Mao were, in many ways, the least self-reliant.[3] Indeed, rural industry in Wuxi and Songjiang Counties received significantly more state support than is commonly understood and certainly more than is implied by the slogan of "self-reliance." By contrast, rural industry in Yueqing County received relatively little state support and was arguably much closer to the Maoist ideal of self-reliance. Ironically,

---

[1] Chapter 3 details changes in the post-1978 institutional environment.

[2] "Self-reliance (*zili gengsheng*)" refers to the use of local resources to meet local needs, while "walking on two legs (*liangtiao tui zoulu*)" refers to the simultaneous promotion of traditional and modern industries in rural and urban areas, respectively.

[3] Christine Wong (1991a) was the first to make this point. The existence of some state support was also noted by early analysts of rural industry, although it received little attention. See, for example, Riskin (1971; 1978). Here, I differentiate the nature and degree of state support for rural industry received by particular communities.

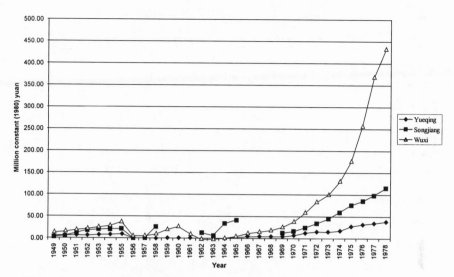

Figure 2.1. Gross value of industrial output (GVIO), township (commune) and village (brigade) level and below, 1949–78.
Note: Data on Songjiang for the periods 1959–61 and 1966–8 are not reported.
Sources: *Songjiang xianzhi* (1991: 11–12; 426; 454–5); *Yueqing sishi nian 1949–1989* (1989:76ff); *Wuxi xian gongye zhi* (1990: 25–8).

however, it was Yueqing that was most frequently and vehemently attacked during the Maoist period for its "capitalist excesses."

The gap in industrial output among the three locales widened dramatically during the Maoist period. As Figure 2.1 illustrates, industrial output of commune- and brigade-enterprises (CBEs) in Wuxi far exceeded that in Songjiang and Yueqing by 1978.[4] Examined in per capita terms (Figure 2.2), industrial output of CBEs in less populous Songjiang was strong, but Wuxi, despite its large population, still outperformed Songjiang even in per capita terms by the end of the Maoist period. The gap between Wuxi and Songjiang, on the one hand, and Yueqing, on the other, also widened (Table 2.1). The disparity is evident not only in terms of industrial output but also in terms of the share of employment generated by rural industry. As of 1978, more than 12 percent of the population was employed in industry in Wuxi, compared with 11 percent in Songjiang and only 3 percent in Yueqing.[5] The Maoist

[4] Commune- and brigade-enterprises were the precursors of township- and village-run collectives.

[5] These employment figures include county-run industry. See *Songjiang xianzhi* (1991:426; 454), *Yueqing sishi nian 1949–1989* (1989:76), and *Wuxi xian tongji nianjian 1990* (1991:87).

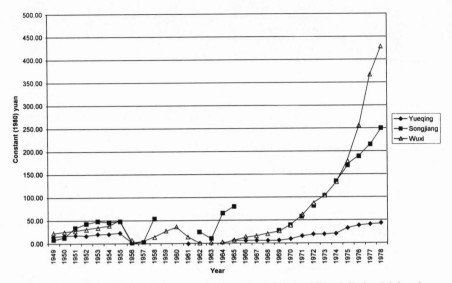

Figure 2.2. GVIO per capita, township (commune) and village (brigade) level and below, 1949–78. *Note*: Data on Songjiang for the periods 1959–61 and 1966–8 are not reported. *Sources*: See Figure 2.1.

era enhanced a legacy of robust rural industrial development in Wuxi and, to a somewhat lesser extent, in Songjiang, while it left a legacy of weaker rural industrial development in Yueqing.

Many scholars of Chinese development have uncritically accepted the Maoist rhetoric of "self-reliance." The conventional wisdom holds that rural industry was financed through local accumulation of capital from agriculture, that inputs were acquired from within the local economy, and that the products of rural industry were consumed locally – completely outside of state plans. Edward Steinfeld (1998:12–13), for example, characterizes CBEs as self-sufficient, market-oriented enterprises. By contrast, Christine Wong (1991a) highlights the central role of the state in promoting rural industrial development during the Maoist period. Her research shows that "rural industrialization . . . was a program initiated from the top, which determined the scope and objectives of the program and provided many resources for its implementation."[6] Building on Wong's findings, this book challenges the conventional wisdom and argues

[6] Joseph, Wong, and Zweig (1991:11). Wong argues that the high degree of reliance on state funds calls into question claims about the efficiency of rural, small-scale industry in the pre-reform period.

Table 2.1. *Gross Value of Industrial Output, 1949–78 (million constant 1980 yuan)*

	Yueqing County						Songjiang County						Wuxi County					
	Total	Subtotal[a]	County	Township	Village	Other	Total	Subtotal[a]	County	Township	Village	Other	Total	Subtotal[a]	County	Township	Village	Other
1949	5.95	5.95			2.46	3.49	12.22	3.05	9.17			3.05	16.59	16.59				16.59
1950	7.30	6.95	0.35		2.73	4.22	16.26	5.10	11.16			5.10	18.24	18.24				18.24
1951	8.36	7.79	0.57		3.41	4.38	25.78	13.96	11.82			13.96	20.61	20.61				20.61
1952	9.66	7.20	2.46		2.76	4.44	32.13	18.11	14.02			18.11	25.24	22.68	2.56			22.68
1953	12.54	9.02	3.52		3.24	5.78	37.12	20.47	16.65			20.47	28.27	25.77	2.50			25.77
1954	12.43	9.25	3.18		3.77	5.48	38.73	19.63	19.10			19.63	36.47	30.23	6.24			30.23
1955	16.98	10.67	6.31		2.87	7.80	40.74	21.64	19.10			21.64	47.26	39.80	7.46			39.80
1956	17.88	0.68	17.20		0.68		47.93	0.80	47.13			0.80	35.90	6.44	29.46			6.44
1957	21.87	1.92	19.95		1.92		48.08	1.50	46.58			1.50	43.02	5.30	37.72			5.30
1958	30.48	0.00	30.48				54.87	25.46	29.41			25.46	54.79	12.15	42.64	12.15		
1959	36.57	0.00	36.57				67.08	n/a	n/a				81.83	22.48	59.35	22.48		
1960	37.51	0.00	37.51				94.98	n/a	n/a				88.33	28.39	59.94	28.39		
1961	25.11	0.28	24.83		0.28		100.28	n/a	n/a				52.18	12.16	40.02	12.16		
1962	22.53	0.32	22.21		0.32		60.14	12.59	47.55	1.75		10.84	44.61	0.16	44.45	0.16		
1963	20.36	0.77	19.59		0.77		48.19	6.06	42.13	1.64		4.42	42.91	0.14	42.77	0.14		
1964	21.27	0.71	20.56		0.71		56.59	34.46	22.13	2.74		31.72	54.53	2.72	51.81	0.19	2.53	
1965	26.48	5.00	21.48		5.00		72.16	42.71	29.45	3.10		39.61	64.56	5.56	59.00	0.21	5.35	
1966	24.87	5.00	19.87		5.00		49.18		n/a				74.89	13.42	61.47	5.59	7.83	
1967	26.35	5.00	21.35		5.00		64.71		n/a				78.74	15.97	62.77	7.52	8.45	
1968	28.24	5.00	23.24		5.00		65.52		n/a				77.42	20.61	56.81	9.96	10.65	
1969	28.62	5.00	23.62		5.00		67.06	12.51	54.55	8.44	4.07		95.75	27.32	68.43	13.26	14.06	
1970	33.17	8.21	24.96	2.71	5.50		85.95	17.23	68.72	12.92	4.31		112.98	39.91	73.07	18.75	21.16	
1971	42.81	12.84	29.97	5.84	7.00		115.50	25.41	90.09	18.20	7.21		155.78	60.18	95.60	34.18	26.00	
1972	51.31	15.82	35.49	7.82	8.00		135.72	35.40	100.32	25.71	9.69		193.73	85.07	108.66	52.44	32.63	
1973	53.48	16.00	37.48	9.00	7.00		155.64	45.54	110.10	31.16	14.38		227.60	100.08	127.52	61.79	38.29	
1974	55.81	17.47	38.34	10.47	7.00		183.06	59.59	123.47	41.14	18.45		272.88	131.74	141.14	77.89	53.85	
1975	62.24	27.80	34.44	13.80	14.00		207.63	75.10	132.53	51.38	23.71		349.02	177.93	171.09	100.05	77.88	
1976	60.83	32.46	28.37	17.46	15.00		225.75	84.67	141.08	56.99	27.86		460.47	256.49	203.98	140.00	116.49	
1977	74.66	35.50	39.16	20.00	15.50		247.70	97.85	149.85	65.21	32.65		592.57	369.26	223.31	199.71	169.55	
1978	91.33	38.36	52.97	22.02	16.34		271.81	114.57	157.24	77.53	37.04		667.44	432.80	234.64	243.25	189.55	

[a] Subtotal includes township (commune) level and below.

Sources: Songjiang xianzhi (1991:11–12; 426; 454–5). *Yueqing sishi nian 1949–1989* (1989:76ff). *Wuxi xian gongye zhi* (1990:25–8).

43

that it is impossible to explain the varied trajectories of rural industrial development in the 1980s and 1990s without a more accurate and nuanced assessment of development from the 1950s through the 1970s.

This chapter provides an overview of the Maoist legacy in rural industry and highlights the significance of state support for rural industry during this period. It challenges the notion that all rural industry under Mao was self-reliant: it demonstrates that, in Wuxi and Songjiang, commune and brigade industry received budgetary grants and bank loans and benefited from direct and indirect incorporation into state economic plans. In contrast, this chapter also shows that rural industrial development in Yueqing during the Maoist period was hampered by the relative absence of such state support. It demonstrates the relatively high degree of self-reliance of rural industrial initiatives in Yueqing – initiatives that were condemned as "capitalist" because many of them were private rather than state-led. Thus, for better and for worse, state intervention during the Maoist period was a key determinant of the strength of rural industry as of 1978.

This chapter begins with a brief discussion of the historical literature on rural industrialization in pre-1949 China, followed by an overview of national policy toward CBEs after 1949. It then traces the development of rural industry in each of the three research sites in order to demonstrate how and why the gaps among the three locales widened so dramatically in the lead-up to 1978. The conclusion of the chapter highlights the importance of Mao-era initiatives for the development of rural industry during the reform period.

HISTORICAL ACCOUNTS OF RURAL INDUSTRIALIZATION

The fact of and likely reasons for the failure of industrial takeoff in the late nineteenth and early twentieth centuries are subjects of intense dispute among historians and economists.[7] The debate is relevant to this study to the extent that scholars make an historical leap, employing arguments about pre-1949 developments to explain the success of rural industry in the 1980s. However, the relative lack of scholarly attention to the thirty-year period of Maoist rule, during which the state actively promoted rural industry, has led analysts across disciplines to underestimate the critical role of the Chinese state in rural industrialization during the twentieth century.

---

[7] This literature has been reviewed extensively elsewhere. See, for example, R. Bin Wong (1997:13–70). See also Philip Huang (1991), Ramon Myers (1991), and R. Bin Wong (1992).

Historians agree that traditional handicraft industries flourished and that at least a few modern industries had been established in rural areas before the Japanese invasion of 1937, particularly in the region of the lower Yangzi River. Furthermore, some historians suggest that pre-1949 patterns of economic growth hold the key to explaining the success of rural industry after 1978. As Madeleine Zelin (1991:59) states,

> The recent upsurge in small-scale entrepreneurship and the large part it has played in the expansion of China's GDP provides [sic] striking evidence of the reemergence of older patterns of economic interaction in response to structural givens that have not changed dramatically despite forty years of Communist rule. . . . The regions that have been most successful in the establishment of small-scale and handicraft industries are, not surprisingly, the same towns whose geographic location and transportation endowment made them centers of trade in the late Qing.

Yet Zelin also argues that the commercial patterns of the late Qing "did not produce the basis for modern industrial growth" (Zelin 1991:56). Thus, it is not clear from her account how the capital and technology for the modern growth of rural industry were generated. Thomas Rawski (1989:82) addresses this point with his argument that the high degree of integration of urban and rural markets in prewar China naturally led to the spread of industrial capital and modern production techniques and that such "spread effects" explain the growth of rural industry in both the pre-1949 and post-1978 periods.

In such historical accounts, however, there is surprisingly little discussion of the development of rural industry during the nearly three decades of Mao's rule after 1949. Concomitantly, there is little analysis of the ways in which the Maoist state shaped the subsequent development of rural industry. This omission is significant, because the existence of sources of capital and technology necessary to underpin modern industrial growth is a key issue in the historical debates.[8] In contrast to Rawski, Philip Huang

---

[8] As Jan Svejnar and Josephine Woo (1990:73–4) point out in the World Bank's rural industry study, "The size, structure, and performance of . . . [rural nonstate enterprises] depend greatly on geographic and historical factors, the availability and types of local resources, the quality and size of the local labor force, access to technology and capital, and the policies pursued by the central and especially the local government." Despite this recognition, little research has been conducted to date on the role of the state apparatus in promoting rural industry under Mao. The work of Christine Wong is a notable exception.

(1990) argues that commercialization of the prewar rural economy failed to provide the capital and technology needed to bring about transformative economic growth.[9] Rather, according to Huang, "What finally powered genuine development . . . was diversification, especially by industrialization. . . . It was the opening up of commune and brigade jobs that finally reversed the six-centuries-long pattern of involution . . ." (P. Huang 1990:318). However, Huang provides only a hint of how such a transformation came about. He notes that "significant advances were made in the late 1960s and early 1970s, during the Cultural Revolution years, as urban industry began to forge processing links with communes or to send phased-out equipment to the communes" (Ibid). Thus, Huang goes further than other historians in delving into the developments of the Maoist period; nevertheless, he provides little analysis of the role of the state beyond the commune in developing rural industry.

In general, state intervention can affect both the pace and direction of development and can be consonant with or at odds with market forces (Wade 1990). In the rural industrial sector under Mao, some developments appear to have been consonant with rural factor endowments identified by Rawski (1989:82), namely "relatively low wages and land costs," and thus with the direction market forces might have dictated. Other developments were clearly at odds with what market forces would have indicated. As Barry Naughton (1995:145) points out, many rural industries developed under Mao were more capital-intensive than would be expected given rural factor endowments. This chapter demonstrates that, during the Maoist period, local state officials intervened to facilitate access to capital, technology, and distribution channels for rural collectives in certain locales, thus shaping the trajectory of rural industrial development.

CENTRAL STATE POLICY TOWARD RURAL INDUSTRY

The Great Leap Forward

The new communist state's First Five-Year Plan (1953–57), with its emphasis on urban heavy industry, did little to further rural industrial-

---

[9] Huang characterizes the Chinese economy in the late nineteenth and early twentieth centuries as subject to involutionary growth. In other words, output expanded due to intensified production in both agriculture and handicraft industries, but in the face of a rapidly expanding labor force, the marginal return to labor did not increase beyond the subsistence level.

ization or even the narrower goal of agricultural mechanization. It was only with the beginning of the Second Five-Year Plan that a new approach to rural industry emerged in the context of the Great Leap Forward and the strategy of "walking on two legs." Under this strategy, small-scale, labor-intensive industry employing simple technologies would be developed simultaneously with large-scale, modern industry.[10] The Chengdu Conference at the outset of the Great Leap in April 1958 stipulated that production of relatively sophisticated equipment for agricultural mechanization would be the responsibility of provincial-level governments and that counties and townships should establish workshops for simple machine repair and manufacturing of spare parts.[11] Local agricultural producers' cooperatives (the precursors of people's communes) would be charged with putting the new equipment to use in order to achieve the goal of gradually mechanizing agriculture. However, by August (only four months later), newly invented people's communes had become the focus of the Great Leap strategy.[12] They were intended to change the course of development by combining agricultural and industrial production in a single organization.[13]

The Sixth Plenum of the Eighth Central Committee in December 1958 established a more explicit link between communes and broader industrial development with the slogan: "People's communes should go in big for industry (*renmin gongshe bixu da ban gongye*)."[14] In an effort to jump-start commune industries, many communes acquired industrial assets by administrative fiat. Communes took over the operations of handicraft cooperatives and small workshops previously run by agricul-

---

[10] On the strategy pursued by industrial planners during the Great Leap Forward, see Bachman (1991).

[11] Zhonggong zhongyang weiyuanhui, "Guanyu nongye jixiehua wenti de yijian (Opinion on the Question of Agricultural Mechanization)," in *Nongye jitihua zhongyao wenjian huibian* (1982:17–18).

[12] People's communes attempted to organize rural life on a heretofore unimagined scale and to fuse rural administration, agricultural and industrial production, and the rural militia into a single organization. Communes combined dozens of agricultural producers' cooperatives and encompassed thousands of households at their extreme. On communization, see Chan, Madsen, and Unger (1992).

[13] Zhonggong zhongyang weiyuanhui, "Guanyu zai nongcun jianli renmin gongshe wenti de jueyi (Resolution on the Question of Establishing People's Communes in Rural Areas)," in *Nongye jitihua zhongyao wenjian huibian* (1982:69); and "Zhonggong zhongyang zhengzhiju zai Beidaihe juxing de kuoda huiyi (CCP Central Committee Politburo Holds Expanded Meeting at Beidaihe)," *Renmin ribao*, September 1, 1958.

[14] Zhongguo gongchandang, "Guanyu renmin gongshe ruogan wenti de jueyi (Resolution on Several Questions regarding People's Communes)," in *Nongye jitihua zhongyao wenjian huibian* (1982:117).

tural producers' cooperatives (*Dangdai Zhongguo de xiangzhen qiye* 1991:36–7). Even industrial assets of some existing state and collective entities were transferred to commune control. Subsequent criticism of "the indiscriminate transfer (*yi ping er diao*) of resources" in the development of commune industry highlights the conflicts generated by this approach. To attenuate some of the conflicts, the Shanghai Conference of April 1959 stipulated that assets taken over from former agricultural producers' cooperatives should be turned over to production brigades (one level down from communes). This change actually did little to reduce conflict, but the phenomenon of rural enterprise was thus expanded to include operations at both the commune and brigade levels (Ibid).

From its inception, commune- and brigade-run industry was intended to use local materials to meet local needs, but it was not intended to compete with modern, urban industry.[15] By late 1959, however, additional conflicts had emerged between state-run, county-run, and commune-run industries, because communes were holding back raw materials for processing themselves and, in some cases, diverting resources from state projects. A subsequent indictment of Great Leap rural industry asserted that "the money, materials and construction forces devoted to [these] projects are mostly obtained through improper channels . . . those people claiming reliance on their own resources actually impair the State's interests and thwart the completion of planned projects. . . ."[16] Indeed, an account of rural industrial development in Wuxi County describes personnel from local material bureaus scouring the country for informal access to industrial inputs during this period (*Wuxi xian gongye zhi* 1990:75).

In response to such practices, a national conference held in December 1959 attempted to reprioritize the functions of commune industry in terms of the "two locals and four serves."[17] The "two locals" reinforced the principle that communes should employ local materials to meet local needs. The "four serves" prioritized the broader functions of commune enterprises. First, communes should serve agriculture by concentrating

---

[15] Zhongguo gongchandang, "Resolution on Several Questions regarding People's Communes," in Ibid.

[16] *Nanfang ribao* (Southern daily), May 15, 1962, as cited in Riskin (1978:81).

[17] Zhongguo gongchandang, "Guanyu renmin gongshe guodu wenti – si shengshi zuotanhui jiyao (Transitional Questions regarding the People's Communes – Abstract of a Four-Province Meeting)," in *Nongye jitihua zhongyao wenjian huibian* (1982:275ff).

on the production of things such as agricultural tools and machinery, fertilizer, pesticide, and silage. Second, they should serve commune members' daily needs by engaging in traditional handicrafts and services such as grain processing, sewing, and cobbling. Third, they should serve large-scale industry and, fourth, they should serve exports – in both cases by undertaking only simple processing. All advanced processing of raw materials was to remain the province of urban industry.

As the disaster caused by the Great Leap became increasingly apparent, central policy toward commune- and brigade-run industry began a gradual reversal.[18] Beginning in 1960, assets previously transferred to communes from existing state and collective enterprises were returned to their original units (*Dangdai Zhongguo de xiangzhen qiye* 1991:39). The proportion of the rural labor force engaged in nonagricultural pursuits was also subject to new limits.[19] Finally, during the autumn of 1962, the Tenth Plenum of the Eighth Central Committee revised the regulations governing rural people's communes and established the policy that "in general, communes should not establish enterprises (*gongshe... yiban de buban qiye*)."[20] Where conditions were not ripe for nonagricultural development, existing enterprises were to close. Any remaining enterprises were to be transferred back to revived handicraft cooperatives or to management and operation by production teams, households, or individuals. Communes could continue to manage and operate enterprises only with the express approval of the county leadership and the commune representative assembly. Moreover, any remaining commune-run enterprises were not to interfere with agricultural production or with state procurement of agricultural products or other raw materials. The revised regulations represented the end of the first, abortive stage of development for commune- and brigade-enterprises.

---

[18] The attempt to develop industry and agriculture simultaneously in an ideologically charged atmosphere resulted in the diversion of essential agricultural labor into nonagricultural pursuits and in the excessive procurement of grain from the rural sector by the state. The outcome was an agricultural crisis that resulted in tens of millions of deaths from famine between 1959 and 1961.

[19] Zhonggong zhongyang weiyuanhui, "Guanyu nongcun renmin gongshe dangqian zhengce wenti de jinji zhishi xin (Urgent Letter of Instruction regarding Current Policy Questions on Rural People's Communes)," in *Nongye jitihua zhongyao wenjian huibian* (1982:377–87, esp. 383).

[20] Zhongguo gongchandang, "Nongcun renmin gongshe gongzuo tiaoli xiuzheng caoan (Revised Draft Working Regulations for Rural People's Communes)," in *Nongye jitihua zhongyao wenjian huibian* (1982:628–49).

The Post-Leap Period and the Cultural Revolution

The hiatus in rural industrial development was relatively brief, although the official policy that held that communes should not establish industrial enterprises remained in force, and the "four cleans" campaign, which targeted corrupt rural cadres, created a hostile political environment for enterprise development. As Carl Riskin (1978:84) points out, "The revival of rural industries seems to have begun by 1963, when the recovery of the national economy as a whole was well under way." Indeed, despite the hostile environment created by the "four cleans," in April 1964, Premier Zhou Enlai accompanied a foreign delegation to the Shanghai suburban county of Jiading to tour Malu Commune, where a handful of enterprises had continued to function even after 1962 (*Dangdai Zhongguo de xiangzhen qiye* 1991:43). A policy statement on the development of agricultural sideline industries the following year (1965) created a further opening for the renewed development of commune- and brigade-run enterprises.[21] By 1966, Mao himself was once again calling on communes to establish collective industries where conditions allowed.[22] A conference on agricultural mechanization held during the summer of 1966 gave lip service to the Great Leap slogan of "self reliance" while at the same time calling for state support for commune and brigade enterprises in the form of budgetary grants, bank loans, planned material supply, and technical training (Fang 1984:412–13). This conference paid particular attention to the development of the "five small industries," that is, the five relatively capital-intensive, producer-good industries that were seen as critical to further agricultural development: iron and steel, chemical fertilizers, machinery, cement, and electric power generation (Wong 1979:9). As will be demonstrated in greater detail in the subsequent section, the dramatic growth of commune-run industry in Wuxi County dates from the mid-1960s.

Other central policies indirectly facilitated the growth of rural industry during the 1960s. Two waves of rustication provided valuable intangible resources to the countryside that would prove instrumental to the

---

[21] Zhonggong zhongyang guowuyuan, "Guanyu dali fazhan nongcun fuye shengchan de zhishi (Instructions regarding Vigorously Developing Rural Sideline Production)," in *Nongye jitihua zhongyao wenjian huibian* (1982:846–50).

[22] "Mao Zedong tongzhi gei Lin Biao de xin (Comrade Mao Zedong's Letter to Lin Biao)," in *Nongye jitihua zhongyao wenjian huibian* (1982:860). See also *Dangdai Zhongguo de xiangzhen qiye* (1991:46).

further development of rural industry. During the "three bad years," 1959–61, in the aftermath of the Great Leap Forward, an estimated twenty million cadres, workers, and urban residents were sent back to rural areas, and in 1968, Mao again called for party cadres and intellectual youth to go to the countryside (*Dangdai Zhongguo de xiangzhen qiye* 1991:45–7). In each instance, former urbanites brought with them information, connections, and technical skills that they were able to exploit in the service of commune and brigade enterprises.[23] Moreover, as urban factories were disrupted by Cultural Revolution turmoil, the output of urban industry declined (by 14 percent in 1967 and 5 percent in 1968), resulting in pent-up demand for industrial products – demand that some rural industries stepped in to fill (Ibid).

While the early openings in the mid-1960s allowed some commune and brigade enterprises to develop and expand, the real watershed for rural industrial development during the Maoist period came in 1970. The National Work Conference on Finance and Banking held in July of that year called for actively supporting the development of the "five small industries" (*Dangdai Zhongguo de jingji tizhi gaige* 1984:143; Fang 1984:467). "Active support" had three components. First, the conference called for the allocation of 8 billion yuan in earmarked funds to be used over the next five-year period. Second, loss-making enterprises could receive tax exemptions or reductions or receive subsidies from the public finance bureau. This policy was formally implemented in 1972 when the right to determine tax exemptions or reductions for the "five small industries" and for all commune- and brigade-run enterprises was decentralized to the local level (*Dangdai Zhongguo de jingji tizhi gaige* 1984:145; Fang 1984:494). Third, enterprises could seek loans from banks or credit cooperatives for development of the "five small industries." While loans were to be directed primarily to county-run enterprises, they were also available to commune- and brigade-run firms (T. Xu 1996:346). Indeed, by 1976, bank loans for commune and brigade enterprises and agricultural mechanization had reached 2.1 billion yuan, accounting for more than 50 percent of all rural loans outstanding (Ibid:348).

The 1970 North China Agricultural Conference that followed the finance and banking conference reaffirmed the policy of "walking on two

---

[23] The contributions to the long-term development of rural industry made by rusticated urbanites are not inconsistent with the fact that they were often perceived in the short-term as a burden by the agricultural communities that had to support them by providing them with food and shelter. See, for example, Jacka (1997:38).

legs" and again emphasized development of the "five small industries" in the service of agricultural development.[24] The following year the State Council held another conference to implement the goals for agricultural mechanization set in 1970.[25] The conference stipulated that an average of 590 million yuan per year in grants should be allocated in the Fourth Five-Year Plan to support mechanization projects specifically at the commune level (*Dangdai Zhongguo de xiangzhen qiye* 1991:49). Central party and government organs mobilized support for commune and brigade enterprises through both policies and the allocation of funds.

As Christine Wong (1991a:185) indicates, "New information now available on the Cultural Revolution period paints a vastly different picture of how rural industrialization was carried out . . . statistics show the share of total investment financed by state funds to have been surprisingly large." As her research on the five small industries demonstrates, budgetary grants for new construction and renovation accounted for roughly two-thirds (8 billion yuan) of total investment in small nitrogenous fertilizer plants during the years 1958 to 1979. Similarly, budgetary grants financed more than half (8 to 9 billion yuan) of total investment in farm machinery production between 1966 and 1978.

Furthermore, a substantial amount of state resources flowed to commune and brigade enterprises through informal channels. In 1967, control over all enterprise depreciation funds was decentralized to the local level. "Throughout the Cultural Revolution period, these funds were commonly pooled by local governments and industrial bureaus and diverted to investment in new enterprises" (Wong 1991a:188). In addition, local officials often directed existing state and collective enterprises to support the development of commune enterprises, with the cost of equipment, materials, and personnel borne by the existing enterprises and, indirectly therefore, by the state plan. Wong concludes that "local governments took advantage of the informal channels to finance the bulk of investment in rural industry with state funds . . ." (Ibid:194). Such practices underscore the positive relationship between the existence of

---

[24] The conference also reproduced the rhetoric of "self-reliance." Zhonggong zhongyang weiyuanhui, "Pizhuan guowuyuan guanyu beifang diqu nongye huiyi de baogao (Approval and Transmission of the State Council Report on the North China Agricultural Conference)," in *Nongye jitihua zhongyao wenjian huibian* (1982:886–95, esp. 893).

[25] Guowuyuan, "Guanyu jiakuai shixian nongye jixiehua wenti de baogao (zhaiyao) (Report concerning Several Questions on Speeding Up the Realization of Agricultural Mechanization [Abstract])," in *Nongye jitihua zhongyao wenjian huibian* (1982:902–13).

local county-run industry and the development of commune and brigade industry – a relationship that will be highlighted in the case studies that follow. By 1975, the role of urban industry in promoting the development of rural enterprises had become official policy, and by 1976, the promotion of rural industry had become further institutionalized through the establishment of a Rural Industry Management Bureau within the Ministry of Agriculture (*Dangdai Zhongguo de xiangzhen qiye* 1991:56).

LOCAL STATE POLICY TOWARD RURAL INDUSTRY

The preceding section outlined central policy toward commune and brigade industry during the Maoist period. In accounting for local variation, however, it is also important to take into account how *local* officials created and exploited opportunities for industrial development.

A brief assessment of the three research sites at the time of the founding of the People's Republic presents a somewhat equivocal picture of their comparative development potential. As of 1949, industrial output per capita, including output at the county, township, village, and household levels, in Songjiang exceeded that in both Wuxi and Yueqing (Table 2.2). On the other hand, Songjiang trailed both Wuxi and Yueqing in per capita agricultural output with 79 yuan, compared with 350 yuan in Wuxi and 132 yuan in Yueqing. Philip Huang (1990) argues that none of the three locales had reached the point of "takeoff" for sustained industrial development by 1949. Indeed, as sociologist Fei Hsiao T'ung (1986:38–9) notes, "Certain external factors were required to set the phenomenon in motion. . . . The establishment of industry requires materials, labour, money, equipment, technology, and a market for its products." As the subsequent sections of this chapter demonstrate, local state policies were crucial in promoting rural industrial development during the Maoist period.

Wuxi County: Creating Links between City and Countryside

Wuxi enjoyed many favorable conditions for the development of rural industry at the beginning of the Maoist period. First, it boasted a highly productive agricultural sector that provided an important foundation for rural industrial development. Indeed, the start-up capital for some of the smaller collective firms came from revenues generated by collective

Table 2.2. Gross Value of Agricultural and Industrial Output Per Capita, 1949–78 (yuan)

	Yueqing County			Songjiang County			Wuxi County		
	Total	Agriculture	Industry	Total	Agriculture	Industry	Total	Agriculture	Industry
1949	146	132	15	110	79	31	374	350	23
1950	155	138	18	141	101	40	439	413	26
1951	173	153	20	170	107	63	425	397	29
1952	187	164	23	198	121	77	475	440	35
1953	195	166	29	210	123	87	495	457	39
1954	189	160	29	210	121	89	468	419	49
1955	209	171	38	216	124	92	531	468	62
1956	203	165	39	235	128	107	535	488	47
1957	251	206	46	237	131	105	460	405	55
1958	253	192	62	274	157	117	506	434	72
1959	244	172	72	287	145	142	522	415	107
1960	230	156	74	345	146	200	509	392	117
1961	198	149	49	357	146	211	352	283	69
1962	196	154	42	268	143	125	387	331	57
1963	204	167	37	245	148	97	428	376	53
1964	216	179	38	297	185	112	479	413	65
1965	211	165	45	284	145	139	592	516	76

1966	214	173	41	344	219	125	602	516	87
1967	179	137	42	389	226	163	514	423	90
1968	199	155	44	403	242	161	499	411	88
1969	200	157	43	422	260	162	557	451	106
1970	223	175	48	455	251	204	662	540	122
1971	225	165	61	552	279	273	723	557	166
1972	240	169	71	636	317	319	881	676	205
1973	229	157	72	683	321	362	929	691	237
1974	215	142	74	701	280	421	1,032	750	282
1975	209	128	80	716	242	473	1,176	820	356
1976	202	125	77	786	276	509	1,426	961	465
1977	228	136	92	793	242	551	1,626	1,034	593
1978	269	158	111	918	319	599	1,868	1,206	662

Note: Industrial output includes county, township (commune), and village (brigade) levels and below.

Sources: See Table 2.1.

agriculture and accumulated at the commune or brigade level. Furthermore, industries such as textiles and food processing relied for inputs on
raw materials provided by the agricultural sector. Second, a low land-to-
labor ratio in Wuxi contributed to a ready supply of surplus labor. Third,
Wuxi was favorably situated astride the Nanjing–Shanghai transportation corridor with relatively good road, water, and rail transport. It was
also proximate to the cities of Suzhou, Wuxi, and Changzhou and to the
industrial port city of Shanghai. Fourth, Wuxi boasted a long tradition of
handicraft production of cotton and silk textiles as well as recent experience with early modern industry in the decades before 1937 (Bell 1985).
Nevertheless, prior to 1949 and into the early communist period, these
conditions had not resulted in what Philip Huang refers to as "transformative rural development."[26]

Existing handicraft production did provide a foundation for Maoist
rural industry, however. With the start of the Great Leap Forward, all
handicraft cooperatives in Wuxi were turned over to commune control
by order of the county party committee. Employing assets from handicraft cooperatives and other existing assets, the county was able to establish a remarkable number of commune enterprises in a relatively short
time. Supplementing these assets were grants in excess of 7 million yuan
made by township-level public finance offices to support the development of commune-run industry during the first three years of the Great
Leap (*Wuxi xian gongye zhi* 1990:59). By the end of 1958, Wuxi County
reported the establishment of 541 commune enterprises, employing
nearly seven thousand people (Ibid). By 1959, the number of commune
factories had been consolidated to 14, while employment swelled to more
than sixteen thousand.

That year, officials from Wuxi City and Wuxi County together crafted

---

[26] As Philip Huang (1990:130) writes, "even in the case of vigorously modernizing Wuxi,
as has been seen, crop production and handicrafts continued down involutionary paths.
The great abundance of cheap female and child labor powerfully shaped the nature of
agrarian change. The new sericulture still yielded smaller marginal returns per workday
than rice. . . . So even for Wuxi, it will not do to project on the countryside the predictions of the classical model: of mutually reinforcing and spiraling urban and rural development with commercialization. I do not want to contend that genuine development
could not have taken place in due course. Had off-farm employment in Wuxi continued
to the point where even auxiliary household labor became scarce and incomes per
workday in peasant crop and handicraft production rose, and had the resulting surplus
been available for capitalizing investments in rural production, transformative change
in peasant livelihood could probably have come to the Wuxi countryside, as it was to do
in the 1980s. But that point was far from being reached in the 1930s, despite the impressive modernization of agriculture that was taking place."

a policy that would continue to shape rural industrial development for the remainder of the Maoist period and into the reform period. The policy entailed "creating linkages between city and countryside, factory and commune; supporting rural areas; and developing industry" (*Wuxi xian gongye zhi* 1990:7).[27] Under this policy, the county was able to expand the industrial sectors in which commune enterprises were engaged during the Great Leap Forward beyond agriculture-related sectors to include electronics, paper, glass, plastics, and printing. Links between rural industry and the urban, state-run, planned economy started early in Wuxi; in subsequent years these linkages grew extensively and took a variety of forms. Moreover, Wuxi's experience highlights the significance of the development of state enterprises and urban collectives for commune and brigade industries; as larger, urban enterprises developed, the opportunities for expansion of smaller, rural enterprises also grew.[28]

Following a brief retrenchment during the immediate post-Leap period, rural industry in Wuxi quickly resumed its new development trajectory.[29] A number of factors contributed to the rapid reemergence of rural industry. One critical factor was the pro-active stance of local party and government organs. Several local government agencies, including the county party committee, the economic committee, the industry bureau, and the material supply bureau, played unusually active roles in rural industrial development throughout the Cultural Revolution period. Spurred by a record grain harvest in 1965, the county party committee made the development of the rural economy – and rural industry in particular – a policy priority. At the same time, the county economic committee put forward a draft plan for "appropriately developing commune industry and consolidating the collective

---

[27] Administratively, Wuxi County was subordinate to Wuxi City from 1958 through 1962; however, during the years 1962 to 1983, it was shifted to the jurisdiction of Suzhou Prefecture. Despite the administrative changes, urban–rural linkages continued to play a crucial role in rural industrial development in the county.

[28] One issue that demands further research is the significance of variation in the backward and forward linkages of particular industrial sectors. County industries in certain sectors may have created more opportunities for linkages with rural industries than others.

[29] Beginning in 1961, some commune enterprises were temporarily transferred to county control; the number of county enterprises increased between 1961 and 1965, while the number of commune enterprises fell, although a few commune enterprises did continue to function. Another group of commune enterprises (especially ones involving the processing of agricultural products) were turned over to production brigades, where their output was accounted for as part of the gross value of agricultural output until 1964. Although official statistics do not provide data on the number of brigade-run enterprises

economy."[30] As of 1965, Wuxi County boasted thirty-five commune- and brigade-run industrial enterprises with output value of 5.6 million yuan (Liu 1990:900). As Table 2.1 shows, by 1966, the output value had jumped to 13 million yuan.

Leading cadres responsible for industry, who were displaced at the height of Cultural Revolution turmoil in the late 1960s, were reinstated by the end of 1970, and they continued to coordinate and promote rural industrial development directly from the county level (*Wuxi xian gongye zhi* 1990:9). Following the North China Agriculture Conference of 1970, the county party committee formulated the slogan "successfully develop industry to promote agriculture" (Ibid). According to a World Bank study, "In the early 1970s, after an intense debate, county authorities [in Wuxi] decided not to abandon [rural industry], even though in accordance with the spirit of the times they stressed the development of agriculture and grain production" (Svejnar and Woo 1990:73–4). Serving agriculture provided a justification to develop agricultural tools and machinery, fertilizer and pesticides, plastic sheeting, construction materials, and even electrical equipment.[31]

Officials at both the prefectural and provincial levels also offered political support for Wuxi's initiatives in rural industry. According to Fei Hsiao T'ung, leaders in Suzhou (which at the time included Wuxi within its jurisdiction) expressed the belief that "it is essential to support rural industries. For example, their supply of raw materials and energy and the sale of their products should be included in state plans if possible [and] they should be favored with low-interest loans" (Fei 1986:75). Similarly, provincial leaders also advocated active support for commune and brigade industry. In August 1975, provincial leaders openly promoted

before 1970, other measures indicate that brigade-run industries began to reemerge as early as 1964, when they were reported to have produced 2.53 million yuan in industrial output (*Wuxi xian gongye zhi* 1990:8; 27). See also Zhang Jianhong (1988:76).

[30] The document was entitled: "Shidang fazhan sheban qiye, gonggu nongcun jiti jingji de yijian (caoan) (Opinion on Appropriately Developing Commune-run Enterprises [and] Consolidating the Rural Collective Economy)," in *Wuxi xian gongye zhi* (1990:76).

[31] Moreover, as David Zweig points out, local officials also began to promote brigade-run industry in particular as an acceptable alternative to more radical proposals supported by the extreme left. Leftists sought to shift control over economic activity and ownership of the means of production to higher levels. Specifically, they sought to shift the accounting unit in agriculture from the team to the brigade. Local officials who promoted brigade-run industry could demonstrate compliance with calls to emphasize the brigade level without disrupting agriculture or agricultural production teams. As Zweig (1989:178) notes, "Brigade and commune factories remain the only Great Leap policy innovation to have developed during both radical and reform eras."

Wuxi's success with rural industry at a province-wide conference on industry and transportation, and in 1977, even as Dazhai Commune was touted as the national model for "taking grain as the key link," Jiangsu leaders promoted rural industry (*Wuxi xian gongye zhi* 1990:10). They insisted on "continuing the correct direction of bringing together industry and agriculture, city and countryside; aggressively developing commune and brigade industry; and more quickly realizing commune industrialization and agricultural mechanization" (*Dangdai Zhongguo de xiangzhen qiye* 1991:60–1). The provincial party secretary at that time, Hu Hong, paid a symbolic public visit to Wuxi County to drive the point home (*Jiangsu sheng dashiji* 1988:352–4). More concretely, officials at the provincial level also developed a set of preferential policies to promote commune and brigade industry. These policies included (1) expanded tax exemptions and reductions, (2) 50 million yuan in interest-free loans to help communes and brigades establish industrial enterprises, (3) political support for the use of local budgetary funds and agricultural loans to finance new investment in rural industry, (4) inclusion of commune and brigade enterprises in the province's sectoral development plans, and (5) official encouragement for many forms of urban–rural industrial linkages.[32]

Another critical set of factors were the extensive urban–rural linkages in Wuxi. Rusticated urbanites played a fortuitous role in the development of rural industry in Wuxi (Tao 1988:24; Zhang 1988:75). During the retrenchment following the Great Leap Forward, approximately thirty-three thousand urban workers relocated to Wuxi County following the slogan "return to the countryside to engage in agriculture (*huixiang*

---

[32] A total of nine forms of urban–rural industrial links were specified: (1) transferring product lines from urban to rural enterprises, (2) dispersing parts production for state firms among rural enterprises, (3) final processing of materials provided by state enterprises, (4) preliminary processing of raw materials by rural enterprises, (5) establishing long-term production and purchase agreements with rural enterprises (*dingdian shougou*), (6) supplying equipment and industrial by-products to rural enterprises, (7) training rural enterprise personnel in technology and skill development, (8) establishing subsidiary workshops by state enterprises in rural firms, and (9) encouraging colleges and research institutes to develop new products with rural enterprises (*Dangdai Zhongguo de xiangzhen qiye* 1991:61). The preferential policies were codified subsequently in the provincial "Regulations on Several Questions regarding Advancing the Development of Commune and Brigade Industry," promulgated in February 1978. Even in the face of a national campaign to readjust the economy in 1979, the Jiangsu provincial party committee continued to issue documents calling for support for commune and brigade industry in terms of funds, equipment, technology, and raw materials (Tao 1988:24; 160).

wunong)" (*Wuxi xian gongye zhi* 1990:10). As of 1970, an estimated one-third of the work force in commune and brigade enterprises in Wuxi was composed of skilled, formerly urban workers (*Dangdai Zhongguo de xiangzhen qiye* 1991:45). Sent-down youth also became a valuable resource for the development of industry. The following example documented by Fei Hsiao T'ung (1986:39) illustrates the impact of sent-down youth on rural industrialization in Sunan: "A chemical factory . . . was started from scratch in 1968, with the help of the father of a city youth who settled down in the commune that year. . . . The city chemical factory . . . supplied raw materials, technology, equipment, *and even part of the funds* the commune required to set up the chemical factory" (emphasis added). As Fei notes, "Examples of this kind are typical of many of the rural factories in southern Jiangsu Province" (Ibid.). Finally, sent-down cadres (*xiafang ganbu*) – including twenty-four hundred such cadres sent to Wuxi in 1970, many of whom had experience in engineering and operations – provided key managerial and technical personnel for commune enterprises (*Wuxi xian gongye zhi* 1990:9).

Such fortuitous connections, combined with the conscious policy of linking urban and rural industry, created opportunities for commune and brigade enterprises in Wuxi to acquire resources from and ultimately become players in the planned economy. Urban industry was a major source of equipment for rural factories. When the county public finance bureau or industrial bureau provided funds for new equipment purchases by state or collective enterprises, these enterprises commonly transferred their older production lines to commune operations (Ibid:51–2). The welding materials factory in Dongtan Town, for example, was established in this way in 1966 (Ibid:59; Informant 199). Thus, much of the equipment acquired by CBEs during the mid- to late-1960s was the old equipment of state factories originally financed through the state budget and transferred to the CBEs at little or no cost.

By the early 1970s, CBEs in Wuxi had also begun to process materials supplied through the plan on behalf of county-run state enterprises. Among the earliest state-owned enterprises (SOEs) to send processing orders to CBEs were the county-run tractor factory and the diesel equipment factory in Wuxi. As of 1971, thirty-six different commune factories were producing parts on behalf of the tractor factory (*Wuxi xian gongye zhi* 1990:67). Such processing arrangements quickly spread beyond the county. By the mid-1970s, 942 CBEs in Wuxi County were processing 1,140 types of products worth approximately 150 million yuan for 513

SOEs in Wuxi City (*Dangdai Zhongguo de xiangzhen qiye* 1991:61). Expanding the scope of processing even further, county officials established a special office to take processing orders from outside the Wuxi area. In 1975, for example, CBEs in Wuxi undertook processing work for the Wuhan Steel Factory and the Shanghai Sea Transport Bureau, among others. These processing arrangements provided local firms with planned materials, such as steel, iron, coke, and other raw materials (Wu and Ju 1994; *Wuxi xian gongye zhi* 1990:68). By 1980, CBEs were providing parts worth 217 million yuan to urban industry, accounting for 26 percent of CBE output. In many cases, occasional processing contracts grew into more formal types of cooperative production arrangements (*dingdian xiezuo*) between urban and rural firms.

In addition to plan materials acquired through production arrangements with SOEs, the county industry bureau and material supply bureau were also actively involved in arranging inputs for CBEs. Capital posed a particular problem. During the late 1960s and early 1970s, virtually every commune and brigade in the county sought to establish new factories using a variety of financial resources. Some funds were accumulated from agricultural activities by communes and brigades. At the same time, county leadership organs mobilized county government units and county-run enterprises to help lagging communes and brigades to establish new factories by providing grants of capital, equipment, and technology (*Wuxi xian gongye zhi* 1990:60). The public finance bureau made both grants and loans to commune and brigade enterprises, although precise data on amounts are not available. Data are available on outstanding loans made to commune and brigade industry from records maintained by the local branch of the Agriculture Bank. These loans grew from a paltry 60 thousand yuan in 1970 to 2.03 million yuan in 1975. By 1980, loans outstanding had already reached an impressive 50 million yuan.[33] Figures provided by the Agriculture Bank indicate that new commune investments in industry financed by remitted profits of existing enterprises also reached their height between 1976 and 1980; investment financed in this way totaled 50 million yuan in both 1979 and 1980 but declined steadily thereafter.[34] The key

---

[33] The exact figure was 49.76 million yuan (*Wuxi xian gongye zhi* 1990:60). Further research is required to determine the nature of the relationship between household incomes, savings rates, and Agriculture Bank lending to CBEs during the Maoist period.

[34] These figures were reported in *Wuxi xian tongji nianjian 1990* (1991:98). During the years from 1976 to 1979, commune enterprises consistently remitted about 80 percent of net profits, and 40 to 50 percent of these funds were channeled into new investments.

point is that the scale of capital initially provided to CBEs by the state and subsequently generated by CBEs themselves during the 1970s gave Wuxi's enterprises a significant head start compared to CBEs in other locales.

County officials in Wuxi also arranged a high degree of integration of CBE output into state plans at various levels. One means by which CBE output gained entrée into plan channels was through production agreements with state-owned enterprises. In addition, the county economic committee, along with the industry bureau at the county level, played a direct role in the management of commune and brigade enterprises by stipulating product types, product specifications, output volume, and even trademarks. In many cases, products of commune industries were subject to monopoly purchase by local commercial organs (*Wuxi xian gongye zhi* 1990:76–7). Machine tools, electrical machinery, and most products for export were put under county plans, while agricultural equipment, machine parts, and construction materials were put under ministerial, provincial, or prefectural plans. By 1976, fully 63 percent of CBE output value was included directly or indirectly in ministerial, provincial, prefectural, or county plans, leaving only 37 percent to be sold outside the plan.[35] These percentages remained stable through the end of the 1970s. With reform, however, the percentage of rural industrial output marketed within the plan gradually decreased to 34 percent by 1985 and continued to decrease thereafter.

Clearly, commune and brigade enterprises in Wuxi broke out of the confines of self-sufficiency and "using local materials to meet local needs" well before the end of the Maoist period. Moreover, CBEs exceeded county-run state and collective enterprises in gross value of industrial output as early as 1975. By 1978, CBEs accounted for fully 65 percent of industrial output in Wuxi.

---

[35] According to Wuxi County records, 30.3 percent of output value was included in state plans directly; 32.5 percent was included indirectly through various agreements with state enterprises; and 37.1 percent was sold outside the plan (*Wuxi xian gongye zhi* 1990:77). A 1975 article in the official party magazine *Hongqi* (Red flag) claimed that 80 percent of the output of CBEs in Wuxi County was included in central or local plans. This estimate is likely to be exaggerated. "Da you xiwang de xin sheng shiwu – Jiangsu sheng Wuxi xian fazhan shedui gongye de diaocha baogao (New Born Things Full of Promise – Investigation Report on the Development of Commune and Brigade Industry in Wuxi County, Jiangsu Province)," *Hongqi* (Red flag) No. 10 (1975), pp. 27–30.

Songjiang County: Developing Industry in
Shanghai's "Distant" Suburb

Of the three research sites, Songjiang had the greatest per capita industrial output as of 1949. A number of factors contributed to its early industrial development. Although the county (initially under the jurisdiction of Jiangsu Province) has been described as a "distant" rather than a "near" suburb of Shanghai, it is located only forty kilometers from Shanghai's city center and, like Wuxi, enjoyed a good natural water transportation network. Songjiang boasted a vibrant traditional handicraft industry and even a few modern factories, the earliest of which had been established in 1905 (*Songjiang xianzhi* 1991:5). On the eve of the founding of the People's Republic, Songjiang County had 144 small factory workshops (most employing only five to thirty people) and more than 5,000 handicraft workshops. Together the factory and handicraft workshops, most of which were to be classified as county-run enterprises after 1949, produced a gross value of industrial output of 12.22 million yuan in that year.[36]

At the outset of the Great Leap Forward, Songjiang County was shifted out of Jiangsu Province and put under the jurisdiction of Shanghai Municipality with the intention of developing it into an industrial satellite of the city. As part of the dramatic changes wrought by the Great Leap, the county's roughly three hundred agricultural producers' cooperatives were converted into seventeen people's communes in September 1958 (*Songjiang xianzhi* 1991:5). As in Wuxi, existing assets were used to jump-start commune industrial development. Forty-four factories and handicraft cooperatives were transferred from the county to the commune level, and many of these workshops served as the basis for nascent commune machine-building efforts – focusing mainly on agricultural equipment (Ibid:412; 455). The county public finance bureau supported these efforts indirectly by financing the purchase of more than one million yuan in agricultural equipment, in part from local producers (Ibid:659). It also provided a 60-thousand-yuan grant to build a pesticide plant. Between 1959 and 1961, the municipal and county public finance offices together supplied funds for interest-free loans to support the development of the collective economy in communes and brigades,

---

[36] This figure corresponds to the figure of 31 yuan per capita in Table 2.2.

including industrial assets, totaling 63.35 million yuan (Ibid:667). Furthermore, the county public finance office made grants totaling 17 million yuan for investment in the five small industries.[37] As a result of the mobilization of these resources, 201 rural enterprises were in operation, employing 17,563 people at the height of the Great Leap.

The Great Leap industrial "boom" in Songjiang was short-lived, however, and the industrial development effort appeared less coordinated than Wuxi's. Workshops that were decentralized from the county to the commune level lacked access to inputs, sales and marketing channels, and technical and managerial expertise. For example, the pesticide plant previously mentioned never went into operation and was ultimately written off as a complete loss. The plant had been initiated without the express approval of municipal authorities, and county officials never succeeded in acquiring the raw materials necessary for it to function (*Songjiang xianzhi* 1991:659). With the readjustment policies of 1962, other enterprises were merged or transferred back to higher levels. Available statistics on industrial output during and after the Great Leap show that county-, commune-, and brigade-run industry together reached a local peak of 100 million yuan in output in 1961 (a level that would not be reached again until 1971), declining to 60 million yuan in 1962 and 48 million yuan in 1963, before beginning a slow and unsteady recovery (Table 2.1). Some commune and brigade enterprises did survive the post-Leap retrenchment, contributing 12 million yuan to output in 1962 and 6 million yuan in 1963 and rebounding to produce 34 million yuan in output in 1964.

Agricultural initiatives provided an opening for the renewed development of commune enterprises in the mid- to late-1960s. For example, local officials in Songjiang began to redevelop chemical fertilizer and pesticide production as early as the late 1960s (*Songjiang xianzhi* 1991:458). Another spur to CBE development was the establishment in 1970 of a three-level agricultural equipment repair network in which communes and brigades set up workshops for repairs and the production of spare parts (Ibid:412). This initiative reflected the Cultural Revolution ideal of commune self-sufficiency as well as the slogan, "major repairs don't leave the commune; minor repairs don't leave

---

[37] *Songjiang xianzhi* (1991:659). To put state provision of resources in perspective, the 63 million yuan and the 17 million yuan together are equivalent to 30 percent of the gross value of output of all industry in the county between 1959 and 1961.

the brigade" (Yang 1988:237). However, there was little equipment to repair, and idle workshops quickly became a drain on commune resources.

At the same time, urban industrial production was disrupted by the Cultural Revolution; in this situation, idle rural workshops increasingly sought to fill processing orders for urban industry. Even as urban industries began to recover from the Cultural Revolution turmoil, they maintained links to rural industry as a route to enterprise expansion (Yang 1988:236–55). For example, the machinery industry in rural Songjiang began taking on processing orders for state enterprises in the early 1970s, and by 1978, processing orders accounted for the majority of output value in this sector (*Songjiang xianzhi* 1991:455). As Philip Huang recounts, based on his research team's interviews in Songjiang's Huayang Commune, the commune's first industrial enterprise (an agricultural implement factory) was established during the Great Leap. Beginning in 1971, it "contracted with a Shanghai factory to make a nozzle for fire hoses, a clamp for irrigation pumps, and bushings for spinning machines. The Shanghai factory supplied the equipment and materials and saw to the marketing; Huayang furnished the labor and the processing site" (P. Huang 1990:253–4). The factory's work force expanded to four hundred to fulfill the growing processing orders. The same was true of Songjiang's garment industry (*Songjiang xianzhi* 1991:459; Informants 1, 3, and 4). Links to rural enterprises presented a way for urban industry to overcome the constraints of limited factory space and restrictive quotas on the hiring of new permanent SOE employees; for rural enterprises, it provided capital, equipment, and entrée into the planned economy. Such ties were gradually formalized into urban–rural joint ventures (*gongnong lianyingchang*). As representatives of both the agriculture committee of the Shanghai Municipal party committee (which governed rural industry) and the Songjiang County Planning Commission emphasized, during the late 1970s and into the 1980s, such joint ventures played a crucial role in facilitating access to material inputs and distribution channels governed by the plan (Informants 39 and 109).

As in Wuxi, rural industrialization in Songjiang also benefited from the rustication of urban residents. Between 1961 and 1963, during the retrenchment following the Great Leap, roughly thirteen thousand workers were laid off from state-run enterprises in the county, and among those more than five thousand were sent to rural areas within the county itself. In addition, from 1968 to 1977, more than three thousand educated youth from the city of Shanghai settled in rural areas of Songjiang, and roughly nine thousand youth were rusticated from the county seat to communes in more remote areas of the county (*Songjiang xianzhi* 1991:705). As in Wuxi, skilled workers and educated youth brought with them technical skills, information, and connections to urban factories.

Although rural industry in Songjiang received less vigorous official support than in Wuxi, the state nevertheless contributed to the reemergence of commune and brigade enterprises in the post-Leap period. Between 1962 and 1977, the municipal and county public finance bureaus provided 5.2 million yuan in interest-free loans specifically targeted at commune industry in Songjiang.[38] And during the period of rapid expansion in the mid-1970s, local budgetary grants to the five small industries (including both county-run and commune-run enterprises) totaled 2.5 million yuan.[39] As of 1977, outstanding bank loans to commune industry had reached 4.5 million yuan, accounting for more than 10 percent of all loans to industrial enterprises in Songjiang.[40] Furthermore, preferential tax policies were implemented beginning in 1978 that provided tax benefits to CBEs. In that year, 106 commune industrial projects received tax exemptions and reductions worth 270 thousand yuan. Commune enterprises also received 1.36 million yuan in tax credits to offset the cross-subsidization of agriculture (Ibid:666).

By the end of the Maoist period, machinery, textiles, garments, and chemicals – all sectors with close links between urban and rural industries – were the most important industrial sectors in Songjiang, accounting for the lion's share of industrial output at the commune and brigade levels. Overall, as of 1978, CBEs already accounted for 42 percent of the gross value of industrial output in the county, compared to 65 percent in Wuxi.

---

[38] Although the funds came from the public finance system, they were administered by the Agriculture Bank and the network of Rural Credit Cooperatives until 1984, when their administration returned to the public finance bureau (*Songjiang xianzhi* 1991:667).

[39] The 2.5 million yuan figure covers the period between 1972 and 1977. The figure for the entire post-Leap/pre-reform period from 1958 to 1978 was 4.3 million yuan (*Songjiang xianzhi* 1991:659–60). Elsewhere, the figure of 10.5 million yuan is reported. The difference appears to reflect the inclusion of investment financed by extrabudgetary revenues (Ibid:700). This does not include grants and subsidies for the purchase of farm tools and machinery totaling 2.5 million yuan and 1.1 million yuan, respectively.

[40] By 1983, only five years later, the proportion had jumped to 49.8 percent (*Songjiang xianzhi* 1991:683).

Yueqing County: Sharing Trousers with Capitalism

While Songjiang had greater total industrial output than Yueqing as of 1949, much of it was generated at the county level. Focusing only on the township level and below, Yueqing's rural industrial output was actually greater than Songjiang's in 1949 (Table 2.1). However, during the period from 1949 to 1978, commune and brigade industry in Songjiang and Wuxi grew at twice the rate of growth in Yueqing. By 1978, Yueqing had only one-third the rural industrial output of Songjiang and one-tenth that of Wuxi at the township level and below; it had fallen even further behind relative to Songjiang and Wuxi in per capita terms (Figure 2.2).

Why was the trajectory of rural industrial growth different in Yueqing? Like the other research sites, Yueqing traditionally relied on commerce and handicrafts as a crucial supplement to agricultural pursuits, especially since arable land per capita was limited. Yet despite the existence of vibrant and closely integrated commerce and handicraft production in Yueqing through the early 1950s, Yueqing failed to keep pace with such counties as Songjiang and Wuxi during the Maoist period. Part of the reason for the widening gap was the less favorable geographic location of Yueqing. More importantly, Yueqing suffered from a relative lack of state support for state and collective industry. Throughout the Maoist period, prefectural- and county-level state and collective industries were consistently weaker in Yueqing than in the other research sites and thus failed to undergird rural industrial growth. At the same time, private initiatives were eliminated or driven underground.

Yueqing, a rural county located across the Oujiang River from the center of Wenzhou, enjoys relatively good water transport that historically has facilitated commerce. Indeed, Wenzhou was opened to foreign trade as a treaty port in 1876, and it would later become one of China's open coastal cities in 1984. In other ways, however, Yueqing – like Wenzhou more generally – was isolated. Surrounded by mountains and coastline, it had no proximate rail or highway links to major industrial centers. Only in the late 1990s did the development of such transportation links begin.[41] But perhaps the most critical geographic feature of Wenzhou during the Maoist period was its location across the Taiwan Straits from the island of Taiwan.

---

[41] The Wenzhou airport opened in 1992, and a rail connection to Wenzhou was established in 1998.

What was initially a "cold war" across the Taiwan Straits in the 1950s became a "hot war" in the 1960s with the PRC's shelling of the islands of Quemoy and Matsu off the mainland coast. As tensions increased, investment declined. In part as a result of Wenzhou's location on the front line in the unresolved civil war between the communists on the mainland and the Nationalists on Taiwan, the central and provincial governments on the mainland were unwilling to commit significant resources to industrial development in Wenzhou. Several sources make a comparison between Wenzhou and Ningbo, another port city farther north along the Zhejiang coast, to illustrate the point (Wang and Zhu 1996:4; Yuan 1987:6; Zhang and Li 1990b:11). In 1957, Wenzhou and Ningbo had comparable levels of industrial output, but as investment in state industry lagged in Wenzhou, it fell behind, posting only about one-third the industrial output of Ningbo by the end of the Maoist period. With only a fraction of the fixed-asset investment of Ningbo, urban industry in Wenzhou had few "hand-me-downs" for the development of rural industry in places like Yueqing. As a result, urban industry provided little in the way of capital, technology, or material inputs to support the development of rural industry in the counties surrounding Wenzhou (Yuan 1987:18; Zhang and Li 1990b:24).

This and other factors converged to lead the rural areas surrounding Wenzhou in a more truly self-reliant direction. In 1956, many communities in Wenzhou conducted experiments in contracting agricultural output to the household (*baochan daohu*) (Wang and Zhu 1996:18; Yuan 1987:11–13; Zhang and Li 1990a:93; Informant 174). Although these experiments attracted hostile national attention and resulted in political attacks on Wenzhou, they reportedly continued illicitly in some places, allowing households to accumulate resources in private hands.

Beginning in 1958, existing handicraft cooperatives were amalgamated into what passed for collective "factories" that employed a small core of workers; most rural residents were expected to work exclusively in agriculture (*H. zhenzhi* 1993:131).[42] Those rural residents who continued to conduct business independently were variously accused of "running underground factories," "abandoning agriculture for commerce," and "restoring capitalism" and were subject to suppression (He 1987:41; Yuan 1987:7). In the aftermath of the Great Leap Forward, collective "factories" were dissolved, and handicraft cooperatives and private

---

[42] Where published sources would identify the name of a town- or township-level research site, an abbreviation is used in lieu of the pseudonym regularly employed in the text.

workshops reemerged. However, private workshops became a target once again in the "four cleans" campaign of the early 1960s (Yuan 1987:16; Zhang and Li 1990b:14).

With the onset of the Cultural Revolution in 1966, even the small towns of Yueqing were thrown into turmoil. For example, Hualing Town's handicraft industry office was attacked in the early years of the Cultural Revolution as a "hideout for speculation, profiteering and capitalist exchange." It was occupied by Maoist factions who attacked independent handicrafts as "unapproved activities (*wuzheng jingying*)." Rebel groups confiscated tools and closed down the workshops of independent tradesmen (*H. zhenzhi* 1993:131). Under the slogan "take grain as the key link," nonagricultural activities were strictly limited (Wang and Zhu 1996:90). Private, small-scale industry was branded with the now-familiar epithet, "the tails of capitalism (*ziben zhuyi de weiba*)," and cadres who supported such activity were accused of "sharing trousers with capitalism (*yu ziben zhuyi chuan liandangku*)" – that is, colluding with capitalists – and were subjected to criticism and struggle (Yuan 1987:16). At the same time, the height of Cultural Revolution turmoil resulted in a vacuum of state authority in some communities that, ironically, created an opening for private household industry (Wang and Zhu 1996:43).

As order was restored in the early to mid-1970s, there was a period in which collective organization of agriculture and industry did hold sway (Ibid:51). In Hualing, two workshops that had been established earlier by independent craftsmen were taken over by collectives. In 1971, in Hualing Town, six people from the metal-working handicrafts cooperative established their own metal shop; they began by using scrap materials to fabricate drawer handles. In the mid-1970s, the independent workshop was converted to a town-run collective that ultimately became the Yueqing Instrument Parts Factory (*H. zhenzhi* 1993:132; 145; Informants 144 and 146). Similarly in 1972, a group of individuals in Hualing's Village Number Seven pooled their resources to establish a workshop where they produced simple electrical fuses. In 1974, the village took over the factory, which later became the collective Yueqing Sewing Machine Factory (*H. zhenzhi* 1993:132; 135; Informant 147). In other cases, villages provided collective sponsorship (*guakao jingying*) for independent workshops, although such sponsorship did not become widespread until after the initiation of reform at the Third Plenum in 1978.[43]

---

[43] He (1987:41). I touch on the issue of collective sponsorship again briefly in the discussion of the evolution of property rights in Chapter 4.

Yueqing employed few formal state resources in the development of rural industry during the Maoist period. State and collective enterprises in Wenzhou received little state investment themselves and had little to pass on to the rural industrial sector. In fact, the output of county-run industry in Yueqing stagnated during the 1960s and actually declined briefly in the mid-1970s – in marked contrast to the steadily increasing output of county-run industry in Wuxi and Songjiang (Table 2.1). The few collective factories that existed as of 1976 in Yueqing's Hualing Town had been taken over from private initiatives. As the example of Hualing's private metal shop illustrates, scrap materials were a common source of inputs. Other small workshops used scrap materials – for example, spinning workshops used materials from cloth scraps. Other workshops, such as those making straw mats, relied on local agricultural raw materials for inputs.[44] As analysts of Wenzhou's development emphasize, it was truly "self-reliant" – in many ways closer to the Maoist ideal than Wuxi or Songjiang. As a result, however, Wenzhou's growth rate during the Maoist period was slower than those of the other research sites, and it emerged from the Maoist period with little accumulated capital or technology under collective control. By 1978, per capita output of commune- and brigade-enterprises was 47 yuan in Yueqing – only about half the national average of 81 yuan. By contrast, per capita output values in Wuxi and Songjiang were well above the national average, with 430 yuan and 253 yuan, respectively.

CONCLUSION: THE LEGACIES OF THE MAOIST ERA

The evidence presented in this chapter challenges the commonly accepted idea that all rural industry embodied the Maoist ideal of self-reliance during the pre-reform era. It shows that in Wuxi and Songjiang, commune and brigade industry received substantial state support through budgetary grants, bank loans, and direct and indirect inclusion in state plans. Moreover, there is evidence from the central level, as indicated by national policy guidelines for grants and loans to CBEs, that such support was not limited to these counties. Nor was such support universal, however. Yueqing, located as it was on the front line against Taiwan, received little state support for the development of rural industry. As a result, the development trajectories of Wuxi, Songjiang, and

---

[44] Wang and Zhu (1996:90). There are also scattered references to black markets for production materials during the 1970s. See, for example, Zhang and Li (1990b:14ff).

Yueqing had diverged quite dramatically by 1978, leaving Yueqing with a weak endowment of collectively owned industrial assets and Songjiang and especially Wuxi with remarkably strong endowments.

These legacies from the Maoist era form an important piece of one of the major puzzles in this book. They help to explain the distinctive regional diversity in property rights forms that has characterized the rural industrial sector during the reform period. As we will see in Chapter 4, the endowment of rural industrial assets in each community at the beginning of reform shaped and constrained the choices of local officials as they sought to promote economic development in a new institutional environment. Before turning to the evolution of property rights after 1978, however, we need to examine the institutional environment of local officials at the outset of the reform period. The incentives created by this institutional environment are the subject of Chapter 3.

3

Incentive Structures and Local Cadre Behavior

THIS chapter provides the foundation for arguments made throughout subsequent chapters of the book by examining the factors that shaped local cadre behavior from the mid-1980s through the mid-1990s. The most powerful of these factors were the incentives contained in the revenue-sharing fiscal system and the cadre evaluation system. First, the fiscal system created a revenue imperative for local officials by requiring that local governments be largely self-financing, and since township governments were heavily dependent on industry to meet their revenue requirements, they had a strong incentive to promote local industrial development. At the same time, the nature of the division of fiscal revenue among levels of government and the inability of higher levels to credibly commit to fiscal contracts created incentives for local governments to evade central tax policy as a means of retaining more revenue at the local level.[1] Second, the cadre evaluation system powerfully shaped local official behavior by linking both the remuneration and advancement of local leaders to performance on economic as well as sociopolitical norms. Economic norms centered around the promotion of industrial development, while sociopolitical norms mandated the financing and provision of public goods and thus reinforced the revenue imperative facing local leaders.[2] These features of the

---

[1] Credible commitment refers to the assurance that one party to a contract will not, by its future actions, reduce the value of the contract to the other party (North 1990).

[2] A public good is defined as a good the consumption of which is nonexcludable and non-divisible. In other words, it is impossible or impractical to exclude individuals from consuming the good, and relatedly, it is impossible or impractical to measure how much of the good any given individual consumes. The classic example is a public sidewalk. Because of these characteristics, a private provider of a public good cannot readily reap the returns of her investment. Provision of public goods suffers from the "free-rider" problem, and,

cadre evaluation system, put in place beginning in 1979, are among the often-overlooked aspects of political reform – albeit *not* democratic political reform – that occurred at the outset of the reform process in China.[3]

The revenue-sharing tax system and the cadre evaluation system are taken to be exogenous to the model of local institutional change developed in the core of this study.[4] Thus, the present chapter describes these factors in detail, although it does not seek to explain how the revenue-sharing tax system came about or why the cadre evaluation system is structured the way it is. Rather, these factors are introduced because they shaped the behavior of interest in subsequent chapters. The chapters that follow describe the specific ways in which township cadres in each locale responded to the incentives to generate revenue for local political purposes. The incentives described here apply to township cadres in Shanghai, Wuxi, and Wenzhou generally, although specific examples are presented for illustration.

The following discussion of the fiscal system focuses on the period prior to 1994. The nature and impact of the tax and fiscal reforms instituted in 1994 are treated in Chapter 7. The problems produced by the pre-1994 system, described in this and subsequent chapters, were a major part of the impetus for the 1994 reforms. Moreover, as Chapter 7 will demonstrate, the legacy of problems continues to shape the implementation of the post-1994 system.

The first part of this chapter outlines the incentives structured by the fiscal system, while the second part focuses on the incentives created by the cadre evaluation system. The data presented here also bear on our understanding of the township more generally. The chapter concludes with a critical evaluation of analogies drawn between the behavior of the township government as a corporate entity and that of a capitalist corporation.

---

as a result, such goods are typically undersupplied. Therefore, public goods are best provided by the state, which can finance their provision through taxation. Here I subsume merit goods, like education, under the general rubric of public goods. Typically, at market prices, society consumes less of a merit good than would be socially desirable. For example, without publicly funded education, children would likely receive fewer years of schooling than would be desirable (Musgrave and Musgrave 1984).

[3] Earlier path-breaking studies of reforms in personnel management include Huang (1996) and Manion (1985; 1993).

[4] Other exogenous variables, including the legacy of public enterprise development and the national political and market environments, are discussed in Chapters 2 and 4, respectively.

THE TOWNSHIP FISCAL SYSTEM

The incentive structure confronting township officials was shaped by the sources of funds on which they depended in order to function and to meet the performance criteria set by the cadre evaluation system.[5] Township fiscal accounts from the 1990s reveal three strong but in some cases perverse incentives created by the fiscal system. First, the imperative of self-financing, combined with overwhelming reliance on rural industry as a revenue source, created an incentive for township cadres to vigorously promote the development of rural industrial firms.[6] Second, the division of revenues into those shared with higher levels of government and those retained primarily or exclusively at the township level created incentives for township cadres to collude with enterprises in evading taxes, shifting revenues from the former category to the latter. The intensity of these incentives depended upon the nature of the contract by which revenues were divided. Moreover, the inability of higher levels of government to make credible commitments to fiscal contracts created yet another incentive for township leaders to evade taxes as a means of shielding revenues from the extracontractual claims of higher levels.[7] Third, the differences

---

[5] This section draws on interviews with township- and county-level finance and tax bureaus in Shanghai, Jiangsu, and Zhejiang. Relevant issues were also addressed in interviews with village-, township-, and county-level party and government leaders; representatives of management and administration offices (*jingying guanli bangongshi*) at the township and county levels; and village accountants. See Appendix 1 for a complete list of interviews. Documentary sources are cited in the text.

[6] Two factors made industry especially important to local government revenue. First, through the 1980s, state-set prices created artificially high profits in many light industrial sectors, which township- and village-run collectives entered in large numbers (Naughton 1995:236). However, by 1992, gradual price reforms and increasing competition had effectively eliminated artificially high profits in these sectors. Second, China had an "industry-centered tax structure" in which the most important revenue-generating taxes were levied on the industrial tax base (Wong 1997:175). Thus, up through the early 1990s, "distortions in the price and tax structures caused resources to be channeled to [particular industrial] sectors, creating excess capacity in processing industries where rates of return [were] high" (Wong 1991b:709). Others have examined the incentives to promote industry as well. See Byrd and Gelb (1990), Oi (1992), Song and Du (1990), and C. Wong (1992).

[7] Barry Weingast (1990), in his discussion of the problem of credible commitment, focuses on two possible outcomes. The first is a negative outcome – the creation of disincentives to invest in the economy. The second is a positive result – the development of state institutions to make commitments more credible. The findings reported here highlight a third possibility: that is, the creation of incentives to evade the fiscal claims of higher levels of government while maintaining investment in the economy. This finding more closely parallels the conclusions of Hilton Root (1989).

74

in the types of fiscal revenue produced by private and collective enterprises created incentives for differential treatment of these enterprises by township governments. The following discussion illustrates the origins in the fiscal system of each of these incentives.

Fiscal Reform: An Overview

The nature of tax administration in China made the division of revenues particularly contentious. The Chinese government operated a unified tax system in which the central level had the exclusive right to determine tax policy (including the scope of taxation and tax rates) for all levels, while each lower level of government was responsible for collecting taxes from the enterprises under its jurisdiction. (The formal government administrative hierarchy in the research sites is shown in Figure 1.2.) To the extent that lower-level governments enjoyed any discretion in tax administration, they exercised it mainly through implementation rather than through formation of policies and regulations.

For much of the Maoist era of economic planning, China functioned under a system of "unified income and expenditure (*tongshou tongzhi*)." Under this system, each level of government turned over virtually all tax receipts and profits from state-owned enterprises to the central government. Lower levels then looked to the central government for budgetary allocations to finance local government expenditures.[8] Unlike state enterprise profits, however, the profits of township and village enterprises (formerly commune and brigade enterprises) – like those of other collectively owned enterprises – accrued directly to their de facto owners, not to the central government.[9] These nonbudgetary funds supplemented budgetary allocations from the central government.[10]

---

[8] This generalization obscures variation over time in the type and degree of central control over local spending. On this, see Oksenberg and Tong (1991). For a description of the system at the level of the commune during the Maoist period, see Song and Du (1990:345).

[9] For example, in Songjiang County prior to 1983, commune- and brigade-run enterprises handed all profits and available funds over to the commune or brigade (*Songjiang xianzhi* 1991:467).

[10] As the State Council regulations on developing commune and brigade enterprises stipulated, the profits of these enterprises were to be used by communes and brigades for building new enterprises or expanding existing ones, developing agricultural land, purchasing agricultural machinery, providing support for poor production teams, and developing social welfare projects. Guowuyuan, "Guanyu fazhan shedui qiye ruogan wenti de guiding (shixing caoan) (Regulations regarding Several Questions on the Development of Commune and Brigade Enterprises [Provisional Draft])," in *Zhongguo xiangzhen qiye nianjian 1978–1987* (1989:427–32).

The major fiscal reform of 1980, popularly referred to as "eating in separate kitchens (*fenzao chifan*)," made each subnational level of government primarily responsible for its own revenues and expenditures.[11] The 1980 fiscal reform was followed in 1983 by the transition from commune and brigade administration (in which party, government, and economic functions were intentionally unified) to township and village administration (in which these functions were, in principle, to be separated).[12] Fiscal reform was extended to the township level after new administrations were established.

By the late 1980s, most townships had superficially completed the separation of party, government, and economic functions by establishing "economic conglomerates (*jingji lianheshe*)." The conglomerate typically encompassed all collectively owned enterprises in the township and was nominally distinct from township party and government organs. However, township officials regularly described the conglomerate as a "hollow (*kongxu*)" structure, indicating the continued lack of separation of party, government, and economic management.[13] Indeed, in every research site but one, either the township executive or the township party secretary served concurrently as the director of the conglomerate.[14] As a central state official explained,

---

[11] *Caishui gaige shinian* (1989:15). This discussion of fiscal reform builds on and engages both Chinese- and English-language studies of fiscal reform. Among the most valuable English-language accounts are Brean (1998), Oi (1992), Oksenberg and Tong (1991), Shue (1984), Wong (1991b, 1992, 1997), Wong, Heady, and Woo (1995), and World Bank (1990b).

[12] See Zhonggong zhongyang, "Dangqian nongcun jingji zhengce de ruogan wenti (zhaiyao) (Several Issues of Current Rural Economic Policy [Abstract])," in *Nongcun shiyong fagui shouce* (1987:68–83). See also Zhonggong zhongyang guowuyuan, "Guanyu shixing zhengshe fenkai jianli xiang zhengfu de tongzhi (Announcement regarding the Implementation of the Separation of Party and Government and the Establishment of the Township Government)," in *Xiangzhen caizheng shouce* (1987:1–3).

[13] Local officials pointed to the absence of a regular administrative hierarchy in explaining why the conglomerate was not a viable organizational structure. Indeed, there was no corresponding organizational structure at the county level or above. In the Chinese context in which authority flows downward from the center, the absence of an administrative superior was regarded as strongly indicative of organizational weakness (Informants 97, 126, and 127). See also "Guanyu wanshan xiang jiti jingji zuzhi jigou de tansuo (A Probe into Improving Township Collective Economic Organizational Structures)," in *Jiading nianjian 1989–1990* (1991:140–2).

[14] As one scholar quipped, these enterprises are "*xiangzhang qiye bushi xiangzhen qiye* (the township head's enterprises not township enterprises)" (Informant 11).

In the rural areas, there is the entire historical legacy of the people's communes in which the government and the enterprise were unified. They have already abolished the commune and established the township, but they have still not achieved the separation of the government and the enterprise. The same is true at the village level. It's not just that the township leaders are the political leaders of the enterprise managers. It's also that the enterprises have to hand over profits and undertake other of society's financial burdens (Informant 167).

Thus, the organizational structure was a hollow shell established to comply – superficially – with the intentions of central reform directives to separate the functions of party, government, and economic administration.[15]

The same 1983 decision that converted communes into townships called for the establishment of a township-level public finance office. The Ministry of Finance codified this decision in 1985 with guidelines on the establishment of public finance offices and with regulations on township fiscal management.[16] While virtually all townships (98 percent) had established public finance offices by the mid-1990s, only 30 percent of

---

[15] A 1991 document issued jointly by the township government and party committee in Chenjiaqiao Township, Chuansha County, Shanghai, outlining the functions of each organ, highlights the lack of separation. One of the functions of the party committee was to set "specific policies and measures (*juti zhengce he cuoshi*)" regarding economic work. Chuansha xian C. xiangwei xiangzhengfu, "Guanyu dang zheng she zai jingji gongzuozhong zhize fengong de shixing guiding (Provisional Regulations regarding the Division of Responsibility for Economic Work among the Party, Government, and Economic Conglomerate)," Mimeo, April 23, 1991.

[16] Caizhengbu, "Guanyu banfa xiang(zhen) caizheng guanli shixing banfa de tongzhi (Announcement regarding Issuance of Township Finance Provisional Management Methods)," in *Xiangzhen caizheng shouce* (1987:6–8). As the lowest formal level of government in the Chinese administrative hierarchy, the township is also responsible for collecting taxes at the village level and below. However, in general, the village retains control over the profit remittances of collective, village-run enterprises. The rationale for this system is that the village is not officially considered to be part of the state. It is governed by a "villagers' committee," and technically, the leader of this committee is elected by the members of the village. In the villages investigated for this study, however, the appointments of the village leader and the village party secretary were effectively decided at the township level. (See the discussion of the cadre evaluation system in the second part of this chapter.) Below the village is the production team (now often referred to as a "villagers' small group"). Some teams operate collective, team-run enterprises; as at the village level, the team retains control over the profit remittances of these firms.

townships had established their own government treasuries, leaving the remaining 70 percent of townships to deposit tax receipts in the treasury at the county level (Guan 1996; Informant 53).[17]

Under the post-1980 fiscal system, fiscal revenues were shared upward, from the township to the central government, based on fiscal contracts signed between administrative levels. After revenue sharing was extended to the township level, the township government continued to collect taxes (as set by the central government) from the enterprises under its jurisdiction. As before, these tax revenues were technically the property of the central government; however, the township government received a share of the revenues it collected based on a multiyear contract negotiated with the county-level government (the next higher level in the administrative hierarchy). These funds were intended to cover the township government's budgetary expenditures; thus, the township no longer looked to higher levels for funds to cover all regular budgetary outlays. The fiscal reforms thereby strengthened the incentives to promote local industry, because the reforms brought budgetary as well as nonbudgetary revenues into the calculus of local officials (Jiang 1996:6–7). Moreover, as Christine Wong's (1991b) research demonstrates, not only did local governments become self-financing, but responsibility for financing many public goods devolved to local governments as well, thus rendering the revenue imperative even more acute. In addition, subnational governments were prohibited in principle from running budget deficits. In this way, fiscal reform intensified the revenue imperative faced by local governments.

It is important to make clear that, even with revenue sharing, China maintained a unitary tax system. Taxes were intended to be collected according to central tax law regardless of the impact of revenue-sharing arrangements on the ultimate division of revenues.[18] Within this framework, the township government enjoyed circumscribed but broadly interpreted authority to grant preferential tax treatment and tax relief to the enterprises under its jurisdic-

---

[17] Township treasuries were actually set up as special accounts held at the local branches of the Agriculture Bank or the Industrial and Commercial Bank (C. Wong 1997).

[18] A May 1988 State Council circular states that tax policy must be implemented according to the letter of the law, regardless of the revenue-sharing tax system. See Guowuyuan bangongting, "Guanyu jiaqiang shuishou gongzuo de jinji tongzhi (Urgent Notice regarding Strengthening Tax Work)," in *Zhili zhengdun shenhua gaige zhengce fagui xuanbian* (1990:152). See also "Qieshi jiaqiang shuishou baozhang caizheng shouru (Conscientiously Increase Tax Revenues, Guarantee Fiscal Revenues)," *Jiefang ribao*, May 16, 1988, p. 1.

tion.[19] As will be discussed in subsequent sections, the potential for abuse of this authority was great in part because the township government was the de facto owner of the collective enterprises under its jurisdiction with a claim on the profits of these enterprises, while at the same time it was a tax collection agent of the central government.

Incentives to Promote Rural Industry

Faced with the necessity of self-financing, townships in Shanghai, Wuxi, and Wenzhou were overwhelmingly reliant on rural enterprise – and rural industry in particular – for revenue. Under the post-1980 system of public finance, townships received revenue via three formal channels, designated "budgetary (*yusuannei*)," "extrabudgetary (*yusuanwai*)," and "self-raised (*zichou zijin*) revenue."[20] Reliance on revenue generated by rural enterprise characterized all three channels. In addition, rural enterprise also financed the activities of an array of township party and government bureaus through profit remittances and sanctioned and unsanctioned levies outside the purview of the formal system of public finance. This section documents the extent of township government reliance on rural enterprise, examining each revenue channel in turn, in order to demonstrate the powerful incentive to promote the development of these firms.

Sources of Budgetary Revenue. Rural enterprise, via the revenue-sharing tax system, became the primary source of budgetary revenue. Budgetary revenues were those funds governed by the fiscal contract (*caizheng baogan*) between the township and the county.[21] The form of fiscal con-

---

[19] There were four main categories of tax relief for township- and village-run enterprises. These categories included tax exemptions or reductions for newly established enterprises, new products, enterprises in difficulty, and enterprises run by schools or those employing a certain percentage of handicapped workers. In general, private enterprises were not granted tax relief. These issues are treated in detail in Chapter 5.

[20] See Caizhengbu, "Guanyu banfa xiang(zhen) caizheng guanli banfa de tongzhi (Ministry of Finance Announcement regarding Issuance of Township Finance Management Methods)," *Caizheng* No. 3 (1992) pp. 52–4. This version of the central regulations governing township revenues was issued on December 29, 1991; it replaces the regulations issued in 1985 cited in note 16.

[21] Contractual forms varied somewhat among counties in Shanghai, Jiangsu, and Zhejiang. However, minor variations in contractual forms did not affect the basic incentives described here. The extent to which contract variations affected the *ways* in which incentives shaped cadre behavior will be discussed in the text where it is relevant. This section draws primarily on data from the fiscal accounts of Nantang Township, Jiading County, Shanghai, to illustrate the incentives created by the fiscal system. Nantang was selected because informants in this site provided the most detailed accounting of township finances. Data drawn from other townships are cited where particularly illustrative.

tract between counties and townships most commonly encountered in the Shanghai area, for example, can be described as "quota remittance with growth."[22] The contract contained two main elements: township remittances of tax revenues to the county, a portion of which was returned to the township, and annual grants by the county to the township for expenditures guaranteed in the contract. In general, the contract set a specific base level of revenue to be remitted, calculated as the difference between township income and expenditure in the base year.[23] Target remittance levels increased by a certain percentage over the base level each year, reflecting anticipated growth in the tax base over the course of the contract, which was usually to cover five years. A fixed percentage of above-target remittances (100 percent in most Shanghai sites) was returned to the township and became one element of the township's budgetary revenues.[24]

As Panel 1 in Table 3.1 shows, in 1991, Nantang Township derived over 95 percent of all tax receipts governed by the fiscal contract from the turnover and income taxes paid by township- and village-run enterprises.[25] Even at the county level, rural enterprises accounted for nearly 60 percent of total tax receipts.[26]

---

[22] This is literally rendered as "fixing base levels of income and expenditure [and] remitting an increasing revenue quota, set for a five-year period."

[23] Remittances governed by contracts included a wide array of taxes collected at the township level. In general, these included direct and indirect taxes on rural enterprises (including the income tax and the product, value-added, and business taxes) as well as a number of minor taxes (including the urban maintenance and construction tax, the arable land-use tax, the vehicle and boat tax, the housing tax, the slaughter tax, and the agriculture tax, among others). In addition to these taxes identified by tax and public finance officials, other taxes listed in the national regulations among those to be shared between townships and counties included the market trading tax, the livestock trading tax, and the contract tax. See *Xiangzhen caizheng shouce* (1987:6–8).

[24] An example of an alternative contractual form commonly employed between counties and townships in Jiangsu Province is referred to as "sharing total revenues." The township retains a percentage (determined by the ratio of expenditure to revenue in the base year) of the target revenue level and a slightly higher percentage of above-target revenues. As under other contractual forms, the revenue target level increases by a certain percentage every year. In this case, however, the township hands over to the county specific *percentages* of both target and above-target revenues rather than a specific *amount* (quota) of revenue.

[25] Although the data do not allow one to separate the tax payments of industry and services, data based on turnover taxes alone show that industrial firms accounted for approximately 75 percent of tax receipts from township- and village-run enterprises in Nantang in 1991.

[26] This figure ranged from nearly 60 percent in Jiading County, Shanghai, where rural enterprise was predominantly collectively owned to as high as 90 percent in Yueqing

Table 3.1. *Nantang Township Fiscal Accounts, 1990–91 (million yuan)*

Panel 1

Year	Turnover Taxes	Income Tax	Other Taxes[a]	Agriculture Tax	Total Tax Receipts
1990	7.083 (52%)	5.990 (44%)	0.053 (0.4%)	0.488 (3.6%)	13.614 (100%)
1991	7.309 (62%)	3.953 (33%)	0.050 (1%)	0.487 (4%)	11.799 (100%)

Panel 2

Year	Contract Target[b]	Contribution to Center	Contribution to County	County Risk Fund	Total Paid to County
1990	9.690	0.223	0.100	0.121	10.134
1991	9.750[c]	0.223	0.000	0.017	9.993

Panel 3

Year	Above-Target Funds	Fixed County Grant	Total Budgetary Funds
1990	3.480 (79%)	0.902 (21%)	4.382 (100%)
1991	2.056[d] (70%)	0.902 (30%)	2.958 (100%)

Panel 4

| Year | Self-raised funds: | | | Total Nonbudgetary Funds | Total Township Revenues |
	Four Fees[e]	Enterprise Profits	Extrabudgetary Funds		
1990	3.209 (76%)	0.993 (24%)	n/a	4.202 (100%)	8.584
1991	3.550 (88%)	0.502 (12%)	0.200[f]	4.052 (100%)	7.010

Panel 5

| Year | Budgetary Expenditures: | | | Fixed County Grant | Total Budgetary Expenditures |
	Health and Education	Agriculture	Other		
1990	1.494 (37%)	0.672 (17%)	0.958 (24%)	0.902 (22%)	4.026 (100%)
1991	1.398 (40%)	0.41 (12%)	0.825 (23%)	0.902 (25%)	3.535 (100%)

Panel 6

| Year | Nonbudgetary Expenditures: | | | Total Nonbudgetary Expenditures | Total Township Expenditures |
	Health and Education	Agriculture	Other		
1990	0.529 (12%)	1.535 (34%)	2.405 (54%)	4.469 (100%)	8.495
1991	0.391 (9%)	1.547 (35%)	2.492 (56%)	4.430 (100%)	7.965

(Continued)

Table 3.1. (*cont.*)

Panel 7

Year	Budgetary Surplus/ Deficit	Nonbudgetary Surplus/ Deficit	Total Township Surplus/ Deficit	Accumulated Township Surplus/ Deficit 1988–Present
1990	0.356	−0.267	0.089	4.293
1991	−0.577	−0.378	−0.955	3.338

[a] In Nantang this includes the urban maintenance and construction tax, the vehicle and boat tax, the housing tax, and the slaughter tax.

[b] The base figure of 8.61 million yuan is the difference between township income and expenditure in the base year, 1987. The remittance target increases 4 percent per year. Thus the 1988 remittance target was 8.95 million yuan, the 1989 target 9.31 million yuan, the 1990 target 9.69 million yuan, and the 1991 target 10.07 million yuan.

[c] A special reduction in target amount granted by the county reduced the target from 10.07 million yuan to 9.75 million yuan.

[d] This includes a special allowance from the county of 250 thousand yuan.

[e] The four fees, which are paid by rural collectives, include the fee to support agriculture (220 yuan per year per employee); the fee to support agricultural subsidiaries (84 yuan per year per employee); the rural education fee (2 percent of gross profits); and the social expenditures fee (7 percent of taxable profits).

[f] Extrabudgetary funds are not included in the total because, based on the arrangement between the township and the county, those funds are deducted from the amount of the county grant.

Source: Informant 135.

The lion's share of township budgetary revenue came from the return to the township of above-target tax remittances (Table 3.1, Panel 3).[27] These above-target remittances accounted for 70 percent of budgetary revenues in 1991 and for nearly 80 percent in 1990. The importance of above-target funds is also apparent on the expenditure side, where they accounted for approximately 75 percent of total budgetary expenditures in 1991. As Panel 5 of Table 3.1 shows, of this 75 percent, 40 percent went to education; 12 percent went to agriculture; and 23 percent went to other expenses, including township construction and payment of salary, administrative, and welfare expenses not covered by the county grant. A comparison of budgetary revenues and expenditures (Table 3.1, Panels 3 and 5) reveals a budget deficit in 1991. In this instance, the township was able to finance additional spending using the budgetary surpluses produced by large above-target revenues generated during the boom years of 1988 and early 1989 (Table 3.1, Panel 7). Thus, the above-target tax revenues

County, Wenzhou, where rural enterprise was predominantly privately owned. Dependence on rural enterprise characterized public finance in the sites investigated regardless of the dominant form of ownership.

[27] This was characteristic of most wealthy areas under the post-1980 fiscal system.

produced by rural enterprises were key to financing the township's budgetary expenditures.

The only major source of revenue not directly associated with rural enterprise was the budgetary grant made to the township by the county as part of the fiscal contract. However, this grant represented only a fraction of total revenue, and the township did not have complete discretion over the use of grant funds. The grant, referred to by local cadres as the "meal ticket *(chifan caizheng)*," was intended to finance the base salaries of state cadres *(guojia ganbu)*, basic administrative expenses (including educational administration), and (in some cases) certain minimal welfare benefits. However, the grant was far from adequate to cover even these costs, particularly since the amount of the grant, based on expenditures for these items in the base year, was fixed over the term of the contract, while costs were continually increasing. Even the costs of officially sanctioned increases in salaries for state cadres, for example, had to be borne solely by the township. Moreover, the actual number of cadres involved in township administration far exceeded the number authorized by the state to be on the state payroll *(guojia bianzhi)*, and the salaries of these additional cadres, referred to as "collective cadres *(jiti ganbu)*," had to be paid out of the township's nonbudgetary funds.[28] As Table 3.1 shows for Nantang Township, the county grant constituted only 30 percent of budgetary funds and only 13 percent of total revenues in 1991. (The county grant accounted for even smaller shares in 1990: 21 percent of budgetary funds and 11 percent of total revenues.) In terms of expenditures, the county grant accounted for only 25 percent of budgetary expenditures and 11 percent of total expenditures in 1991. The

---

[28] There were 24 cadres on the state payroll in Nantang (Informant 133). Although a complete payroll breakdown is not available for Nantang Township, 1989 data on nearby Xuhang Township may provide an indication of the inadequacy of budgetary funds. Xuhang is similar to Nantang; also in Jiading County, the township ranked seventeenth out of twenty based on per capita income of 1,127 yuan, while Nantang ranked fourteenth with per capita income of 1,231 yuan. In Xuhang a total of 170 people were employed directly by the township government: 55 in governmental administrative offices (of whom only 23 were state cadres), 57 in nonprofit public institutions such as schools, and 58 in the township's various corporations in charge of industry, agriculture, and trade. In 1989, salaries, benefits, and basic office expenses totaled 1.7 million yuan. Only 10 percent of the cost was covered by budgetary funds. The remainder was covered by nonbudgetary funds: 48 percent by self-raised funds and 42 percent by extrabudgetary funds. The data on Xuhang are reported in Sang and Wu (1991:27–9). Similarly in Songyang Town, Songjiang County, Shanghai, there were 127 cadres in total; 29 were state cadres, including 21 in party and government organs and 8 in the military, which operated a base within the jurisdiction of the township (Informant 97).

inadequacy of the county grant intensified the revenue imperative for the township government. Consequently, the township turned to nonbudgetary funds derived from rural enterprise to make up for the shortfall.

Sources of Nonbudgetary Revenue. Throughout the 1980s and into the 1990s, nonbudgetary revenues played an increasingly important role in township finances. These revenues included both officially sanctioned and reported extrabudgetary and self-raised funds as well as unsanctioned and unreported "off-budget" levies (Fan 1998; Wong 1998). The largest component of nonbudgetary revenue, self-raised funds, derived almost exclusively from rural enterprise, and the sources of these funds were, in turn, divided into two main categories: profit remittances and fees.[29] The township government effectively controlled 100 percent of the profits of collective, township-run enterprises.[30] Profit remittances were shared between the township industrial corporation – that is, the arm of the township government responsible for overseeing rural industry – and the public finance office. Only the amount turned over to the public finance office, usually about 10 to 20 percent of net profits, became self-raised revenue.[31] The rationale for the remission of collective enterprise profits to the township government was based on the notion that these firms were owned by all citizens of the township and that these citizen-owners were represented by the township's party and government apparatus.[32] This notion reinforced the lack of separation between party, government, and enterprise. Indeed, one local official noted that the actual level of enterprise profits in his jurisdiction was impossible to calculate, because the enterprises paid directly for so many of the local government's expenses. (I return to this issue in Chapter 5 and briefly in this section in the discussion of unsanctioned, "off-budget" levies.)

---

[29] Here, profits refer to formally declared profits. As will become clear, local officials had significant influence over the level of formally declared profits in collective firms.

[30] Although national regulations stipulated that profit remittances not exceed 40 percent of a collective enterprise's net profits, township government claims often exceeded this share. For the official regulations, see "Zhonghua renmin gongheguo xiangcun jiti suoyouzhi qiye tiaoli (People's Republic of China Regulations on Township and Village Collectively Owned Enterprises)," *Guowuyuan gongbao* No. 11 (July 10, 1990), pp. 387–93.

[31] The industrial corporation's share of profit remittances is discussed in the subsequent section.

[32] The same logic applies to profit remittances by village-run enterprises at the village level.

Rural enterprises also paid a number of officially mandated fees that accrued to local governments as self-raised funds.[33] While specific fees varied slightly from province to province, the general categories were broadly similar. In Shanghai Municipality, for example, collective enterprises paid four fees that became self-raised revenues of the township government.[34] These fees levied on industry included (1) fees to support the development of agriculture (*yigong bunong*), (2) fees to subsidize agricultural sideline products, especially pork (*yigong bufu*), (3) fees to finance rural education (*nongcun jiaoyu fujia fei*), and (4) fees to fund social welfare expenditures (*shehuixing zhichu fei*).[35] The fees paid by township-level enterprises accrued almost entirely to the township government. Only the fee to support agriculture was divided among the township and the county and municipal governments, with the township retaining nearly 75 percent of the total. The township also shared in a

---

[33] The central government sanctioned the deduction of these legally mandated fees from the pretax profits of rural firms; thus, they entailed a de facto subsidy equivalent to the income tax revenue foregone by the central government, and the use of these funds was restricted, in principle, to purposes sanctioned by the central government.

[34] The national regulations sanctioning the collection of the rural education fee were promulgated in December 1984. See Guowuyuan, "Guanyu choucuo nongcun xuexiao banxue jingfei de tongzhi (Announcement regarding Raising Operating Funds for Rural Schools)," in *Xiangzhen caizheng shouce* (1987:245–7). For central guidelines on fees for social welfare expenditures, see Zhonggong zhongyang guowuyuan, "Guanyu jinyibu huoyue nongcun jingji de shixiang zhengce (Ten Policies for Further Enlivening the Rural Economy)," in *Zhongguo xiangzhen qiye 1978–1987* (1989:501–4). With respect to fees to support agricultural development, see Zhonggong zhongyang guowuyuan, "Guanyu yijiubaliunian nongcun gongzuo de bushu (zhailu) (Plan regarding Rural Work for 1986 [Abstract])," in Ibid (1989:511–12). For local regulations, see Shanghai shi renmin zhengfu, "Pizhuan shinongwei guanyu zai xiangzhen qiyezhong jianli 'yigong bunong' zhuanxiang zijin de baogao de tongzhi (Notice of Approval and Transmission of the Report by the Municipal Agriculture Commission on Establishment of an Earmarked Fund 'Using Industry to Support Agriculture' in Township- and Village-run Enterprises)," in *Shanghai shi jingji tizhi gaige wenjian huibian* (n.d.:154–6).

[35] Some township governments also levied a labor substitution fee (*yizidailao*) to be paid by rural residents. Apparently, however, not all townships levied this fee, and its assessment varied by township as well. This fee had its origins in the "Sixty Articles on the People's Commune," a document that states that each resident owes twenty days of labor to the commune. Where this fee was revived, it was intended explicitly "to reduce the burden on public finances" in light of declining budgetary revenue (Informant 56). There is no record of this levy in Nantang Township, but in Luhang Town, Shanghai County, for example, a fee of 60 yuan per year was levied on rural enterprise employees only. By contrast, in Meilin Town, Shanghai County, a fee of 40 yuan was levied on farmers, 60 yuan on rural enterprise employees, and 80 yuan on private entrepreneurs. Meilin collected about 500 thousand yuan in labor substitution fees in 1991, of which it used about 300 thousand yuan to hire outside laborers from poorer regions to maintain irrigation ditches and repair roads.

portion of the fees paid by village-run enterprises, including the fee to support agriculture (52 percent) and the social welfare expenditures fee (30 percent). Technically, the township did not have complete discretion over the uses of self-raised funds. However, one public finance official reported that, in practice, these funds were deposited into a general account that the township used at its discretion (Informant 70).

Distinct from self-raised funds, extrabudgetary funds derived primarily from the income of administrative agencies (*xingzheng danwei*) and public nonprofit institutions (*shiye danwei*) that were not generally subject to direct or indirect taxes. Extrabudgetary funds commonly included user-fees charged to clients by units such as the labor service bureau and the local health clinic. In these cases, income beyond what was necessary to cover salaries and expenses of the unit became extrabudgetary income for the township. The township also derived income from some regulatory offices, such as the trademark fees charged by the industrial and commercial bureau. In addition, some funds came from punitive fees charged, for example, for violation of family-planning policies. Also falling under the rubric of nonprofit institutions were certain rural enterprises such as "social welfare factories," which employed handicapped workers and were operated by the township civil affairs office, and "school-run factories," which were affiliated with some township schools.[36] These enterprises enjoyed tax-exempt status and, in addition to providing funds for the units that ran them, turned a portion of their profits over to the township government. These profits then became extrabudgetary income for the township.[37] In addition, limited shares of both the agriculture tax and the special agriculture and forestry products tax were returned to townships for use as extrabudgetary funds.

As Table 3.2 shows, nonbudgetary funds in Nantang Township increased, albeit erratically, to well over 50 percent of total revenue. As Tables 3.3 and 3.4 show, nonbudgetary revenues also accounted for a sub-

---

[36] In the case of school-run factories, the relationship between the school and the factory appeared to be a strictly financial one.

[37] The profits of these enterprises could be quite large, particularly in light of their tax-exempt status. For example, the Xiafei Cosmetics Company in Chuansha County, Shanghai, famous locally for its provocative television ad campaigns, was a welfare factory affiliated with the township civil affairs office. Between 1985 and 1990, it received approximately 10 million yuan in tax exemptions and other benefits in a township where the gross profits of all township-run enterprises over the same period totaled about 80 million yuan.

Table 3.2. *Total Revenues in Nantang Township, Jiading County,*
Shanghai, 1988–91

	Budgetary		Nonbudgetary	
Year	Above-Target Funds	County Grant	Self-Raised Funds	Total
Million yuan				
1988	2.67	0.90	3.73	7.31
1989	5.82	0.90	5.25	11.97
1990	3.48	0.90	4.20	8.58
1991	2.06	0.90	4.05	7.01
Percent of total				
1988	37	12	51	100
1989	49	8	44	100
1990	41	11	49	100
1991	29	13	58	100

Note: Township extrabudgetary funds, which totaled 200 thousand yuan in 1991, are not included because, based on the arrangement between Nantang Township and Jiading County, these funds were deducted from the county grant.
Source: Informant 135.

stantial and growing portion of total revenue in other Shanghai townships for which data are available. (In comparison, nonbudgetary funds consistently accounted for about 30 percent of total revenue in Hualing Town in Yueqing County under Wenzhou City, where rural enterprise was mainly privately owned. In the case of Hualing, these funds came mainly from contributions by private entrepreneurs.) In general, self-raised funds composed the largest share of nonbudgetary revenue. In Nantang Township, all nonbudgetary revenue derived from self-raised revenue, that is, the official fees and profit remittances paid by rural enterprises.[38] In 1991, the four officially mandated fees accounted for 88 percent of nonbudgetary revenue and over 50 percent of total revenue,

---

[38] As noted at the beginning of this section, nonbudgetary revenues were, according to official definitions, comprised of both extrabudgetary and self-raised funds, but the arrangement between Nantang Township and Jiading County required that the amount of extrabudgetary revenues be deducted from the county grant paid to the township. Therefore, extrabudgetary revenues represented no net increase in revenue to the township in this particular case. However, the profits of tax-exempt rural enterprises operated by schools or civil affairs offices could be an important source of extrabudgetary revenue in other townships.

Table 3.3. *Total Revenues in Songyang Town, Songjiang County, Shanghai, 1989–95*

| | Budgetary | | Nonbudgetary | |
Year	Total Budgetary Funds	Extra-Budgetary Funds	Self-Raised Funds	Total
Million yuan				
1989	2.85	0.89	1.90	5.64
1990	5.86	0.96	2.19	9.01
1991	4.54	0.62	2.01	7.18
1992	4.15	1.25	1.87	7.26
1993	5.25	1.10	3.89	10.25
1994	5.19	1.15	5.82	12.16
1995	5.62	2.02	5.98	13.61
Percent of total				
1989	51	16	34	100
1990	65	11	24	100
1991	63	9	28	100
1992	57	17	26	100
1993	51	11	38	100
1994	43	9	48	100
1995	41	15	44	100

Note: Comparable data are available for Songyang Town through 1995.
The fiscal reform (*fenshuizhi*) initiated nationwide in 1994 was not fully
implemented at the township level until 1996.
Source: *S. tongji nianjian* (1991:36; 1992:45; 1993:57; 1994:55; 1995:44; 1996:46).

Table 3.4. *Sources of Township Revenue, 1991 (Million Yuan)*

| | Shanghai | | | Wenzhou |
	Nantang	Luhang	Meilin	Hualing
Budgetary funds	2.958 (42%)	2.726 (49%)	4.797 (62%)	1.81 (69%)
Of which:				
Above-target funds	2.056	1.710	3.647	0.62
County grant	0.902	1.016	1.150	1.19
Nonbudgetary funds[a]	4.052 (58%)	2.860 (51%)	3.000 (38%)	0.80 (31%)
Total	7.010 (100%)	5.586 (100%)	7.797 (100%)	2.61 (100%)

[a] These figures exclude extrabudgetary funds, i.e., funds levied by government agencies that
do not accrue to the public finance office. Therefore, the share of total nonbudgetary funds
is most likely even greater than reported here.
Sources: Informants 56, 70, 135, 160, and 167.

while collective enterprise profits accounted for 12 percent of nonbudgetary revenue and 7 percent of total revenue.[39] Local cadres relied heavily on these funds to meet the performance targets set for them at the county level. In Nantang Township in 1991, 9 percent of nonbudgetary funds were dedicated to health and education, 35 percent to agriculture, and the remaining 56 percent to other expenditures including urban construction, welfare benefits, and salaries for collective cadres (Table 3.1, Panel 6). Thus, official nonbudgetary funds financed a wide array of public goods ranging from schools, clinics, and cultural centers to roads, bridges, and irrigation projects.[40]

Beyond these officially reported revenue sources, townships also made demands on enterprises to "amass capital (*jizi*)," make so-called "voluntary contributions (*juankuan*)," pay "unsanctioned levies (*tanpai*)," and provide goods and services in kind in order to finance and build major projects. These demands tended to be erratic, driven by the need to finance particular projects, and therefore varied substantially from year to year. They were also seldom reflected in formal township fiscal accounts. According to a 1995 report by the Ministry of Agriculture, such exactions financed public projects ranging from rural roads to primary and middle schools, government office buildings, and water treatment plants.[41] At the same time, however, since there was little accountability for such unsanctioned levies, they also contributed to official corruption at the local level.[42]

The powerful incentive for township cadres to promote rural enter-

---

[39] In Nantang Township a set number of enterprises were assigned to make profit remittances exclusively to the public finance office. The remaining enterprises made profit remittances to the industrial corporation. By contrast, in Meilin and Luhang Towns, the public finance office received a certain percentage of the profits of each enterprise.

[40] Even in cases in which the county and municipal governments provided ad hoc grants for major township projects, such as the development of a system to provide running water throughout a township, the township government was required to provide a certain percentage of matching funds from both budgetary and nonbudgetary revenues. See Whiting (1999a) and C. Wong (1997).

[41] Lu and Li (1996), B. Xu (1996), and Ye (1996) contain summaries of the Ministry of Agriculture report. See also Whiting (1999a).

[42] Central documents explicitly link "off-budget" levies and corruption. Corruption is defined in the documents as misappropriation of funds and commercialization of legitimate government functions for private personal benefit or profit (*ba quanli shangpin hua*). See, for example, Zhonggong zhongyang bangongting guowuyuan bangongting, "Guanyu zhuanfa caizhengbu 'guanyu zhili luan shoufei de guiding' de tongzhi (Notice regarding Transmission of Ministry of Finance 'Regulations on Controlling the Chaotic Levying of Fees')," in Ding (1996:7).

prise is clear from this review of every major revenue source for township governments. In the case of Nantang Township, a conservative estimate based on the data presented in Table 3.1 suggests that about 90 percent of total revenue (including budgetary, extrabudgetary, and self-raised revenue channels) came from rural enterprise. All of these revenue channels contributed substantially to the provision of public goods and services. Thus, rural enterprise was essential to the ability of township cadres to achieve the performance criteria set for them at the county level and was essential to their political success.

Sources of Township Revenue beyond the Purview of the Public Finance Office. Rural enterprise also played a major role in financing township activity beyond regular fiscal channels through the profits controlled by the township industrial corporation. The industrial corporation rivaled the public finance bureau in the scale of funds it controlled, funds that derived solely from rural enterprise. In the case of Luhang Town, Shanghai County, Shanghai, for example, the public finance office took in 5.59 million yuan in total revenues in 1991, while the industrial corporation took in 3.17 million yuan in profits, depreciation, and technical development funds from the township-run collective enterprises under its jurisdiction. This figure does not include the profit remittances of village- and team-run collectives that accrue to the village and the team, respectively. Taking into account all three levels, profit remittances from collective enterprises totaled 5.80 million yuan in Luhang in 1991, leaving less than 1 million yuan in profits to be retained by the enterprises themselves. Nor does this sum include the management fee paid to the township industrial corporation by collective enterprises at the township, village, and team levels.[43] The fee, calculated at 0.25 to 0.4 percent of the total value of output, produced revenues to cover the operating expenses of the industrial corporation. The industrial corporation used remittances of profits and depreciation funds primarily to finance new projects and in some instances to repay the debts of loss-making enterprises, since it commonly served as guarantor on bank loans to township- and village-

---

[43] See "Xiangzhen qiye guanli fei tiqu jiejiao he guanli banfa (Exaction and Payment of and Management Methods for the Township- and Village-Run Enterprise Management Fee)," in *'Zhonghua renmin gongheguo xiangcun jiti suoyouzhi qiye tiaoli' xuexi zhidao* (1991:405–7).

run enterprises.[44] Whether facilitating access to bank loans or making new investments, the functions performed by the industrial corporation, financed by the profits and fees paid by subordinate enterprises, were intended to maintain the breakneck pace of rural industrial growth. High growth rates were key to the ability of township leaders to meet the continually increasing output and profit targets on which bases their performance was evaluated.

Many other bureaus of the township government relied on rural enter- prise as a source of funds through the unsanctioned levying of various exactions above and beyond the funds they received through formal channels.[45] Although the central government repeatedly declared these exactions to be illegal, they continued to occur on a large scale.[46] A study conducted from 1987 to 1988 in the suburban counties surrounding Shanghai identifies 188 different fees levied on rural enterprises, only 59

---

[44] However, as I demonstrate in Chapter 6, the township's role as loan guarantor was fre- quently characterized as "empty (*kongde*)," since it often shirked its obligations to local banks when local collective enterprises failed to repay loans.

[45] A special central government investigation identified 143.7 billion yuan (equivalent to 2.5 percent of GDP) in unofficial "off-budget" revenues in 1995 (Whiting 1999a).

[46] Prohibitions against unsanctioned levies were issued in 1985, 1986, 1988, 1990, 1993, 1996, and 1997, but such levies were "repeatedly prohibited but not stopped (*lüjinbuzhi*)." See Zhonggong zhongyang guowuyuan, "Guanyu zhizhi xiang nongmin luan tankuan, luan shoufei de tongzhi (Notice regarding Prohibiting Chaotic Exactions and Chaotic Fees on Farmers)," cited in Ding (1996); Guowuyuan, "Guanyu jianjue zhizhi xiang qiye luan tanpai de tongzhi (zhaiyao) (Notice regarding Resolutely Halting the Uncon-trolled Levying of Exactions on Enterprises [Abstract])," in *Xiangzhen caizheng shouce* (1987:319–21); Guowuyuan, "Jinzhi xiang qiye tanpai zanxing tiaoli (Provisional Regu- lations Prohibiting Unsanctioned Levies on Enterprises)," in Ding (1996); Zhonggong zhongyang guowuyuan, "Guanyu jianjue zhizhi luan shoufei luan fakuan he gezhong tanpai de jueding (Decision regarding Resolutely Halting the Uncontrolled Imposition of Fees, Fines, and Exactions of All Kinds)," *Guowuyuan gongbao* No. 23 (January 15, 1991), pp. 838–42; Guowuyuan, "Guanyu qieshi jianqing nongmin fudan de tongzhi (Notice regarding Conscientiously Reducing Farmers' Burdens)," in Ding (1996); Zhong- gong zhongyang guowuyuan, "Guanyu zhuanfa caizhengbu 'Guanyu zhili luan shoufei de guiding' de tongzhi (Notice regarding Transmission of Ministry of Finance 'Regula- tions on Controlling the Chaotic Levying of Fees')," in Ding (1996); Zhonggong zhongyang guowuyuan, "Guanyu qieshi zuohao jianqing nongmin fudan gongzuo de jueding (Decision regarding Conscientiously Doing Well the Work to Reduce Farmers' Burdens)," *Guowuyuan gongbao* No. 12 (April 21, 1997), pp. 563–8; and Zhong- gong zhongyang guowuyuan, "Guangyu zhili xiang qiye luan shoufei, luan fakuan he gezhong tanpai deng wenti de jueding (Decision regarding Rectifying Uncontrolled Fees, Fines, and Exactions on Enterprises and Other Issues)," *Guowuyuan gongbao* No. 24 (August 6, 1997), pp. 1078–80. Because TVEs are governed by the Ministry of Agricul- ture, the TVE burden was, in some cases, addressed in documents on farmers' burdens.

of which – about one-third – had official approval from the county- or provincial-level government (Wu and Gu 1988:51–2).[47] A similar survey of rural industrial enterprises conducted in Wuxi County in 1987 reveals that more than 40 percent of enterprise profits went to fees and exactions, only about one-third of which had legal grounding (Yu and Li 1989:22–6).[48] A broader, national study conducted by the Ministry of Agriculture in 1995 identified 204 types of fees levied by more than sixty different government agencies and determined that at least 46 percent of the fees were unsanctioned. While these studies focus primarily on the exactions suffered by collective enterprises, other studies, as well as enterprise interviews, demonstrate that private firms face some of the same kinds of illegal levies.[49] Overall, however, township agencies appear to approach collective enterprises more readily; as a result, the incidence of unsanctioned levies appears to be somewhat lower for private firms.[50]

Exactions took a multitude of forms. Regulatory offices exacted special inspection fees and levied fines for alleged policy violations, while administrative offices demanded contributions for schools, athletic events, and holidays commemorating youth, teachers, and the elderly. Tax and industrial-commercial bureaus required enterprises to purchase subscriptions to for-profit publications put out by these bureaus, while banks sold tea leaves to enterprises for profit before reviewing loan applications. Township health clinics required representatives of rural enterprises to attend conferences for which fees were charged as a means of financing new equipment purchases. Officials in Shanghai, Jiangsu, and Zhejiang attributed the problem in part to increases in the size and number of government offices at the local level, which caused the local

---

[47] See also Sang and Wu (1991:27–9) and "Jiading xian xiangzhen gongye xianzhuang he duice diaocha de zonghe baogao (Comprehensive Report on the Investigation into the Status of and Policies for Jiading County Township and Village Industry)," in *Jiading nianjian 1989–1990* (1991:193–8).

[48] It should be noted that the vast majority of surveys conducted by Chinese government agencies and academic institutions are not representative sample surveys. They can be useful to the extent that they provide illustrations of particular empirical phenomena, but they cannot serve as the basis for valid descriptive inferences about the characteristics of the relevant population (Manion 1994).

[49] See, for example, Shen (1992).

[50] Preliminary evidence from a 1997 pilot survey in a random, stratified sample of 130 enterprises of all ownership types in one prefecture in Hebei Province conducted by the author under the auspices of the Asian Development Bank indicates that private firms in the sample faced a lower incidence of unsanctioned levies than did state or collective enterprises. See Whiting (1999a).

bureaucracy to expand beyond the ability of the public finance office to support it (Chen 1991; Wu and Gu 1988). Thus, one local party official, referring to the proliferation of unsanctioned levies, described rural enterprise as a "second treasury."[51]

Officials in all township government offices depended on the revenues provided by rural enterprise – whether via budgetary, extrabudgetary, or self-raised channels; via profit remittances to the industrial corporation; or via illegal exactions – in order to function. This dependence created an overwhelming incentive to promote rural enterprise development. However, the incentive was often manifested in dysfunctional ways.

Incentives to Evade Taxes

The system of public finance, in addition to creating incentives to promote rural industry, also created a number of incentives for the township government to evade taxes in order to increase the share of revenue retained at the local level. These incentives stemmed from (1) the distinction between revenues shared with higher levels of government and those retained exclusively at the township level; (2) the absence of a credible commitment to fiscal contracts on the part of higher levels of government; and (3) the level of extraction, relative to the tax base, contained in the tax contract.

The township government served as both tax collector and de facto owner of collective enterprises. As such, it received both tax revenues, which were shared with the county government according to the terms of the fiscal contract, and profits, which were controlled solely by the township government itself. Particularly when the above-target sharing formula was less than 100 percent, the township government had an incentive to collude with the collective enterprises under its jurisdiction to evade taxes. By shifting revenue out of taxable channels, more funds were left in the enterprise, where the township government could control these funds in their entirety, rather than receiving only a lesser share of the same funds through the fiscal system.[52] Given the revenue impera-

---

[51] Chen (1991:28). Indeed, dependence on rural enterprise for funds has spawned an array of metaphors for these firms from "money trees (*yaoqianshu*)" to "the flesh of a Tang monk (*tangsengrou*)," the latter a reference to the belief, found in the Chinese mythological tale *Journey to the West*, that those who consume the flesh of a monk can live forever.

[52] Two authors make this point explicitly. See Guan and Jiang (1990:187). Yasheng Huang (1990) identifies a similar phenomenon with respect to bank loans.

tive facing township officials, the incentive to collude in tax evasion was strong. In fact, even in situations in which the above-target sharing formula was 100 percent – meaning that all tax receipts above the target level were returned to the township – officials still had an incentive to collude in tax evasion. If township officials collected taxes according to the tax code without regard to the base remittance level specified by the fiscal contract and in so doing exceeded the target amount, they revealed greater fiscal capacity, increasing the potential for a ratchet effect in the base remittance level to be determined in the next contract round. The desire to avoid or diminish such a ratchet effect created an incentive for the township to hide revenue. Moreover, by exposing greater fiscal capacity, the township increased the risk of facing extracontractual levies from higher-level governments.[53]

The experiences of townships in the suburban Shanghai counties provide good examples of the inability of higher levels of government to make credible commitments to fiscal contracts. This lack of credible commitment created the incentive for the township government to evade taxes as a means of shielding revenues from the extracontractual claims of the county, provincial, and central levels. Two types of post hoc contractual changes were common. First, higher levels of government, when faced with fiscal difficulties, exacted involuntary "contributions (*gong-xian kuan*)" from subordinate levels of government. As Panel 2 of Table 3.1 illustrates, Nantang Township made extracontractual "contributions" to both Jiading County and the central government in 1990. Indeed, the director of Nantang's public finance office reported making "contributions" to the central government in 1989, 1990, and 1991, and to the county government in 1989 and 1990. Other townships reported making extracontractual "contributions" to the central government during this period as well. According to an official of the public finance office in Meilin Town, Shanghai County, the town's contribution to the central government was deducted from the above-target tax revenues that, based on the fiscal contract, should have been returned to the town (Informant 70).

A second common practice was for the county government unilaterally to adjust the base figure for revenue remittances during the course of a contract period. For example, in Chenjiaqiao Township, Chuansha County, Shanghai, 1990 tax receipts totaled 22.8 million yuan, far exceed-

---

[53] Moreover, as of the early 1990s, township tax receipts in the research sites were still held in the county treasury, since township treasuries had not yet been established.

ing the contracted base figure of 8.9 million yuan. In response, the county revised the base figure, requiring the township to remit a minimum of 15.47 million yuan. Townships in Songjiang County, Shanghai, reported similar experiences.[54] Officials in Songyang Town, Songjiang County, reported that the share of above-target revenues returned to the town was reduced from 100 to 50 percent during the course of the first contract period. An official of the county public finance bureau noted explicitly that such changes had undermined the intended incentive effects of the fiscal contract (Informant 112). Unilateral changes in the fiscal contract destroyed the credibility of the commitment by higher levels of government to abide by the contract, thereby creating the incentive for the township government to evade taxes in order to conceal its revenue potential.

The final key to the incentives to evade taxes contained in the fiscal contract is the base level of revenue, relative to the tax base, to be remitted to the county. Differences in revenue-sharing arrangements were ramified throughout the fiscal system. Government and tax bureau officials in Nantang Township, for example, drew a comparison between their situation in Jiading County, Shanghai, and that in neighboring Kunshan, a county-level city just across the border in Jiangsu Province (Informants 133 and 139). The officials pointed out that, while the levels of economic development and population sizes in both places were quite similar, Jiading had a remittance target several times the size of Kunshan's. Although the 1991 gross domestic products and, by implication, the tax bases in Jiading and Kunshan were virtually identical (2.45 and 2.44 billion yuan, respectively), Jiading's county-level tax receipts were 480 million yuan, while Kunshan's were only 123 million yuan.[55] The officials suggested that townships or counties which, like

---

[54] See also the discussion of this issue in Jiading County in Lu (1990:9) and Shao and Zhu (1991:142–3).

[55] The populations of the two counties were approximately 510 thousand and 560 thousand in Jiading and Kunshan, respectively; thus, per capita GDP was 4,803 yuan in Jiading and 4,357 yuan in Kunshan. Although the officials' claim was that the difference was due to the incentives inherent in the base level of target remittances, the difference might also be due to differing statutory tax rates across sectors, reflecting differences in the economic structure in the two counties. However, Kunshan County appears to be only slightly less industrialized; agriculture, industry, and services represent 19, 61, and 20 percent of the economy, respectively, in Kunshan and 12, 65, and 23 percent of the economy in Jiading. Indeed, the pattern of lower tax receipts appears consistent across even highly developed Jiangsu counties. Although Wuxi County, Jiangsu, has a gross domestic product (4.74 billion yuan) nearly twice that of Jiading and an even more highly industrialized economic structure (with agriculture, industry, and services representing

---

Kunshan, could easily meet their base remittance targets essentially faced a lower cost to tax evasion. The base remittance level was an important threshold, particularly since some fiscal contracts contained penalty clauses that required local governments to make up any shortfall using their own funds. Thus, townships or counties with high base remittance levels relative to the tax base were forced to reveal more of their fiscal capacity simply to fulfill their contractual obligations.

This account of intergovernmental fiscal relations is not to suggest that township officials had no influence over fiscal contracts. Township officials could argue for a low base remittance level in fiscal contracts. Although the county could initiate changes in fiscal contracts unilaterally, township officials could respond by bargaining for other concessions to balance the effects of such changes. In a parallel to findings of the literature on central–provincial relations (Lieberthal and Oksenberg 1988), status as a major revenue contributor could give a township influence with the county as well as subjecting it to tighter control. Bargaining represented another means by which township officials strived to retain as much revenue as possible at the local level.

Clearly, the fiscal system contained a number of dysfunctional features that, especially in combination, created powerful incentives to evade taxes. The conflict of interest inherent in the township government's dual status as de facto enterprise owner and tax collector, the absence of a credible commitment to fiscal contracts, and, in certain locales, a low base remittance level relative to the tax base all encouraged the township government to collude with collective firms in tax evasion. The ways in which these incentives were manifested in policy implementation are discussed in Chapter 5.

Incentives for Differential Treatment of Private and Collective Firms

Several features of the public finance system account for the incentives for differential treatment of private and collective firms by township governments. The absence of a formal claim on private enterprise profits, the

---

12, 75, and 13 percent of the economy, respectively), Wuxi's tax receipts were only 394 million yuan – 86 million yuan less than Jiading's. (I have not located the figure for the remittance target in Kunshan [the Jiading County 1990 remittance target was 236 million yuan] necessary to confirm the officials' claim. Nevertheless, the other readily available data presented here do tend to confirm it.) These issues are reexamined and evaluated with quantitative data in Chapter 5.

Table 3.5. *Township Government Funds Derived from Collective and Private Firms*

Revenue Source	Collective	Private
Budgetary		
Turnover taxes	yes	yes
Income taxes	10%–55%	35%
Urban maintenance tax	yes	yes
Nonbudgetary		
Profit remittance	yes	no
Legally mandated fees		
Agriculture fee	yes	no
Agricultural subsidiaries fee	yes	no
Social welfare fee	yes	no
Rural education fee	yes	yes
Nonlegally mandated fees	yes	yes
Other		
Management fee	yes[a]	yes[b]

[a] Paid to the township industrial corporation.
[b] Paid to the industrial and commercial bureau at the township level.
Source: Interview data.

different treatment of private and collective tax revenues in fiscal contracts, and the existence, before 1994, of different tax rates for private and collective firms all created incentives to treat private firms prejudicially.

The township government had no direct institutional incentive to collude with private enterprises in tax evasion. Unlike collective enterprises – which in Shanghai paid four legally mandated fees that became self-raised funds of the township government – private enterprises paid only the rural education fee (Table 3.5).[56] More importantly, township governments had no legitimate claim on the after-tax profits of private enterprises. Thus, the direct conflict of interest that fostered collusion between the township government and collective firms in evading the taxes to be shared with higher levels of government did not exist with respect to private firms. Nevertheless, the township

---

[56] The rural education fee paid by private enterprises was assessed as a 1.5 to 4 percent surcharge on turnover taxes rather than on gross profits as for collective enterprises. Private enterprises also paid a management fee to the industrial and commercial bureau (1.5 to 2 percent of total sales).

government and other agencies did benefit from the exaction of extralegal fees and contributions from private firms. As subsequent chapters will show, extraction from private firms in all forms was costly to local governments, and since private firms received little support in the form of bank loans, their ability to absorb extralegal fees was more limited than it was for collective firms, which had softer budget constraints.

The division of private enterprise tax revenues contained in the fiscal contract also shaped the behavior of the township with respect to the taxation of private firms. Even within Shanghai Municipality, there were differences in the manner in which the taxes paid by private enterprises were treated in fiscal contracts. In Nantang Township, for example, private enterprise taxes were not included in the fiscal contract until 1989. Prior to that year, private enterprise taxes were turned over directly to the county, leaving the township with little incentive to pursue private enterprise tax collection vigorously. The fiscal contract devised for private firms in 1989 took 1988 receipts as the base figure; the base target was remitted to the county, and above-target remittances were shared, with 50 percent returned to the township. Thus, the new arrangement increased the township's incentive to collect private enterprise taxes. By contrast, in Songjiang County, where private enterprises represented a slightly larger proportion of firms than in Jiading, private firms had consistently been included in the regular fiscal contract. In that situation, local officials already had a strong incentive to pursue the taxation of private firms.

Differences in the maximum income tax rate also created incentives for differential treatment. While all private enterprises paid a 35 percent income tax on profits, collective enterprises earning income over 10 thousand yuan paid income tax at a rate that increased incrementally from 35 percent to a top rate of 55 percent paid by collectives earning more than 200 thousand yuan annually.[57] The wide gap between private and

---

[57] On private enterprises, see "Zhonghua renmin gongheguo siying qiye suodeshui zanxing tiaoli (People's Republic of China Provisional Regulations on Private Enterprise Income Tax)," in *Zhongguo xiangzhen qiye nianjian 1989* (1990:134). On collective enterprises, see "Zhonghua renmin gongheguo jiti qiye suodeshui zanxing tiaoli (People's Republic of China Provisional Regulations on Collective Enterprise Income Tax)," in *Xiangzhen caizheng shouce* (1987:120–4); and Caizhengbu, "Guanyu banfa 'Zhonghua renmin gongheguo jiti qiye suodeshui zanxing tiaoli shixing xice' de tongzhi (Detailed Rules and Regulations for Implementation)," in Ibid (1987:124–34).

collective tax rates created an additional incentive for the township government to collude with collective enterprises in tax evasion in order to level the playing field in competition against private firms. Furthermore, in areas where the township government traditionally relied upon collective enterprises for revenue, it had an incentive to protect the profits of collectives and, concomitantly, its own revenues by prohibiting the entry of private firms.[58] Township governments could prohibit entry locally by refusing, for example, to license firms in sectors where collective firms were already established.

Summary

Local governments were heavily dependent on rural enterprise for revenue. Townships responded to the revenue imperative strengthened by the post-1980 revenue-sharing fiscal system by actively promoting the development of rural enterprise. From the perspective of the central state, rural enterprise, as the leading growth sector in the economy, was a tremendous success. The distinctive patterns of private and collective enterprise development that emerged as a result of incentives to promote rural enterprise are described in the next chapter.

However, other less felicitous consequences also accompanied the promotion of rural enterprise. The same incentive structure contained a number of dysfunctional elements that undermined the capacity of the central state to regulate the economy. The preceding analysis has revealed a number of incentives for township cadres to collude with collective firms in tax evasion. The ramifications of tax evasion in one of the economy's most dynamic sectors were serious. Tax evasion contributed to the growing budget deficits faced by the central government

Footnote 57, cont.: Collective enterprise income tax rates

Income level (yuan)	Tax rate (percent)
Less than 1,000	10
1,000–3,500	20
3,500–10,000	28
10,000–25,000	35
25,000–50,000	42
50,000–100,000	48
100,000–200,000	53
More than 200,000	55

[58] This argument corresponds to one made by Barry Naughton (1992a:14–41) with respect to state enterprises.

throughout the late 1980s and early 1990s, which in turn reduced the center's ability to redistribute income or to finance central investment in key areas such as infrastructure development. Furthermore, as one World Bank study points out, "the 'tax levers' the central government designs may be a far cry from the fiscal measures which are actually implemented, leaving the central government significantly weakened in its use of a fiscal policy instrument" (World Bank 1990b:18). Moreover, to the extent that the drive to promote rural enterprise motivated local officials to interfere in the allocation of bank loans to collective firms without regard to credit ceilings or borrower qualifications, the central government's ability to implement monetary policy was similarly undermined. Indeed, the extent of taxes, profit remittances, fees, and levies paid by collective enterprises in some cases "bled them dry."[59] As a result, many collectives were "anemic" and heavily reliant on "transfusions" in the form of bank loans (Qin 1991a:189). Chapters 5 and 6 examine in detail the nature of tax and credit policy implementation that resulted from the incentives described here.[60]

THE CADRE EVALUATION SYSTEM

The cadre evaluation system had a powerful independent influence on local cadre behavior, because, at root, local leaders sought to maintain their positions of power, and the cadre evaluation system structured the way local cadres pursued this goal.[61] Ironically, the system created incen-

---

[59] One study conducted in Jiading County estimated that rural collectives retained less than 6 percent of gross profits on average (Shen and You 1991:187–8).

[60] Christine Wong's research, while touching briefly on issues of soft credit and tax evasion and avoidance, suggests other problems stemming from the incentive to promote rural industry, such as protectionism on the part of regional officials who have an interest in preserving the market for the products of local enterprises. See Wong (1991b:709).

[61] The assumption that local officials pursue career success has substantial empirical support. This section is based primarily on interviews with twenty-eight county, township, and village leaders in Shanghai, Jiangsu, and Zhejiang. Relevant issues were also addressed in interviews with twelve representatives of county and township offices of management and administration (*jingying guanli bangongshi*) and policy research (*zhengce yanjiushi*). (See Appendix 1 for a complete list of interviews.) Detailed data on the terms by which cadres were evaluated were acquired for five townships and seven villages. Furthermore, based on a survey of village leaders in Jiangsu and Hubei provinces, Scott Rozelle (1994:115) reports that "most young village leaders want to advance within the bureaucratic hierarchy. . . . only one of the village leaders stated that he would not take a position in the township if it were offered (that was a leader of the most successful village in the Jiangsu study area)." Similarly, Philip Huang (1990:322) indicates that in Songjiang County there was a high degree of identification with the

tives for cadres not only to promote the rapid development of rural industry but also to distort central tax and credit policies and to interfere in enterprise management, reinforcing the lack of separation between party, government, and enterprise. Township leaders were extremely sensitive to the criteria by which they were evaluated, because their performance on these criteria determined their level of remuneration and influenced their tenure in office and opportunities for promotion. The salience of performance criteria is demonstrated by the fact that cadres in the research sites were aware at all times of where they stood in terms of fulfilling their key performance targets and where they stood relative to leaders of other townships and villages in their areas.

Background: The Development of the Post-Mao Cadre Evaluation System

Central-state leaders began to address the problem of evaluating local cadres shortly after the initiation of reform in 1978. In November 1979, the Organization Department of the CCP Central Committee issued a document calling for the establishment of a new system of evaluation for cadres.[62] This initial statement stipulated that evaluations should cover political thought, organizational and leadership abilities, familiarity with substantive issues, and "democratic" work style, as well as actual achievements (*gongzuo de shiji chengxiao*). Moreover, evaluations should be linked to both material and nonmaterial rewards, as well as promotions or transfers. A subsequent national organization work conference held in 1983 built on the foundation put in place in 1979. Notably, however, it placed greater weight on the assessment of concrete achievements rather than political attitudes or work style and reiterated the importance of concrete achievements in determining material rewards and penalties as well as promotions (*Zhongguo renshi nianjian* 1991).

---

state among cadres above the level of the natural village (i.e., the team, in this part of the country). "Brigade cadres in Huayangqiao, with good prospects of advancing up the bureaucratic ladder of the party-state, tended to identify more with the state apparatus than [with] their home communities. This was all the more true of commune and county cadres; most of them, in any case, came from other localities, a modern version of the good old-fashioned rule of avoidance for county magistrates."

[62] Zhonggong zhongyang zuzhibu, "Guanyu shixing ganbu kaohe zhidu de yijian de tongzhi (Notice of Opinions regarding the Implementation of a Cadre Evaluation System)," in *Renshi gongzuo wenjian xuanbian* (1987:12–15).

The commentary surrounding the establishment of the new evaluation process during the early to mid-1980s helps to put the changes in context. Commentators emphasized the importance of moving away from the subjective evaluations of political attitudes that characterized the Cultural Revolution toward specific, measurable, and quantifiable indicators of performance.[63] Furthermore, they pointed out that

> Using concrete achievements as the main standard to assess both cadre ability and political integrity will help to negate the phenomenon of cadres who do more and less, perform well and poorly, all eating from the same "big pot" and to negate the phenomenon of cadres who simply try to make no mistakes but achieve nothing, passing their days in office in mediocrity sitting in an "iron armchair."[64]

Thus the cadre evaluation system was seen in part as a means to break the paralysis of many local cadres following the Cultural Revolution and to actively mobilize them to pursue specific goals.

By 1988, the CCP Organization Department had established official guidelines for the annual evaluation of party secretaries and government executives at the county and township levels.[65] The national guidelines for evaluation criteria included indicators ranging from the gross value of industrial output, tax remittances, and procurement of agricultural products, to realized infrastructure investment, population growth rates, and completion rates for nine-year compulsory education. (The 1988 national guidelines are reproduced in Table 3.6.) These guidelines were an attempt to standardize and systematize evaluation of cadre performance on a range of government functions at the local level. Moreover, they explicitly sought to encourage competition (*guli jingzheng*) among

---

[63] See also Li Lei, "Shiji shi kaocha ganbu de weiyi biaozhun (Actual Practice Is the Primary Standard for Evaluating Cadres)," *Gongren ribao* (Workers' daily), September 13, 1985, reprinted in Han and Yue (1987:506–8); and Yang Bohua, "Jianli yange de ganbu kaohe zhidu (Establish a Strict Cadre Evaluation System)," *Beijing ribao* (Beijing daily), July 15, 1985, reprinted in Ibid (1987:509–13).

[64] Jiang Zhaoyuan, "Xuanba kaocha ganbu yao zhuzhong gongzuo shiji (Selecting and Evaluating Cadres Should Focus on Actual Work)," *Renmin ribao* (People's daily), July 9, 1985, reprinted in Han and Yue (1987:503–5).

[65] Zhongyang zuzhibu, "Guanyu shixing difang dangzheng lingdao ganbu niandu gongzuo kaohe zhidu de tongzhi (Notice regarding Implementation of the Annual Job Evaluation System for Leading Cadres of Local Party and Government Organs)," in *Zhongguo renshi nianjian 1988–1989* (1991:529–40); and He, Wei, and Lin (1991:175–82).

Table 3.6. *National Guidelines for Performance Criteria of Local Party and Government Leaders*

Category
Gross national product
Gross value of industrial output (not including any output below the village level)
Gross value of agricultural output (not including any output below the village level)
Gross value of output of township- and village-run enterprises
National income per capita
Rural income per capita
Taxes and profits remitted
Fiscal income
Labor productivity of state and collective enterprises
Procurement of agricultural and subsidiary products
Retail sales
Infrastructure investment realized
Natural population growth rate
Grain output
Local budgetary income
Local budgetary expenditures
Forested area
Nine-year compulsory education completion rate

Note: Each category was to be assessed by the relevant government organ and data on both level and rate of increase were to be provided.

Source: Zhonggong zhongyang zuzhibu, "Guanyu shixing difang dangzheng lingdao ganbu niandu gongzuo kaohe zhidu de tongzhi (Notice Regarding Implementation of the Annual Job Evaluation System for Leading Cadres of Local Party and Government Organs)," in *Zhongguo renshi nianjian* (1991).

party secretaries and government executives at the same level of the administrative hierarchy.

At the township level, the cadre evaluation system was designed to make party and government leaders responsible for the performance of the township in economic as well as social and political terms. In most cases, performance criteria (*kaohe zhibiao*) were set by the county office of management and administration. The criteria did not exhaust the full range of functions performed by township leaders; rather, they reflected the priorities of county leaders and were one means of conveying these priorities to township officials – and through them to village leaders. This approach facilitated cadre management at the county level by reducing the complex issues of township development to a few key indicators. Such a system also allowed county officials to compare the performance of township leaders across locales and helped identify the most competent cadres for promotion.[66] Promotions, demotions, and transfers across townships within the county were not uncommon for township leaders, who were selected from a countywide pool. Indeed, of the twelve government executives and party secretaries at the township level interviewed for this study, eight had served in similar capacities in other townships within the same county. Thus, they were not tied to their township of origin. By contrast, village leaders, including all twelve of those interviewed for this study, typically served in their home villages.

Township executives and party secretaries were state cadres, who received a base salary from the state payroll. For these cadres, the performance criteria affected only their bonuses, which, nevertheless, usually accounted for the largest single share of their incomes.[67] In practice, the growth of rural industry (whether measured primarily by output value, profits, or sales) was the single most important determinant of local officials' bonuses. Yet in addition to industry, the provision of public goods, such as education and public order, were also considered in evaluating overall performance under the cadre evaluation system. In principle, strong performances on specific indicators resulted in bonus increments, while weak performances resulted in bonus deductions. Performances on the full range of indicators were recorded in officials' personnel files and therefore could affect their promotion prospects. Thus, the cadre evaluation system reinforced the incentives, created by the fiscal system, to promote rural industry in order to generate revenue; at the same time, it constrained township leaders to dedicate at least some resources to the provision of public goods.

[66] Jiading party document (Jiaweifa [1989] # 8) promulgated on March 3, 1989: see Zhonggong Jiadingxian wei Jiadingxian renmin zhengfu, "Guanyu wanshan 1989 nian xiangzhen dang zheng jiguan ganbu kaohe jiangli banfa de tongzhi (Announcement regarding Improvement of the Methods of Evaluation and Reward for Cadres in Township Party and Government Organs for 1989)," in Jiadingxian nianjian bianji weiyuanhui, *Jiading nianjian 1988–1990* (Jiading yearbook 1988–1990) (Shanghai: Tongji daxue chubanshe, n.d.), pp. 44–5.

[67] In Luhang Town, Shanghai County, for example, the township executive's bonus accounted for 60 percent (2,510 yuan) of his total 1991 income of 4,180 yuan, the basic salary accounted for 34 percent (1,420 yuan), and subsidies accounted for 6 percent (250 yuan) (Informant 66). The top government and party leaders at the township and village levels were usually evaluated on the same terms and received the same level of remuneration.

Although the CCP Organization Department produced national guidelines for performance criteria, there was significant variation in specific performance criteria at the grass roots. Table 3.7 reproduces the performance criteria for township government executives and party secretaries in Jiading County, Shanghai, for 1989.[68] The emphasis on rural industry is reflected in the first set of indicators, which assigns highest priority to increases in the gross value of industrial output and industrial profits. The second set of indicators focuses on the provision of agricultural and agricultural subsidiary products to the state and to the urban market. Since many agricultural tasks had, by 1989, devolved to households that contracted directly with the village for land and other inputs, the inclusion of agriculture among the performance targets for township officials was most likely intended to shape their interactions with village leaders.[69] The third set of indicators covers "party building," which refers to communist party functions, including the recruitment and education of party cadres, the maintenance of party discipline and exemplary behavior among party members, and the organization of activities for nonmembers that inculcate party values. The fourth set of indicators focuses on education and contains an item that explicitly evaluates township leaders on the scale of funds they dedicate to education in the community. The fifth performance indicator, and the only one related to health care, is family planning, suggesting the importance placed on birth control by county officials.[70] The final indicator is public order, which was evaluated separately by the politics and law leadership small group.

Like its counterpart at the county level, the township office of management and administration set the criteria used to evaluate both village leaders and collective enterprise managers, and in this way, incentives created at higher levels were ramified down through the administrative

[68] The county instituted this kind of evaluation process beginning in 1986, although the specific indicators changed somewhat from year to year. Township leaders in other counties also reported being evaluated using similar criteria. In Luhang Town, Shanghai County, for example, economic items accounted for 60 out of a possible 100 points, sociopolitical items accounted for 40 (Informant 66). However, township leaders emphasized that industrial performance carried the most weight in determining their bonuses.

[69] While many facets of agricultural management (irrigation, application of fertilizer, etc.) affect how much is produced and available for sale, the performance indicators set by county officials reflect only their "bottom-line," i.e., were sales targets for grain, etc., met or not.

[70] In bureaucratic terms, the relationship between public health and family planning is indirect since they were handled by separate offices at the township level.

Table 3.7. *Performance Criteria for Township Government Executives and Party Secretaries, Jiading County, Shanghai, 1989*

Category	Points	County-level unit responsible for evaluation of target fulfillment[a]	
Township- and village-run industry	33		
Increase in gross value of industrial output		10	rural industry bureau
Increase in industrial profits		10	rural industry bureau
Increase in profit rate on gross value of output		5	rural industry bureau
Township ranking by profit rate on total capital		4	rural industry bureau
Increase in total value of exports		4	rural industry bureau
Agriculture	30		
Sales to the state of grain and vegetables		15	grain bureau/vegetable office
Sales to the urban market of pigs		10	animal husbandry bureau
Sales to the state of oil-bearing crops		3	grain bureau
Sales to the state of leather and cotton		2	supply and marketing cooperative
Party building	21		
Building of party organizations		7	CCP organization section
Building of party spirit and discipline		7	discipline inspection committee
Education of party members		7	CCP propaganda section
Education	9		
Completion rate for compulsory education		3	education committee
Participation rate for worker training		3	education committee
Scale of funds dedicated to education		3	education committee
Family planning	7		
Family planning compliance rate		7	family planning office
Public order		[b]	politics and law leadership small group
Total	100		

[a] In most cases, this unit performs the actual evaluation. The county statistical bureau is also involved in the evaluation of fulfillment of all targets for industry and agriculture. The county party committee's policy research office oversees the compilation of data at the end of the year.

[b] According to the document, "the performance of township party and government cadres with respect to their public order responsibilities is to be evaluated separately by the county's 'politics and law leadership small group (*zhengfa lingdao xiaozu*)'."

Source: Jiading party document (Jiaweifa [1989] # 8) promulgated on March 3, 1989. *Jiading nianjian 1988–1990* (n.d.: 44–5).

hierarchy. Village leaders and enterprise managers were usually collective cadres, who received no basic salary from the state. For them, the performance criteria determined their entire incomes. In all seven villages for which detailed data are available, the gross value of industrial output and industrial profits were the key targets in determining the incomes of village leaders. The case of a village party secretary in Nantang Township, Jiading County, illustrates how contract incentives were structured. According to his contract for 1991, his starting salary was pegged (based on a step function) to the level of industrial output achieved in the village that year. Because the village's total output value exceeded a 2 million yuan threshold, he received a starting salary of 5,100 yuan. (Less successful village leaders received lower starting salaries; the minimum possible starting salary was 2,800 yuan.) In addition, he received 50 yuan for every 10 thousand yuan of profit over and above the village's target level of 1.85 million yuan. Village enterprises produced total profits of 2.5 million yuan; therefore, he received a profit bonus of 3,250 yuan. These two items accounted for the lion's share (about 85 percent) of his income, which totaled 9,960 yuan. By directly linking income and industrial performance, the cadre evaluation system created a very direct incentive for local cadres to take a personal interest in economic management.

Like township leaders, village leaders were evaluated on a range of performance indicators, but their incomes were most closely linked to industrial performance. To the extent that village enterprises generated revenue via industry, the village had more resources at its disposal to apply to other village functions. Such resources could finance agricultural equipment purchases for use by villagers, irrigation, roads, and other infrastructure projects, and subsidies for village schools and health clinics, in addition to further industrial development.[71]

While cadres benefited from strong economic performances, they also paid a high price for weak economic showings. Moreover, a leader's remuneration was contingent upon the performance of other township or village leaders, thus pitting local cadres in competition with one another. Strong performance in one township or village tended to drive up target levels for the others. This characteristic of the evaluation system encouraged cadres to innovate in order to improve their performance relative to others. In two of the seven villages for which detailed data are

---

[71] These expenditures were reflected in the accounts of a village in Songyang with several successful industrial enterprises, for example (Informant 87).

available, village leaders' remuneration fell in light of declining relative performance and failure to meet rapidly increasing targets. A village in Nantang Township, Jiading County, offers an example of the importance of this link. The village leader presided over a period of declining economic performance relative to other villages in the township during the late 1980s and early 1990s. As a result, his 1991 income of 4,046 yuan was 20 percent less than his 1988 income of 5,040 yuan, achieved three years earlier (Informant 122). Similarly, a village in Luhang Town, Shanghai County, had been ranked third in the township in terms of output in 1989, but by 1991 had dropped to ninth. The income of the village party secretary, who failed to meet his industrial targets, fell by several thousand yuan to 2,950 yuan, while higher-ranked village party secretaries earned more than 6,000 yuan each in 1991 (Informant 62). Similar performance-based income differentials occurred among township leaders. For example, in Songjiang County in 1995, the party secretary and government executive of the township with the strongest economic performance each earned 17,500 yuan, while those of the township with the weakest performance each earned 6,000 yuan (Informant 214). Clearly, there were very real costs to failure to achieve the norms set by the cadre evaluation system.

Not only were the incomes of township and village leaders determined by their performance in rural industry, but their tenure in office and opportunities for advancement were to some extent as well. According to an official of the Shanghai suburban industry management bureau, which governed township- and village-run industry, county leaders appointed township executives and party secretaries with the intention that they would participate directly in decision making with respect to these enterprises. As this official put it, they "rise or fall on the basis of economic success" (Informant 37).[72]

Consistent with this intention, the contract terms for collective enterprise managers were also designed to align their incentives with those of township leaders.[73] Although contracts contained many detailed targets,

---

[72] Susan Shirk (1993:189–90) identifies a similar phenomenon at the provincial level. "Under the post-1980 incentive structure, the political ambitions of individual local officials became closely identified with the economic accomplishments of their domains. ... Whether officials aimed to climb the ladder of success to Beijing or to become leading figures on the local scene, their reputation was enhanced by industrial growth and local building projects."

[73] Managers of township- and village-run collectives were typically selected from relatively small pools within the township or village, respectively. Two early studies of rural col-

the operative ones for determining managers' incomes were output value and profits.[74] For example, in Songyang Town, Songjiang County, if a factory met the targets for output value and profits set by the town, the manager and party secretary would receive 180 percent of the average worker's wages as their base salaries. Beyond that, they would receive a one-thousand-yuan bonus for each one million yuan in output value over the target level and a two-thousand-yuan bonus for each one hundred thousand yuan in profits over the target level. Meeting other targets for improving product quality, repaying bank loans on time, meeting safety standards, improving the circulation of funds, and reducing the level of uncollected accounts-receivable merited a flat increment of only 50 yuan each. Some contracts also stipulated bonus deductions for failure to pay specified minimum amounts to the local government in terms of fees levied to support agriculture, agricultural subsidiary products, rural education, and social welfare and for failure to make contributions to community health insurance and pension plans.[75] These obligations roughly

lective managers in Jiangsu Province indicate that the vast majority (93 to 95 percent) were selected from within the township or village where the enterprise was located (He 1991:184; Meng 1990:302). Moreover, managers tended to be selected from among those with experience as party or government cadres. One multiprovince study of 200 rural industrial enterprises reports that 60 percent of managers had served previously as local government cadres (Qiu 1988:758). Analysts attributed such career paths to the importance placed on political reliability and ability to achieve the goals of township leaders (Du 1992:119; Qiu 1988). As one enterprise manager in Songyang Town put it, "those who follow the township leaders thrive, while those who oppose them fail (*shunzhe chang nizhe wang*)" (Informant 77). Interviews in Nantang Township revealed a particularly distinctive career pattern among the first generation of collective managers who rose from team leader to village (brigade) accountant or village party secretary to a position in the township (commune) government before assuming the position of manager. More broadly, among the research sites for this study, more than 90 percent of the collective enterprises for which information was available were managed by party members. (Firms were considered to be managed by party members if the general manager was a party member or if the enterprise had a full-time party secretary who served concurrently as a vice general manager. However, only 55 percent of collective firms provided an answer to this question. Questioning about party membership was considered sensitive by most informants. Indicative of this sensitivity was that officials and managers of local collectives who concurrently held both government and party positions sought to identify themselves to foreigners solely on the basis of their nonparty positions. Such sensitivity likely contributed to the number of managers who evaded questions about party membership.)

[74] See, for example, Shao (1991:186) and S. zhen renmin zhengfu, "Guanyu yijiujiuyi niandu gongye shengchan zerenzhi de yijian (Opinion regarding the 1991 Industrial Production Responsibility System)," Mimeo.

[75] This was the case, for example, in the contract for the manager of a collectively owned bicycle parts factory in Nantang Township (Informant 129).

paralleled the responsibilities of township leaders under the cadre evaluation system. Overall, contract incentives for managers were closely aligned with the incentives for township leaders.

The Unintended Consequences of the Cadre Evaluation System

While the cadre evaluation system encouraged township leaders to foster the development of the local economy and to provide certain public goods, it also perpetuated reliance on administrative rather than market guidance of enterprises, undermined enterprise autonomy, contributed to the distortion of central credit policies, and produced a number of other dysfunctional incentives. As an official in Luhang Town put it, "In evaluating performance, [the county] emphasizes economic targets; so, of course the party secretary wants to meddle (*ganyu*) in the economy" (Informant 46). Furthermore, township leaders were appointed for three-year terms, creating a relatively short time horizon.[76] They vied with one another to exceed targets and to complete projects that would set them apart from other local leaders and improve their chances of promotion.

There was intense pressure to meet and surpass the rapidly increasing targets set within the cadre evaluation system. Such intense pressure created incentives for cadres to distort central credit policies in order to meet the goals set for them. For example, expectations regarding economic performance increased dramatically in February 1992, following the promulgation of a central party document that ushered in a fast-growth campaign characterized by the ratcheting up of economic targets. According to a bank official in Songjiang County, "Last year [1991], targets increased about 25 percent. This year they will increase a minimum of 30 percent. Townships cannot meet targets without new enterprises. New enterprises increase output value in one fell swoop, whereas old enterprises are doing well if they increase 10 percent in a year" (Informant 84). The bank official further suggested that such high growth rates could be attained only by relying on bank loans. Township officials, scrambling to meet rapidly increasing targets, had a powerful incentive to employ political leverage to pressure local offices of state-

---

[76] Margaret Levi (1988:32) employs the notion of a "discount rate" to assess, based on a leader's security of office, the extent of his concern for future benefits; those leaders with little security of office "will be less concerned with promoting the conditions of economic growth and increased revenue *over time* than with extracting available revenue...."

run banks and rural credit cooperatives to grant loans for new enterprises, even in violation of central regulations regarding loan ceilings,
sectoral distribution of credit, and borrower qualifications. Not only did
local cadres have the incentive to influence the implementation of credit
policy, but their authority – via party channels – over bank officials gave
them the means to do so.[77]

The content of the targets themselves created incentives for township
and village leaders to interfere in the economy in counterproductive
ways – a version of the moral hazard problem.[78] For example, where the
number of joint venture contracts signed was an important criterion of
performance, local officials again had an incentive to intervene in local
bank decision making in order to secure bank loans for the foreign
partner, regardless of the suitability of the proposed project or the creditworthiness of the borrower. The use of output value as a performance
indicator for township leaders provided an even more prominent
example. Although, as of the early 1990s, the importance of output value
as a performance indicator was gradually giving way to emphasis on sales
and profits, the disproportionate attention it had received up to that
point had resulted in several undesirable consequences. According to a
study conducted in Jiangsu Province, the focus on output value created
an incentive for township leaders to expand productive capacity without
sufficient attention to the efficiency of production or the salability of
products (He 1991:121).[79] Figures 3.1 and 3.2, which originally appeared
in a Shanghai newspaper, comically illustrate these problems. The
problems became particularly serious during recessionary periods when
unsold goods accumulated in inventory while production continued
apace.

The prominence of output value as a performance indicator can be
understood in the context of the structure of taxes.[80] Turnover taxes –
specifically the product tax and the value-added tax – were paid at the
point of production and were later included in the sales price of a good.[81]

---

[77] This issue is addressed in detail in Chapter 6.
[78] Such problems arise when the principal relies on proxies to measure the behavior of an
agent. The agent then has an incentive "to redirect his efforts toward the proxy measure"
rather than toward the "abstract goals" of the principal (Moe 1984:755).
[79] See also Shao (1991:185–7). At least some officials at the Ministry of Agriculture were
aware of the hazards of this approach. See Guo and Liu (1991:84).
[80] I am indebted to Christine Wong for this insight.
[81] In other words, turnover taxes were paid on the value of output regardless of whether
the output was sold (World Bank 1990b).

Figure 3.1. Newspaper cartoon illustrating lack of attention to efficiency. The truck is labeled "Enterprise X." The cargo falling off the bed is labeled "Efficiency." The caption reads, "This is the way to go fast." *Source*: *Shanghai gongye jingji bao*, December 8, 1988, p. 2.

As Table 3.8 shows, income taxes composed a small and decreasing share of tax revenues from township- and village-run enterprises, while, conversely, turnover taxes, which already constituted the bulk of tax revenues, were becoming even more important. Thus, county officials – who shared in the tax receipts but not the profits of these enterprises – tried to ensure adequate performance on taxes by making the readily measurable indicator of output value a centerpiece of township executives' contracts. Although some county officials employed tax receipts as a performance indicator as well, one county executive commented that he considered it unwise to push tax collection through performance criteria directly (Informant 103). He reasoned that if county-level tax receipts were too high, the provincial level would be likely to increase the minimum amount of taxes it expected the county to hand over. By focusing incentives on output value, county officials hoped to ensure adequate tax revenues, while leaving themselves room to maneuver through the selective approval of tax breaks after the minimum level of tax receipts was met. Since county and township governments faced similar incentive structures, the county had to strike a delicate balance in revenue extraction. Revenues that entered tax channels revealed greater fiscal capacity to higher levels of government, including, but not limited to, the

Figure 3.2. Newspaper cartoon illustrating lack of attention to salability of products. The sacks on the conveyer belt are labeled "Blind production." The barge is labeled "Market." The caption reads, "Oblivious to what's going on outside the window – It's full! Don't push the button any more!" *Source*: *Shanghai gongye jingji bao*, October 24, 1988, p. 2.

county level. At the same time, the county, like the township, could tap into enterprise resources outside of regular fiscal channels – especially if such resources were protected from formal taxation.[82]

Revised economic performance criteria, found in three of the five townships for which detailed data are available, placed less emphasis on output value and greater emphasis on sales and profits. For example, in

---

[82] With the implementation of a new tax and fiscal system in 1994, tax types were clearly assigned to particular levels of government. Strikingly, after the implementation of these reforms, county officials began to include relevant tax types in the performance criteria of township leaders (Informant 214). This issue is addressed in Chapter 7.

Table 3.8. *Taxes Owed by Township- and Village-run
Enterprises, 1978–97*

Year	Total tax liability (billion yuan)	Profit tax liability (billion yuan)	Profit taxes as share of total taxes
1978	2.20	0.74	33.6
1979	2.26	0.70	31.0
1980	2.57	0.79	30.7
1981	3.43	0.95	27.7
1982	4.47	1.25	28.0
1983	5.89	1.89	32.1
1984	7.91	2.63	33.2
1985	10.86	3.27	30.1
1986	13.73	3.86	28.1
1987	16.94	4.44	26.2
1988	23.65	5.98	25.3
1989	27.25	6.09	22.3
1990	27.54	5.71	20.7
1991	33.38	6.81	20.4
1992	47.32	9.55	20.2
1993	87.73	16.78	19.1
1994	n/a	23.13	n/a
1995	130.17	27.87	21.4
1996	143.90	30.47	21.2
1997	156.24	40.81	26.1

Sources: *Zhongguo xiangzhen qiye nianjian* (1989:638; 1990:106; 1991:186; 1992a [1990 data]:194; 1992b [1991 data]:200; 1993:232; 1994:364; 1996:99; 250; 1997:121; 248). *Zhongguo tongji nianjian* (1993:396; 1995:366; 1998:422).

Jiading County, the township cadre evaluation system was first implemented in 1986; the biggest problem, as identified by a 1989 party document, was that profit had not been employed as the most important indicator of economic performance.[83] This problem was echoed elsewhere. A representative of Songyang Town, Songjiang County, noted that, "Up to now, leaders have only worried about output value, but that's not what counts. What counts is profit" (Informant 99). In response to this problem, officials in Songjiang County shifted the emphasis from

[83] See Zhonggong Jiading xianwei Jiading xian renmin zhengfu, "Guanyu wanshan 1989 nian xiangzhen dang zheng jiguan ganbu kaohe jiangli banfa de tongzhi (Announcement regarding Improvement of Methods of Evaluation and Reward for Cadres in Township Party and Government Organs for 1989)," in *Jiading nianjian 1988–1990* (1991:44–5).

output value to sales during the early 1990s, but by 1995 settled on a measure that combined output value and profits. Officials in Jiading County also adjusted their performance criteria to reflect profitability more closely.

While the new focus on profits avoided some of the pitfalls associated with the disproportionate emphasis on output value, it nevertheless invited significant direct involvement on the part of township and village officials in both bank and enterprise management. Not only did local leaders have a relatively short time horizon, but they also lacked market information and adequate means to evaluate the potential profitability of investments. Imitation appeared to be a common, if imperfect, strategy for identifying potentially profitable investments in this information-poor environment. For example, in their quest for quick profits, officials in Nantang Township, Jiading County, Shanghai, used bank loans garnered through political manipulation to rush into investments in production lines for latex rubber gloves, which had been profitable elsewhere. The resulting duplication of capacity resulted in massive losses and the inability to repay bank loans.[84] The World Bank identified the same phenomenon in the development of excess capacity in aluminum extrusion and processing plants in townships in Wuxi County, Jiangsu, in the mid-1980s (Wang 1990:241). The incentives on the part of local officials to meet and exceed performance targets thus had serious negative consequences for enterprise autonomy and implementation of credit policy.

Balancing Political, Social, and Economic Incentives

The necessity of maintaining public order constituted a political constraint on the revenue maximizing behavior of local cadres. As Douglass North (1981) suggests, leaders often face a trade-off between political considerations and considerations of economic efficiency in producing revenue. Accordingly, the evaluation of cadre performance in maintaining public order led township cadres to balance concerns about local employment levels and economic efficiency. It was common practice for township officials to interfere in collective enterprise management by assigning quotas that indicated the number of jobs each factory was to

---

[84] Informant 131. See also "Shijiao sifenzhisan rujiao shoutao shengchanxian tingchan (Three Quarters of the Production Lines for Latex Rubber Gloves in Suburban Shanghai Cease Production)," *Shanghai gongye jingji bao,* June 15, 1989, p. 1.

provide for local residents each year and by preventing managers from firing redundant local workers.[85] On the other hand, the same concern could be seen as creating even greater demand for revenue on the part of township cadres. Rather than allowing failing factories to close their doors and lay off their employees, township officials had an incentive to intervene with bank officials to arrange soft credit or to intervene with tax officials to arrange tax concessions, beyond the bounds of central policy, in order to protect local jobs.[86] Thus, the financial responsibility for providing public goods and social welfare at the local level reinforced incentives for township cadres to distort central tax and credit policies.

Social targets were yet another factor in evaluating cadres' performance, and although interviews suggest that they were not the most important factor, financial demands of local social programs contributed to the burdens on local enterprises (Chen 1991; Lu and Li 1996; B. Xu 1996; Ye 1996). The more revenue officials extracted from local enterprises, the more resources they could commit to educational programs, family planning campaigns, and so on. As the first part of this chapter demonstrates, the budgetary funds of township governments were far from sufficient to enable officials to meet their obligations as defined by the cadre evaluation system, forcing them to levy various exactions on enterprises beyond the boundaries of the regular public finance system.[87]

While the cadre evaluation system did encourage productive invest-

---

[85] This prohibition typically did not apply to workers who were not *local* residents (*bendi ren*). As the manager of one village-run factory in Nantang Township commented, "This factory has a few workers from Anhui, and I would like more because I can fire them if they're bad. If they're from my own village, I'm stuck with the bad ones; I can't fire them (Informant 126). On this, see also Du (1992:109), Guo and Liu (1991:89), He (1991:183), and Meng (1990:302).

[86] This finding challenges general notions of the flexibility of rural enterprise employees who still maintained ties to agriculture and who could therefore readily return to farming full- or part-time when demand for labor in rural firms declined. See, for example, He (1991:184). At least in the relatively wealthy coastal townships where this study was conducted, the employees of rural collectives came to resemble their counterparts in state-run enterprises in that they held the expectation that employment in nonagricultural pursuits should be available to them. As one Shanghai study points out, overstaffing contributed to thinner profits and great reliance on soft credit by rural collectives (Sang and Wu 1991:28).

[87] See also Whiting (1999a) and C. Wong (1997). A report issued by the Institute of Rural Development of the Chinese Academy of Social Sciences makes the same point. See Sun, Zhu, and Hu (1993:26).

ments and provision of public goods and social welfare, it did not preclude the pursuit of narrowly personal benefits by local cadres. Blatant official corruption occurred, although it risked both social and political-legal censure as recent, high-profile campaigns against official corruption demonstrate. Moreover, while official corruption was unquestionably a serious problem, reports of widespread corruption must be balanced by consideration of China's strong performance on basic development indicators. As a recent World Bank study demonstrates, literacy, infant survival rates, and life expectancy in China are better than in most other countries at comparable levels of GDP, "suggesting relatively efficient service delivery in education, health services, and water and sanitation. Output indicators of these and other government services also compare well to other developing countries: primary and secondary enrollment rates, access to sanitation and safe drinking water, and access to paved roads are usually at levels similar to [those of] middle income countries" (World Bank 1999:4 as cited in Whiting 1999a). These indicators, in many cases, corresponded to specific performance criteria for local officials.

At the same time, local cadres could readily pursue certain personal benefits within the system with relatively little risk to their positions and careers. Nonproductive expenditures such as lavishly appointed government office buildings equipped with heating and air conditioning and staffed by an expanding number of employees with connections to local officials, luxury cars at the disposal of government officials, and large entertainment budgets were commonly justified, for example, in terms of the need to attract foreign investors. Such expenditures were financed by rural enterprises, and the excessive extraction necessary to pursue these types of projects often left insufficient retained earnings for normal enterprise development. Collective firms in particular, which remitted profits in addition to paying taxes and fees, were left with very few retained earnings, thereby limiting their ability to provide for their own fixed or working capital needs or to repay bank loans. As the World Bank study on rural industry shows, the share of profit remittances used by township governments for productive investments in new or existing enterprises declined beginning in the mid-1980s (Wang 1990). This decline contributed to interference in the allocation of bank loans as a means of compensating for the undercapitalization of enterprises.[88] Thus, while the cadre evaluation system oriented official attention toward eco-

---

[88] This issue is addressed in greater detail in Chapter 7. See also Y. Huang (1990).

nomic development and public goods provision, it did not completely preclude manipulation of the system for personal benefit on the part of local leaders.

Summary

The cadre evaluation system encouraged township officials to pursue the generation and extraction of revenue for local political purposes. In addition, it reinforced the lack of separation between party, government, and enterprise, and created incentives for local cadres to subvert the intent behind central regulations regarding tax exemptions and reductions. It similarly created incentive to distort central credit policies regarding loan ceilings, sectoral allocation of investment, and borrower qualifications. To the extent that local bank branches exceeded their credit ceilings, for example, the central government was forced either to reduce credit allocations to its own priority sectors (such as transportation and energy) in order to contain inflationary pressures in the economy or to risk inflation by allowing the total supply of credit to expand. Moreover, the type of local cadre behavior described here weakened the ability of the center to guide the sectoral orientation of local investment. From the perspective of the central state, therefore, the incentives were highly dysfunctional. These problems were important factors motivating the banking and fiscal reforms undertaken in the mid-1990s.

CONCLUSION: REEVALUATING THE
"TOWNSHIP AS CORPORATION" MODEL

In interpreting the growth of collectively owned rural enterprises, a number of analysts have suggested an analogy between the township as a corporate entity and a capitalist corporation (Byrd and Lin 1990; Oi 1992). This concluding section evaluates this analogy in light of the foregoing discussion of the fiscal system and the cadre evaluation system. The township resembled a corporation in that township officials, as de facto owners of collective enterprise assets, exercised significant control over the firms under their jurisdiction. They were de facto owners because township governments had (1) authority to decide how enterprise assets would be used, including control over the appointment and remuneration of managers, the nature and scale of investment, and the size of the work force; (2) effective claim on all collective enterprise profits; and (3) authority to dispose of enterprise assets by transfer, sale, or dissolution of the firm. According to William Byrd and N. Zhu (1990:89),

> At the community [township] level the industrial corporations responsible for supervising community [collective] enterprises function in many ways like financial conglomerates, holding companies, or the headquarters of loosely managed multidivisional corporations. The key financial roles of the industrial corporations include pooling enterprises' after-tax profits for investment and directing other resources (from local banks and credit cooperatives) to particular investment projects; cushioning subordinate enterprises from short-term fluctuations; serving as a short-term financial intermediary by transferring funds from enterprises with surpluses to those with deficits; and facilitating the issuance of short-term bonds to local residents.

However, the incentive structures described throughout this chapter suggest that the township also differs from a corporation in three important respects. First, township officials owed their positions not to de jure ownership of capital but to the county-level officials who appointed them. The power that township officials exercised as de facto owners of collective firms lasted only as long as they held political office. As political leaders, township officials pursued sociopolitical as well as economic goals. One survey of township and village leaders identifies producing revenues to finance government activities, increasing local employment opportunities, and increasing the incomes of local residents as their top three goals with respect to rural enterprises (Qiu 1988). Unlike real owners, the goals of township officials were determined in part by the performance criteria associated with their political office.

Second, the township government derived revenues from its collective enterprises via many channels other than profit remittances. The township retained a share of the direct and indirect taxes paid by the firms under its jurisdiction; it also received an array of legally mandated fees and illegal exactions paid by collectives. Thus, township officials tended not to seek single-mindedly to maximize the profits of the enterprises under their control. Rather, as Wong (1988a:104) argues, "local governments try to maximize net revenues, which consist of profits and taxes [and fees] paid by the firm. They would be willing to allow the survival of money-losing firms as long as sufficient tax revenues [and fees] were generated to offset the losses."

Third, not only did township officials have an incentive to levy sanctioned and unsanctioned fees that reduced the level of taxable profits, but they also had an incentive to employ discretion in the implementation of central tax policy in order to shift revenues from shared tax channels to other channels that the township alone controlled. The institutionalized practice of tax evasion implies a concomitant softening of the budget constraint (Kornai 1979:806; 1986:1697). Similarly, given the political oversight exercised over local bank and credit cooperative offices by township leaders, these leaders had both the incentive and the opportunity to manipulate the allocation of bank loans, again softening the budget constraint.

Given these caveats, the potential for soft budget constraints at both the township and enterprise levels is clear.[89] As Song and Du (1990:355) note in their report for the World Bank,

> As chief owner of the assets of township [collective] enterprises, the township government, as part of its function, should oversee the operational behavior of the enterprise in the same way as boards of directors in Western countries do. . . . But close examination reveals that governments' duty to their enterprises is motivated by their own financial needs and by pursuit of wider community goals.

The next chapter discusses the ways in which the incentives contained in the fiscal system and the cadre evaluation system helped to shape the evolution of property rights in the research sites. Chapters 5 and 6 demonstrate how the same incentives led local cadres to manipulate central tax and credit policies for local political purposes.

---

[89] By contrast, Che and Qian (1998) argue that townships have relatively hard budget constraints.

4

Incentives, Constraints, and the Evolution of Property Rights

THE three counties of Wuxi, Songjiang, and Yueqing were similar in that they were among the wealthiest counties in the country as of the early 1990s, but they differed dramatically in the forms of property rights that characterized the rural industrial sector – the main source of wealth in each of the three local economies. Local government-run firms dominated rural industry in Wuxi and Songjiang,[1] while privately run firms dominated in Yueqing. This chapter employs a case study approach to construct a theoretical explanation for this empirical puzzle. Local officials responded to incentives to generate revenue through the promotion of rural industry by supporting particular forms of property rights within their jurisdictions. However, their choices about what forms of property rights to support were constrained by distinct local resource endowments inherited from the Maoist era and shaped by the nature of national political-legal and market institutions during the reform period.

In the relatively inhospitable political and economic climate of the early reform period, local officials in Yueqing County, Wenzhou, faced a particular challenge in attempting to specify private property rights in order to promote private investment in industry. They responded to the challenge by innovating aggressively in the area of property rights, drafting local regulations that allowed several different forms of private investment to coexist. Most private investors in Yueqing chose to adopt cooperative shareholding (*gufen hezuo*) – a form of ownership that entailed some attenuation of full private property rights – rather than private (*siying*) ownership – an ownership form that did not entail the

---

[1] Government-run firms also dominated the prosperous rural industrial sectors in the supplementary research sites of Shanghai, Jiading, and Chuansha counties.

same attenuation. This chapter explains the aggressive innovation by local officials and the apparently anomalous choice of private investors in terms of credible commitment. It demonstrates that only the cooperative shareholding form met the prerequisites for credible commitment to private property rights by the central state during the first decade and a half of reform.

Some scholars (e.g., Clarke 1996:55) have questioned the significance of secure property rights given the growth witnessed in the private sector even in the absence of a more credible commitment to the rights of private enterprises (*siying qiye*).[2] The case study data presented in this chapter suggest that, without such a commitment, problems remained in eliciting long-term, large-scale private investment in industry. In contrast to commercial assets, industrial assets were relatively immobile. Therefore, insecure property rights posed greater risks to industrial investors, risks that local state officials actively sought to diminish by supporting property rights to which the central state would credibly commit.

A number of sociologists and legal scholars have approached this problem by focusing on social definitions of property rights (Ellickson 1991; Lin and Chen 1994; Nee and Su 1996; Wank 1995; 1996). In their view an investor's claim on assets is socially defined and recognized – often in the context of the interpersonal networks in which entrepreneurs are embedded. However, the importance placed on explicit, politically recognized definitions of property rights by private investors and local officials in the Wenzhou site suggests that socially defined rights alone were insufficient to protect the interests of private entrepreneurs. As the subsequent discussion will show, explicit, politically recognized rights were particularly important in interactions with actors from outside the local community – interactions that occurred in the context of political campaigns and in the context of expanding supply and marketing areas.

The first part of this chapter explains the emergence of a distinct spatial pattern of property rights across the three locales. It combines the

---

[2] One rationale for private investment in the *absence* of secure property rights may be the sheer magnitude of the potential gains in the booming Chinese economy. When a *very small* fixed investment (representing a very small potential loss) can produce potentially large gains, even a low probability that property rights are secure may motivate a rational investor to invest. In other words, one might expect to find private investment under conditions such that $p \cdot G$ is greater than $(1 - p) \cdot L$, where p is the probability that property rights are secure, G is the potential gain if property rights are secure, and L is the potential loss if they are not. See Coleman (1990:104) and Whiting (1998:173).

analysis of incentives and constraints found in institutional economics with empirical material introduced here and in Chapters 2 and 3 to explain the nature of rural industrial development in Yueqing, Songjiang, and Wuxi during the first decade and a half of reform. The second part of the chapter demonstrates that property rights backed by credible commitment on the part of both central and local state officials were particularly important in encouraging private investment in industry. It draws on theories developed by institutional economists and political scientists in order to identify the prerequisites for credible commitment to property rights and to explain the actions taken by local officials and private entrepreneurs in Yueqing.

THE SPATIAL PATTERN OF PROPERTY RIGHTS

A focus on the incentives and constraints facing local officials helps to explain the distinct pattern of property rights that emerged in China's rural industrial sector. The demands of the cadre evaluation system and the nature of the revenue-sharing fiscal system created a real revenue imperative for local officials at the outset of the post-Mao reforms. As of the early 1980s, local governments in Wuxi and Shanghai already had a strong base of commune- and brigade-run enterprises and therefore a ready source of revenue. Given the revenue imperative, local officials had a strong incentive to nurture the development of these firms with continued investment and to protect them against encroachment by private firms. By contrast, the local government in Wenzhou had only a weak base of commune- and brigade-run enterprises as of the early 1980s and lacked the resources to invest further in the development of these firms. Therefore, local cadres in Wenzhou responded to the revenue imperative by trying to encourage private enterprise development. Thus, the approach to promoting rural industry in each locale was constrained by distinct resource endowments inherited from the Maoist period. After the initiation of reform, moreover, rural industrial development was further shaped by national political and legal environments hostile to private ownership, by the incomplete nature of markets for land, capital, and other scarce inputs, and by restrictions on access to markets for many products.

More than a decade after the initiation of reform, this combination of incentives and constraints had produced distinctly different patterns of enterprise ownership in Wuxi and Shanghai as opposed to Wenzhou. At the county level as of 1990, firms with private investment accounted for

8 percent of industrial enterprises in Wuxi County, Wuxi; 21 percent in Songjiang County, Shanghai; and more than 90 percent in Yueqing County, Wenzhou.

This section begins by reviewing the literature in institutional economics that provides a theoretical basis for understanding how property rights are specified. The remainder of the section examines the differing dispositions toward private enterprise on the part of local governments in Wuxi, Shanghai, and Wenzhou in light of the legacy of industrial assets inherited from the Maoist period, the nature of the national political-legal environment, and the nature of the national market environment.

Property Rights Theory

Property rights can be defined as a set of exclusive but not unrestricted rights governing the ownership and control of assets. They include the right to use and make decisions about the use of an asset, the right to alienate (sell or destroy) an asset, and the right to earn income from the use or sale of an asset (Eggertsson 1990:34–5; Furubotn and Pejovich 1974:4). As Armen Alchian and Harold Demsetz (1973:18) point out, this set or "bundle" of rights is divisible. In other words, one party may hold some of these rights but not others.

Property rights evolved in response to the incentives for local officials to develop local sources of revenue. As Douglass North (1981:20–9) argues, state officials are driven by the need for revenue in order to finance state functions. They therefore have an interest in developing the revenue base by specifying property rights that generate revenue as efficiently as possible. However, North also emphasizes that efficiency is not the only consideration; the state also faces a number of constraints in specifying property rights. There may be higher transaction costs (that is, the costs of "monitoring, metering, and collecting" revenue) associated with more efficient forms of property rights (Ibid:29).[3] Put another way, although a given form of ownership may generate revenue very efficiently, if it is difficult or costly for the state to extract that revenue, the state may choose not to support that form of ownership. In addition, it may be necessary to appease certain powerful groups in

---

[3] More generally, transaction costs characterize contracts between parties who have conflicting interests and for whom acquiring information is costly. They include the costs of acquiring information, negotiating agreements, measuring resources, monitoring behavior, and enforcing performance.

society that have vested interests in less efficient forms of property rights. Finally, past developments limit the opportunity set (the range of policy options) available to state officials at any given point in time. According to North (1990:5), "both what organizations come into existence and how they evolve are fundamentally influenced by the institutional framework. In turn they influence how the institutional framework evolves."

The broader political-legal environment also shapes the ways in which property rights evolve. The political-legal environment refers to the degree of ideological support and official recognition accorded particular forms of property rights. This environment is composed in part of state policies, regulations, and laws; it constitutes the official set of "justificatory principles" indicating what forms of property rights are considered legitimate by the state (Stark 1996:1013). However, the political-legal environment cannot simply be reduced to official rules. As John Litwack (1991:78) emphasizes, legality is a social phenomenon that depends on the belief of the population in the stability and enforceability of the law. Thus, formal changes in the legal framework are important, but they may not be sufficient to guarantee property rights (Clarke 1992). As North (1990:6) points out, "Although formal rules may change overnight as the result of political or judicial decisions, informal constraints embodied in customs, traditions, and codes of conduct are much more impervious to deliberate policies." Furthermore, political or judicial decisions themselves often contain contradictions and tensions. In sum, the larger political-legal environment constrains but does not determine the choice of local state officials regarding the specification of property rights.

Finally, property rights are shaped by the broader economic environment and the nature of factor and product markets. The extent to which goods are allocated by bureaucratic decisions rather than by prices limits the ability of private entrepreneurs – who function for the most part outside formal bureaucratic channels – to realize the full value of their investments. As Victor Nee (1996:910–11) notes,

> In the state socialist redistributive economy officials act as monopolists who specify and enforce the rules of exchange by administrative fiat and exclude private entrepreneurs from taking part in legitimate economic activities. . . . The more developed the market economy, the greater the breadth and diversity of opportunities that develop outside the boundaries of the redistributive economy.

The perpetuation of bureaucratic control over the allocation of resources and the slow pace of marketization for factors and products constrain the effective exercise of private property rights over productive assets and shape the particular forms of property rights adopted in industry.

Thus, choices about property rights are shaped by the incentives of local state officials to promote rapid industrial development and by the constraints posed by available community resources and broader political and economic environments.

Like the national states described by North, local governments in China faced a very real revenue imperative during the period under study. As illustrated in Chapter 3, township government officials were dependent on funds from rural industry to meet their revenue needs. Given this imperative, local officials had a particular incentive to promote township-run collective enterprises, *ceteris paribus*.[4] While the township government received taxes and fees from all rural enterprises, as de facto owner of township-run collectives, it also received profit remittances from these firms.[5] The local government also faced lower costs in extracting revenue from collective than from private firms.[6] Furthermore, collective enterprises were officially regarded as a legitimate part of the socialist system and were, in some ways, better integrated into the planned economy. For these reasons, local governments seeking to generate and control as much revenue as possible would prefer to promote collective industry – other things being equal. However, other things were not equal.

The Maoist Legacy Revisited

The three counties covered by this study – Wuxi, Songjiang, and Yueqing – had very different economic endowments at the beginning of the

---

[4] These firms are called "collective" for historical reasons, but they are essentially local, government-run firms for which the local government provides the investment capital either directly or indirectly (e.g., by serving as the guarantor for loans from state-run banks).

[5] Operationally, the concept of ownership employed in this study is consistent with the Chinese principle of "whoever invests is the owner and receives the benefits (*shei touzi, shei suoyou, shei shouyi*). Thus, for analytical purposes, firms with government investment are considered to be owned by the government, while firms with private investment are considered to be privately owned regardless of the type of license the enterprise holds. Nevertheless, as will become clear in the subsequent discussion, the form of property rights and the type of license are significant both politically and economically. For the Chinese principle, see Dong (1989:13) and Du (1989:1031). See also the discussions in Clarke (1992:292–3) and Granick (1990:36–7).

[6] This issue is explored in detail in Chapter 5.

reform era. As Jan Svejnar and Josephine Woo (1990:73–4) point out in the World Bank's rural industry study, "the size, structure, and performance of the [rural enterprise] sector in each county depend greatly on geographic and historical factors, the availability and types of local resources, the quality and size of the local labor force, access to technology and capital, and the policies pursued by the central and especially the local government." Chapter 2 demonstrated the influence of these factors in each of the three research sites in the years leading up to 1978, but the legacy of the Maoist era continued to shape the trajectory of rural industrial development during the post-Mao period.

Table 4.1 illustrates the disparity in public enterprise development in the three counties in terms of the gross value of industrial output. As of 1978, the gross value of industrial output of township and village (then commune and brigade) industry was 38 million yuan in Yueqing (47 yuan on a per capita basis), compared to 115 million in Songjiang (253 yuan per capita), and 516 million in Wuxi (511 yuan per capita).[7] Thus, Yueqing produced less than 10 percent of what Wuxi produced and roughly 20 percent of what Songjiang produced on a per capita basis.[8] In terms of the value of fixed assets of collectively owned industrial enterprises at the township and village levels combined, Yueqing similarly had less than 10 percent of the fixed assets of Wuxi as of 1981, the first year for which data are available (Table 4.2). By 1985, the disparity had grown, leaving Yueqing with only 3 percent of the fixed assets of Wuxi. Such a weak legacy of collective enterprise made it very difficult for local officials in Yueqing to develop successfully on the basis of the collective model.

As of the early 1980s, townships and villages in Wuxi, and to a somewhat lesser extent in Songjiang, already had a relatively strong collective revenue base that enabled them to invest even more in collective enterprise development and gave them an incentive to protect this revenue base. According to the World Bank's assessment, "Wuxi's

---

[7] There is a slight difference between the 1978 figure for gross value of industrial output in Wuxi reported in *Wuxi xian gongye zhi* (1990:28) and in *Wuxi xian tongji nianjian* (1991:89), but it does not affect the substance of the argument.

[8] Demonstrating even greater disparity, the gross profits of commune- and brigade-run collectives were less than 10 million yuan (11 yuan on a per capita basis) in Yueqing, compared to nearly 50 million yuan (107 yuan per capita) in Songjiang and 178 million yuan (175 yuan per capita) in Wuxi (*Yueqing sishi nian* 1989:106; *Songjiang xianzhi* 1991:455; *Wuxi xian tongji nianjian* 1991:95).

Table 4.1. *Gross Value of Industrial Output, by Ownership Type, Township Level and Below, 1978–97*

| | Yueqing County, Wenzhou | | | | | Songjiang County, Shanghai | | | | Wuxi County, Wuxi | | | |
| | Total | Township-run Collective | Village-run Collective | Private Shareholding Cooperative | Private, Individual, and Other | Total | Township-run Collective | Village-run Collective | Private, Individual, and Other | Total | Township-run Collective | Village-run Collective | Private, Individual, and Other |
Year													
(Level, million yuan)													
1978	38.36	22.02	16.34			114.57	77.53	37.04		515.81	289.91	225.90	
1979	50.62	28.01	22.61			149.67	99.37	50.30		664.24	375.31	288.93	
1980	121.31	38.33	78.98		4.00	194.93	122.97	71.96		986.70	515.17	471.53	
1981	178.42	41.12	131.30		6.00	267.42	185.82	81.60		1,132.25	595.07	537.18	
1982	139.29	43.11	90.51		5.67	316.18	232.14	84.04		1,198.60	669.97	528.63	
1983	208.39	70.24	126.53		11.62	383.87	278.96	104.91		1,532.45	829.65	702.80	
1984	284.41	93.10	174.24		17.07	442.72	316.46	126.26		2,442.88	1,278.07	1,164.81	
1985	354.72	74.13	83.11	165.12	32.36	635.61	440.06	195.55		4,169.35	2,089.35	2,080.00	
1986	421.10	78.44	119.00	196.11	27.55	848.65	604.11	244.54		5,293.61	2,754.20	2,539.41	
1987	558.86	101.28	173.06	253.91	30.61	1,218.78	855.61	358.96	4.21	7,198.25	3,658.37	3,539.88	
1988	799.30	79.47	108.60	487.77	123.46	1,697.73	1,149.13	542.08	6.52	9,536.28	4,924.30	4,611.98	
1989	881.46	82.14	93.09	575.22	131.01	2,072.07	1,392.10	664.59	15.38	10,324.49	5,313.92	5,010.57	
1990	838.15	90.65	81.23	524.99	141.28	2,287.65	1,639.48	615.90	32.27	11,692.74	5,832.46	5,860.28	
1991	1,082.52	144.25	100.88	712.18	125.21	3,606.51	2,666.86	884.93	54.72	14,842.02	7,505.54	7,336.48	
1992	1,868.46	284.34	126.73	1,220.80	236.59	4,849.77	3,585.75	1,117.85	146.17	30,362.28	1,4698.60	15,663.68	
1993	4,284.43	520.64	144.88	1,970.15	1,648.76	7,653.93	5,641.45	1,854.46	158.02	43,610.40	2,2483.42	20,773.20	353.78
1994	5,672.68	383.39	173.59	2,615.74	2,499.96	11,699.59	8,420.22	3,005.48	273.89	59,721.44	3,0335.54	28,868.84	517.06
1995						17,352.38	12,148.24	4,813.21	390.93	74,994.57	3,9627.12	34,065.68	1,301.77
1996						19,226.61	12,092.01	4,307.79	2,826.81				
1997	1,7340.13	1,055.20	14.18	8,165.30	8,105.45	24,151.03	14,891.46	4,510.81	4,748.76	60,758.13	3,4125.37	24,895.60	1,737.16

(Percentage share)

Year													
1978	100.0	57.4	42.6	0.0	0.0	100.0	67.7	32.3		100.0	56.2	43.8	
1979	100.0	55.3	44.7	0.0	0.0	100.0	66.4	33.6		100.0	56.5	43.5	
1980	100.0	31.6	65.1	0.0	3.3	100.0	63.1	36.9		100.0	52.2	47.8	
1981	100.0	23.0	73.6	0.0	3.4	100.0	69.5	30.5		100.0	52.6	47.4	
1982	100.0	30.9	65.0	0.0	4.1	100.0	73.4	26.6		100.0	55.9	44.1	
1983	100.0	33.7	60.7	0.0	5.6	100.0	72.7	27.3		100.0	54.1	45.9	
1984	100.0	32.7	61.3	0.0	6.0	100.0	71.5	28.5		100.0	52.3	47.7	
1985	100.0	20.9	23.4	46.5	9.1	100.0	69.2	30.8		100.0	50.1	49.9	
1986	100.0	18.6	28.3	46.6	6.5	100.0	71.2	28.8		100.0	52.0	48.0	
1987	100.0	18.1	31.0	45.4	5.5	100.0	70.2	29.5	0.3	100.0	50.8	49.2	
1988	100.0	9.9	13.6	61.0	15.4	100.0	67.7	31.9	0.4	100.0	51.6	48.4	
1989	100.0	9.3	10.6	65.3	14.9	100.0	67.2	32.1	0.7	100.0	51.5	48.5	
1990	100.0	10.8	9.7	62.6	16.9	100.0	71.7	26.9	1.4	100.0	49.9	50.1	
1991	100.0	13.3	9.3	65.8	11.6	100.0	73.9	24.5	1.5	100.0	50.6	49.4	
1992	100.0	15.2	6.8	65.3	12.7	100.0	73.7	23.0	3.0	100.0	48.4	51.6	
1993	100.0	12.2	3.4	46.0	38.5	100.0	73.7	24.2	2.1	100.0	51.6	47.6	0.8
1994	100.0	6.8	3.1	46.1	44.1	100.0	72.0	25.7	2.3	100.0	50.8	48.3	0.9
1995						100.0	70.0	27.7	2.3	100.0	52.8	45.4	1.7
1996						100.0	62.9	22.4	14.7	100.0	56.2	41.0	2.9
1997	100.0	6.1	0.1	47.1	46.7	100.0	61.7	18.7	19.7				

Sources: Yueqing sishinian 1949–1989. Yueqing tongji nianjian. Songjiang xianzhi. Songjiang tongji nianjian. Wuxi xian tongji nianjian. Xishanshi nianjian.

Table 4.2. *Original Value of Fixed Assets in Industry (Million Yuan)*

	County-run Firms	Township- and Village-run Firms	Township-run Firms	Village-run Firms
1981				
Yueqing	45.36	21.31	11.96	9.35
Wuxi	119.95	278.06	171.96	106.10
1985				
Yueqing	77.53	25.59	13.72	11.87
Songjiang		280.87		
Wuxi	225.36	807.12	459.17	347.95

Note: 1981 and 1985 provide the earliest data available.

Sources: *Yueqing sishi nian* (1989:95–107). *Songjiang xianzhi* (1991:453). *Wuxi xian tongji nianjian* (1991:96).

administrative climate makes it virtually impossible for large industrial private enterprises to emerge (Byrd and Lin 1990a:8)."[9] This view was echoed in 1992 by a representative of the Ministry of Agriculture, which oversees rural industrial development. "In Sunan they limit private enterprises because they're afraid that the most capable people will leave their positions in collective enterprises. They're afraid of competition (Informant 188)."[10]

By contrast, townships and villages in Wenzhou had a relatively weak collective revenue base, which left them with few resources to invest in further developing collectively owned enterprises. Rather, local cadres turned to society and attempted to encourage the development of a private revenue base through the mobilization of privately held resources.[11] As one researcher at the Zhejiang Academy of Social Sciences commented, "Wenzhou could not rely on the Sunan model. If it

[9] See also *Jingji gongzuozhe xuexi ziliao* (Study Materials for Economic Administrators) reprinted in *Renmin daxue fuyin baokan ziliao – Jingji tizhi gaige* (Reprints of periodical materials – Economic system reform) 3(1989):61.

[10] In the narrow sense, "Sunan" refers to the area encompassing Suzhou, Wuxi, and Changzhou in southern Jiangsu Province, and Wuxi County is often seen as the epitome of the Sunan model. Some scholars use the term more broadly to represent the larger Yangzi River delta region.

[11] A vast secondary literature has emerged on Wenzhou; see, for example, Fei and Luo (1988), He (1987), Yuan (1987), and Zhang and Li (1990a; 1990b). In English, see A. Liu (1992), Y. Liu (1992), Nolan and Dong (1990), Parris (1993), and Young (1989).

had, it would still be poor. Objective economic conditions forced it [onto its present path]" (Informant 174).[12] Despite the apparent advantages of pursuing a collective development path, the range of policy choices open to officials in Wenzhou was constrained by the limits on collective resources.

While the weakness of the state and collective sectors left little revenue in official hands, there were some financial and other resources in private hands in Wenzhou even in the early 1980s. These sources of private capital accumulation may have had their roots in early experiments contracting land to the household and allowing household workshops to exist in the 1950s and 1960s (Wang and Zhu 1996:18; Yuan 1987:11–13; Zhang and Li 1990a:93). Although these practices were attacked as capitalist and suppressed in 1957 and 1962, respectively, scholars at the Zhejiang Academy of Social Sciences suggest that some workshops continued to exist underground throughout the Cultural Revolution (Informant 174). Other sources point to the renewal of petty commerce and trade practices in Wenzhou after the initiation of reform (Fei and Luo 1988:6). Beginning around 1980, laborers from Wenzhou returned to traditional practices, traveling throughout the country offering services door-to-door and working on construction teams. By 1983, cash remittances from these workers came to more than 500 million yuan for Wenzhou Municipality as a whole – or more than 40 million yuan per county on average (Zhang and Li 1990b:32).[13] These networks not only provided financial resources and information about market demand but also developed into supply and marketing networks as local industrial production expanded. After 1979, when the militia was removed from fishing boats working off the coast, a lively smuggling trade arose between Wenzhou and Taiwan fishermen.[14] Using the networks already developed, Wenzhou traders profited by marketing transistor radios and tape recorders produced in Taiwan in exchange for antiques and other valuables for which there was demand in Taiwan. These networks also provided private sources of raw material outside plan channels as traders collected scrap material from state enterprises

---

[12] See also Wang and Zhu (1996:18).
[13] To put this figure in perspective, 40 million yuan is greater than the total profits and taxes generated by township- and village-run collectives in Yueqing in the same year (*Yueqing sishi nian* 1989:107).
[14] Although none of the written sources identified here address the issue of smuggling, both a local government official and a private entrepreneur identified it in interviews as one important early source of capital (Informants 5 and 165). See also A. Liu (1992).

around the country and marketed it in Wenzhou. Finally, Wenzhou residents benefited from remittances from the large number of Wenzhou natives living overseas (Zhang and Li 1990b:32). The availability of capital for private investment likely contributed to the relative success of private enterprise in Wenzhou as compared to other areas poorly endowed with state and collective enterprises where private enterprise was allowed to emerge.

An Alternative Perspective. There is debate surrounding the question of why Wenzhou pursued a private model of development, and one perspective focuses on the cultural and historical traditions unique to the Wenzhou coastal region.[15] Yia-ling Liu (1992), for example, suggests that Wenzhou is unique in the coincidence of interests between local cadres and local residents. This coincidence, she argues, stems from the fact that Wenzhou was liberated by local guerrilla forces in 1949 and continued to be governed by local cadres even after 1949. In Liu's formulation, the strength of private property rights in Wenzhou, therefore, reflects the continued role of local cadres who respected and perpetuated local values and traditions. The implication is that outside cadres would have responded differently to the challenge of developing the tax base in Wenzhou. However, scholars at the Zhejiang Academy of Social Sciences note that outside, "southbound" cadres intermingled with the local cadres who liberated Wenzhou. They found that some outside cadres supported private initiatives, while some local cadres opposed them, depending on the economic situation. Thus, they interpret their findings to suggest that it was objective economic conditions that shaped the developmental path taken in Wenzhou (Informant 174). This view is shared by researchers such as Wang and Zhu (1996:18), who argue that Wenzhou's development path is a response to economic conditions rather than a reflection of a unique culture.

[15] A full examination of the cultural–historical argument is beyond the scope of this study. Such an examination would focus on the orientation of community norms and values and would explore the nature of lineage organization and its relation to political authority in each locale, the patterns and foci of community protests, and the background and role of party and government cadres in each locale in both the pre- and post-1949 eras. The first of these issues was suggested by participants in the panel on "Property Rights, Institutions, and Social Structure in China," at the Annual Meeting of the Association for Asian Studies, Boston, March 24–27, 1994, where this research was first presented. The second issue is developed for the southern Jiangsu region in the historical research of Kathryn Bernhardt (1992). The third issue is raised in the work of Yia-ling Liu (1992) and is touched on briefly here.

Summary. While the factors contributing to Wenzhou's uniqueness may account for Wenzhou's success relative to other predominantly private areas, the argument put forward here suggests that they do not account for the favorable disposition toward private enterprise itself. Indeed, evidence gathered by the World Bank indicates that, even beyond Wenzhou, private enterprise played a proportionally greater role in poorer areas with few collective resources, lending weight to the revenue-driven, resource-constrained model (Byrd and Gelb 1990). The varied endowments of industrial assets inherited from the Maoist era decisively shaped the disposition of local cadres toward the development of private firms in Wuxi, Songjiang, and Yueqing.

The National Political-Legal Environment

The weak ideological and policy support accorded private enterprises by the central state heightened the risks faced both by private investors and by local officials who supported the private sector. In contrast to the status of private enterprises, the status and legitimacy of township- and village-run collectives were affirmed early in the reform process. Although these firms did not enjoy the same political status as state-run enterprises, the State Council issued a major document in 1979 affirming their significance and calling for their continued rapid development.[16] The important position of township- and village-run collectives in the national economy was even more firmly established by a 1984 document that mandated the closer integration of these firms into the state planning system. Indeed, the document stated that "township- and village-run enterprises should be treated the same as state-run enterprises and should be given all necessary support."[17] These early state regulations were ultimately formalized with passage of the law on

---

[16] Their development was promoted with a highly favorable profit tax rate of 20 percent and liberal terms for tax exemptions and reductions. Guowuyuan, "Guanyu fazhan shedui qiye ruogan wenti de guiding (shixing caoan) (Regulations on Several Questions regarding the Development of Commune- and Brigade-Enterprises [Provisional Draft])," in *Zhongguo xiangzhen qiye nianjian 1978–1987* (1989:427–32).

[17] Along with the integration of rural collectives into the mainstream economy, profit tax rates were brought into line with those of urban collectives and small state-run enterprises through the implementation of an eight-grade progressive tax ranging from 10 to 55 percent. Zhonggong zhongyang guowuyuan, "Zhuanfa nongmuyuyebu 'Guanyu kaichuang shedui qiye xin jumian de baogao' de tongzhi (Notice of Transmission of the Ministry of Agriculture's 'Report on Initiating a New Phase for Commune and Brigade Enterprises')," in *Zhongguo xiangzhen qiye nianjian 1978–1987* (1989:422–7).

township- and village-run enterprises by the National People's Congress in 1996.[18]

In comparison, central state policy toward the private economy conveyed extreme ambivalence and, at times, open hostility. From 1981 to 1987, central state policy restricted the open development of the private economy and limited the number of employees that private individuals could hire. At the same time, however, it took an increasingly ambivalent stand toward larger private firms that exceeded the official limits.

In 1981, the State Council established provisions governing private investment in the form of individual household firms (*getihu*) in cities and towns and limited the number of employees to seven – two assistants and no more than five apprentices.[19] Central party document (1983) #1 extended these provisions to rural areas. At the same time, the document insisted that no system of exploitation would be allowed to exist, even as it acknowledged an important role for hired labor and anticipated the emergence of new economic forms, such as cooperative ventures.[20] In April 1983, the State Council promulgated regulations governing cooperatives (*hezuo jingying zuzhi*), allowing these firms to employ up to ten apprentices.[21] The document distinguished cooperative from individual ownership in two ways: (1) the voluntary pooling of the assets (such as labor and capital) of more than one person to form a new cooperative entity, and (2) the acknowledgment that some portion of the total assets belonged to that new entity and not to any single investor. That portion of the assets was referred to as "public accumulation." Thus, it affirmed that cooperative ventures were "socialist" in

---

[18] Township and village enterprises were defined in the law as rural *collective* economic organizations or firms located in rural areas with majority investment by rural residents that undertook a financial obligation to support agriculture. As noted in Chapter 3, private enterprises did not undertake this obligation (Table 3.5). "Zhonghua renmin gongheguo xiangzhen qiyefa (People's Republic of China Law on Township and Village Enterprises)," *Fazhi ribao*, October 29, 1996. The belated passage of the law on TVEs should be seen as indicative of the low status of law (*fa*) rather than the low status of TVEs.

[19] Guowuyuan, "Guanyu chengzhen feinongye geti jingji ruogan zhengcexing guiding (Several Policy Regulations regarding the Nonagricultural Individual Economy in Cities and Towns)," in *Nongcun shiyong fagui shouce* (1987:728–31).

[20] Zhonggong zhongyang, "Dangqian nongcun jingji zhengce de ruogan wenti (Several Questions on Current Rural Economic Policy)," in *Nongcun shiyong fagui shouce* (1987:68–83, esp. 74–5).

[21] Guowuyuan, "Guanyu chengzhen laodongzhe hezuo jingying de ruogan guiding (Several Regulations on Cooperative Laborers in Cities and Towns)," in Ibid:724–7.

nature and could legitimately be considered part of the collective economy.

Grudging acknowledgement of growing private investment was reflected in central party document (1984) #1. It maintained the principle of limiting employment levels in firms with private investment but, at the same time, openly acknowledged that enterprises of various forms already exceeded the limit.[22] Without explicitly condemning those enterprises, the document placed special emphasis on cooperative forms of investment and reiterated that private investment that took the form of a cooperative would *not* be regarded as "capitalist" (and therefore politically suspect) in nature. Nevertheless, the absence of any regulations governing private investment in enterprises employing more than the allowable number of workers became a source of conflict in some rural communities, as it drove private investors to register as "fake collectives."[23]

Central leaders responded to the demand for legislation governing private enterprise in May 1986 by proposing the establishment of several experimental zones, including one in Wenzhou that would focus on developing regulations governing rural reforms and especially reforms in ownership.[24] By July 1986, the Wenzhou industrial and commercial bureau had proposed the relaxation of policies toward an array of private enterprise forms, including, for example, the lifting of restrictions on the number of employees in firms registered as individual enterprises.[25] These measures were followed at the central level by statements

---

[22] Zhonggong zhongyang, "Guanyu yijiubasinian nongcun gongzuo de tongzhi (Notice regarding Rural Work for 1984)," in Ibid:54–67. Shortly thereafter, State Council document (1984) #26, promulgated in February, reiterated the restrictions on employment in individual enterprises. See Guowuyuan, "Guanyu nongcun geti gongshangye de ruogan guiding (Several Regulations regarding Rural Individual Industry and Commerce)," in Ibid:720–3.

[23] "Fake collectives" are treated in detail in subsequent sections. For concerns about the absence of regulations governing private enterprise in the mid-1980s, see, for example, Lin (1987) and Luo, Quan, and Gao (1989).

[24] Before the end of 1986, the Zhejiang provincial party committee and government had submitted a "Request for Instructions regarding the Establishment of the Wenzhou Experimental Zone" to the Central Committee and State Council; the zone was initiated officially as of 1987 (Zhang 1990:178). See also Pan (1988). For a discussion of the elite politics surrounding the establishment of the experimental zone, see Parris (1993:255).

[25] "Guanyu gongshang xingzheng guanli bumen ruogan zhengce fangkuan de jianyi (Opinion regarding Relaxation of Several Policies by Industrial and Commercial Administrative Agencies)," in *Wenzhou zhi lu congshu: Kaituozhe de guiji – Wenzhou shi difang fagui jianbian* (1989:40–6).

reflecting increasing official tolerance and acknowledgment of private enterprise. Central party document (1987) #5, promulgated in January 1987, employed the concept of the "primary stage of socialism" (which became the central theme of the Thirteenth Party Congress later that year) to justify a greater role for private enterprise.[26] It stated explicitly that private enterprises (at that time referred to as *siren qiye*) employing more than the official limit of seven workers would be allowed to exist and develop. However, foreshadowing future tensions, the document also identified contradictions between public and private ownership and pointed to cooperative enterprises as one means of gradually *socializing* private investment.

Beginning in 1987, experimental policy progressed along three tacks. In rapid succession, the municipal government in Wenzhou promulgated three sets of provisional regulations governing household firms affiliated with collective enterprises (*guahu jingying*), private enterprises (*siren qiye*), and cooperative shareholding enterprises (*gufen hezuo qiye*).[27] The provisional regulations governing private enterprise defined it as an entity with one or more investors, investing a minimum of 30 thousand yuan, operating at a fixed place of production, using privately owned production materials, and employing eight or more workers. It sought to guarantee the owners' rights to use, receive income from, and dispose of the firm's assets. However, according to the regulations, private enterprises would be required to reinvest fully 50 percent of after-tax profits. And while private firms would still be required to pay income taxes at the same high rates as individual household firms, they would receive reductions for any assessments over 50 thousand yuan. Individual owners would also be liable for the individual income adjustment tax. In order to encourage "fake collectives" to make explicit their claims to

---

[26] Zhonggong zhongyang zhengzhiju, "Ba nongcun gaige yinxiang shenru (zhaiyao) (Deepening Rural Reform [Abstract])," in *Zhongguo xiangzhen qiye nianjian 1978–1987* (1989:518–21). For the endorsement of private enterprise at the Thirteenth Party Congress, see Zhao Ziyang, "Advance along the Road of Socialism with Chinese Characteristics," *Beijing Review*, November 9–15, 1987, pp. 23–49, esp. p. 36.

[27] Wenzhou shi renmin zhengfu, "Wenzhou shi guahu jingying guanli zanxing guiding (Wenzhou Provisional Regulations on the Management of Household Firms Operating in Affiliation with Collective Enterprises)," "Wenzhou shi siren qiye guanli zanxing banfa (Wenzhou Provisional Methods for Management of Private Enterprises)," and "Guanyu nongcun gufen hezuo qiye ruogan wenti de zanxing guiding (Provisional Regulations regarding Several Questions on Rural Shareholding Cooperatives)," in *Wenzhou zhi lu congshu: Kaituozhe de guiji – Wenzhou shi difang fagui jianbian* (1989:140–3; 160–4; 165ff). The development of affiliated households has been treated elsewhere. See Y. Liu (1992), Parris (1993), and Young (1989).

private ownership, supplemental regulations allowed these firms to register as private enterprises while continuing to pay lower collective tax rates.[28]

After the Thirteenth Party Congress in the fall of 1987, the central state moved quickly to pass central legislation guaranteeing private property rights. In April 1988, the National People's Congress revised the constitution to recognize the legitimacy of private enterprise.[29] This action was followed in June by the passage of central regulations governing private enterprise.[30] While Wenzhou's experimental regulations served as a basis for the central version, the tax regulations accompanying the latter stipulated that private firms would pay a flat 35 percent income tax. With the passage of central regulations, private enterprises operating under the guise of collectives nationwide were required to re-register (Ma 1988:88). Thus, outright private ownership did not receive official recognition from the central state until 1988, fully ten years after the initiation of reform.

Even in light of the constitutional amendment and private enterprise regulations of 1988, however, continued attacks called into question the state's commitment to private enterprise. An especially hostile set of attacks was associated with the economic rectification campaign of late 1988 through 1991, even though the attacks were part of a long series of campaigns with anti-private elements, including the anti-spiritual pollution campaign of 1983 and the anti-bourgeois liberalization campaign of 1987. The Fourth Plenum of the Thirteenth Central Committee in June 1989 initiated an attack on "individual and private entrepreneurs who use illegal methods to seek huge profits and thereby create great social disparity and contribute to discontent among the public."[31] The State

---

[28] Wenzhou shi renmin zhengfu bangongshi, "Guanyu guanche shishi 'Wenzhou siren qiye guanli zanxing banfa' disige zanxing guiding (banfa) de tongzhi (Notice on Thoroughly Implementing 'Provisional Methods for Managing Private Enterprises')," in *Wenzhou zhi lu congshu: Kaituozhe de guiji – Wenzhou shi difang fagui jianbian* (1989:184–6).

[29] For the revised text, see: "Zhonghua renmin gongheguo xianfa xiuzhengan (Draft Revision of the Constitution of the People's Republic of China)," in *Zhongguo nongye nianjian* (1989:538).

[30] See "Zhonghua renmin gongheguo siying qiye zanxing tiaoli," "Zhonghua renmin gongheguo siying qiye suodeshui zanxing tiaoli," and Guowuyuan, "Guanyu zhengshou siying qiye touzizhe geren shouru tiaojie shui de guiding," *Jingji ribao*, June 29, 1988, p. 2.

[31] See Guowuyuan, "Guanyu dali jiaqiang chengxiang geti gongshanghu he siying qiye shuishou zhengguan gongzuo de jueding (State Council Decision regarding Vigorously Strengthening Tax Collection Work in Urban and Rural Individual Industrial and Commercial Enterprises and Private Enterprises)," *Guowuyuan gongbao* No. 16 (September 20, 1989), pp. 626–9.

Council responded in August 1989 with a decision to launch a series of investigations into the taxation of individual and private firms.[32] The decision targeted all private firms but particularly those that continued to register falsely as collectives and those that operated under affiliation with state or collective enterprises.[33] The decision emphasized the political as well as economic significance of the action. Indeed, during the same period, the Communist Party decreed that private entrepreneurs engaged in exploitation and would therefore be barred from party membership.[34] This decision signaled a serious political setback for private entrepreneurs, a number of whom had already been inducted into party.[35] The Fifth Plenum of the Thirteenth Central Committee in November 1989 determined that unspecified aspects of private development were "not beneficial" to socialism and would be limited.[36] In conjunction with an aggressive campaign to reinvigorate state enterprises, the plenum emphasized public ownership as the mainstay of the socialist economy, strongly implying that private enterprise would not be allowed to grow beyond certain unpublished limits. Not surprisingly, Wenzhou in particular came under explicit attack during this period for its "capitalist" practices.

The end of the economic rectification campaign of late 1988 to 1991 and its associated ideological orthodoxy was marked by Deng Xiaoping's "southern tour *(nanxun)*" in February 1992. During the tour, which was featured prominently on the nightly news broadcasts of state-run television, Deng visited some of the most advanced factories in South China built with private and foreign investment, giving them his imprimatur. Thus, his tour significantly relaxed the political climate for private investment in industry.

---

[32] Ibid.

[33] For the local regulations applying to Wenzhou, see Zhejiangsheng gongshang xingzheng guanliju, "Guanyu qingli 'jia jiti' he dui hezuo jingying qiye ruhe dengji guanli de tongzhi (Notice regarding Cleaning Up 'Fake Collectives' and How to Register and Manage Cooperative Enterprises)," in *Gufen hezuo jingji wenjian huibian* (1991:52–4).

[34] Central party document (1989) #9 is cited in Nongcun jiceng dang zuzhi diaocha yanjiu ketizu, "Guanyu Wenzhou gufen hezuo qiye dang zuzhi jianshe de kaocha baogao (Regarding the Report on the Investigation into the Establishment of Party Organizations in Wenzhou's Shareholding Cooperative Enterprises)," *Zhejiang shehui kexue*, No. 4 (1992), p. 38.

[35] The discomfiture of private entrepreneurs who had already been inducted into the party was evident in interviews, as was the unease of other private entrepreneurs who took the decision as a sign of things to come (Informants 5 and 89).

[36] See Zhonggong zhongyang, "Guanyu jinyibu zhili zhengdun he shenhua gaige de jueding (Decision regarding Advancing Rectification and Deepening Reform)," in *Shiyijie sanzhong quanhui yilai jingji tizhi gaige zhongyao wenjian huibian* (1990:598–9).

Nevertheless, as late as September 1995, the Fifth Plenum of the Fourteenth Central Committee reiterated the position that "keeping the public sector of the economy as the dominant one and allowing diverse sectors to develop side by side is the basic principle we have upheld for a long time. Any practice that shakes or forsakes the dominant position of the public sector is a departure from the socialist orientation" (Yang 1995:17). The relatively hostile political environment – evident both before and after the passage of central regulations on private enterprises in 1988 and both before and after Deng's "southern tour" of 1992 – influenced the kinds of property rights that local officials were willing and able to support during the first fifteen years of reform.

The Nature of Markets for Factors and Products

Finally, choices about property rights were constrained by the market environment – by the nature of markets for inputs into industry and by the nature of markets for industrial products.[37] The private sector was virtually shut out of the state's planned distribution channels. Although the rural collective sector as a whole was never fully integrated into state economic plans, it also was never fully excluded. Early in the reform process when the plan's influence over supply and marketing was at its greatest extent, access to plan channels was key to realizing the full value of investments in industry.

Beginning in 1979, the State Council encouraged local planning commissions and industrial bureaus at the county level and above to extend their management to include township- and village-run enterprises.[38] For instance, management functions came to include arranging for production permits (*shengchan xukezheng*). Central production ministries in Beijing not only established standards for products within each ministry's bailiwick but also sought to limit production by issuing a limited number of permits for each product line. In cases in which production permits were required, firms without such permits could not legally sell their products – at least not to state-run commercial or industrial firms. Managers of rural collectives seeking production permits began to

---

[37] Access to loan capital is addressed in detail in Chapter 6.

[38] Guowuyuan, "Guanyu fazhan shedui qiye ruogan wenti de guiding (shixing caoan) (Regulations on Several Questions regarding the Development of Commune- and Brigade-Enterprises [Provisional Draft])," in *Zhongguo xiangzhen qiye nianjian 1978–1987* (1989:427–32).

receive assistance not only from the township industrial corporation but also from the county rural enterprise management bureau and the county planning commission (Informants 45, 97, 164, and 191).

In 1984, the CCP Central Committee and State Council directed state planning agencies, materials bureaus, and transportation bureaus "to increase the proportion of TVE inputs and outputs that are directly or indirectly covered by state plans" and encouraged state commercial and foreign trade organs to include TVEs in their purchasing meetings.[39] In addition, they directed education bureaus to include TVE needs in planning for vocational training and in the assignment (*fenpei*) of technical personnel with postsecondary credentials.

Inputs. To illustrate, as of 1979, commune- and brigade-run collectives in Wuxi County acquired 72 percent of petroleum, 26 percent of steel, 23 percent of coal, 21 percent of lumber, and 13 percent of pig iron inputs through plan channels (*Wuxi xian gongye zhi* 1990:78–81). Starting in 1984, central planners created a "dual track" economy by freezing plan targets at 1984 levels; as the economy began to "grow out of the plan," an increasing proportion of materials began to circulate at "negotiated prices (*yijia*)" beyond plan channels (Naughton 1995:182). Thus, by 1988, rural collectives in Wuxi acquired only 18 percent of petroleum, 2 percent of steel, 12 percent of coal, 2 percent of lumber, and 4 percent of pig iron via the plan. Similarly, in Shanghai in the late 1980s and into the early 1990s, state plans provided access to roughly 20 to 30 percent of the steel and 10 percent of the coal, in addition to varying amounts of the copper and aluminum used by rural collectives (Informant 39).[40]

By contrast, privately owned firms existed within "the crevices of the public ownership system" (Zhang and Qin 1989:63).[41] Not surprisingly, the growth of the private economy in Wenzhou depended upon the

---

[39] Zhonggong zhongyang guowuyuan, "Zhuanfa nongmuyuyebu 'Guanyu kaichuang shedui qiye xin jumian de baogao' de tongzhi (Notice of Transmission of the Ministry of Agriculture's 'Report on Initiating a New Phase for Commune and Brigade Enterprises')," in *Zhongguo xiangzhen qiye nianjian 1978–1987* (1989:422–7).

[40] See also S. zhen qiye guanli bangongshi, "Qiye guanli qingkuang jiaoliu (Exchange on the Situation in Enterprise Management)," No. 7 (July 27, 1991). The report discusses the difficulties faced by rural collectives in adjusting as the prominence of planned supply declined.

[41] The World Bank study on rural industry found that in Wuxi, only 5 percent of the small private enterprise sector could obtain raw materials at below-market prices, while fully 79 percent of the collective sector could do so (Song and Du 1990:349).

emergence of informal markets specializing in steel, lumber, cement, and other inputs (He 1987; 1989; Informant 169). These informal markets were supplied by private purchasing agents who specialized in acquiring scarce materials in small amounts from state enterprises around the country. However, the informal markets were vulnerable to official crackdowns during retrenchment campaigns. When orders from the State Administration of Industry and Commerce forced the closure of Wenzhou's commodities markets for a brief period in the mid-1980s, local prices for steel, lumber, and cement "went through the roof" (Informant 169). When the informal markets finally reopened, renewed competition among purchasing agents gradually drove prices down again. Nevertheless, even in periods of relative permissiveness, the supply of raw materials through such informal markets was erratic and constituted a constraint on the growth of private firms.

Product Markets. A multiprovince study of 200 rural enterprises conducted during the mid-1980s found that close to 25 percent of the goods produced by rural collectives were purchased by foreign trade or materials bureaus or were guaranteed purchase (*baoxiao*) by state-run industrial or commercial companies (Du 1987:273). Inclusion in binding plans was desirable, because the plans protected firms from the volatility of the emerging market. For this reason, the World Bank reports that during the 1980s, some local authorities sought to ensure the stability of sales for rural collectives "by increasing the proportion of product orders covered by state planning" to the extent possible (Luo 1990:159). As Chapter 2 illustrated, Wuxi experienced an unusually high degree of plan integration even during the Maoist period. In 1979, at the beginning of the reforms, 65 percent of the industrial products manufactured by rural collectives in Wuxi were marketed through plan channels. As China's "dual track" reform of the planned economy progressed, the percentage declined and, by 1988, had fallen to 32 percent (*Wuxi xian gongye zhi* 1990:77). In Shanghai most products sold through the plan were produced by rural collectives engaged in joint ventures with urban state-run enterprises. As of the early 1990s, nearly 50 percent of rural collective output was produced in state–collective joint ventures. Twenty percent of this output was governed by binding state plans, with another 50 percent governed by nonbinding guidance planning (Informant 39). Some older TVEs were included in state plans even without having established joint ventures with state enterprises. For example, the output of some TVEs was subject to guaranteed purchase by state-run companies such as the Shanghai Electrical Equipment Corporation and the Shanghai Construction Metals Corporation (Informants 47 and 67).

To the extent that rural collectives, like private enterprises, relied on market channels to sell their products, however, they faced intense competition. A majority of TVE managers questioned in the World Bank study on rural industry characterized competition as "relatively," "very," or "extremely fierce" (Byrd and Zhu 1990:90–2).[42] This impression is reinforced by the widespread phenomenon of falling prices in markets for TVE products during the 1980s and again in the mid- to late-1990s (Naughton 1995). Market pressure led to tactics on the part of some local officials to protect local markets for collective enterprises. These protectionist tactics ranged from "excluding outside products from local markets to threatening local enterprises with cutoffs of funds and bank loans, supplies of fuel, etc. should they dare to buy the products of competitors" (Wong 1988a:104). While it appears that these forms of protectionism had declined by the 1990s, they highlight the closely linked interests of local officials and their collective enterprises.

In sum, the choices of local officials regarding the forms of property rights they would support were constrained by distinct local resource endowments inherited from the Maoist era and shaped by the nature of national political-legal and market institutions during the reform period.

Disposition toward Private Enterprise in Wuxi and Songjiang

Local government officials in Wuxi and Songjiang were openly hostile to the interests of private investors. To illustrate this point, subsequent paragraphs examine the treatment of private firms in two townships in Wuxi and Songjiang, focusing on the period after the 1988 passage of the constitutional amendment affirming the legitimacy of private enterprise and the promulgation of regulations governing its development.

Dongtan Town in Wuxi County represented an extreme case of official defense of collective-sector interests. As of the early 1990s, the township industrial and commercial bureau had not granted a single private enterprise license in the industrial sector.[43] Even at the county level, private firms accounted for only 8 percent of the total in that sector in

---

[42] See also Du (1987:272–3).

[43] Interviews reveal the existence of a small number of individually contracted (*geren chengbao*) collectives in Dongtan Town. To the extent that these firms actually relied on private sources of investment they could be considered private firms with "fake" col-

1990. An official of the township industrial and commercial bureau referred to a 1992 document issued by the township party committee that set the minimum level of registered capital for private enterprises at 500 thousand yuan, and he described having recently denied the application of private investors prepared to invest 300 thousand yuan in a printing business. The official commented that the party secretary did not care about what higher levels said about "private and collective wheels turning together (*geti jiti yiqi shang, qige lunzi yiqi zhuan*)"; he did not want any private industry in his town (Informant 193). Indeed, to the extent that competition from private enterprises would have reduced the sales revenues of township collectives, there would have been fewer collective resources for the township government to tap.

By contrast, Songyang Town in Songjiang County boasted one of the highest concentrations of private enterprises among townships in the Shanghai suburban counties, with private firms accounting for 21 percent of firms in the industrial sector as of 1990. Nonetheless, private enterprise development was still highly restricted. Although the minimum registered capital required was only 50 thousand yuan, private firms were not granted licenses in any industry in which a collective factory was already operating (Informant 111). The only exception to this rule was if the anticipated production runs were so small that no collective firm would accept contracts in that product line (Informants 89 and 94). The restriction was enforced through the effective veto power of the township industrial corporation over private enterprise license applications.[44] In addition, although regulations allowed private enterprises to enter into joint ventures with foreign firms, as of the early 1990s, no applications had received approval (Informant 89).

Access to land and other inputs was also a major constraint on private enterprise development in Wuxi and Songjiang. As World Bank researchers point out,

> Partly because of the success of industrial township and village community enterprises, local authorities [in Sunan] were reluctant to

---

lective licenses. In most cases, however, an individual leased the collective assets of a loss-making village-run or school-run collective enterprise for a fixed sum (Informants 191, 192, and 193). This form of enterprise management will be addressed in more detail in the context of taxation in Chapter 5.

[44] Regulators also denied licenses to private firms that affected the use of electricity by collectives (Informant 94).

encourage development of private enterprises that might give community enterprises too much competition.... Private enterprises
are tolerated, but their development has been constrained by limits
on loans, restricted access to inputs, and environmental and other
regulations (Svejnar and Woo 1990:79–80).

In Shanghai, for example, it was local policy to limit both the use of land
and the scale of factory buildings for private enterprises (Informant 52).
Based on the experiences of the private enterprise owners in Songyang
Town during the early 1990s, the only options were to operate out
of one's own home or to rent an abandoned building or shed from
the village. Even in cases in which private entrepreneurs won approval
to expand existing workshops, their investments were minimal because
of the belief that the state could repossess the land and buildings at
any time, causing the owners to lose their assets (Informants 89 and
94). Similarly, neither the Agriculture Bank nor the local credit cooperative in principle granted loans to private enterprises; in practice,
however, about half the private enterprises in the township had received
small, short-term loans from the credit cooperative, none exceeding
10 thousand yuan.[45] According to a representative of the credit cooperative, total loans to private firms accounted for approximately
0.2 percent of the credit cooperative's total loans outstanding in 1991
(Informant 99).

Given the strong endowment in collective assets as of the early 1980s,
the dependence of the local government on rural enterprise for fiscal
revenue, and the close financial ties between collective firms and the local
government, local officials in the Sunan region resisted the development
of private firms by creating relatively effective barriers to entry and
growth.

Disposition toward Private Enterprise in Wenzhou

By contrast, the overriding concern of local government officials in
Wenzhou was fostering private economic development. Because of the
historical legacy of weak collective development, the actions of local officials were guided by the desire to promote private investment. As an official of the tax and public finance bureau in Yueqing County, Wenzhou
stated, "We must encourage investment on the part of individuals

[45] On this, see Chapter 6.

144

because the county doesn't have enough money itself" (Informant 167).[46]
Subsequent paragraphs examine efforts on the part of local officials in
Wenzhou to promote private enterprise since the early 1980s. They
describe the interplay of the national political and market environments,
on the one hand, and the actions of local cadres and private entrepreneurs, on the other. The discussion demonstrates that, despite the
increasingly relaxed policies of the central government, local efforts to
promote private investment were hindered by the failure of the state as
a whole to make private property rights secure.

The evolution of private property rights began much earlier in
Wenzhou than in Sunan, with local cadres broadly interpreting reform
edicts that only narrowly expanded the allowable scope of economic
activity on the part of private individuals and households. As North
(1990) suggests, institutional change often begins with the lax enforcement of rules that stand in the way of change.[47] Local officials in
Wenzhou describe their approach as proceeding "not according to higher
levels, not according to documents, but rather according to reality (*bu
wei shang, bu wei shu, yao wei shi*)" (Informant 168). Accordingly, a wide
array of essentially private ownership forms emerged in the industrial
sector beginning in the late 1970s and early 1980s with the knowledge
and support of subprovincial local officials but well ahead of the regulations and laws designed to govern them.[48] However, none of the early
guises under which private investment arose provided a reliable guarantee of private property rights.

The earliest practice was for private investors to register illicitly as
"fake" collective enterprises. According to the Yueqing County rural
enterprise bureau, it was common as of 1980 for individual investors in
Yueqing to pay the village for both access to village buildings and for
authorization to register as a village-run collective enterprise (Informant
164). This practice also facilitated trade. At that time, private investors
could not obtain the status of juristic persons (*faren*) and therefore could

---

[46] Kristen Parris's (1993:255) research on Wenzhou provides implicit support for this view.
[47] "Frequently, evading the law in the context of lax enforcement was a successful strategy" for initiating institutional change (North 1990:88).
[48] These forms included household enterprises affiliated with collectives (*guahu*), joint
household enterprises (*lianhu*) (a type of cooperative [*hezuo jingying qiye*]), individual
household enterprises (*getihu*), private enterprises (*siying qiye*), private partnerships
(*siren hehuo qiye*), shareholding cooperatives (*gufen hezuo qiye*), and individual and
private firms that falsely registered as collectives. Here, the focus is on the "larger" end
of the spectrum, i.e., industrial enterprises with private investment employing eight or
more workers.

not sign valid contracts or open commercial bank accounts, because these privileges were reserved for units within the official state bureaucratic hierarchy.[49] Commercial bank accounts were essential to conducting business with the larger state-run economy, because state enterprises could only issue payments via state-run banks, accompanied by official receipts. In addition to providing access to bank accounts, therefore, the sponsoring unit would provide the entrepreneur with such items as letters of introduction and official receipts.[50] The affiliated firm could also pay taxes at the low, collective rate. Officials emphasized that the practice of affiliation increased local tax receipts, because without affiliation, some firms would not exist or would be driven underground given the absence of explicit legal standing in the early 1980s (Informant 169).

However, those private investors registered as "fake" collectives had no guarantees of their rights as owners.[51] In some cases, village leaders made claims on the assets of the firms – particularly those assets accumulated after the initial investment – and private investors had no legal basis on which to challenge these claims (Luo, Quan, and Gao 1989).[52] As one legal scholar notes, local officials "could suddenly demote the founders and investors to mere employees with no right to a return on the capital that they had invested" (Clarke 1992:305). For example, in Hualing Town, Yueqing County, two now fully collective enterprises had been founded with private investment and were later taken over by the local government – with the original investors receiving compensation only for the value of their initial investment and not for the full value of the firm (including reinvested profits) at the time of collectivization (Informants 146 and 147). In other cases, village sponsors repudiated their relationships with private entrepreneurs when disputes with clients arose (He 1987:45).[53] Finally, given private owners' technically illegal

---

[49] On juristic persons, see Clarke (1992:305). See also the description of the problems stemming from the lack of *faren* status in He (1989:95).

[50] These services were later enshrined in experimental regulations governing affiliated households. See Wenzhou shi renmin zhengfu, "Wenzhou shi guahu jingying guanli zanxing guiding (Wenzhou Municipality Provisional Regulations on Affiliated Household Firms)," in *Wenzhou zhi lu congshu: Kaituozhe de guiji – Wenzhou shi difang fagui jianbian* (1989:140–3). See also the discussion in Parris (1993).

[51] This problem is discussed as historical background in Du (1989) and Jisen Ma (1988:87).

[52] See also the similar problem discussed in Lyons (1994:150).

[53] See also "Wenzhou shi mingxi chanquan shidian gongzuo huibaohui jiyao (Minutes of the Follow-up Meeting on the Experiment to Clarify Property Rights in Wenzhou Municipality)," Mimeo, June 15, 1989, p. 13. These sources present differing perspectives on this problem depending on whether the injured party was the private entrepreneur or the client.

position, they had no recourse if village sponsors increased collective "management fees" and other exactions to extortionary levels.[54]

Alternatively, private firms could register as individual enterprises or as cooperatives (as of 1983), but in either case those with more than a few employees were operating outside the bounds of official policy. According to officials of the rural enterprise bureau, by the mid-1980s, informal cooperatives among relatives and friends engaged in small-scale industry had begun to emerge in Yueqing (Informants 164 and 165). Such informal cooperatives not only allowed individual entrepreneurs to pool capital and skills but also seemed to be an answer to the discrimination (*qishi*) against and limitations (*xianzhi*) on outright private investment in industry (He 1987:69–75). These enterprises came to be referred to in Wenzhou as cooperative shareholding enterprises (*gufen hezuo qiye*), and they were licensed as cooperatives (under a loose interpretation of the 1983 regulations) at the discretion of the industrial and commercial bureau. However, in November 1986, the State Administration for Industry and Commerce issued a document stating that virtually all enterprises currently registered as cooperatives (*hezuo jingying zuzhi*) were in actuality private partnerships (*geren hehuo qiye*) – that is, *not* cooperative in nature – and would be required to re-register as individual household firms (*getihu*) since no legislation governing private partnerships existed (Luo, Quan, and Gao 1989:378). The change meant that these enterprises would be subject to the punitively high income tax rates imposed by central state policy on individual enterprises, which could reach as high as 80 percent (Informant 174). Although the policy was not vigorously enforced in Zhejiang, it was clearly intended to limit the development of private firms. Moreover, private enterprises that continued to register as cooperatives faced problems similar to those of "fake collectives"; in some cases, owners lost their claims to enterprise assets, since according to the 1983 regulations, true cooperatives required a significant proportion of "public accumulation."

The lack of any effective guarantee of property rights directly affected the behavior of private investors. Entrepreneurs were uncertain how long their firms could continue to exist or how large their firms would be allowed to grow. They worried about being attacked as ideologically suspect and feared losing their investments through expropriation (Luo, Quan, and Gao 1989:373–4). As a result, some investors adopted

---

[54] This was the experience in 1987 related by one private entrepreneur (Informant 5). See also Luo, Quan, and Gao (1989).

"hit-and-run" strategies of investment – making small investments, reaping the profits, and then closing down to live on the profits for some period of time before starting a new venture.[55] Reports indicate that private entrepreneurs who remained in business through the mid-1980s were unwilling to increase their investments beyond a limited scale (Zhang 1987:32). "Reportedly, the seriousness of the legal issue was brought home to the top leadership ... when they learned that private entrepreneurs in Wenzhou were afraid to expand their assets beyond the one million (yuan) mark and preferred to dismiss workers while spending their money on extravagant homes or even ancestral tombs."[56] In addition, the inability of many private investors to gain access to the energy, raw materials, bank financing, or land necessary for expansion placed an effective ceiling on their firms' development (Informants 148, 149, 155, and 169).

From the perspective of local government officials in Wenzhou, the fact that private investors were unwilling to make larger-scale, longer-term investments implied stasis, not development. Encouraging such investment on the part of private entrepreneurs was a challenge for Wenzhou cadres – despite their willingness to tolerate unofficial forms of private enterprise locally – because of the lack of credible commitment to the rights of private investors.

The difficulties facing Wenzhou cadres in encouraging investment on the part of private entrepreneurs continued even after the passage in 1988 of the national regulations governing private enterprise in the form of *siying qiye*. One private entrepreneur interviewed in Wenzhou in 1991 stated explicitly that he was holding back on new investments until he was more certain that policy would not change (Informant 5). Another described the great psychological pressure (*sixiang yali*) he felt as a private enterprise owner (Informant 149). These findings are reflected in a study conducted by the Economic Policy Research Center of the Ministry of Agriculture in several sites including Wenzhou (K. Gao 1991). The study reports that from 1989 to 1990, significant numbers of private entrepreneurs reduced the scale of funds invested in their enterprises or even ceased operation because they perceived that the policy toward the private sector was changing.[57] According to the study, the registered

---

[55] This pattern was reflected in the experiences of a number of private entrepreneurs interviewed (Informants 5 and 148).

[56] "The Privately Run Enterprises," *China News Analysis* No. 1382 (April 1, 1989), p. 5.

[57] Researchers at the Zhejiang Academy reached the same conclusion (Informant 174).

capital of private enterprises in Wenzhou declined by 5 percent in 1989 alone. The study also identifies several cases of private entrepreneurs successfully liquidating their assets and taking them abroad. Echoing the same theme, Wenzhou party secretary Liu Xirong highlighted the problem of private capital flight in a June 1990 speech (Liu 1991).

Similarly, private entrepreneurs continued to exhibit "short-term behavior" such as "excessive consumption," suggesting a lack of confidence in the policies intended to protect their rights and interests. Researchers at the Zhejiang Academy of Social Sciences attributed extremes of lavish consumption to the high degree of risk faced by private entrepreneurs in the political climate of the early 1990s (Informant 174). Other surveys also draw links between the "fear of policy change" and the increasing proportion of entrepreneurs' income spent on consumption (Wu 1989). An official of the tax and finance bureau in Yueqing County lamented in 1992 that private entrepreneurs were afraid to invest in large-scale projects there (Informant 162). As North (1990:110) points out, "If organizations . . . devote their efforts to *unproductive activity*, the institutional constraints have provided the incentive structure for such activity."

Local officials were also concerned by private investors who shifted funds out of production and into savings. Two reports link this trend to the lack of confidence on the part of private investors (K. Gao 1991; Z. Gao 1991). Official concern arose because of the existence of official limits on the scale of lending in the Wenzhou region by the state-run banking system. Because of such lending limits, funds deposited in Wenzhou were transferred through the state-run banking system to other locales (Informants 158 and 174). Shifts of funds out of private investment into private savings in state-run banks were thus a cause of concern to local cadres, because local private savings did not necessarily directly translate into loans to be made *locally* but rather contributed to loan capital in other locales.

I argue that the forms of disinvestment behavior observed in Wenzhou reflected the continuing absence of credible commitment to private property rights on the part of the state. Consistent with the preceding theoretical discussion, private entrepreneurs reduced or withheld investments because of the belief that, as private investors, they would not be able to reap the returns of those investments. Thus, the passage of the 1988 regulations on private enterprise was a necessary but not sufficient condition for credible commitment to private property rights. In terms of Litwack's (1991) analysis, a belief by the population in the stability and enforceability of the rules had not developed with respect to private investment as of the early 1990s.

Furthermore, a credible commitment on the part of the state to private property rights was also necessary for the development of impersonal trade. Even in the 1980s, rural enterprises – both private and collective – sought markets across provincial boundaries for a growing proportion of their output (Byrd and Zhu 1990; Du 1992:90; Du 1987:272). However, according to an official of the Hualing Town industrial office in Yueqing County who oversaw the activities of larger privately owned and collectively owned industrial firms, even with the passage of private enterprise legislation, many firms outside Wenzhou were still unwilling to sign contracts with private enterprises (Informant 145). In addition, private entrepreneurs felt they had no legal recourse in resolving contract disputes since courts refused to recognize their claims. Indeed, in some cases courts interpreted the economic claims of private investors as being not merely without merit but criminal. As I argue in a subsequent section, the regulations governing private enterprises in the form of *siying qiye* failed to meet the criteria for credible commitment on the part of the state. Central leaders apparently perceived the cost of attacking *siying qiye* – particularly in the industrial sector – as acceptably low.

An Alternative: The Sociological Approach

Sociologists have developed an alternative approach to understanding the development of rural enterprise by focusing on the clientelist networks in which entrepreneurs are embedded. In their view, an investor's claim on assets is socially defined and recognized. Victor Nee and Sijin Su (1996:113) focus on "longstanding social ties based on frequent face-to-face interactions" as an important basis for trust and cooperation between entrepreneurs and the government in the Chinese political economy. In a similar vein, David Wank (1995; 1996) highlights clientelist ties to government officials as a key source of protection for private investors in the absence of strong legal guarantees. "Long-term relations, by increasing the degree of trust and concern for mutual benefit, reduce the likelihood of opportunistic behavior by official-patrons vis-à-vis entrepreneur-clients" (Wank 1995:178). Finally Nan Lin and Chih-jou Chen (1994) emphasize thick relationships based on familial ties.

Interpersonal networks clearly played a role in private enterprise development. As noted earlier, interpersonal networks were a factor in the development of informal commodity markets in Wenzhou during the early 1980s. Similarly, personal connections affected the ability of a few private investors to acquire small bank loans in Songjiang. Nevertheless, reliance on personal connections clearly did not result in unconstrained private sector development or in equal levels of private sector development across locales. Moreover, there is no evidence to suggest that the density or quality of personal networks varied systematically by region; such networks seemed to pervade every region and to pervade the public and private sectors alike. Indeed, as Armen Alchian (1977:129) suggests, property rights "in any society are to be construed as supported by the force of etiquette, social custom, [and] ostracism, [in addition to] formal legally enacted laws supported by the states' power of violence of punishment."

The sensitivity to the formal institution of property rights on the part of both private investors and local state officials in the Wenzhou site suggests that cultivation of clientelist networks was insufficient to protect the interests of private investors.[58] As both Litwack and North emphasize, reliance on personal networks to guarantee the enforceability of contracts severely limits the potential scope of private enterprise development (Litwack 1991; North 1990). The inadequacy of reliance on personal networks held particularly true for interactions with actors outside the local community – whether in interactions with representatives of the central state industrial-commercial administration or in contracts with state enterprises across local and provincial boundaries. Sole reliance on personal connections for every approval, license, and contract was both costly and insecure. Finally, the cultivation of personal networks cannot account for the distinct spatial pattern of private investment, since reliance on personal networks seemed to pervade business practices across locales and across ownership forms.[59]

THE QUEST FOR CREDIBLE COMMITMENT: AGGRESSIVE POLICY INNOVATION AND PRIVATE INVESTOR CHOICE IN WENZHOU

Local cadres in Wenzhou had an institutionally defined interest in promoting private investment. They innovated aggressively in the area

---

[58] Many analysts of Chinese business practices argue that a cultural practice like the cultivation of personal networks (*guanxi*) alone cannot explain investment behavior; the political environment is a crucial variable (Hamilton and Biggart 1988; Whyte 1995).

[59] For a fuller elaboration of this critique, see Whiting (1998).

of private property rights in response to the tentative investment behavior exhibited by private entrepreneurs throughout the 1980s. After taking initial steps in 1986, the Wenzhou municipal government in 1987 approved three major pieces of local legislation, each representing a different approach to guaranteeing the rights and interests of private investors. The three included (1) regulations formalizing the relationship between affiliated household firms (*guahu*) and their collective sponsors, (2) regulations guaranteeing for the first time the rights of private investors in explicitly private firms (*siying qiye*) with eight or more employees, and (3) regulations guaranteeing the rights of private investors in somewhat attenuated form in shareholding cooperatives (*gufen hezuo qiye*).[60] Private entrepreneurs in the Wenzhou research site opted overwhelmingly for the most attenuated form of ownership, that is, the shareholding cooperative. The reason behind this otherwise anomalous choice is that the shareholding cooperative form provided the highest degree of credible commitment to private property rights, albeit in somewhat attenuated form. As the subsequent discussion will demonstrate, only this form met the prerequisites for credible commitment by the central state. Of the three forms of ownership, only the shareholding cooperative form offered private investors an independent and legitimate *collective* license.[61] Only a collective license linked the minority interests of local officials and private entrepreneurs in Wenzhou to the majority interests of local officials and de facto owners of township- and village-run collectives, which were the pillars of the rural economy throughout China. While "private" and "collective" labels were clearly important in Chinese politics (Y. Liu 1992:302), this section makes the argument that the collective license was more than just a mere label reflecting symbolic politics. Rather, the discussion shows that there were concrete interests behind the symbols.

The section begins by reviewing the relevant theoretical literature and then examines specifically how national regulations governing shareholding cooperatives contributed to credible commitment by linking the interests of private investors to those of the larger rural collective economy.

---

[60] See note 27.

[61] Affiliated households received a permit (*guahu jingying xukezheng*) attesting to their status, while private enterprises received a private license (*siying qiye yingye zhizhao*).

The State and Credible Commitment: Theoretical Issues

Political scientists and institutional economists suggest that incentives to generate revenue are only effective if there is a credible commitment to property rights on the part of the state. If an investor is not confident that he can reap the gains of his investment at some future point, that assessment reduces the value of the investment and undermines the incentive to invest.

> For economic actors to undertake costly actions necessary for economic development, they must expect to garner the return of their efforts. The potential redistribution of these returns – whether through a substantial tax increase, a wholesale reversal of the reform process, or outright confiscation – reduces the expected private return to these actions (Weingast 1993:2).[62]

Where such a credible commitment to property rights is absent, investment tends to be smaller-scale and shorter-term than would otherwise be the case.

> We have only to contrast the organization of production in a Third World economy with that in an advanced industrial economy to be impressed by the consequences of poorly defined and/or ineffective property rights. Not only will the institutional framework result in high costs of transacting in the former, but insecure property rights will result in using technologies that employ little fixed capital and do not entail long-term agreements. Firms will typically be small (except those operated or protected by the government) (North 1990:65).

Thus, credible commitment to property rights is an important factor in promoting economic development.

However, the issue of credible commitment to property rights contracts is especially problematic since one of the parties to the contract is the state. Because the state enjoys a monopoly over the legitimate use of violence, it is difficult to constrain its behavior, as North's (1990:35) research on early modern Europe demonstrates: "[T]he state was as often an increasing source of insecurity and higher transaction costs as it was protector and enforcer of property rights."

---

[62] This point is also made by others. See Eggertsson (1990:247; 275; 341).

The theory of credible commitment suggests that constraints on state behavior are credible only when they are self-enforcing. In other words, it is necessary to "create a set of arrangements that alter incentives so that carrying out the original bargain – rather than behaving opportunistically *ex post* – is compatible with the incentives facing the actors after the fact. Contracts of this form are said to be *self-enforcing* and therefore represent a credible commitment" (Weingast 1993:4).

Barry Weingast (1993) identifies two key criteria that create the conditions for credible commitment on the part of the state. First, members of the national community must react against state transgressions in a way that punishes the state. Second, community members must share common ideas about what constitutes transgressions by the state so that they react against them in concert. Reactions that punish the state could entail dissent on the part of important supporters of the regime (such as local party and government leaders), for example. This reaction is analogous to Albert Hirschman's (1979) notion of voice. However, members of the national community need not be conscious of punishing the state or even aware of acting in concert with other community members. Disinvestment does not depend on knowledge of others' actions but only on an individual calculation based on one's own structural situation. The aggregation of many individuals or communities in the same structural situation withholding or withdrawing investment (and consequently the tax revenues and employment opportunities that go along with investment) also punishes the state. This reaction is analogous to Hirschman's notion of exit. As reflected in Weingast's second criterion, however, such "punishment" would have a significant impact only if inflicted on the state by large numbers of individuals or communities reacting simultaneously to a similarly perceived transgression. For example, the cost (in terms of lost jobs and revenue) to the central state of undermining property rights contracts would be great both politically and economically if enterprise owners and local officials all over the country – not just in Wenzhou and not just in the private sector – reduced or withheld investment. In summary, the state can make a credible commitment to property rights when they are structured such that it is in the interest of the state to respect them.

Of course, the role of the state is important in underpinning other kinds of contracts besides property rights. The state can facilitate trade by acting as a neutral third party that can and will enforce contracts between firms. However, if the state does not regard private firms as legitimate, it is less likely to play the role of a neutral third party in enforcing contracts in which private firms are involved. To the extent that trade contracts must therefore rely on personal connections (or other informal means) for enforcement, the scope of trade is severely limited (North 1990:12).

The Development of Shareholding Cooperatives

The litany of problems associated with private enterprise, along with increasingly virulent attacks on "fake collectives," gave heightened importance to the third policy element in Wenzhou's three-pronged approach to governing private investment – the regulations governing shareholding cooperatives. Indeed, the overwhelming majority of private investors in the Wenzhou research site had chosen this form of investment as of the early 1990s, despite the fact that it entailed some attenuation of the rights they could enjoy as investors. This section employs the theory of credible commitment to explain this choice.

The development of experimental local regulations governing shareholding cooperatives began in 1987 not only in Wenzhou but also in several other locales. These multiple experiments had very different underlying intents and involved very different types of enterprises – privately run firms in Wenzhou and local government-run collective firms elsewhere – both of which would ultimately be governed by the same national regulations, thereby linking private and collective interests in a common policy.

The Government-run Variant of Shareholding Cooperatives. As in Wenzhou, local leaders in several other locales, working under the guidance of the Central Committee Secretariat Rural Policy Research Office and the State Council Rural Development Research Center, also developed experimental regulations governing rural shareholding cooperatives (Du 1989; Pan 1988). Outside Wenzhou, however, shareholding cooperative experiments focused on township- and village-run collective enterprises. Central Committee document (1987) #5 on "Deepening Rural Reform" highlighted the need to separate government and collective enterprises and to end the legacy of fused political and economic control lingering from the commune era.[63] The document explicitly identified shareholding cooperatives as a means of

---

[63] Zhonggong zhongyang zhengzhiju, "Ba nongcun gaige yinxiang shenru (zhaiyao) (Deepening Rural Reform (Abstract))," in *Zhongguo xiangzhen qiye nianjian* (1989:518–21).

limiting government interference and increasing the autonomy of township- and village-run collectives from the local government. Thus, the experiments were intended to reduce the interference of local leaders in the operations of collective firms and to separate the functions of township governance from enterprise management (*zhengqi fenkai*) in order to make enterprise managers more responsive to market forces. However, these goals appear rarely to have been met during the first decade of implementation between 1987 and 1996.[64]

In practice, the experiments facilitated two processes that were unintended by central policy makers. First, they allowed local party secretaries and township executives to translate their political power into ownership of a relatively large number of individual shares in the most valuable firms, often at highly favorable prices.[65] As a result, local officials developed a vested interest in the success of shareholding cooperatives. Their interest in local shareholding cooperatives was based not only on their official positions as township party secretaries or township executives (and therefore overseers of government shares in the firms), but also on their ownership of their own individual shares. This interest constitutes one element in the establishment of credible commitment. If the enterprise loses, the officials lose.[66]

Second, local officials implemented shareholding cooperative reforms in such a way as to channel new sources of investment capital into collective enterprises, while preserving their control over the collective economy. The experiments entailed transforming the existing assets of local government-run firms into shares held by the local government (*jiti*

---

[64] Only in cases in which the shares controlled by the township government were balanced by the shares controlled by outside government agencies with interests distinct from those of the township did there appear to be any disciplining effect on the behavior of the township government.

[65] In the case of the Jiabao Company in Jiading County, for example, individuals were, in principle, entitled to purchase thirty individual shares each. However, according to a township official, employees in the newly transformed collective were only allowed five shares each, while the township party secretary and township executive (among other officials) acquired hundreds of shares each (Informants 138 and 143). Similar experiences were reported regarding other of the most desirable government-run shareholding cooperatives (Informant 197). Jiabao was exceptional, however, in that it became one of the first rural enterprises whose shares were to be traded on the Shanghai stock exchange; the shares of the vast majority of firms were not publicly traded.

[66] Most shareholding cooperatives were not publicly traded. However, threats to the ability of the enterprise to pay dividends would reduce the value of their personal shares.

gu) and then mobilizing firm employees and local residents to invest in shares to be held by individuals (*geren gu*), while ensuring that the government continued to hold the majority of shares.[67]

One of Shanghai's earliest experiments with shareholding cooperatives in rural collectives began in the Chuansha Printing and Dyeing Machinery Factory in Chengzhen Township in 1989. Although the experiment was begun with the express goal of expanding firm autonomy, an internal report of the Chuansha County party committee policy research office highlighted the mobilization of idle capital in the hands of enterprise employees into productive investment within the firm as a key outcome of the experiment.[68] Indeed, the experiment was begun during a period in which the firm was experiencing an acute shortage of capital in part because of the failure of its largest state-owned client to make payments on completed orders (Informant 24).[69] Moreover, it coincided with a national austerity program (the economic rectification campaign of 1989 to 1991) that restricted access to bank loans via the state-run banking system.[70] Through the shareholding experiment, new share offerings to employees in 1989 and 1991 were successful in generating a total of 759 thousand yuan in new investment – roughly 1,500 yuan per employee.[71]

The report of the Chuansha County party committee policy research office was equivocal in its assessment of the initial effect of the experiment on enterprise autonomy, since the early share offerings were structured to maintain township control over a majority of voting shares. In addition, the party branch continued to exercise veto power over the appointment or transfer of all enterprise-level cadres. Indeed, the firm had a long history of active involvement by the local officials, and

---

[67] The experimental regulations also set guidelines governing the distribution of after-tax profits. According to the earliest guidelines, 45 percent of after-tax profits were to be distributed to shareholders, 40 percent were to be dedicated to reinvestment, 8 percent to the firm welfare fund, and 7 percent to the worker bonus fund (Informant 24). See also Zhu and Yin (1992).

[68] Chuansha xianwei zhengce yanjiushi, "Guanyu Chuansha yinran jixie chang shixing gufen hezuo zhi de diaocha he sikao (An Investigation into and Reflections on the Implementation of the Cooperative Shareholding System in the Chuansha Printing and Dyeing Machinery Factory)," *Chuansha diaoyan* No. 7 (April 20, 1991), pp. 1–11.

[69] This client accounted for 80 percent of sales in 1989. In 1990, orders by the same client were cut by 70 percent (falling from 16 million yuan to 4.8 million yuan).

[70] On this, see Chapter 6.

[71] For a more detailed account of corporate governance in shareholding cooperatives, see Whiting (1999b).

the township continued to set the firm's output and profit targets, to determine the salary and bonus of the manager, and to set the total wage bill for the factory. This problem was reflected in broader criticism of shareholding experiments in collective enterprises for "changing the path but not changing the system (*zhuan gui bu zhuan zhi*)" (Chen 1995).

Beginning in 1992, experiments with shareholding cooperatives were extended to a total of 593 enterprises in Shanghai, the majority of which were in the rural industrial sector. The experiments were explicitly intended to attract new capital investment into the rural enterprise sector.[72] They generated more than 700 million yuan in new investment capital, an average of nearly 1.2 million yuan per enterprise. Still, as of 1992, most township- and village-run collectives involved in experiments with shareholding cooperatives in the Shanghai area maintained local official dominance by restricting new investment in such a way as to preserve local officials' majority control over voting shares.

The implementation of shareholding cooperative reforms in Songjiang was consistent with this pattern. As in the case of the early experiment in Chuansha County, reforms were implemented in the context of what local leaders perceived to be a shortage of capital confronting the rural collective sector. Local documents described "amassing capital (*jizi*)" from local workers as the "most important function (*zuida gongneng*)" of shareholding cooperatives. As of 1996, there were 274 shareholding cooperatives in Songjiang, of which 131 were newly established firms and 143 were existing firms that underwent conversion; the latter had attracted 77.4 million yuan in new investment from workers and others. Of the 274 firms, the local government was the controlling shareholder in 214 firms (78 percent).[73] Not surprisingly, there was little change in the nature of corporate governance. As one manager in Songyang Town put it, "There has basically been no change in the way the enterprise is managed (*jingying guanli meiyou shenme duoda de bianhua*)" (Informant 217). This view was reflected in a 1996 report by the county

---

[72] As one report put it, the experiments made a breakthrough by directly attracting funds from employees, local residents, and society more broadly. See "Shanghai jiaoqu nongcun gufen hezuo ruogan wenti yanjiu (Research on Several Issues regarding Rural Shareholding Cooperatives in the Shanghai Suburbs)," *Caijing yanjiu* No. 6 (1993), pp. 24–30.

[73] Indeed, a 1992 document of the Songjiang County Party Committee set forth the principle that shares held by collective entities (including the local government) should constitute, at minimum, 50 percent of the total. Moreover, the output of these firms continued to be reported under the category of "collective."

executive in charge of industry: "Government and enterprise have still not been separated. . . . the township still holds the majority of the shares, the government still directly appoints the manager and directly interferes in production and operations, and the manager still seeks political intervention whenever he runs into difficulties."[74]

Thus, in Shanghai, the interest of local officials in developing shareholding cooperatives had two main objectives: (1) acquiring individual shares in the most valuable firms and (2) bringing new investment capital into firms controlled by the local government.

The Private Variant of Shareholding Cooperatives. In Wenzhou, by contrast, local officials designed local regulations governing shareholding cooperatives to promote private investment by addressing the ongoing concerns of private investors about the security of their property rights.[75] The Wenzhou experimental zone leadership small group and the municipal system reform commission took charge of drafting the regulations.[76] According to an official of the system reform commission, his office directly consulted more than twenty private entrepreneurs in order to ascertain what they wanted before they would invest more actively (Informant 171). He reported that they were most concerned about two issues: (1) the determination of the "political nature" of the enterprise (*dingxing*) and (2) the disposition of firm assets. Specifically, the entrepreneurs wanted their firms to be considered legitimately collective in nature, which was seen as essential to their security and ability to conduct business. In addition, they wanted to be able not only to control but also to dispose of the firm's assets. Wenzhou party secretary Liu Xirong summarized the entrepreneurs' position as follows: "A collective enterprise is too public; a private enterprise is too private – if too public, one fears domination; if too private, one fears having one's 'capitalist tail' cut off. Shareholding cooperatives are both

---

[74] "Zai woxian qiye gaizhi huiyishang de jianghua (Speech to the Conference on Reforming the Enterprise System in My County)," Mimeo, June 16, 1995.

[75] Local officials in Wenzhou also conducted some experiments on local government-run firms, but experiments in Wenzhou were primarily oriented toward the private variant. For a discussion of the government-run variant in the context of predominantly private experiments, see Wenzhou shi nongwei jingying guanli ke, "Gufen gongsi jiang yuelaiyueduo (There Will Be More and More Stock Companies)," in Lin (1987: 295–305).

[76] Other key players included the municipal industrial and commercial management bureau, the tax and finance bureau, the rural enterprise bureau (now corporation), and the local branch of the People's Bank of China.

public and private combined and are [therefore] the most appealing" (Liu 1991:3).

The first version of local regulations (Wenzhou municipal government document [1987] #79) defined a shareholding cooperative enterprise as an entity with a minimum of two investors that faced *no restrictions* regarding the number of employees but met certain guidelines regarding the distribution of after-tax profits. These guidelines set a limit of 25 percent on the share of profits that could be divided among investors; required that a minimum of 50 percent be reinvested in the firm in the names of the investors; and stipulated that the remaining portion be committed to public accumulation (*gonggong jilei*), collective welfare within the firm (*jiti fuli*), and worker bonuses.[77] Public accumulation referred to assets that could not be liquidated or claimed as the personal property of the investors; however, it is important to note that this portion of the assets did *not* belong to the local government but rather to the firm as a collective entity.[78] According to the document, the firm would be considered a part of the cooperative economy (*hezuo jingji zuzhi*); would be taxed at collective rates; and would be eligible for tax deductions, exemptions, and reductions, as well as bank loans according to the rules governing collective enterprises.[79]

---

[77] Wenzhou shi renmin zhengfu, "Guanyu nongcun gufen hezuo qiye ruogan wenti de zanxing guiding (Provisional Regulations on Several Questions regarding Rural Shareholding Cooperative Enterprises)," in *Wenzhou zhi lu congshu: Kaituozhe de guiji – Wenzhou shi difang fagui jianbian* (1989:165). Compare the experimental guidelines for the private variant with those for the government-run variant of shareholding cooperative enterprises in note 67. The latter has no "public accumulation" fund ostensibly because the township government is already the majority shareholder.

[78] Later regulations clarified that in the event of the dissolution of the firm, that portion of the assets accounted for under the "public accumulation" fund could be applied to a variety of uses at the discretion of the owners. However, that portion of the assets could not be liquidated and distributed either to the individual owners or the workers. The approved uses for that portion of the assets included developing in a new enterprise, investing in an existing enterprise, developing agriculture, or establishing an independent welfare and insurance fund for firm employees. Wenzhou shi renmin zhengfu, "Pizhuan 'guanyu gufen hezuo qiye guifanhua ruogan zhengce guiding de baogao' de tongzhi (Notice of the Approval and Transmission of the Report regarding Several Policy Regulations on the Standardization of Shareholding Cooperative Enterprises)," in *Gufen hezuo jingji wenjian huibian* (1991:28–33). Despite these clarifications, some differences of opinion remain. I will return to this point in the subsequent discussion.

[79] As with regular collective enterprises, tax-exempt funds were, in principle, to be used only for enterprise development.

With the promulgation of these experimental regulations, a national debate ensued over whether shareholding cooperatives should be considered a form of private or collective ownership. The determination that these firms were indeed collective in nature was essential for the regulations to serve the purpose of calming the political fears of private investors in light of ongoing attacks on private firms. Therefore, following the promulgation of document #79 in November 1987, Wenzhou officials issued an explanation that sought to distinguish these firms (1) from the agricultural producers' cooperatives of the mid-1950s – because they were not entirely voluntary,[80] (2) from run-of-the-mill collectives – because they had no clear individual owners, and (3) from private partnerships – because they had no public accumulation and therefore did not qualify for a legitimate collective license (Song and Huang n.d.). The first two points were likely directed at private investors, while the third point was likely directed at the policy's detractors from the public camp. The explanation cited as its authority central party document (1983) #1 and the 1983 State Council regulations on cooperatives that followed.[81] These two central documents, Wenzhou officials reasoned, provided three justifications for considering shareholding cooperatives to be a legitimate element of the socialist system. First, the State Council document had emphasized the voluntary nature of any pooling of assets in cooperatives. Second, it had made clear that individuals who "invested capital or other assets in a cooperative venture *retained private ownership* of those assets (*rugu de zijin huo qita caiwu reng shu geren suo you*)." Third, it had stipulated that any firm that had "definite" public accumulation (*gonggong jilei*) was a legitimate part of the socialist cooperative economy.

Nevertheless, the centrally oriented (*tiaotiao*) industrial and commercial bureau (the local arm of the State Administration of Industry and Commerce) continued to regard shareholding cooperatives as private entities and to issue private licenses, while the locally oriented (*kuaikuai*) territorial government insisted on their collective nature.[82] Thus, even at the lowest level, divisions could be found in the state

---

[80] For a discussion of coercion in the establishment of agricultural producers' cooperatives in the 1950s, see Shue (1980:309).

[81] See notes 20 and 21.

[82] Guowuyuan yanjiushi diaochazu, "Zhejiang Wenzhou shixing gufen hezuo de qingkuang (The Situation Surrounding the Implementation of Shareholding Cooperatives in Wenzhou, Zhejiang)," in *Gufen hezuo jingji wenjian huibian* (1991:39–42).

apparatus, highlighting the difficulty of making private property rights secure.[83]

County and township governments in Wenzhou attempted to make registration as a shareholding cooperative as palatable as possible for private investors. This effort often entailed very loose implementation of stipulations regarding public accumulation funds. Many firms failed to clearly delineate funds for "public accumulation" and distributed more than the allowable share of profits among investors. However, the loose implementation of this and other stipulations – such as the required standardization of financial accounting practices[84] – fueled the challenges to the collective status of these firms.[85] In response to these challenges, the Wenzhou municipal government issued a document in November 1989 calling for the "standardization" of shareholding cooperatives.[86] The document reiterated the importance of public accumulation funds in distinguishing collective from private firms and specified that fully 15 percent of after-tax profits must be dedicated to this purpose. In order to appease critics, a distinction was made between those enterprises that had complied fully with the standardization criteria and those that had complied only partially. The former would be registered simply as "collective enterprises (*jiti qiye*)," while the latter would be registered as "collectively owned cooperative enterprises (*jiti suoyouzhi hezuo qiye*)" (Liu 1991).

In reality, there was little difference in the day-to-day management and operation of private firms before and after the transition to the shareholding cooperative form. In most cases there was no separation between ownership and management; owners were usually directly involved in the management of the firm. Decision making was not an

---

[83] Other analysts have also noted the more conservative, central orientation of the industrial and commercial bureau. See, for example, Bruun (1993:112) and A. Liu (1992:706).

[84] These firms resisted maintaining official account books for fear of revealing illegal practices. Many had gotten a foothold in the marketplace by hosting banquets, giving gifts, and employing kickback schemes for clients. While these practices were also common among township- and village-run collectives, collective firms often operated in collusion with the local government and tax office. Private investors were not confident of receiving the same degree of protection.

[85] Wenzhou party secretary Liu Xirong (1991:5) made reference to Li Peng's dissatisfaction with the handling of shareholding cooperatives in a 1991 speech.

[86] Wenzhoushi renmin zhengfu, "Guanyu gufen hezuo qiye guifanhua ruogan wenti de tongzhi (Notice regarding Several Questions on the Standardization of Shareholding Cooperatives)," in *Gufen hezuo jingji wenjian huibian* (1991:22–7).

institutionalized process, and firm accounting practices, while clear internally, seldom met government standards. However, there remained the possibility that private entrepreneurs would not, at some point in the future, be able to liquidate fully 100 percent of the firm's assets, since some portion of the assets belonged, in theory, to the firm as a collective entity.

Local officials in Wenzhou won the first battle for collective status in February 1990 when the Ministry of Agriculture promulgated national regulations on shareholding cooperatives that governed both the private variant found in Wenzhou and the government-run variant found in predominantly collective areas such as Shanghai. The regulations stipulated that these enterprises were socialist in nature and were to be issued collective licenses.[87] A front-page editorial in the official, state-run newspaper *Jingji ribao* underscored the "socialist nature" of shareholding cooperatives, explicitly encompassing both those entities in which private individuals owned the majority of shares and those in which the local government was the majority shareholder.[88] The status of all shareholding cooperatives as legitimate parts of the "socialist collectively owned sector" was affirmed again in a Ministry of Agriculture document in 1997.[89] This status was seen as essential to protecting Wenzhou's private investors from shifts in the political winds.

The Creation of Credible Commitment. The governance of both the private and government-run variants of shareholding cooperatives under one regulatory framework created the conditions for credible commitment. As Weingast (1993:20) argues, constraints on state behavior are credible only when local communities "react in concert against the government in the face of violations."

> Success requires the conjunction of two aspects of citizen behavior: First, that citizens react to violations by punishing the government, and second, that they hold sufficiently similar views about the

---

[87] Nongyebu, "Nongmin gufen hezuo qiye zanxing guiding (Provisional Regulations on Rural Shareholding Cooperatives)," *Guowuyuan gongbao* No. 4 (March 23, 1990), pp. 121–8. Although the Ministry of Agriculture specified higher percentages for public accumulation funds, it inserted a clause allowing localities to adjust this figure based on local conditions.

[88] *Jingji ribao*, March 29, 1996.

[89] Nongyebu, "Guanyu woguo xiangzhen qiye qingkuang he jin hou gaige yu fazhan yijian de baogao (Report regarding the Situation of Township and Village Enterprises and Opinions on Future Reform and Development)." *Renmin ribao*, April 24, 1997.

appropriate bounds on government so that they react in concert" (Ibid).

Local government officials and entrepreneurs in both predominantly private and predominantly collective locales shared a common interest in the security of shareholding cooperatives. Indeed, in the face of threats by the State Administration of Industry and Commerce not to license shareholding cooperatives as collectives, local cadres from predominantly collective areas such as Shanghai also weighed in to defend the collective nature of these firms. For example, a report of the Chuansha County party committee policy research office regarding its own experiment with the government-run variant of shareholding cooperatives argued that shareholding by individuals did not in and of itself constitute private ownership and that shareholding cooperatives were clearly a collective form of ownership.[90]

In theoretical terms, transgressions by central leaders against shareholding cooperatives could elicit reactions, whether in the form of voice or exit, that would "punish" the central government. Voice would punish the central government by revealing dissent among members of an important political support group – local party and government officials. Exit – the withholding or withdrawal of investment in these firms – would punish the central government in terms of revenue and employment forgone. Linking the interests of private investors in Wenzhou to those of local government officials in Shanghai and elsewhere raised the cost to the central government of challenging these interests. While undermining the development of long-term, large-scale investment by private individuals in Wenzhou cost the central government relatively little either politically or economically, the risk of undermining the vested interests of local officials throughout the larger, rural collective economy likely entailed costs high enough to constrain the actions of central leaders.

Overcoming the Limitations of the Political and Market Environments. With the greater perceived legitimacy of the shareholding cooperative form of ownership, it became the dominant form in many townships and counties in Wenzhou (K. Gao 1991). With a legal, collective license,

---

[90] Chuansha xianwei zhengce yanjiushi, "Guanyu Chuansha yinran jixie chang shixing gufen hezuo zhi de diaocha he sikao (An Investigation into and Reflections on the Implementation of the Shareholding Cooperative System in the Chuansha Printing and Dyeing Machinery Factory)," Chuansha diaoyan No. 7 (April 20, 1991), pp. 1–11.

private investors in Yueqing had greater faith in the security and enforceability of their rights under political conditions of the 1980s and early 1990s. One clear indicator of the political legitimacy of shareholding cooperative enterprises was the eligibility of their owners for party membership. While the owners of private enterprises registered as *siying qiye* were barred from party membership, private owners of shareholding cooperatives continued to be eligible.[91]

Moreover, for shareholding cooperatives, status as a legitimate member of the public sector facilitated access to factor and product markets that were characterized by bureaucratic allocation and subject to significant political control. In Yueqing, greater access was particularly evident in certain restricted product markets and in restricted markets for land and capital.

Access to Product Markets for Shareholding Cooperatives. Status as a shareholding cooperative facilitated access to highly regulated product markets. Industrial production in Yueqing was concentrated in electrical components and related products – many of which were governed by production permits (*shengchan xukezheng*) issued by the Ministry of Electronics or, in some cases, by the Ministry of Posts and Telecommunications. To receive a production permit, a firm had to meet certain standards for equipment and technical personnel, and products had to meet certain quality standards. Moreover, applications for production permits had to pass through an initial screening process by the relevant industrial management bureaus at the county and provincial levels before being passed on to the central level.[92] Bureaucratically, shareholding cooperatives (*gufen hezuo qiye*) were better situated than outright private enterprises (*siying qiye*) to receive the technical and political support necessary to obtain production permits. Unlike private enterprises in the form

---

[91] Nongcun jiceng dang zuzhi diaocha yanjiu ketizu, "Guanyu Wenzhou gufen hezuo qiye dang zuzhi jianshe de kaocha baogao (Investigation into the Establishment of Party Organizations in Wenzhou's Shareholding Cooperative Enterprises)," *Zhejiang shehui kexue* No. 4 (1992), p. 38.

[92] These included both the relevant production bureau (*chanpin guikou guanli bumen*) and the local economic commission (*difang jingwei*). Guowuyuan, "Implementing Rules for Production Permits for Industrial Products," in *Nongcun shiyong fagui shouce* (1987:773–6). Since shareholding cooperatives paid a management fee to the enterprise management office, while *siying qiye* paid a management fee to the industrial-commercial bureau, the incentives were also aligned such that the enterprise management office would more actively support shareholding cooperatives.

of *siying qiye*, for which the industrial and commercial bureau served as the supervisory bureau (*zhuguan bumen*), shareholding cooperatives came under the auspices of the enterprise management office that governed all collective enterprises engaged in industry and was part of the larger industrial management structure at the county level and above.[93]

In Yueqing, the first enterprises to receive official production permits in 1987 were shareholding cooperatives.[94] Local officials were instrumental in helping these firms obtain new equipment and attract the needed technical personnel in order to obtain production permits for five types of low-voltage electrical components. Owners of shareholding cooperatives in Hualing Town described how the Hualing enterprise management office worked closely with the Yueqing County rural enterprise bureau and the Yueqing County electronics company in appointing technical specialists to assess and improve the quality of products.[95] The Hualing enterprise management office also guided the applications through the approval process at the county and provincial levels to help ensure that the central ministry issued the permit (Informant 164). By the mid-1990s, county officials had assisted more than 460 shareholding cooperatives to obtain production permits and related certifications. By contrast, no production permits were granted to private enterprises registered as *siying qiye* before 1992. After 1992, some private enterprises also obtained production permits, but they accounted for a small fraction of permit holders in Yueqing.[96]

Access to Factor Inputs for Shareholding Cooperatives. Of the key factor inputs, land was the last in which a functioning market began to develop in Yueqing, and the absence of a commercial real estate market posed a real constraint on enterprise development. The shareholding cooperative framework played an important role in

---

[93] See notes 77 and 86.

[94] "Yueqing shi gufen zhi shiqinian fazhan toushi (A Perspective on Seventeen Years of Development of the Shareholding System in Yueqing)," Mimeo, 1996, pp. 3–4.

[95] Informants 151, 155, 156, 236, 237, 239, and 240. By contrast, a private enterprise owner complained in 1992 about the absence of such support from the town industry office (Informant 149).

[96] Informants 149, 152, 164, and 247. See also Yueqing xian, "Guanyu yinfa guifanhua gufen hezuo qiye ruogan zhengce buchong guiding de tongzhi (Notice on Several Supplemental Policy Regulations for Standardizing Shareholding Cooperatives)," in *Gufen hezuo jingji wenjian huibian* (1991:56–9).

meeting the need for land on the part of privately invested firms.[97] All land transactions of 3 *mu* or more had to be approved at the county level or above; the county established nineteen industrial parks and provided shareholding cooperatives with preferential access to land in these zones, while limiting the access of private enterprises registered as *siying qiye*.[98] Virtually all of the more than 600 enterprises granted approval to build production facilities in county industrial parks between 1993 and 1996 were shareholding cooperatives.[99]

With respect to loan capital, local offices of the Agriculture Bank and the Industrial and Commercial Bank in Yueqing allowed shareholding cooperatives access to bank loans on the same preferential terms as township- and village-run collectives, which set shareholding cooperatives (*gufen hezuo qiye*) apart from private enterprises registered as *siying qiye*, particularly in the years leading up to 1992.[100] Owners of *gufen hezuo qiye* and *siying qiye* interviewed in Yueqing were unanimous in their perception that the former enjoyed better access to fixed-asset and working-capital loans, at lower interest rates, and for longer loan periods.[101]

Nevertheless, the long-term concern for credible commitment appears

---

[97] Ibid. The visual contrast between the three- and four-story factory buildings of shareholding cooperatives in Wenzhou and the cramped informal workshops of private enterprises in Shanghai or even Wenzhou was striking. However, some private enterprises registered as *siying qiye* in Wenzhou were successful in getting access to land for new factory buildings. Those exceptions were much rarer in Shanghai.

[98] As of the mid-1990s, Yueqing County could approve transactions involving up to 3 *mu*, Wenzhou Municipality up to 5 *mu*, and Zhejiang Province up to 10 *mu* (Informant 243).

[99] Four of Yueqing's industrial parks, housing about 120 enterprises, were located in Hualing Town. In Hualing, *gufen hezuo qiye* were also given preference in the allocation of land in the industrial parks. The first private investors to get approval to purchase land and build factory space in the industrial park explicitly linked their status as *gufen hezuo* enterprises to receipt of the necessary bureaucratic approval (Informant 148). The owner of the largest *siying qiye* in the town, an electrical equipment factory, reported being unable to acquire the necessary approval to purchase land in the industrial park until he established a shareholding cooperative and submitted the application under its name (Informant 235).

[100] As noted previously, Deng Xiaoping's "southern tour (*nanxun*)" in February 1992 marked a significant liberalization of policy toward *siying qiye* in Yueqing and elsewhere.

[101] In the early to mid-1990s, however, reforms in the banking system began to make state-run commercial banks more attuned to profitability; as a result, loans were increasingly allocated on the basis of credit worthiness rather than on the basis of politically defined criteria, and this change may have increased the availability of loan capital to *siying qiye*. Nevertheless, *gufen hezuo* status performed a key function in facilitating access to capital for private investors during the first decade and a half of reform.

to play a greater role in a private investor's choice of ownership form than does the consideration of short-term benefits. Indeed, local officials in Wenzhou expressed the willingness to provide access to such benefits as bank loans, land, and tax breaks to private investors registered as private enterprises, but the local officials were often constrained by pressure from higher levels, particularly during campaigns such as the economic rectification campaign of 1988 to 1991. With the end of the rectification campaign, marked by Deng's "southern tour" in February 1992, local officials moved to accommodate private investment in the form of *siying qiye* even more, particularly with access to bank credit, land, and approval for tax reductions (Informant 167). The continued importance of the role of the cooperative shareholding form after 1992 suggests greater concern on the part of private investors with the long-term issues of credible commitment to private property rights (Chen 1994:406).

The Predominance of Shareholding Cooperatives in Yueqing. By the mid-1980s shareholding cooperatives had become the dominant form of ownership in Yueqing. Table 4.1 illustrates the evolution of property rights through changes in industrial output by ownership category. The large increase reported under "village-run collectives" from 1980 to 1984 likely reflects the output of private firms conducting business under the nominal sponsorship of village-run collectives, a practice that became common in Wenzhou around 1980. Between 1980 and 1984, this category accounted for 60 to 70 percent of industrial output. However, the practice of informal affiliation with village-run collectives did not provide adequate security to private investors. Private investment in the form of shareholding cooperatives began to emerge in Wenzhou during the mid-1980s, and experimental regulations were promulgated in 1987. As Table 4.1 shows, private investment in the form of shareholding cooperatives surged beginning in 1985 and increased sharply in 1988. Since 1985, privately invested shareholding cooperatives have accounted for at least 45 percent of industrial output in Yueqing, growing to 65 percent in the late 1980s and early 1990s. The atmosphere for private investors improved somewhat following Deng's "southern tour" in 1992, and the share of investment in industry with outright private ownership (*siying qiye*) increased after that, but privately invested shareholding cooperatives have continued to predominate. Table 4.3 provides additional detail on the ownership breakdown with 1991 data on the

Table 4.3. *Ownership Breakdown of Large-scale Rural Industry,*
Hualing Town, Wenzhou, 1991

	Firms (Units)	(%)	Employment (Thousand)	(%)	Output Value (Million Yuan)	(%)	Tax Receipts (Million Yuan)	(%)
Total	275	100	7.84	100	177.78	100	20.76	100
Township-run	13	5	0.64	8	34.46	19	4.13	20
Village-run	11	4	1.05	13	33.21	19	4.38	21
Cooperative shareholding	220	80	5.56	71	89.58	50	100.43	50
Private	31	11	0.59	8	20.53	12	1.83	9

Source: Informant 144.

number of firms and the level of employment, output value, and tax receipts in Hualing Town. The data demonstrate the importance of shareholding cooperatives for building a strong tax base. Indeed, county officials indicate that the share of cooperative enterprises was even higher in other townships. This point is supported by the data on countywide industrial output in Table 4.1.

Table 4.4 details the growth of shareholding cooperatives with private investment in Yueqing County as a whole from 1985 to 1994. While the number of enterprises grew slowly between 1985 and 1994, the value of fixed-asset investment increased steadily at double-digit rates – even during the years of economic rectification from 1989 through 1991 (Figure 4.1). This growth was supported by increases in bank loans; the value of total loans outstanding increased every year except 1990, as did the average size of loans. With the exception of 1990, at the height of the economic rectification campaign, output growth was strong, and tax receipts increased apace. Although employment levels fluctuated, total employment doubled in the period between 1985 and 1993 to reach nearly 75 thousand employees. Finally, net profits increased every year, and the rate of profit on capital was steady. These figures suggest that shareholding cooperative status benefited private investors at the same time that local officials also reaped benefits in terms of revenue and employment generated.

However, neither the development of the private variant of the shareholding cooperative nor the development of officially recognized private enterprise fully resolved the problem of credible commitment to the rights of private investors. Clearly, there was a trade-off for private

Table 4.4. *Growth of Shareholding Cooperatives, Township Level and Below, Yueqing County, Wenzhou, 1985–94*

Level	1985	1986	1987	1988	1989	1990	1991	1992	1993	1994
Number of firms	2,311	2,224	2,261	2,947	2,959	2,723	2,770	2,972	3,636	4,370
Total employment	36,753	39,439	21,545	64,787	54,248	50,808	52,088	60,127	73,185	n/a
Average employment per firm	16	18	10	22	18	19	19	20	20	n/a
Average wage	835	963	2111	1,235	1,566	1,515	2,050	2,782	2851	n/a
Gross value of output (million yuan)	165.12	196.11	253.91	487.77	575.22	524.99	712.18	1220.80	1970.15	2615.74
Taxes (million yuan)	12.05	14.94	19.81	42.30	50.29	46.37	67.80	89.13	146.01	n/a
Net profits (million yuan)	8.56	8.95	11.72	32.79	34.27	35.36	49.59	73.27	165.33	n/a
Average net profits per firm	3,704	4,024	5,184	11,127	11,582	12,986	17,903	24,653	45,470	n/a
Average bank loans outstanding per firm	1,177	4,195	4,980	8,426	9,605	8,898	17,628	30,784	45,547	45,437
Average value of fixed assets per firm	n/a	9,159	10,398	16,430	23,917	32,956	42,368	71,174	118,328	187,526
Profitability (net profits/total capital)	0.14	0.13	0.14	0.17	0.12	0.12	0.13	0.10	0.13	n/a

Percent increase over previous year	1986	1987	1988	1989	1990	1991	1992	1993	1994
Number of firms	-3.8	1.7	30.3	0.4	-8.0	1.7	7.3	22.3	20.2
Total employment	7.3	-45.4	200.7	-16.3	-6.3	2.5	15.4	21.7	n/a
Average employment per firm	11.5	-46.3	130.7	-16.6	1.8	0.8	7.6	-0.5	n/a
Average wage	15.3	119.1	-41.5	26.8	-3.3	35.3	35.7	2.5	n/a
Gross value of output	18.8	29.5	92.1	17.9	-8.7	35.7	71.4	61.4	n/a
Taxes	24.0	32.6	113.5	18.9	-7.8	46.2	31.5	63.8	n/a
Net profits	4.6	30.9	179.8	4.5	3.2	40.2	47.8	125.6	n/a
Average net profits per firm	8.6	28.8	114.7	4.1	12.1	37.9	37.7	84.4	n/a
Average bank loans outstanding per firm	256.4	18.7	69.2	14.0	-7.4	98.1	74.6	48.0	-0.2
Average value of fixed assets per firm	n/a	13.5	58.0	45.6	37.8	28.6	68.0	66.3	58.5
Profitability (net profits/total capital)	-7.5	4.4	20.1	-25.9	-6.9	15.2	-23.8	28.4	n/a

Source: Yueqing tongji nianjian.

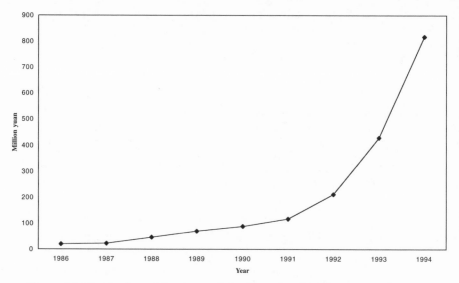

Figure 4.1. Total value of fixed assets of private shareholding cooperatives, Yueqing County, Wenzhou, 1986–94. *Sources*: See Table 4.4.

investors between the undesirable attenuation of property rights entailed in the public accumulation fund and the desirable security of a legitimate collective license. Despite the local regulations clarifying the disposition of the public accumulation fund, the industrial and commercial bureau in the Wenzhou research site asserted that, upon dissolution of the firm, the public accumulation fund, would accrue to the township government, although there were no recent cases in which this had occurred (Informant 157). Officials from the rural enterprise bureau also acknowledged the ongoing debate over this issue (Informant 164). Such contradictions contributed to doubts on the part of some private investors.[102] Indeed, one private investor whose firm was registered as an outright private enterprise (*siying qiye*) explained his choice precisely in these terms. His firm did not become a shareholding cooperative enterprise because the investors were unwilling to give up the right to liquidate and distribute all of the firm's assets (Informant 149). His assessment was that the risk of losing control over that portion of firm assets designated as the public accumulation fund was greater than the risk he faced by maintaining a private as opposed to collective license.

[102] See note 91.

Importantly, this firm was relatively small in scale; it had not made any major investments in factory buildings (it was still operating out of a dwelling structure); and its suppliers and clients were almost exclusively local, suggesting that personal networks may have played a greater role in underpinning property rights and resolving disputes.

CONCLUSION: THE EVOLUTION OF PROPERTY RIGHTS

This chapter demonstrates that concerns on the part of local government officials about revenue – and therefore concerns about investments that develop the tax base – were a major force shaping the evolution of property rights in Wuxi, Songjiang, and Yueqing. As the next chapter demonstrates, property rights, in turn, had a significant influence on the development of extractive institutions in the three research sites.

Property rights evolved in response to revenue imperatives and in light of existing resource constraints. Hence there was a greater incentive to encourage private investment in relatively poor areas where local governments had few collective resources. However, promoting private enterprise posed a challenge for local cadres in Yueqing because of the lack of credible commitment by the Chinese state to the property rights of private investors. Local officials fought to overcome this problem by developing regulations that granted private investors a legitimate, collective license. By linking the minority interests of private investors to the majority interests of local government investors in other locales, the shareholding cooperative form of ownership created the conditions for credible commitment to private investment. The majority of private investors in Yueqing chose to accept, at least nominally, an attenuation of their private property rights in order to attain the greater security associated with this collective form of ownership. The evolution of property rights was also shaped by the nature of the broader political and market environments. In the relatively hostile political and economic climate of the early reform period, shareholding cooperatives provided private investors not only with greater political legitimacy but also with better access to land, capital, and highly regulated product markets.

As of 1994, shareholding cooperatives with private investment accounted for the lion's share (46 percent) of industrial output in Yueqing. Private investment in all forms accounted for fully 90 percent of industrial output in Yueqing, compared to 2.3 percent in Songjiang and 0.9 percent in Wuxi (Figure 4.2). This chapter has provided

173

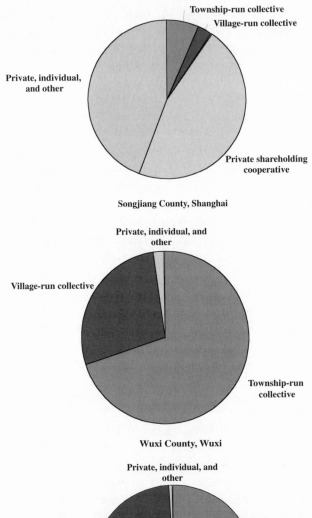

Yueqing County, Wenzhou

Township-run collective

Village-run collective

Private, individual, and other

Private shareholding cooperative

Songjiang County, Shanghai

Private, individual, and other

Village-run collective

Township-run collective

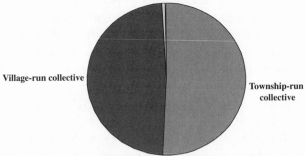

Wuxi County, Wuxi

Private, individual, and other

Village-run collective

Township-run collective

Figure 4.2. Gross value of industrial output by ownership, 1994. *Sources*: See Table 4.1.

theoretical explanations for both the nature of and variation in property rights in rural industry. The next chapter addresses the impact of property rights on the design and effectiveness of state extractive institutions. Chapter 7 takes up the evolution of property rights in the post-1994 period.

5

Stasis and Change in
Extractive Institutions

L OCAL extractive institutions evolved in response to a complex set
of incentives and constraints. While all local governments faced a
common revenue imperative, their particular institutional arrangements
for revenue extraction were shaped by the constraints associated with
the local structure of property rights. Different structures of property
rights were associated with different levels of transaction costs and different distributions of bargaining power within the local community.
Under collective forms of ownership, information about the resources of
firms was held by agents situated within a local hierarchy headed by local
state officials. Collective ownership entailed lower costs of revenue
extraction to the local state, because it provided institutional arrangements that internalized transactions, creating "enforceable norms for
the transmission of information" (Evans 1995:26).[1] By contrast, under
private forms of ownership, information was held within a firm that was
at arm's length from the local state, raising the cost of revenue extraction. As Nicholas Van de Walle (1989:607) points out, information costs
are likely to be higher for state regulation than for state ownership,
because regulation of an industry requires the acquisition of such extensive information about an industry's costs and technologies. Therefore,
as private firms became an increasingly important part of the local
economy, local state officials had an incentive to innovate, developing
new institutional arrangements to cope with those costs. However, the
nature of new institutions for revenue extraction from private sector
firms was influenced not only by the informational costs involved but
also by the bargaining power of private firms within the local economy.
Where private firms carried more weight in the local economy, they could

---

[1] The insight derives from Coase (1937).

be expected to win greater accommodation from the local state. Thus, there was a relationship of mutual dependence between private firms and the local state: the firm was dependent on the state to support the firm's claim on its assets, while the state was dependent on the firm to generate revenue. The resulting institutional arrangements reflected the interests of powerful actors in both the local state and the economy.

Local institutional arrangements also had implications for the ability of the central state to extract revenue from the grass roots. In the course of China's transition from a planned to a market-oriented economy, one of the most fundamental challenges facing state officials at every administrative level has been to create a revenue system that can effectively tap the resources of a rapidly evolving economy. During the first decade and a half of reform, the central government in China presided over one of the fastest-growing economies in the world. The rural industrial sector, encompassing both collective and private ownership forms, was one of the most important contributors to that growth. During the same period, however, total budgetary revenue declined as a percentage of GNP, and the central government faced persistent budget deficits. Thus, the center clearly had difficulty mobilizing revenue into budgetary channels. Although its share of total budgetary revenue fluctuated during this period, in general, the central government could exercise relatively more effective control over revenue once it entered budgetary channels. Therefore, from the perspective of the central state, a key issue was how effective local institutional arrangements were in mobilizing revenue into budgetary channels.

This chapter examines the evolution of local institutions for revenue extraction and explores the implications of local institutional change for achieving the central state goal of improved fiscal control. It demonstrates that state building went hand-in-hand with the development of market institutions such as private enterprise. This discussion focuses on the period framed by the Third Plenum of the Thirteenth Central Committee in September 1988, which launched a thorough-going economic rectification campaign, and the Third Plenum of the Fourteenth Central Committee in November 1993, which initiated major tax and fiscal reforms. The period was punctuated by Deng Xiaoping's southern tour in February 1992, which signaled the beginning of a new cycle of freewheeling economic expansion, but which was quickly followed by the renewal of austerity beginning in 1993. A focus on this period provides a good test of the center's ability to implement tax policy, since one of the goals of the economic rectification campaign was to crack down on violations of policy in the private and collective sectors.[2]

The first section of this chapter provides background on the institutional legacy of the centrally planned economy. The next two sections trace the development of new institutional arrangements to deal with the challenge of taxing the newly emerging private sector and the existence of resistance to institutional change in the collective sector. The following section looks at the impact on local revenue extraction of the larger, provincial regulatory frameworks in which all local governments were embedded. The final section of this chapter uses quantitative data to test the implications of the case study data presented in the preceding sections.

THE INSTITUTIONAL LEGACY OF THE CENTRALLY PLANNED ECONOMY

Despite the predominance of the state in the pre-reform economy, the institutions of tax administration were relatively underdeveloped. In the classic command economy, taxation played only a secondary role in

[2] On economic rectification in the private sector, see Guowuyuan, "Guanyu dali jiaqiang chengxiang geti gongshanghu he siying qiye shuishou zhengguan gongzuo de jueding (Decision regarding Vigorously Strengthening Tax Collection Work in Urban and Rural Individual and Private Enterprises, August 30, 1989)," *Guowuyuan gongbao* No. 16 (September 20, 1989), pp. 626–9. See also "Rural Enterprises and the Private Economy: Rectification," *China News Analysis* No. 1405 (March 1, 1990). On the collective sector, see Guojia shuiwuju, "Guanyu yange jianshui mianshui guanli de guiding (Regulations regarding Strict Management of Tax Reductions and Exemptions, August 18, 1988)," in *Zhili zhengdun shenhua gaige zhengce fagui xuanbian* (1990:155–6); Guowuyuan bangongting, "Zhuanfa guojia shuiwuju guanyu qingli zhengdun he yange kongzhi jianshui mianshui jijian de tongzhi (Notice of Transmission of State Administration of Taxation Opinion regarding Rectification and Control of Tax Reductions and Exemptions, November 30, 1988)," *Guowuyuan gongbao* No. 1 (February 1989), pp. 23–5; Guowuyuan, "Guanyu zhengdun shuishou zhixu jiaqiang shuishou guanli de jueding (Decision regarding Rectifying Tax Procedures and Strengthening Tax Management, December 27, 1988)," in *Zhili jingji huanjing zhengdun jingji zhixu quanmian shenhua gaige dang zhongyang guowuyuan youguan zhengce fagui, diyiji* (1990:364–7); Guojia shuiwuju, "Guanyu qingli zhengdun he yange kongzhi jianshui mianshui de juti shishi yijian (Opinion regarding Specific Measures to Rectify and Strictly Control Tax Reductions and Exemptions, March 9, 1989)," in *Zhili zhengdun shenhua gaige zhengce fagui xuanbian* (1990:168–72); Guowuyuan, "Pizhuan guojia shuiwuju guanyu jinyibu tuijin yifa zhishui jiaqiang shuishou guanli baogao de tongzhi (Notice of Approval and Transmission of State Administration of Taxation Report regarding Further Advancing Administration of Taxes according to Law [and] Strengthening Tax Management)," *Guowuyuan gongbao* No. 43 (January 1992), pp. 1496–1501.

the extraction of revenue and was even less important as a regulatory tool. The pre-reform Chinese state garnered revenue primarily through the combination of state-set prices that discriminated in favor of industry and state monopoly ownership of industrial enterprises.[3] According to World Bank (1990b:8) figures, fully 56 percent of total government revenue came from profit remittances in 1978, whereas by 1988, only ten years later, less than 2 percent derived from that source.[4] Thus, under the pre-reform socialist system in China, the state depended on the profits remitted by state-owned enterprises as its main source of revenue, while it employed plan targets to guide the economy. With the rapid development in the 1980s and 1990s of collective and private enterprises, taxation has become more important both as a source of revenue and as a means of regulating and guiding the economy. Therefore, reform necessitates another phase of state building, requiring the development of a different set of institutions with different capabilities than those put in place with the completion of socialist transformation in the mid-1950s.

Even as of the early 1990s, however, tax bureaus were understaffed by poorly trained personnel, ill-equipped to deal with the explosion in the number of private, collective, and other firms and the emergence of new central laws and procedures to govern them. Indeed, one problem was the sheer complexity of the tax code (Oksenberg and Tong 1991:30). During the period under study, all industrial firms, regardless of their ownership form, were required to pay turnover taxes (including product, value-added, or business taxes); however, the assessment of income tax differed based on the form of ownership.[5] With the promulgation of the central government's private enterprise law and accompanying tax regulations in 1988, private firms

---

[3] Barry Naughton (1992a) notes that before the initiation of reform, collectively owned rural industrial enterprises were prohibited from entering highly profitable sectors.

[4] George Ecklund (1966:23) claims that during the late 1950s, more than 50 percent of the government's budgetary revenue came from profit remittances. David Bachman (1987:127) points out that statistics from the late 1950s are particularly unreliable. He cites figures of 19 percent for 1957 and 46 percent for 1965. Taken together, these sources suggest that profit remittances accounted for close to half of government revenue from the late 1950s to the late 1970s.

[5] See Guowuyuan, "Guanyu fabu chanpin shui deng liuge shuishou tiaoli (caoan) he tiaojie shui zhengshou banfa de tongzhi (zhaiyao)," in *Xiangzhen caizheng shouce* (1987:48–64); and Caizhengbu, "Guanyu banfa chanpin shui deng sige shuishou tiaoli (caoan) shishi xize he ziyuan shui ruogan wenti guiding de tongzhi," in Ibid:64–87. See also *Zhongguo shuiwu daquan* (1990:759ff).

were required to pay a 35 percent tax on income.[6] By contrast, income tax rates for collective enterprises increased incrementally from 10 percent on firms earning less than 1 thousand yuan per year to 55 percent on firms earning more than 200 thousand yuan per year.[7] Collectively owned firms in the rural industrial sector – unlike private enterprises – were also eligible for a range of preferential tax policies.[8] These policies included exemptions or reductions of profit and turnover taxes for periods ranging from one to three years for newly established enterprises, new products, and enterprises in financial difficulty. In addition, collective enterprises established by schools in order to finance school operations and enterprises employing a certain percentage of handicapped workers were completely tax exempt. Finally, collective firms that had incurred bank debt to finance technological upgrading could receive a partial exemption from profit taxes to facilitate the payment of bank loans.[9]

Tax offices at the township level lacked the necessary staff and training to implement such a complicated set of tax policies effectively.[10] The local tax offices investigated for this study governed two or even three townships,[11] and while there were commonly separate tax collection groups for each township, there was often only one team of auditors. In

---

[6] Income was defined as gross receipts minus deductible production costs, sales costs, and indirect taxes. See Guowuyuan, "Zhonghua renmin gongheguo siying qiye suodeshui zanxing tiaoli," in *Zhongguo shuiwu daquan* (1990:808). Prior to 1988, private enterprises had been taxed according to the regulations governing individual household firms (*getihu*). Getihu paid income tax on a ten-level scale, ranging from 7 percent to as high as 60 percent for firms earning over 30,000 yuan. In Shanghai, regulations required that the wealthiest *getihu* pay additional income taxes on a four-level scale with the highest possible tax rate reaching 84 percent for firms earning over 110,000 yuan. See Guowuyuan, "Zhonghua renmin gongheguo chengxiang geti gongshangye hu suodeshui zanxing tiaoli," in Ibid:810; and *Shanghai shi shiyong shuilu shouce* (1991:59).

[7] "Zhonghua renmin gongheguo jiti qiye suodeshui zanxing tiaoli (People's Republic of China Provisional Regulations on Collective Enterprise Income Tax)," in *Xiangzhen caizheng shouce* (1987:120–4); and Caizhengbu, "Guanyu banfa 'Zhonghua renmin gongheguo jiti qiye suodeshui zanxing tiaoli shixing xice' de tongzhi (Detailed Rules and Regulations for Implementation)," in Ibid:124–34.

[8] Tax officials in each research site described the same set of preferential policies (Informants 63, 100, 110, 133, 160, and 194).

[9] Although not a central focus of this discussion, still other types of enterprises found in the rural economy, such as individual household firms and foreign joint ventures, paid taxes according to still different regulations, further contributing to the complexity of the tax code.

[10] Bachman (1987:129–31) emphasizes the same problems during the 1980s.

[11] The townships in this study had populations of 20 to 30 thousand people and were usually home to several hundred industrial enterprises.

the most extreme case, tax collectors in Hualing Town, Wenzhou – where the majority of firms were privately owned – were each responsible for more than one hundred enterprises (Informant 171; He 1987:156). By contrast, in Songyang Town, Shanghai – where only 20 percent of the firms were privately owned – each tax collector was responsible for only about forty enterprises. Nonetheless, even the director of the Songyang tax office considered it impossible for his official staff to effectively monitor and regulate the behavior of all firms – at least at existing staff levels (Informant 100).

At the same time, some of the weaknesses in the implementation of central tax policy stemmed not from staff and training problems but from the fragmented structure of the administrative system at the local level. The director of the township tax office was appointed within the tax hierarchy at the county level, one step up the administrative ladder. This arrangement ostensibly provided the director with some independence from township government leaders. However, the party affairs of the director were governed at the township level where his office was located, and township leaders had to approve his appointment (Informant 194; World Bank 1990b:140). Published descriptions of the duties and functions of tax and finance officials stated that the director of the township-level office was under the leadership (*lingdao*) of the township executive and party secretary, while he received only professional guidance (*yewu zhidao*) from higher level tax and finance organs.[12] Moreover, with the exception of the director,[13] those staffing local tax offices were usually members of the local community; in that context, township leaders could exercise influence over the careers and opportunities of their spouses and children. Thus, local tax officials had dual loyalties – to the local community and to the administrative hierarchy of which they were a part. The conflict of interest was particularly acute with respect to the taxation of collective firms, since community leaders had a direct claim on collective enterprise profits. The most direct supervision by higher levels occurred during the annual tax audit in the fourth quarter

[12] He, Wei, and Lin (1991:85). The members of the tax bureau staff were under the combined leadership of the county- and township-level tax bureaus and received only guidance from township leaders (Ibid:93). Leadership relations confer the authority to issue binding orders, whereas professional relations entail the issuance of guidelines and nonbinding directives (Lieberthal and Oksenberg 1988:148–9).

[13] For example, the director of the tax office responsible for Songyang and Daqiao towns in Songjiang County had recently been transferred there from another township (Informant 100).

of the year.[14] Tax organs at each level organized groups of cadres to perform audits, and the State Council and provincial governments sent out work teams to conduct audits at lower levels. According to central guidelines, audits were to take place in at least 30 percent of the units in each jurisdiction. Included in the scope of the audit were state, collective, private, and individual household firms. However, the rigor of audits conducted by provincial work teams varied. Subsequent sections of this chapter examine the stark variations in provincial regulatory environments and demonstrate how local officials approached the taxation of public and private firms very differently.

THE EVOLUTION OF LOCAL INSTITUTIONS FOR REVENUE EXTRACTION FROM THE NEWLY EMERGING PRIVATE SECTOR

Where private enterprises emerged as an important part of the local economy, local officials had greater incentives to adopt innovative revenue collection mechanisms, because these enterprises enjoyed a higher degree of operational autonomy from the local state and the transaction costs (the costs of acquiring information, measuring resources, monitoring behavior, and enforcing performance) associated with revenue extraction were higher. This section examines the development of new institutional arrangements in Hualing and Songyang – the two sites in Wenzhou and Shanghai, respectively, where private enterprises had become a viable part of the local industrial economy. While both sets of institutional arrangements were innovative attempts to cope with the difficulties of taxing private firms, they differed in the degree to which they accommodated the interests of private capital. The differences were consistent with the bargaining power of private entrepreneurs as reflected in the size of their contribution to the tax base.[15] In neither case were the particular innovations adopted entirely new, however; rather, they were adaptations of various practices used to tax

---

[14] Annual audits were implemented every year beginning in 1985. See, for example, Guowuyuan, "Guanyu kaizhan yijiujiuling nian shuishou caiwu da jiancha de tongzhi," *Guowuyuan gongbao* No. 16 (August 28, 1990), pp. 582–5.

[15] The implicit bargaining power that encourages local officials to take the interests of private firms into account does not depend on organized bargaining activity on the part of private entrepreneurs as long as most private firms are likely to respond to official actions in similar ways (by reducing investment, for example). Moreover, this kind of bargaining power is likely to become even more effective as capital mobility increases. If private entrepreneurs can easily move their businesses to other locales, they then have the ability to "shop around" for the most favorable regulatory environment.

private firms before the private sector was virtually eliminated under communist rule in the 1950s. These actions reflected a boundedly rational approach to the challenges of taxing the private sector (March 1978; Simon 1957). Looking back to past practices provided "cognitive short-cuts" to identifying possible solutions (Pierson 1993:611). Furthermore, borrowing from historical precedent provided solutions that accorded with the limited bureaucratic capacity of the local state. Nevertheless, such innovations contributed to the central state's extractive capacity by bringing more revenue into budgetary channels.

Information costs were a major obstacle to effective taxation of private firms, especially since private entrepreneurs had an incentive to minimize their tax burden by concealing their taxable resources. Rough estimates by the State Council Development Research Center and the State Administration of Taxation suggest that, nationally, about 70 percent of privately owned firms succeeded in evading taxes, resulting in the loss of about 50 percent of the taxes owed.[16] The first challenge to local officials addressing this problem entailed identifying taxpayers. In some cases unlicensed firms operated completely outside the regulatory system.[17] Even more difficult was accurately assessing the tax burden. While private firms were required to maintain account books, retain relevant evidence of income and expenditures, and submit account forms to the local tax office,[18] these records were often incomplete, inaccurate, or missing altogether. Cash and barter transactions left no paper trail, and mismanagement of receipts made it difficult to account for even aboveboard sales. Few private enterprises employed qualified, full-time accountants, and accounting forms commonly reflected deliberately false reporting or simply crude guesses.

The information requirements for turnover and income taxes differed. Accurate information regarding output or sales provided a sufficient

---

[16] See Guowuyuan fazhan yanjiu zhongxin, "Woguo geti siying jingji diaocha baogao (Report on the Survey of China's Individual and Private Economy)," *Jingji gongzuozhe xuexi ziliao* No. 58 (1989), reprinted in *Fuyin baokan ziliao – Jingji tizhi gaige* No. 3 (1990), pp. 60–79. See also *Zhongguo de siying jingji* (1989); and Rong (1989).

[17] In particular, small start-up enterprises, often operating out of private homes, could go undetected. Such firms often began by doing simple processing for larger firms. The problem was exacerbated by the lack of coordination between the tax office and the industrial-commercial bureau, which was responsible for licensing firms.

[18] Regulations promulgated in 1989 restated the 1988 requirement that private enterprises establish and maintain account books for the purpose of taxation as a condition of licensing. See "Decision regarding Vigorously Strengthening Tax Collection Work" cited in note 2.

basis for the assessment of turnover taxes, but the assessment of income taxes required additional, detailed information regarding a firm's costs. Without complete and accurate records, the assessment of a firm's total sales lacked any objective basis, making it difficult for the tax bureau to levy turnover taxes. The cost accounting necessary to assess income taxes presented even greater difficulties, such as monitoring the prices at which inputs were acquired and identifying the actual number of workers employed by a firm. Wage costs, for example, were difficult to monitor because the demand for labor was volatile and because labor turnover was high. A report by the tax bureau in Songjiang County, Shanghai, described the difficulties as follows:

> In one type of enterprise those participating in the private enterprise are the husband and wife and sons and daughters of the family. These people work [in the enterprise] at busy times and at idle times work in agriculture. Or, during the daytime they work in agriculture or do housework and during the nighttime do a few hours of work [in the enterprise]. If everyone is counted as a [full-time] employee, then every enterprise will be a loss-maker. In a second type, workers hired by a private enterprise come from poor areas. Take, for example, the thirty workers at the metal finishing factory (*paoguang chang*). They all come from the owner's ancestral home in Subei, and after spring begins they come to work. At the end of the year they go back to Subei. In between people are always coming and going – there is tremendous turnover. In a third type, although those hired by a private enterprise may be relatively stable, nevertheless the owner uses underhanded methods to report the number of workers – actually having fewer but reporting more. This is relatively hard to find out about.[19]

Similarly, tax officials reported difficulty in monitoring the costs of raw materials: "The power over supply and marketing for private enterprises is all in the hands of the owners. This way it is very difficult to correctly figure the costs of raw materials. Add to that chaotic management and other problems."[20] Thus, the report makes an implicit contrast with col-

---

[19] Songjiang xian shuiwuju jizheng guanligu, "Guanyu Songjiang xian S. zhen jianli siying qiye lianhu jizhang zhan de qingkuang huibao (Report on the Situation surrounding the Establishment of the Private Enterprise Joint Accounting Station in S. Town, Songjiang County)," Mimeo, March 25, 1991.

[20] Ibid.

lective enterprises, in which informational constraints were minor since they were part of a larger collective organizational framework controlled by the township. Informational constraints were magnified by the shortage of well-trained personnel to perform audits (Yuan 1987:185). As the World Bank (1990b:113) points out in its study of revenue mobilization in China, "the system is complicated and difficult to administer; it requires a highly qualified staff for efficient administration, and books of account for smaller firms may be inadequate to the task of determining sales and profits tax activity. This problem will grow as smaller collectives and private businesses become more important."

The ongoing need for revenue on the part of local state officials meant that it was desirable to have an objective basis for extraction. Subjective guesses at the likely revenue potential of the private sector risked either undertaxing, and therefore unnecessarily reducing the resources available to state officials, or overtaxing, and driving an important part of the tax base out of business. Ole Bruun's (1993) study of private business in Chengdu suggests that these problems were commonplace. "The utterly impenetrable principles for tax collection, if principled at all, were a constant source of conflict. There were no consistent methods for assessing turnover and computing taxes, and the tax bureau's statement that it was without the 'scientific means' to determine turnover in many cases appeared to be an excuse for maintaining serious discrimination" (Bruun 1993:122). Particularly where local government was heavily dependent upon a private tax base, it was important for tax officials to have some objective basis for tax assessment, since it directly affected the buoyancy of tax collection efforts.[21]

Institutional Arrangements in Wenzhou

The Daizheng Method. The practice of "*daizhengshui*" (loosely translated as "simultaneous collection of taxes") implemented in Wenzhou represented an accommodation between the local state and private capital and reflected the strength of the private sector, which accounted for the majority of firms in the local economy. On the one hand, it provided an objective basis for tax assessment. On the other hand, by keeping accounting requirements simple, it reduced the

---

[21] Buoyancy refers to the tax yield relative to changes in the tax base. A loss of buoyancy occurs when increases in the tax base are not reflected in tax yields. See World Bank (1990b).

Table 5.1. *Sample Composition of the "Simultaneous Taxation"*
Rate for Private Enterprises in the Electronics Industry,
Hualing Town, Wenzhou

Tax	Rate (Percentage)
Value-added tax	4
Income tax	3.5
Urban maintenance and construction tax	0.2
Energy and transportation tax	0.5
Rural education fee	0.08
Zhejiang provincial grain fee	0.6
Total	8.88

Source: Informant 160.

informational costs associated with revenue extraction to both the local state and private firms, and it afforded private firms greater predictability than did the more subjective methods of revenue extraction employed toward private firms elsewhere.[22]

Under the *daizhengshui* system, all taxes and official fees were calculated together as a simple percentage of the value of each sale. The single rate (usually about 9 to 10 percent) encompassed the turnover tax and additional increments to cover income taxes and other taxes and fees, as shown in Table 5.1.[23] The increment that substituted for the separate assessment of income tax was set by the municipal government based on investigations of the profit rates of a sample of firms in each major industrial subsector (He 1987:184; Informant 162). The government audited the firms in the sample to determine the actual rate of profit. It then used that information to determine the *daizheng* rate at which sales would be taxed, as an administrative shortcut to actually calculating the income tax on gross profits for all firms. (In Table 5.1, that rate for the electronics industry is 3.5 percent.)[24]

[22] Reportedly, most privately owned industrial firms in Hualing Town (including six of the seven privately owned firms investigated in this study for which detailed information on collection methods was provided) were taxed using this method in the early 1990s.

[23] While managers interviewed described the system in the same basic terms, they differed in their accounts of the range of taxes and fees included in the single rate. For example, only a few managers described mandatory contributions to the workers' pension fund managed by the local government as included (Informants 149 and 150).

[24] Informant 160. In Hualing, the *daizheng* rate for private enterprises was set slightly higher than the rate on shareholding cooperatives.

The tax bureau monitored enterprise sales volume (or gross income) by controlling the issuance of official sales receipts. Most privately owned enterprises did not have the authority to write receipts for their sales (Informant 160). Rather, the tax bureau performed this function and deducted the *daizheng* tax based on the record provided by the receipts.[25] Tax officials enforced the *daizheng* policy by policing the transport of goods. The municipal tax bureau established inspection stations at thirty-eight major transportation nodes in the Wenzhou area, and all goods transiting these points were to be accompanied by receipts (He 1987:155; Yuan 1987; Informant 162).

Local government officials defended the practice of *daizhengshui*, even as they acknowledged that it represented an accommodation to the interests of private capital. The Wenzhou municipal system reform commission reported conducting an experiment that compared the standard implementation of the income tax with the *daizheng* method in a sample of private firms. According to a representative of the commission, the firms that paid income tax on the basis of enterprise accounts succeeded in inflating their costs to such a degree that firms paying the 3.5 percent *daizheng* income tax produced more revenue for the local government (Informant 171). Similarly, an official of the Wenzhou municipal industrial-commercial bureau claimed, "Wenzhou really has the highest tax rate in Zhejiang, even though it doesn't meet [the letter of the] tax regulations." He added, "*Daizheng* is [nevertheless] a very lax policy, but state enterprises don't pay what they're supposed to either" (Informant 168).

Clearly, the *daizheng* method benefited the enterprise. Where private entrepreneurs had a choice, they chose to continue using the practice of *daizhengshui*, since it reduced administrative costs to the firm. Privately owned firms in Hualing Town did not submit detailed accounting forms to the tax bureau (Informant 162). As an official of the Hualing tax and finance bureau noted, "it doesn't matter whether costs are accounted for correctly" (Informant 160). *Daizhengshui* also afforded predictability. One entrepreneur explained his choice to continue using *daizhengshui* in terms of the predictability offered by simply estimating the tax burden on the basis of a fixed percentage of sales (Informant 148). In addition,

---

[25] Certain firms in Hualing had been granted permission by the tax bureau to write their own receipts. These were firms with stable clients among urban state-owned firms – clients that generally required receipts in order to account for their own costs. Nevertheless, the record of receipts still provided the basis for collection of the *daizheng* tax (Informants 148 and 160).

the favorable effective tax rates paid by privately owned enterprises using *daizhengshui* allowed the tax base to develop quickly – what one industrial-commercial bureau official referred to as "filling the pond to raise fish (*fangshui yangyu*)" (Informant 168). Indeed, although local regulations on privately held shareholding cooperatives (passed in 1990 during the national economic rectification campaign) required that these firms adopt standardized accounting practices and pay income tax according to standard methods, by 1992 – when implementation of tax policy entered a period of relative relaxation – local officials in Wenzhou allowed private shareholding cooperatives to continue paying according to the *daizheng* method.[26] Moreover, although new policies making private enterprises eligible for certain tax reductions and exemptions were to have been premised on adopting standard accounting practices, the local tax bureau implemented these preferential policies by simply reducing the *daizheng* rate.[27] Finally, while inflating costs as an avenue of tax evasion was closed, other avenues remained open. To the extent that a firm could avoid detection at local inspection stations, it was possible to evade taxation. For example, one entrepreneur described transporting goods via back roads or waterways to avoid the inspection stations surrounding Wenzhou (Informant 12). The effectiveness of the *daizheng* method depended on the strength and quality of receipt management by the tax bureau.

The Precursors of Daizhengshui. The informational constraints and administrative handicaps that necessitated the practice of *daizhengshui* are not new, and the transitional measures adopted by the local government in Wenzhou to compensate for its underdeveloped capacity to tax the booming private sector paralleled certain historical practices. During the early 1950s, local tax bureaus in some locales used methods similar to those just described to overcome the difficulties of taxing private firms. The primary focus was on determining gross income and generating derivative estimates of taxable profits. Where accounts

---

[26] Local tax officials were able to make this choice since the conclusion of the rectification campaign reduced the pressure to implement standardization (Informant 162). Nevertheless, the regulations can be found in Wenzhou shi renmin zhengfu, "Pizhuan 'guanyu gufen hezuo qiye guifanhua ruogan zhengce guiding de baogao' de tongzhi (Notice of Approval and Transmission of Report regarding Several Policy Regulations on the Standardization of Cooperative Stock Enterprises)," in *Gufen hezuo jingji wenjian huibian* (1991:28–33).

[27] This was the practice in the case of Informant 150.

were unavailable, incomplete, or unreliable, local officials employed various means to identify gross income; most practices fell under the rubric of "democratic appraisal (*minzhu pingyi*)" (Diao 1969:173; Ecklund 1966:36–60; Jin, Liu, and Wang 1991:511; *Wuhan shi zhi: shuiwu zhi* 1992:200). A practice that apparently originated in the "liberated areas" controlled by the Chinese Communist Party before 1949, "democratic appraisal" entailed forming a group of officials and business owners in a given sector; the function of the group was to determine the gross income of the firms concerned. The group would select a number of representative firms for a more intensive investigation in order to determine a standard net profit rate (*biaozhun chunyilu*) (*Wuhan shi zhi: shuiwu zhi* 1992:200). The net profit rate would be applied to the gross income of firms in that sector, and the appropriate profit tax rate would be applied to the resulting profit estimate. In some cases the assessment would be applied to a group of firms, and the specific distribution of the tax burden would be determined within the group itself.[28]

The approach taken in Wenzhou in the 1990s resembled the practice from the early 1950s with two distinctions: First, official control over receipts and the establishment of inspection stations at transportation nodes replaced "democratic appraisal" groups for determining gross income levels. Second, and relatedly, tax officials at the township level applied the *daizheng* rate (determined by the municipal government based on sample studies) directly to individual firms and not to groups of firms. Tax officials in Wenzhou began to use the *daizheng* method for taxing individual household firms (*getihu*) in 1978. Given the early strength of the private sector in Wenzhou, there was a natural continuation of the practices used to tax individual household firms as they grew and acquired new licenses as private enterprises – despite the official requirement that private enterprises were to maintain complete accounts and pay taxes on that basis, as specified in the 1988 regulations that legalized the private sector.

Institutional Arrangements in Shanghai

The Private Enterprise Joint Accounting Station. Local officials in Songyang Town, Shanghai took a more adversarial approach to taxing

---

[28] Similar practices had been employed under the Kuomintang (KMT) regime (Lieberthal 1980).

the private sector. Although private firms constituted a relatively small part of the predominantly collective economy, some officials regarded them as a potential threat to the collective sector, which constituted the main source of revenue for the town.[29] Their approach centered on the establishment of a private enterprise joint accounting station (*siying qiye lianhu jizhang zhan*), which was responsible for maintaining the accounts of all private firms in Songyang. In addition, tax and industrial-commercial bureau officials integrated the functions of the accounting station into the normal monitoring and enforcement functions of the corporatist private entrepreneurs' association (*siying qiyejia xiehui*) in a two-pronged approach to overcoming the difficulties of governing the private sector.

The central Chinese state tried to compensate for the lack of bureaucratic control over the private sector by creating corporatist controls over private entrepreneurs through compulsory membership in the individual and private entrepreneurs' associations.[30] Entrepreneurs automatically became members as part of the licensing process. During the first decade of reform private entrepreneurs joined *getihu* in a single organization, the individual entrepreneurs' association (*geti laodongzhe xiehui*), which was mandated by the State Council in 1981.[31] Private entrepreneurs were later organized into a separate organization after the formal legalization of the private sector in 1988. In Songyang Town, for example, a separate branch of the private entrepreneurs' association was established in 1991 (Informant 89). The association was a hierarchically structured national organization with branches reaching down to the township level. At each level, branches were created and supervised by the local tax and industrial-commercial bureaus – the two organs with direct responsibility for oversight of the private sector. While

---

[29] An article published in the Chinese journal *Finance* is indicative of this attitude. The article states that the development of private industry represents an attack on collective industry at the township and village level. Therefore it suggests as a matter of policy that tax officials should guarantee that tax receipts from private firms increase more rapidly than those from collective firms. Moreover, it states that the strict taxation of private firms should become the central focus of their work. "Zhengque chuli sange guanxi shixian caizheng chixu zengshou (Correctly Handle the Three Relationships and Realize Continued Fiscal Increases)," *Caizheng* No. 6 (1989), pp. 21–3.

[30] As this paragraph illustrates, the characteristics of the association are consistent with Philippe Schmitter's (1979:21) definition of state corporatist structures.

[31] Guowuyuan, "Guanyu chengzhen feinongye geti jingji ruogan zhengcexing guiding (Policy Regulations on the Nonagricultural Individual Economy,)" in *Nongcun shiyong fagui shouce* (1987:731).

each branch elected leaders from among its own members, the nominees were chosen directly by the supervisory agencies, and elected leaders received monetary compensation from the state in exchange for their services.

The association, in some cases, performed limited advocacy functions for private entrepreneurs,[32] but in general, it served as an arm of the local tax and industrial-commercial bureaus. The State Council described the association's mandate as "transmitting and organizing the study of party and government policies and enforcing and encouraging the conscientious implementation of state policies, laws, and decrees. . . ."[33] Indeed, in a 1989 decision on strengthening tax collection in the private sector, the State Council explicitly called upon the individual and private entrepreneurs' associations to assist local governments in combating tax evasion.[34] Local descriptions of the association's mandate reflected the same concerns. One description of the association's functions included an explicit statement about assisting the government with fees and tax collection as well as more general statements about furthering professional morals and "civilized business practices" (Informants 89, 93, and 100). However, in Songyang the association was little more than a transmission belt: officials from the tax and industrial-commercial bureaus would explain specific policies and regulations and exhort private entrepreneurs to comply.[35] Thus, in practice, the corporatist structure was comparatively weak, both as a means of control and as a source of information.

Therefore, local officials in Songyang established the private enterprise accounting station specifically to acquire the financial accounting

---

[32] For example, the president of the Songyang private entrepreneurs' association described the case of one private enterprise owner who was unable to collect on several accounts receivable owed by state and collective firms. As a result, he was unable to pay his tax bill on time. The association intervened with the tax bureau and arranged for the private enterprise to pay the tax in installments and to be exempted from part of the late fee.

[33] At the time, the private entrepreneurs' association was subsumed by the individual entrepreneurs' association. Guowuyuan, "Guanyu chengzhen feinongye geti jingji ruogan zhengcexing guiding (Policy Regulations on the Nonagricultural Individual Economy)," in *Nongcun shiyong fagui shouce* (1987:731).

[34] See "Decision regarding Vigorously Strengthening Tax Collection Work," cited in note 2.

[35] Songjiang xian caizheng shuiwuju, "Ruhe jiaqiang qiye de shuishou zhengguan? S. shuiwuzu de zuofa shi: jianli siying qiye lianhu jizhang zhan (How to Strengthen Enterprise Tax Collection? S. Tax Group's Method Is: Establish the Private Enterprise Joint Accounting Station)," *Songjiang caishui jianbao* (Songjiang public finance and tax bulletin) No. 4 (March 18, 1991).

information necessary to monitor and tax private firms more effectively. The accounting station was established in January 1990 at the initiative of the Songyang tax and industrial-commercial bureaus (Informants 92 and 93).[36] By 1992, the station had a staff of four full-time accountants and bore responsibility for the accounts of all thirty-four private industrial enterprises in the town. Unlike private enterprises in Wenzhou, private firms in Songyang issued their own receipts, and the accountants made regular inspections of each firm's production and operations to check for consistency between operations and financial accounts and filed reports with the tax bureau. For instance, accountants would monitor the number of workers employed in private enterprises by checking the identity cards of employees against the wage roll, since wage roll padding was a common way to inflate costs (Informant 89). As outsiders, the accountants had difficulty detecting all but the most egregious errors, but they compensated by developing norms for cost accounting in each industrial sector. For example, they developed an index linking wages and output in various industries as a further means of gauging the accuracy of the wage bills reported by private firms.[37] Tax officials in Songyang innovated aggressively to check wage roll padding and other evasive practices in private firms, while the same practices in collective firms went unchecked, as demonstrated in subsequent sections.

[36] Indeed, the county tax bureau did not learn of the initiative until later. According to a tax bureau report, ". . . we discovered that the fifteen private enterprises [as of 1990] in Songyang Town had a joint accounting station. From January 1990, fifteen private enterprises, with the *help* of the Songyang/Daqiao tax bureau deputy director and an official of the Songyang tax group, together appointed three accountants to work in a centralized way and established the joint accounting station. Now it has already expanded to twenty-four private enterprises [as of 1991] and four accountants. After we discovered this situation, with the support of the bureau's leadership, we investigated to see whether the joint accounting station really strengthened private enterprise management." (The findings of the county's investigation are discussed in subsequent paragraphs in the text.) Despite the euphemistic use of the term "help," it is clear from interviews and other sources that the joint accounting station was established by the Songyang tax group and not by the entrepreneurs themselves. See Songjiang xian shuiwuju jizheng guanligu, "Report on Private Enterprise Joint Accounting Station"; and "How to Strengthen Enterprise Tax Collection," cited in note 35.

[37] Somewhat more arbitrarily, local officials decided that any private enterprise involved in processing industries producing annual output value below 50 thousand yuan would only be granted an individual household (*getihu*) license (to be taxed at higher rates), because, the logic went, 50 thousand yuan in output orders could not have provided enough work for the number of workers (a minimum of eight) required for status as a private enterprise – and, therefore, the firm had to have inflated its wage bill.

Local officials employed the information obtained through the accounting station in conjunction with meetings of the private entrepreneurs' association in order to enforce compliance with tax and other policies. Private enterprise owners in Songyang attended a compulsory meeting on the fifth day of every month at which tax officials reported on each firm's financial performance and assessed each firm's tax liability. Firm owners were then required to make their tax payments at the bank before the seventh of each month. At the same time, industrial-commercial bureau officials used the meetings to collect industrial-commercial fees as well as to mobilize ostensibly voluntary contributions to various local causes such as schools, retirement homes, and athletic events.[38]

Private entrepreneurs had little bargaining power, reflecting their minor position in the local economy, and they were made to bear the costs of monitoring and enforcement. With the establishment of the accounting station, every private firm in Songyang was assessed an additional mandatory fee of 40 yuan per month by the private entrepreneurs' association. The tax bureau used these funds to pay the salaries and overhead of the four accountants. Moreover, the simple fact that the accounting station was intended to tax private firms according to the letter of the rather Byzantine tax code raised the cost of doing business.

The argument presented here operates at the institutional level of analysis. While institutions pattern behavior in consistent ways, their impact is not deterministic. Thus, although this argument focuses on formal institutional change, it does not preclude a role for individual accommodations between local state officials and private entrepreneurs. As one private entrepreneur put it, those who have a personal relationship with a tax bureau official can influence what are considered costs and what are considered profits.[39]

The Precursors of the Songyang Approach. The Songyang approach resembled efforts to assess and extract the wealth of private firms

---

[38] In addition, the monthly association aided in overcoming interbureau communication problems. In the past, according to tax bureau reports, the industrial-commercial bureau had not shared information with the tax bureau, and as a result, a number of licensed firms that had not registered with the tax bureau had gone undetected. See "How to Strengthen Enterprise Tax Collection," cited in note 35.

[39] Informant 5. He gave the example of deducting the purchase of a car (not a legitimate deduction according to the tax regulations), which would substantially reduce a firm's tax liability.

documented for both the pre-Communist period and the early years of the People's Republic before the elimination of the private sector. In the 1980s and 1990s, as in earlier periods, local officials, constrained by the limited bureaucratic capacity of the state, relied on business associations in taxing and regulating the private sector.

Susan Mann, following Max Weber, uses the term liturgical governance to describe the Qing (and later the Republican) government's reliance on merchant organizations to collect revenue and to perform other services on behalf of the state (Mann 1987). Merchant organizations were "held responsible for adjudicating disputes, stabilizing prices, limiting competition, and setting standards for fair trade. Most important, they were often given the power to assess and remit commercial taxes" (Ibid:23–4). Specifically, liturgical organizations such as guilds or other merchant groups bore collective responsibility for the collection of commercial taxes in the form of quotas negotiated with local government officials. Mann makes clear that reliance on liturgical structures reflected "above all, the limited bureaucratic capabilities of the state" at the same time that fiscal demands on the state were increasing (Ibid:154ff). The Qing state lacked both the personnel and the detailed information on commercial activity necessary to employ direct, bureaucratic methods of tax collection. For many of the same reasons, guilds or chambers of commerce continued to perform tax collection functions – at least in some areas – during the Republican era.[40] Similarly, Shaoguang Wang's (1993:10) analysis of the extractive capacity of the Chinese state in the 1950s reveals that the PRC government also relied on guilds to collect taxes in Wuhan during the first years of PRC rule.[41]

In analyzing the historical process of state building in China, Mann identifies three modes of taxation that have appeared in roughly chronological order: (1) liturgical tax management, (2) contract tax farming, and (3) bureaucratic tax collection. As the state came to play an increasingly direct, bureaucratic role in revenue extraction, the relationship between the state and business associations evolved.[42] Wang (1993) describes the transition in Wuhan from the assignment of tax quotas to guilds, to the assessment of taxes on a firm-by-firm basis. The Wuhan municipal gov-

---

[40] In other areas the emergence of professional tax farmers "signaled the absence, or the demise, of liturgical taxing strategies" (Mann 1987:187).

[41] For related practices under the KMT, see Lieberthal (1980).

[42] It is only in the more recent era that the state itself has taken on the responsibility of directly assessing and collecting the taxable wealth of the private business community (Mann 1987:3).

ernment relied on guild organizations in making the transition. For local officials to tax firms directly, the local officials required basic information about each firm's sales and profits – information that, as Mann notes, local officials in the Qing had been unable to tap (Mann 1987:159). Therefore, in 1950, the Wuhan industrial-commercial department and the Wuhan tax department called upon the city's association of industry and commerce (*gongshanglian*) – an umbrella organization bringing together various guilds and merchant organizations from across the city – to join in a campaign to standardize accounting practices. The goal of the campaign was to produce uniform and reliable information as a basis for taxation (Wang 1993:17; *Wuhan shi zhi: shuiwu zhi* 1992:201).

Some parallels may be drawn between the current private entrepreneurs' association and the merchant organizations of the Qing, Republican, and early Communist periods. The organizations have performed similar functions in terms of tax collection and general oversight, and their roles have reflected attempts to overcome constraints – particularly informational constraints – on the ability of the state to tax and regulate the private sector. Similarly, the role of the private enterprise accounting station (in conjunction with the private entrepreneurs' association in Songyang) in establishing standardized accounting systems has parallels to the role played by the association of industry and commerce in Wuhan, as described by Wang. Indeed, the Songjiang County tax bureau sought to extend the institutional arrangements developed in Songyang to other townships following the promulgation by the Shanghai municipal government of regulations requiring that all private firms were to use standard accounting practices by January 1, 1991.[43]

Although the form and functions of the present-day private entrepreneurs' association may have distant roots in a tradition of liturgical governance, two distinctions must be made. First, the differing degrees of autonomy enjoyed by business associations in different historical periods suggest somewhat different models of state–society relations. While the traditional liturgies on which the Qing state depended were largely autonomous from the state *at the local level*, even local branches of the current private entrepreneurs' association are initiated and effectively co-opted by the state.[44] Thus, the definition of a traditional liturgy as a

---

[43] "Establishment of the Private Enterprise Joint Accounting Station," cited in note 19.

[44] Although in 1902 the Qing government transformed many guilds and trade associations into more modern chambers of commerce, granting them legal charters and incorporating them into a national hierarchy, they appear to have maintained significant autonomy at the local level. See Mann (1987:152ff); and Rowe (1984).

societal organ performing governance functions on behalf of the state no longer strictly applies. Second, liturgical governance, as described by Mann, was characterized by collective responsibility, whereas the function of the present-day association is to facilitate the direct taxation of individual firms bearing individual responsibility. Leaders of the private entrepreneurs' association did appear concerned with establishing a reputation for conscientious tax payment as indicated by the association's intervention in cases in which the delinquent payments to private enterprises by state and collective firms impinged on the ability of private firms to make timely tax payments.[45] However, the direct incentives for mutual enforcement created by collective responsibility no longer exist. Nevertheless, as in the case of the *daizheng* approach taken in Wenzhou, the innovative approach to reducing the transaction costs of taxing private firms taken in Songyang also had historical precedents.[46]

Summary

Measurement, monitoring, and enforcement were among the biggest obstacles to effective taxation of the private sector. The task facing the Chinese government, like most developing country governments, is, as Kiren Aziz Chaudhry (1993:261) emphasizes, "nothing less than a thorough reform of the public and private sectors. This entail[s] forging national regulatory, legal, and extractive institutions and their ancillary information gathering and enforcement agencies and creating legal, accounting, and disclosure requirement[s] for private business elites who [have] yet to experience the burdens of regulations." Local officials in both Wenzhou and Shanghai developed new institutional arrangements to cope with transaction costs, but they did so in different ways, reflecting the different distributions of bargaining power within the two communities.

---

[45] See note 32.
[46] Theories of bounded rationality suggest that making reference to historical precedent is one way in which policy makers seek solutions to current problems. However, the evidence presented here provides no explicit statement that local officials in Wenzhou and Songyang knew about past practices or drew on them in any conscious way, although it is likely that local officials were aware of earlier practices. Examining the empirical basis for the parallel between contemporary practices and historical antecedents is a task for future research.

RESISTANCE TO INSTITUTIONAL CHANGE IN
THE COLLECTIVE SECTOR

With respect to township- and village-run collectives in Wuxi and Shanghai, local officials had a vested interest in maintaining the status quo that allowed them to manipulate revenue extraction to retain as much revenue as possible at the local level. The close integration of township- and village-run enterprises into the existing collective organizational structure inherited from the commune era meant that collective enterprise managers enjoyed relatively little autonomy from the local state.[47] Not only were managers subordinates in a hierarchical relationship with local state officials, but also the separation between the budgets of the township or village and its collective enterprises was highly imperfect. As a result, the informational costs faced by local officials in extracting revenue from these firms were relatively low, and they could readily do so – via either budgetary or nonbudgetary channels. Moreover, collective firms directly performed many sociopolitical functions at the behest of the local state. Revenue extraction from collective enterprises was therefore part and parcel of the larger collective organizational structure that harnessed the political and economic resources of the community to the purposes set out by local state officials, and local officials had little incentive to change the existing institutional arrangements.

The first part of this section establishes a consistent pattern of collusion in tax avoidance and evasion between local governments and their collective enterprises.[48] The second part demonstrates that institutional

---

[47] Collective managers had some bargaining power vis-à-vis local officials due to the greater intimacy of their knowledge about the firm, but they were still dependent for their positions as managers upon the continued support of township officials.

[48] The latter entails illegally reducing the tax burden by concealing taxable resources, while the former entails fully exploiting all legally mandated tax reductions and exemptions. The distinction between avoidance and evasion is a fine one, particularly in the Chinese case. In offering a general definition, the World Bank study of revenue mobilization characterizes tax avoidance as an action undertaken by a local government and tax evasion as an action undertaken by a firm. "Local and provincial governments may reduce the amount of taxes due from enterprises by providing special arrangements to help enterprises over hardship periods or by giving tax holidays to encourage new activities. . . . All of these arrangements are well within the spirit and the letter of the law. They represent a form of tax avoidance." However, this distinction ignores the collusion of local governments in tax evasion as well as central government efforts to combat this collusion. Indeed, definitional distinctions tend to become blurred in practice: As the World Bank study points out, "Local governments also can become more lax in their assess-

197

innovations – to the extent that they occurred at all in the collective sector – were applied mainly to quasiprivate firms and that, even then, they generated conflict within the local state.

Tax Avoidance and Evasion

In the twenty-five collective enterprises in Wuxi and Shanghai for which responses to questions about the implementation of tax policy were relatively complete, managers or accountants described practices involving tax evasion in more than 75 percent of the cases.[49] They were willing to discuss these practices to the extent that they did because of the perceived legitimacy of tax evasion in collective enterprises at the local level.[50] One collective manager whose firm inflated costs to reduce taxable profits defended the practice as follows: "This is not tax evasion, because the [central] state didn't invest in this enterprise and because it's for the collective" (Informant 197). Another manager echoed this theme: "[Tax evasion] is no problem because it's not an individual evading taxes for himself" (Informant 195). Township officials had an incentive to collude in tax evasion in order to shift revenues from shared budgetary (tax) channels to nonbudgetary channels that the township alone controlled. Collusion took various forms, driven in part by the preferential policies under which collectives operated. Although the central government mandated preferential tax policies to benefit rural collectives, it also sought to control their application. The State Council and the State Administration of Taxation repeatedly issued documents condemning and prohibiting abuse of preferential policies by local governments.[51] In addition, the central government used the procedure of annual audits to address this problem. The local government practice of exceeding its authority in granting tax breaks was a special target of the

---

ment and collection efforts and can permit enterprises to underdeclare tax liability. This is a form of evasion on the part of *both* the enterprise *and* the local government" (World Bank 1990b:280).

[49] Data are drawn from six firms in Dongtan Town in Wuxi, nine firms in Nantang Township in Jiading County, Shanghai, and ten firms in Songyang Town, in Songjiang County, Shanghai. By township, respondents reported tax evasion in 100, 90, and 50 percent of the cases, respectively.

[50] The willingness of many, though not all, collective enterprise managers and accountants to discuss these issues with relative frankness was striking. This was the case whether interviews were arranged officially (in conjunction with the local government) or unofficially (through friends).

[51] See note 2.

annual tax audit in 1990.[52] A study conducted by a leading economist at the Chinese Academy of Social Sciences estimates that in wealthy coastal regions, tax exemptions typically accounted for at least 15 percent of total tax revenues during the pre-1994 period (Fan 1998:227).

Tax "Avoidance": Abuse of Preferential Policies. Officials throughout township government agencies colluded with enterprise managers to avoid taxes. It was common practice for collective managers to rename the factory, or to rename one of the factory's workshops, and register it with the industrial-commercial bureau as a new enterprise, eligible for a multiyear tax exemption or reduction.[53] The industrial-commercial bureau, which bore responsibility for licensing new firms, did not interfere in such manipulation (Informants 183, 188, and 189). Indeed, in one site an official of the bureau explained the discrepancy between the number of collectives reported by the tax bureau and other township agencies as a result of this practice. Officials of the township industrial corporation (the arm of the township government responsible for management of collective enterprises) governed divided enterprises as one – with one set of performance targets, one manager, a single set of internal account books, and a single bank account (Informants 83, 177, and 180). In Songyang, such divisions and mergers occurred in cycles, with a single enterprise dividing, merging, and dividing again as tax exemptions expired (Informant 83). Moreover, while tax regulations stipulated that tax-exempt funds were to be used for specific purposes within the enterprise, local governments commonly tapped those funds in the form of larger profit remittances to finance other township government activities.[54]

An even wider range of bureaucratic agencies was involved in granting tax exemptions for new products. The product had to be certified as new by either a national- or provincial-level agency. In the case of

---

[52] Guowuyuan, "Guanyu kaizhan yijiujiuling nian shuishou caiwu wujia da jiancha de tongzhi," *Guowuyuan gongbao* No. 16 (August 28, 1990), pp. 582–5.

[53] Informants 67, 123, 124, 180, and 196. Policy analysts at the Ministry of Agriculture, which oversees rural enterprise development, cited the tax exemptions and reductions awarded to newly established enterprises as the most frequently abused of the preferential policies available to rural collectives. Moreover, they characterized such abuse explicitly as a form of tax evasion (Informant 188). This assessment was echoed by researchers at the Chinese Academy of Social Sciences Rural Development Research Institute and at the State Council Development Research Center (Informants 185 and 189).

[54] Informants 194 and 196. As one township official put it, "This phenomenon exists; one only needs to put in a word with the tax bureau."

Shanghai, the science and technology commission was responsible for evaluating new products. As of the early 1990s, the Shanghai tax authority also became involved in the approval process in an attempt to reduce the number of products that received approval despite their failure to meet the relevant criteria (Informant 110). Nevertheless, the county executive in one Shanghai suburban county noted that the county government could still influence the tax bureau by bribing the technical experts to advocate approval (Informant 103). In other cases, the technical approval process was circumvented altogether. The manager of a collective factory in Luhang Town, Shanghai, described how the tax bureau could help older enterprises like his own: "The 'new product' is just with respect to this enterprise; this is special treatment – not exactly according to the regulations – but it was approved by the county tax bureau" (Informant 67). The manager estimated the benefit at 500 thousand yuan per year. Even legitimate tax exemptions were subject to abuse. The manager of a village-run factory in Nantang Town, Shanghai, described receiving preferential treatment for one product – attested to by the awards for technical innovation adorning his office. However, in order to evade taxes on other products, the factory's manager sold the products using receipts written for the new, tax-exempt product, thus illicitly obtaining tax exemptions for a large portion of the factory's total output (Informant 126). The manager pointed out that township officials were aware of the practice and that the enterprise still contributed significantly to meeting the township's tax quota and, more importantly, to supporting the township's nonbudgetary expenditures. Indeed, he reported contributing 80 thousand yuan to the construction of new buildings for the township government and the township industrial corporation.

Welfare and school-run enterprises were also tempting targets for manipulation because of their completely tax-exempt status. Local officials could create welfare factories simply by listing a certain number of handicapped individuals on enterprise payrolls. In response to this practice, higher-level tax authorities stipulated that high value-added products (that is, products generating significant tax revenues) could not be produced in welfare factories (Informants 83 and 110). Nevertheless, in Luhang Town, Shanghai, factory managers and representatives of the industrial corporation reported shifting the most profitable processing work into welfare factories to take advantage of the tax exemption (Informants 46 and 49). In Wuxi, "hanging out a 'school-run' sign (*gua xiao paizi*)" was simply an easy way to obtain tax-exempt status for collective enterprises; according to a township official, the schools that ostensibly sponsored the enterprises in many cases did not even exist (Informant 196). By the early 1990s, there came to be so many "school-run" collectives in Wuxi that county tax authorities finally set a ceiling on the level of exemptions in this category.

In another common practice, the township tax bureau allowed collectives to be in arrears in paying their taxes. The enterprises could then use the money to supplement their working capital funds – interest free. During the years leading up to the 1994 reforms, tax payments in arrears consistently constituted fully 25 percent of the recorded tax liability of township- and village-run collectives nationwide, reaching a high of nearly 23 billion yuan in 1993.[55] The seriousness of the abuse was underscored in a 1990 State Council document forbidding this practice.[56] Nevertheless, all forms of tax avoidance were characterized by at least the outward appearance of compliance with complicated tax regulations. Therefore, the practices were easy to overlook if auditors and other officials chose to do so.[57]

Tax Evasion. Tax evasion resulted in part from the nature of the relationship between local governments and collective enterprises. These firms directly bore the cost of provision of many public goods. As one village leader in Shanghai put it, "It would be hard to identify the true profit rate of the village's four collective enterprises, because they pay [directly] for so many village expenses" (Informant 131).[58] Thus, there was incomplete separation between the operating budgets of the local firms and the local administration. As a result, actual public expenditures were even greater than the sum of budgetary and nonbudgetary revenues reported by local finance offices.

A range of community expenses were regularly borne by collective

---

[55] The figure for tax payments in arrears is the difference between taxes owed and taxes paid. *Zhongguo xiangzhen qiye nianjian* (1994:364). In fact, arrears increased in the post-1994 period. On this, see Chapter 7.

[56] Guowuyuan bangongting, "Zhuanfa guowuyuan lianhe qingli tuoqian shuikuan lingdao xiaozu guanyu zhuajin qingli qianshui jidian yijian de tongzhi (State Council Office Notice of Transmission of Several Opinions of the 'State Council Joint Leadership Small Group on Eliminating Tax Payments in Arrears' regarding the Focus on Eliminating Delinquent Taxes, October 12, 1990)," *State Council Bulletin* No. 23 (January 1991), pp. 850–2.

[57] The issue of broader, subnational regulatory environments is discussed in subsequent sections.

[58] Similar comments were made by other village leaders (Informants 71, 122, and 126).

enterprises. Enterprises commonly financed the wages of township and village cadres by listing them on enterprise payrolls.[59] These cadres included township government officials, township industrial corporation staff, and, most commonly, village cadres, such as those staffing village administration, agricultural equipment services, and irrigation services. One village enterprise manager reported covering approximately 60 thousand yuan in village expenses, including the wages of sixteen village cadres, the outlay for parts and maintenance of village agricultural machinery, and the cost of village electricity, among others (Informant 127). The manager pointed out that he maintained a separate accounting of the expenses so that the proper figures could be used when calculating his fulfillment of profit and other targets for purposes of salary and bonuses. Another village in the same township reportedly padded enterprise wage rolls with thirty names simply as a means of supplementing village resources (Informant 126).

Enterprises covered community capital construction outlays in a variety of ways that allowed the enterprises to deduct the costs from their tax bills. In Nantang, some enterprises covered a portion of the cost of erecting new buildings to house the township government and industrial corporation by deducting from their taxes the costs of construction materials along with the costs of regular enterprise inputs (Ibid). Deductions of community expenditures as enterprise costs were also the subject of negotiation between the township government and the local tax bureaus. For example, officials in Nantang negotiated with both the township and the county tax bureaus to deduct the cost of installing direct-dial phone lines, a cost that was not technically deductible (Informant 139). The county tax bureau allowed 200 enterprises to write 800 thousand yuan in such expenses into costs; the township had to come up with the remaining 700 thousand yuan by other means.

Collective enterprises also performed a community welfare function by providing employment for local residents beyond the labor requirements of the firm. In part for this reason, higher-level tax authorities placed ceilings on allowable deductions for wage expenditures to prevent the tax system from bearing the entire cost of such community welfare programs.[60] Local governments countered by inflating costs – particularly padding wage rolls – to reduce the financial burden on firms. This behav-

[59] Informants 97, 120, 122, 126, 127, and 131.
[60] This rationale is clear, since firms that could demonstrate strict economic reasons for raising wages could do so.

ior is aptly captured in the saying "The higher levels make policies, and the lower levels find ways to get around them (*shang you zhengce; xia you duice*)." Thus, the practice of inflating costs had both diffuse and specific causes. It not only reflected a general strategy to retain more revenue at the local level, but it was also a specific measure designed to increase wages in the face of low ceilings on allowable deductions for wage expenditures in collective firms.

Padding the wage rolls with fictitious names (*mingdan konge*) was a commonly used means of inflating enterprise costs in every research site.[61] As a means of safeguarding tax revenues, central and provincial governments set ceilings on the level of deductible wages to rein in wage and bonus increases in collective firms. In Shanghai Municipality, for example, both the municipal tax and finance bureaus and the agriculture committee of the municipal party committee were involved in setting standards for allowable deductions of wages (Informant 119). At lower levels, however, a division occurred between control over *tax-deductible* wage levels and control over *actual* wage levels. The tax bureau controlled the level of wages that could be deducted from the tax bill.[62] If the average wage level exceeded the ceiling, the additional expenditure had to be covered using after-tax profits.[63] The actual average wage – regardless of how it was covered – was controlled through party channels. At the township level, the party's economic management office (*jingying guanli bangongshi*) exercised control over actual wages.[64]

In most research sites, actual average wages exceeded the limits set by the tax bureau, and padded wage rolls were a means of reducing the additional costs to the enterprise. In 1991, for example, tax regulations in Shanghai and Jiangsu stated that the allowable deduction for average expenditures on the basic wages of collective enterprise employees was 1,440 yuan per year (120 yuan per month). Although certain counties and enterprises received special dispensations allowing higher deductions for

---

[61] Informants 80, 95, 100, 102, 119, 120, 126, 138, 194, 195, 196, 197, 199, 200, and 201 described their experiences in padding wage rolls.

[62] Informants 77, 80, 119, 138, 139, and 142.

[63] There were some exceptions provided for in the regulations. For example, allowable deductions for the wage expenditures of export-oriented firms were higher (Informant 125).

[64] Informants 77, 80, 119, 138, 139, and 196. This office is a party organ under the township party committee, which in turn is under the rural work section of the county party committee.

wage costs,[65] even in these cases actual average wage levels still exceeded deductible limits. One township enterprise manager in Jiangsu employed approximately 500 workers in his factory but officially reported employing over 800 (Informant 195). While in this case the allowable deduction per worker was over 1,900 yuan per year for 1991, the actual average wage was well over 3,000 yuan per year. The 600,000 yuan made available by padding the wage roll was applied to the difference. The same phenomenon was reported by other managers.[66]

Township party and government officials, including officials of the township tax office, played a key role in perpetuating the practice of padding enterprise payrolls. Indeed, township officials themselves approved the number of employees and the total wage bill of each enterprise (Informants 142 and 199). The manager of a township-run firm in Jiangsu explained:

> The industrial corporation sends down the target for the total wage bill for the enterprise. The tax bureau knows that this exceeds the standards for deductible wages. If they want to investigate – go ahead; the industrial corporation and the township [leadership] have already decided. There is a separate settling of accounts with the township party committee. . . . This enterprise treats all its wages as tax deductible. Here we pad the payroll, because the standard for deductibility set by the tax bureau is too low (Informant 199).

Even in cases in which padding wage rolls was part of a general strategy of tax evasion, tax officials at the township level took a passive approach to policy enforcement in collective firms. As one township tax official from a Shanghai site put it, "[Enterprises] evade taxes by submitting fake wage reports. The industrial corporation and the economic management office both know about this in the case of collectives; so, it's okay" (Informant 100).

---

[65] Deductible levels for certain economically advanced areas were increased from 120 to 180 yuan per month (2,160 yuan per year). In addition, certain highly successful enterprises were allowed to increase deductible wage costs at a rate pegged to profit increases (Informant 196).

[66] In another case, the manager employed about 480 workers but officially reported employing over 660. The allowable deduction per worker was 1,440 yuan per year, and actual wages averaged about 2,800 yuan. The 260 thousand yuan made available by padding the wage roll was used to cover the remainder of the wage bill (Informant 197). Other similar cases are among the sources cited in footnote 61.

While apparently not as pervasive as inflating costs, the phenomenon of underreporting sales and output also occurred among collective firms in a variety of forms.[67] One approach was for firms to delay formal licensing – and, concomitantly, tax assessment – well beyond the start of operations. A manager in Nantang who managed to delay formal licensing and taxation for more than a year with the help of township officials described the practice as "reasonable but not legal (*heli bu hefa*)" (Informant 123). Another approach was for firms to make sales without receipts. A village enterprise manager also in Nantang (who served concurrently as village leader) reported that over the past several years, profits from unreported sales had brought in about 2.5 million yuan for the firm (Informant 126). Similarly, a township enterprise manager in Dongtan Town, Wuxi, explained that he used the profits from unreported sales to cover the expenses of entertaining clients and officials at the factory (Informant 195). A village enterprise manager in the same town reported 2.6 million yuan in after-tax profits in an interview, although the tax bureau recorded only 176 thousand yuan in pretax profits (Informants 194 and 197).

A Preliminary Assessment. Tax evasion was the norm among rural collectives. It was particularly acute with respect to profit taxes, as the preceding discussion of inflated costs suggests. A township official in Wuxi described the pervasiveness of the problem: "1991 profit taxes for the entire county were only 20 million yuan. That is very little and it's getting smaller and smaller. It's ridiculous" (Informant 196). Similarly, records for one township in Shanghai show that in 1988, 44 percent of township-run enterprises and 28 percent of village-run enterprises paid no profit taxes. By 1990, those figures had increased substantially, with fully 58 percent of township-run firms and 50 percent of village-run firms paying no profit taxes whatsoever (Informant 141).[68] Without complete information it is impossible to determine definitively the extent of legitimate tax exemptions and reductions, but the case study data presented here suggest that it is unlikely that exemptions on this scale faithfully reflect the policies of the central government. Moreover, the case study findings parallel national trends.

Table 5.2 presents national data on the taxation of rural collectives.

---

[67] Informants 1, 120, 122, 123, 126, 192, 194, 200, and 201.
[68] Percentages are based on data from eighteen township-run and sixty-eight village-run firms for 1988 and from nineteen township-run and sixty-eight village-run firms for 1990.

Table 5.2. *Taxation of Township- and Village-run Collectives, 1978–97*

Year	Net profits (billion yuan)	Total tax liability (billion yuan)	Profit tax liability (billion yuan)	Profit taxes as share of total taxes	Average *rate* of profit tax
1978	8.81	2.20	0.74	33.6	7.7
1979	10.45	2.26	0.70	31.0	6.3
1980	11.84	2.57	0.79	30.7	6.3
1981	11.28	3.43	0.95	27.7	7.8
1982	11.55	4.47	1.25	28.0	9.8
1983	11.78	5.89	1.89	32.1	13.8
1984	12.87	7.91	2.63	33.2	17.0
1985	17.13	10.86	3.27	30.1	16.0
1986	16.10	13.73	3.86	28.1	19.3
1987	18.78	16.94	4.44	26.2	19.1
1988	25.92	23.65	5.98	25.3	18.7
1989	24.01	27.25	6.09	22.3	20.2
1990	23.27	27.54	5.71	20.7	19.7
1991	28.47	33.38	6.81	20.4	19.3
1992	48.13	47.32	9.55	20.2	16.6
1993	n/a	87.73	16.78	19.1	n/a
1994	n/a	n/a	23.13	n/a	n/a
1995	n/a	130.17	27.87	21.4	n/a
1996	173.09	143.90	30.47	21.2	15.0
1997	173.45	156.24	40.81	26.12	n/a

Note: This table represents three distinct regulatory regimes in force between 1978 and 1997: (1) the period before 1986, when uniform national regulations on profit taxes for township- and village-run collectives were first implemented; (2) the period from 1986 to 1993, and (3) the period after 1993, when new tax and fiscal regulations were negotiated and implemented. Data after 1992 are not comparable with data for the preceding years for two reasons. First, in implementing centralizing fiscal reforms beginning in 1994, the central government guaranteed that the consolidated tax revenues available to subnational governments would not fall below 1993 levels. Not surprisingly, the total recorded tax liability of township- and village-run collectives shot up, nearly doubling from 1992 to 1993, in a ploy to ensure a high level of guaranteed revenue after 1993. (Relatedly, tax arrears plummeted from 26 percent in 1992 to 2 percent in 1993 to 1994, before soaring to 43 percent in 1996.) Second, along with fiscal reforms, new accounting regulations and tax rates were implemented beginning in 1994.

Sources: *Zhongguo xiangzhen qiye nianjian* (1989:638; 1990:106; 1991:186; 1992a [1990 data]:194; 1992b [1991 data]:200; 1993:232; 1994:364; 1996:99; 250; 1997:121; 248). *Zhongguo tongji nianjian* (1993:396; 1995:366; 1998:422).

The data in the table represent three distinct regulatory regimes in force between 1978 and 1997: (1) the period before 1986, the year in which uniform national regulations on profit taxes for township- and village-run collectives were first implemented; (2) the period from 1986 to 1992; and (3) the period after 1993, when new tax and fiscal regulations were negotiated and implemented. Focusing on comparable data from 1986 through 1992, profit taxes as a share of total taxes declined from 28 percent in 1986 to 20 percent in 1992.[69] During the same period, net profits increased 20 percent per year on average, while profit tax payments increased only 16 percent. The average profit tax rate wavered, falling from 19.3 percent in 1986 to 16.6 percent in 1992. Of even greater concern from the perspective of the central government was evasion of indirect taxes, since these taxes accounted for the bulk of fiscal revenue. Indeed, an official of the township economic management bureau in Wuxi described the extent of evasion of indirect taxes as "serious" (Informant 196). Manipulation of preferential policies involving exemptions or reductions of indirect as well as direct taxes undermined the center's ability to tap this form of revenue.

Reliance on fiscal contracts at the township level exacerbated the problem. While manipulation occurred throughout the fiscal year, it intensified as local governments neared completion of their fiscal contracts. A State Council circular targeted precisely this behavior on the part of local governments. The circular stated that tax policy must be implemented according to the letter of the law, regardless of the degree of fulfillment of fiscal contracts.[70] Nevertheless, the degree of contract fulfillment continued to influence local government behavior in a variety of ways. This influence was felt to some degree in all townships, but it depended in part on the intensity of monitoring by higher-level authorities.

The relationship between fiscal contract fulfillment and the implementation of tax policy was most apparent in the application of preferential tax polices. Once the fiscal contract was fulfilled, township tax

---

[69] This decline is based on reported tax *liability*. Data on taxes actually *paid* are available only for the years 1988 to 1992, when profit taxes paid as a share of total taxes paid fell from 21.6 percent to 15.9 percent.

[70] Guowuyuan bangongting, "Guanyu jiaqiang shuishou gongzuo de jinji tongzhi (Urgent Notice regarding Strengthening Tax Work)," in *Zhili zhengdun shenhua gaige zhengce fagui xuanbian* (1990:152). See also "Qieshi jiaqiang shuishou baozhang caizheng shouru (Conscientiously Increase Tax Revenues; Guarantee Fiscal Revenues)," *Jiefang ribao*, May 16, 1988, p. 1.

bureaus had greater leeway to grant preferential treatment (Informant 83). This relationship did not always work to the firm's benefit, however. In Nantang Town, Jiading County, Shanghai, for example, managers complained that they were not granted tax exemptions or reductions as newly established firms. The managers explained the failure in terms of the township's difficulties in meeting its annual tax quota and expressed the hope that, once the township had exceeded its quota, they would receive tax breaks retroactively (Informant 120). Officials of the tax bureau stated that if those enterprises had been granted exemptions, then the township would have failed to fulfill its fiscal contract (Informant 133). The same problem occurred in Songjiang County, where local officials did not meet their fiscal target until the final month of the year (Informant 110). The relationship between fiscal contracts and tax policy was also manifest in such situations as tax bureau acquiescence in inflating costs. A county-level official of the rural enterprise bureau in Songjiang noted with respect to the practice of padding wage rolls, "The government must interfere, allowing it when appropriate and not allowing it when inappropriate" (Informant 102). "Appropriate" was determined in part by the ability of the county to fulfill its fiscal quota. As the manager of an enterprise in Wuxi stated, "Under the fiscal contracting system, if the local government can complete its target relatively easily, then it will allow more tax deductions. If it can complete the target only with difficulty, then it will allow fewer deductions" (Informant 200).

The consistent patterns of collusion reported here can be understood by examining the incentives and constraints acting on local officials. It was in the interest of township officials, as both tax collectors and owners of collective firms, to collude in reducing the tax burden, since they could readily tap these revenues through other channels. Since there were few informational constraints on their ability to extract from collective firms, they had little incentive to make changes in existing institutional arrangements for revenue extraction. However, fiscal contracts influenced how much revenue flowed into budgetary as opposed to nonbudgetary channels.

Limited Institutional Innovations

Institutional innovations toward collective firms were limited to the most marginal segment of the collective sector – individually contracted collectives (*geren chengbao jiti qiye*) – and even in these cases, innovations revealed significant tensions within the local state apparatus. Individually contracted collectives represented an arena in which there was neither effective taxation nor significant profit turnover to the state. These firms closely resembled private firms in that the manager laid claim to all residual profits after the terms of his contract were fulfilled.[71] At the same time, however, these enterprises benefited from treatment as collectives – and particularly from lax implementation of tax policy. As one analyst described them, "Individual contractors hang out a collective signpost and hand over a fixed amount of contracted profits. Most of the profits accrue to the individual with the result being that the individual gets rich and the collective is impoverished" (Tao 1988:173–4).

During the economic rectification campaign of the late 1980s and early 1990s, the central government sought to eliminate those firms that openly exploited collective status for private gain or, minimally, to eliminate their collective benefits.[72] Local governments responded in different ways to this central initiative. For example, in some locales, the county rural enterprise management bureau did not allow individual contracts to be renewed once they had expired. Those managers whose contracts did not expire during the period of the campaign were strongly "advised" to return the factory to the collective and to repudiate their individual contracts (Informants 9 and 14). In a number of other research sites, tax officials extended to individually contracted collectives the same innovations that had been designed to tax private firms more effectively. In some cases these extensions elicited resistance from local government executives who sought to prevent encroachment by the tax bureau into the domain of the local collective economy. The cases of resistance to attacks against even marginal members of the collective economy provide a basis for disaggregating the interests of different bureaucratic components of local governments and, concomitantly, for analyzing conflict within the local state. This section examines two cases in which local

---

[71] Technically, individually contracted collectives differed from other collectives, because according to the contract, the manager paid a fixed amount (or fixed percentage) in profit-turnover to the local government and retained all residual profits as his personal income. Moreover, some such firms were, in reality, private firms established with private investment, which through personal deals between managers and local leaders registered as collective enterprises.

[72] See "Decision regarding Vigorously Strengthening Tax Collection Work," cited in note 2; and Guojia shuiwuju, "Guanyu siying qiye shuishou zhengce de ruogan guiding," in *Zhili zhengdun shenhua gaige zhengce fagui xuanbian* (1990:162–3).

tax officials sought, in different ways, to extend innovative practices to individually contracted firms.

Songyang. In Songyang Town, the goal of the tax bureau was to channel individually contracted firms either into the regulatory framework provided by the private enterprise accounting station or into the formal collective sector, which was closely governed by the town's industrial corporation. As of 1992, there were approximately forty individually contracted firms, virtually all of which were team-run enterprises.[73] The rationale articulated by local officials for eliminating individually contracted firms paralleled the one set forth at the center. In Songyang, team-run collectives, unlike township- and village-run firms, were not closely supervised by the industrial corporation. According to the director of the tax bureau, individually contracted team-run firms did not submit account forms to the industrial corporation and were not subject to performance standards either for increasing output value or profits (Informant 100). He noted that the vast majority of these enterprises stayed in business despite showing losses year after year, because they were actually profitable firms that had simply inflated costs to evade taxes.[74] Indeed, like other firms, it was common for individual contractors to evade taxes by such actions as padding wage rolls.[75] Therefore, the tax bureau planned to abolish all individually contracted firms either by forcing them to become full-fledged collectives run by the village and supervised by the township industrial corporation, or by forcing them to become private enterprises subject to the special scrutiny of the private enterprise accounting station.[76] In the words of the director,

Most team-run enterprises are individually contracted. The strong ones must become village-run collectives. This is because right now the industrial corporation doesn't really manage team-run collectives. The weak ones must become private enterprises. . . . Each tax

---

[73] Informant 100. In some places teams had practically faded away since after decollectivization they served few, if any, official functions. In Songyang, teams still typically sponsored one or more small enterprises (Informants 90, 91, and 95).

[74] The tax bureau reported that thirty-six firms consistently showed losses (Informant 100).

[75] Ibid. This was the practice, for example, in the case of Informant 95, who ran an individually contracted firm in Songyang.

[76] In this context, one informant emphasized that, for example, the tax bureau carefully supervised the number of workers in a private enterprise but not in a collective (Informant 89).

collector is responsible for 30–40 firms. They could audit all the team-run enterprises, but [forcing them to become] private is easier because (a) they won't have the safety of collective protection, and (b) they will be supervised by the private enterprise accounting station (Informant 100).

Team leaders and firm managers in Songyang resisted attempts to change the status of individually contracted, team-run firms. Team leaders sought to protect these firms because managers who were often their friends and relatives and because the firms represented financial resources that the team leaders were loathe to forsake. Minimally, teams received a fixed payment from the contractor, and in some cases, team leaders also had a personal stake in the enterprise.

In Songyang, the tax bureau appeared to prevail in its battle against individually contracted collectives, but the conflict between representatives of the tax bureau and local officials was confined to the level of the team, an arena that was marginal to the overall economy of the town. Moreover, there was no question of applying the regulatory resources of the private enterprise accounting station to full-fledged collective firms. Indeed, the director of the tax bureau made a clear distinction between the treatment of tax evasion on the part of semiprivate contracted firms and full-fledged collectives:

> The industrial corporation and the economic management office both know about this in the case of [regular] collectives; so it's okay. Enterprises use this to cover their business expenses.[77] Of course, the tax people still oppose this in principle. [But] individually contracted enterprises use this for themselves; so this is undesirable (Informant 100).

This account illustrates that, although the tax bureau was an arm of the central government, it had little independence at the local level. The tax bureau had more authority to act where its interests coincided with those of the local government – as in the cases of private or contracted firms.

---

[77] Business expenses (*yewufei*) referred to the "cost of doing business," including such items as entertainment and gift giving. Tax regulations limited the tax deductible expenditures in this category to less than 2 percent of sales. Collective managers regularly complained that this was too little, and they commonly inflated tax deductible costs in other categories in order to compensate for this limit.

Dongtan. Tax officials in Dongtan Town, Wuxi County, also applied to individually contracted collectives certain measures initially developed for taxing private enterprises. Beginning in 1992, they instituted a variant of the "simultaneous taxation" method (*fuzhengshui*) used in Wenzhou for all enterprises with total sales volume below two million yuan – encompassing a total of about thirty township- and village-run enterprises. The director of the tax bureau explained the definition of the scope in the following way: "This system will be used especially for individually contracted collectives. The intention is to abolish all the special privileges given these enterprises due to their collective status. . . . This will help to avoid fake reports, and this system makes it harder to evade taxes" (Informant 194). An official of the town's economic management office amplified this explanation by stating that targeted firms included all those in which the manager had a claim on the residual profits (Informant 196).

Resistance from Dongtan Town officials was effective in scaling back the scope of the tax bureau's initiative. The initial plan called for implementing *fuzhengshui* in all enterprises with total sales volume less than five million yuan (Ibid). While the tax bureau's target may have been only those enterprises in which the contracting manager had a claim on residual profits, by defining the scope in terms of enterprise size rather than contractual form, it drew in a wider range of firms, including some regular township- and village-run collectives. Setting the cutoff as high as five million yuan would have resulted in the inclusion of a higher proportion of regular collective firms, thereby reducing the township government's ability to collude in tax evasion with those larger collectives. Local officials succeeded in pressuring the tax bureau to reduce the cutoff to two million yuan. In contrast to the conflict that occurred in Songyang, the intragovernmental conflict in Dongtan took place at the township level, closer to the core of the township economy, and township government officials were able to prevail in reducing the scope of the tax bureau's initiative. Representatives of the tax bureau referred to this behavior as protectionism (*baohu zhuyi*) toward the local collective economy.

In general, township and village leaders exercised significant financial control over regular, township-run, and village-run collective enterprises; therefore, they had little incentive to support changes in the institutional arrangements that facilitated such control. Tax bureau officials were able to establish new institutional arrangements only in the most marginal segment of the collective sector, and even in this context, local leaders resisted the attempts of the tax authorities to establish independent control. As Kathleen Thelen and Sven Steinmo (1992:27) observe, "Conflicts over institutions lay bare interests and power relations, and their outcomes not only reflect but magnify and reinforce the interests of the winners."

SUBNATIONAL REGULATORY FRAMEWORKS

All local government efforts at revenue extraction, whether toward private or collective firms, took place within broader regulatory frameworks defined by the provincial government. In general, central decrees were implemented indirectly via provincial-level authorities, and there is evidence that reveals systematic variation in the implementation of tax policy by province. The provincial environment had a major impact on the regulatory framework – even at the grass roots.

This section uses case study data from Shanghai and Jiangsu to examine contrasts in provincial regulatory environments. The data suggest that the most relevant aspect of the provincial environment in this regard was the perceived nature of the central-provincial fiscal contract (*caizheng baogan*) in the context of the declining profitability of urban, state-run industry. Shanghai was universally regarded by Chinese observers as having a more burdensome fiscal contract with the center than did Jiangsu.[78] The burdensome contract created pressure for more aggressive monitoring of policy implementation at the county and township levels.

Perceived differences in revenue-sharing arrangements were ramified throughout the fiscal system. In 1990, for example, Shanghai's fiscal contract required it to remit about 15 percent of GDP to the center, while Jiangsu's contract required it to remit only about 9 percent. Put another way, although Shanghai's 1990 GDP was only about one-half (56 percent) of Jiangsu's, Shanghai remitted close to the same amount of revenue to the center (*Jiangsu jingji nianjian* 1992; *Shanghai jingji nianjian* 1992). However, the perception of a heavy fiscal burden in Shanghai's fiscal contract with the center failed to take into account that, on a per capita basis, Shanghai's GDP was nearly three times higher than Jiangsu's. More likely, the perception reflected the lingering influence of

---

[78] Lynn White (1989), in his study of taxation in Shanghai, also makes the case that Shanghai bears a heavier tax burden than other provinces, particularly Jiangsu. See also Lin (1994).

Shanghai's decades as a cash cow for the central government. Even after Shanghai had negotiated a more favorable fiscal contract with the center in 1988, the perception remained that Shanghai had gotten a "rotten deal."[79] One response of the Shanghai municipal government to its perceived heavy fiscal burden was to set relatively high base levels for tax remittances in fiscal contracts with county-level units. To illustrate, although Jiading County, Shanghai, and neighboring Kunshan County, Jiangsu, had similar levels of GDP in 1991 (2.45 billion yuan and 2.44 billion yuan, or about 4,800 yuan and 4,300 yuan on a per capita basis, respectively), Jiading collected nearly four times as much in taxes (480 million yuan as compared to 123 million yuan) and remitted significantly more revenue to higher levels.[80]

Moreover, the burden of a weak state enterprise sector was heavier in Shanghai than in Jiangsu, compounding the perceived differences in fiscal contracts. While the absolute size of the state sector was roughly comparable in Shanghai and Jiangsu, producing about 74 billion yuan and 95 billion yuan in gross value of industrial output in 1990, respectively, it represented 64 percent of the total in Shanghai and only 34 percent of the total in Jiangsu. Furthermore, subsidies for planned losses to urban, state-run enterprises in Shanghai (about 3 billion yuan) were almost double the amount in Jiangsu (about 1.7 billion yuan).[81]

The financial pressure exerted by Shanghai's fiscal contract with the center in conjunction with its weak, urban, state-run industrial sector led to more aggressive monitoring of policy implementation at the local level. This was particularly true with respect to rural industry, which was regarded as a fiscal resource capable of compensating in part for the weak performance of the state-run sector. Furthermore, municipal officials in some quarters held rural industry responsible for the declining performance of state industry (Informant 187; Naughton 1992a). The belief that competition from rural, nonstate industry was in part to blame contributed to more aggressive monitoring in this sector. (Aggressive monitoring did not completely preclude collusive behavior between local officials and collective enterprises in Shanghai, however. The costs of

---

[79] *Sheke xingxi jiaoliu* No. 44 (1989), p. 5, as cited in Lin (1994:259). For the 1988 fiscal contract, see *Shanghai jingji nianjian* (1989:477).

[80] Revenue from rural enterprise, collected at the township level, makes a substantial contribution to total revenue at the county level and above.

[81] I am indebted to Christine Wong for her input on this issue.

monitoring necessary to ensure complete compliance would likely outweigh the benefits.)

Aggressive monitoring was manifested in three ways. First, local officials in both Shanghai and Jiangsu reported that representatives of the tax bureau in Shanghai conducted audits and investigations of enterprise accounts with much greater frequency and vigor than did officials in the same position in Jiangsu (Informants 184a and 194). Second and relatedly, the approach to fiscal contract fulfillment taken by local officials in Shanghai was closer to the letter of the law than in Jiangsu. Third, tax deductions for wages and business expenses were much more closely monitored in Shanghai, resulting in consistently lower wage levels and less freewheeling business practices than in Jiangsu. The newspaper *Shanghai gongye jingji bao (Shanghai Industrial Economy)*, a publication of the municipal planning commission, ran a series of articles in 1988 flagging these differences. The articles complained that Shanghai's rural collectives could not compete with those in Jiangsu. One of the reasons given was that Shanghai's rural enterprises were granted fewer, shorter, and smaller tax holidays and thus were less able to attract domestic joint venture partners from among the more technically advanced of Shanghai's state-owned firms. The state-run firms disproportionately sought rural partners from among rural collectives in nearby southern Jiangsu and northern Zhejiang from which they could obtain larger profits.[82] Similarly, Shanghai technical personnel tended to seek employment in rural enterprises outside of Shanghai where they could earn higher salaries.[83] Finally, it was harder for Shanghai's rural industries to woo clients since they could deduct from taxes only a fraction of the business expenses allowable elsewhere. The same problems continued into the early 1990s. The following paragraphs examine the differences in the implementation of tax policy in collective firms in Shanghai and Jiangsu with particular emphasis on the approach to fiscal contracts and on the

---

[82] Feng Jiqun, "Gao yige you tese de Shanghai xiangzhen qiye tiaoli (Produce a Shanghai Statute on Township and Village Enterprises with Special Characteristics)," *Shanghai gongye jingji bao*, January 21, 1988, p. 1; and idem, "Xiangzhen qiye houjin buzu ling ren danyou (The Insufficient Momentum of Township and Village Enterprises Worries Many)," *Shanghai gongye jingji bao*, February 15, 1988, p. 2.

[83] Feng Jiqun, "Jinshui loutai nan de yue (The Waterfront Pavilion Rarely Gets the Moonlight)," *Shanghai gongye jingji bao*, March 10, 1988, p. 2. The title of the article is a pun on the original saying, "moonlight reaches the waterfront pavilion first," meaning that those who are close at hand get the best opportunities. The author is lamenting the fact that although Shanghai's rural enterprises were favorably situated, they were not enjoying the best opportunities.

deductibility of wages and business expenses. The contrasts reflect the higher levels of monitoring found in Shanghai.

Although local governments in both Shanghai and Jiangsu stepped up efforts to hide revenue after meeting their fiscal quotas, the nature and degree of evasion differed significantly in the two locales. Officials in the two locales manifested very different attitudes toward fiscal contracts. The "guiding thinking (*zhidao sixiang*)" in Jiangsu was for local governments to meet but not to exceed their fiscal quotas. According to one local official, "The province already thinks it has to hand over too much. The county has to hand over too much as well, and this affects the rate of urban construction. [Therefore,] after the assignment is completed, the township will approve [additional] tax breaks" (Informant 196). This view was echoed by an official at the county level: "After completing their *baogan* targets, townships do not hand over any more taxes" (Informant 191). As an official of a township-level tax bureau put it, "The tax law became irrelevant after the implementation of the revenue-sharing fiscal system" (Informant 194). He further explained, "You don't want to take in too little, and you don't want to take in too much, but you must complete your quota. . . . My instructions are to ensure the completion of targets. . . . But after meeting the fiscal quota, then we can use existing policies to give enterprises [additional] tax breaks." The official acknowledged that if, by implementing the tax regulations, the township would have exceeded its fiscal quota, then the township should by rights have collected the higher amount; nevertheless, it was standard practice in the township to increase reductions and exemptions instead. As an official of the Ministry of Agriculture Policy Reform Section recognized, "The revenue-sharing fiscal system is not fair or even-handed; the prevalence of tax exemptions is linked to the nature of the fiscal contract" (Informant 188).

By contrast, the "guiding thinking" in Shanghai was to enforce the strict implementation of policy.[84] As of the early 1990s, according to a local official, "Policies had not been relaxed in Shanghai because of the fear that the *baogan* target would not be met."[85] A finance official from

[84] A municipal official in Shanghai described the hiding of revenue as a major source of conflict with county and township leaders (Informant 37).

[85] Informant 138. Similarly, an official of the Ministry of Agriculture Rural Enterprise Section stated, "In Shanghai the tax burden is extremely heavy; so they do not grant tax exemptions or reductions to township- and village-run enterprises." Although clearly an exaggerated statement in view of the evidence, the point is nonetheless clear (Informant 187).

Luhang Town, Shanghai, described the process of revenue extraction in the following manner: "Enterprises still pay first; then if the [township] exceeds [its] target, some [of the revenue] is returned."[86] Indeed, case study data show that Shanghai townships consistently exceeded their minimum revenue-sharing quotas,[87] while townships in Jiangsu avoided overfulfilling their fiscal contracts.[88]

The contrasting approaches to the implementation of tax policy were also starkly reflected in the remuneration of rural enterprise managers, technicians, and shop floor workers. The contrast is captured first in the complaints of an enterprise manager in Songyang Town, Shanghai, and then in the boasts of an official of the county economic commission in Wuxi County, Jiangsu:

> The policies of Shanghai Municipality are not advantageous. [The production of] many products has been lost to Jiangsu and Zhejiang. There remuneration levels are very high. There factory managers earn a lot of money. That is not allowed here. . . . Shanghai wants to control [things], but it controls too much. This destroys township- and village-run enterprises. Shanghai technical personnel can be found everywhere else, but they're not in Shanghai's rural enterprises because of [Shanghai's] policies (Informant 77).

> Rural enterprise managers here can earn up to 100 thousand yuan in income. They are supposed to pay individual adjustment tax, but they don't and no one goes after them for it. Also, many engineers come here from Shanghai to earn more money. Shanghai doesn't want them to leave, but they come because they can earn more money here. It is often technical people from Shanghai who are involved in establishing enterprises here (Informant 191).

In interviews Jiangsu managers consistently reported incomes higher than those reported by Shanghai managers. Among the collective managers in Dongtan Town, Jiangsu, who responded to questions about their income, the highest reported annual income in 1991 was 80,000 yuan,

---

[86] Of course, the official went on to say that "because of other policies, it is not all given back." As noted in the discussion of the fiscal system in Chapter 3, there is a lack of credible commitment to fiscal contracts by higher levels (Informant 70).

[87] Informants 34, 53, 70, 112, and 135.

[88] Informants 181 and 191. Of course, once revenues had entered budgetary channels, higher levels could renege on fiscal contracts and not return the contracted amount. This commonly occurred at the township and county levels in Shanghai in 1990 and 1991.

while the lowest was 17,300 yuan, with an average of 41,075 yuan.[89] By contrast, among the collective managers in Nantang Township, Shanghai, the highest reported annual income in 1991 was 9,900 yuan, and the lowest was 3,800, with an average of 6,580 yuan.[90] These figures are not based on a representative sample, and not all managers responded to questions about their incomes. In addition, underreporting of managers' incomes may have been more prevalent in Shanghai, where local party organs sought to control managerial incomes more closely.[91] By contrast, a local official in Dongtan stated that there were no ceilings on managerial incomes.[92] Nevertheless, a clear pattern emerges. As one Shanghai manager lamented, if only he had been born somewhere else, he would have been making a lot more money (Informant 47).

The same pattern could be found among the wages of shop floor workers. It was not uncommon for the average annual wage in rural enterprises in Jiangsu in 1991 to be over 3,000 yuan, while the average wage in Shanghai's rural enterprises rarely exceeded 2,500 yuan.

The key difference, according to local officials in both Shanghai and Jiangsu, was the extent to which costs were deducted from an enterprise's tax bill. As a tax official in Nantang Town, Jiading County, Shanghai, commented, "There are national regulations regarding costs, but here we use regulations published by Shanghai Municipality. Jiangsu published regulations that were quite strict [on paper], but Jiangsu is passive in implementation. The key is the base of the tax contract. This is why Shanghai is different from Jiangsu" (Informant 133). The difference the official was highlighting was the degree of active enforcement of tax policy. While such actions as the padding of wage rolls did occur in Shanghai, more active policy enforcement prevented such actions from occurring to the same extent as in Jiangsu, resulting in lower average wage levels in Shanghai. By contrast, according to a county official in Wuxi, "The average worker's wage exceeds the deductible standard set by the tax bureau. . . . After all is said and done, all wages are

---

[89] Informants 192, 196, and 197.
[90] Informants 120, 123, 126, 127, and 129. Similarly, in Luhang Town, Shanghai, the income of the highest-paid collective manager was 11,000 yuan while that of the lowest-paid was 4,000 yuan (Informant 66).
[91] Indeed, ceilings on income sometimes prevented managers from ever collecting the bonuses awarded to them on the basis of contract incentives.
[92] Informant 193. Interestingly, the official noted that the goal of the local leadership was to pay managers enough that they would not want to go elsewhere to establish a private enterprise as a means of increasing their income.

deducted as costs, [although] tax should actually be paid on the part which exceeds the deductible standard" (Informant 191). An official of the economic management office in Dongtan Town, Wuxi, was more explicit: "This office is engaged in local policy (*tu zhengce*). This is especially true in terms of remuneration for both managers and workers. The tax policy in this regard has totally lost touch with reality (*tuoli shiji*). ... The amount of tax-deductible wages is too low; so the problem of padding wage rolls, etc., exists" (Informant 96).

Finally, contrasts in implementation were also apparent in the treatment of business expenses (*yewufei*). Facing highly competitive product markets, rural enterprises commonly used entertainment, gifts, and payments to clients to gain footholds in the marketplace. Officials and rural enterprise managers in Jiangsu reported that fully 100 percent of these business expenses were deducted from firms' tax liabilities.[93] Tax regulations limited the deductibility of these expenses to a small percentage of a firm's total sales value; beyond that limit, business expenses were to be deducted from after-tax profits. By contrast, although Shanghai managers also inflated deductible costs to cover business expenses, they reported having to cover at least part of these expenses out of after-tax profits.[94] Thus, more aggressive monitoring of tax policy implementation resulted in less freewheeling business practices and less competitive wages in Shanghai.[95]

A TEST OF THE HYPOTHESES

The case study data presented here suggest two hypotheses about the sources of tax effort at the local level in China. First, the data suggest that the structure of property rights was an important determinant of effort. It operated in part indirectly, through innovative institutional arrangements designed to overcome the difficulties of taxing the private sector, on the one hand, and through collective organizational structures that shielded collective enterprises from strict implementation of tax policy on the other. Second, the case studies show that the provincial environment, manifested in the intensity of monitoring of lower-level behavior, had an important bearing on implementation – even at the grass roots. This

---

[93] Informants 180, 184, 191, and 199.
[94] Informants 79, 80, and 81.
[95] It appears that 1992 may have signaled something of a sea change for Shanghai. Local officials in Nantang Township, for example, projected that managers' incomes would increase by more than three times over 1991. Informant 138.

section presents a preliminary test of these hypotheses using a regression model of the tax ratio for all counties in Jiangsu, Zhejiang, and Shanghai – the three provincial-level units where case studies were conducted.[96] In theory, the tax ratio (defined as total taxes collected as a share of total output) is predicted by two sets of variables: tax capacity and tax effort. Tax capacity is a measure of the readily taxable resources (the tax base) in a given locale. Tax effort, on the other hand, is a measure of the ability or willingness of the government to tap those resources reflected in tax capacity. Most studies of taxation have estimated tax effort only indirectly.[97] As Organski and Kugler (1980:81) in their study of political capacity state with regard to the determinants of tax effort, "What these variables are and how they operate, we cannot discern at present. They are part of the work that remains to be done."

This study directly addresses the issue of tax effort. The following model of the tax ratio specifies variables that account for both tax capacity and tax effort and provides a test of the hypotheses generated through case study research about the implementation of tax policy at the local level in China. Existing studies have operationalized tax capacity in several different ways. One approach reflects the sectoral composition of an economy. For example, agriculture is generally regarded as difficult to tax, since agricultural producers are highly dispersed and generate a relatively small economic surplus. By contrast, oil exports are generally regarded as easy to tax, since producers are usually concentrated in a few large operations and generate a relatively large economic surplus. Therefore, economies highly dependent on agriculture for a large share of GNP would be expected to have lower tax capacities, ceteris paribus, than those that derive a large share of GNP from oil exports. Another approach is to express tax capacity simply using GNP per capita. The rationale is that a

---

[96] Although this study focuses primarily on the township level, township-level data were not available; therefore the regression uses data from the county level.

[97] Most regression approaches predict the tax ratio (as the dependent variable) using independent variables that reflect only tax capacity, leaving tax effort in the error term. They use the coefficients on the capacity variables (produced by the regression equation) in conjunction with actual data to produce an estimate of the expected tax ratio for each case. They then compare the actual tax ratio to the expected tax ratio to construct an index of tax effort. Richard Bird (1978) is highly critical of tax effort studies since they do not take into account "political and administrative realities" in any direct way. This study directly addresses this problem. Among the best known studies of tax effort are: Bahl (1971), Chelliah (1971), Chelliah, Bass, and Kelly (1975), Lotz and Morss (1967), and Newlyn (1985). For a political approach to this issue, see Organski and Kugler (1980). For an application of this approach to the Chinese case, see World Bank (1990b).

high per capita GNP reflects a large taxable surplus. In this study tax capacity is operationalized using the share of agriculture in total output. This operationalization was chosen over GNP per capita because GNP per capita was found to be collinear with the measure of collective ownership, a variable of theoretical interest.[98] The share of agriculture in total output is expected to be negatively related to the tax ratio.

Tax effort is specified using variables that reflect both the form of enterprise ownership and the provincial environment. Form of enterprise ownership is operationalized using the output value of collectively owned rural industrial enterprises as a share of total industrial output value, which is expected to be negatively related to the tax ratio.[99] Provincial environment is operationalized using dummy variables for Shanghai and Zhejiang.[100] The Shanghai variable is expected to be positively related to the tax ratio. The case studies do not suggest strong expectations about the Zhejiang variable, although interviews suggest that the Zhejiang regulatory environment is more lax than that found in Shanghai.[101] The results of the regression are reported in Table 5.3.[102]

The relationships are significant and in the expected directions, and the model accounts for approximately 80 percent of the variance in the tax ratio. As hypothesized, the effect of collective ownership on the tax ratio, holding taxable capacity and provincial environment constant, is negative and statistically significant.[103] Specifically, a 1 percentage point increase in the collective share of industrial output results in a 0.062 percentage point

---

[98] Other sectoral factors such as mining or trade are not included because taxes from these sources do not appear in the numerator of the tax ratio, which is based on industrial and commercial taxes. See the notes to Table 5.3 for complete definitions.

[99] Industrial enterprises constituted the largest part of the tax base during the period under study.

[100] The third province, Jiangsu, is excluded. The coefficients on the included dummy variables are interpreted as the effect of being located in Shanghai (or Zhejiang) as opposed to being located in Jiangsu, other things being equal.

[101] Although Shanghai is a provincial-level city, while Zhejiang is a province, they both enter directly into fiscal contracts with the counties under their jurisdiction. Thus, while Wenzhou City in Zhejiang exercises administrative control over the counties under its jurisdiction, it does not exercise fiscal control.

[102] Ordinary least squares regression was used. Tests for autocorrelation, heteroskedasticity, and multicollinearity were performed using the Durbin-Watson statistic (= 1.66), the Glejser test, and auxiliary R-squares, respectively; no evidence of these potential problems was found. Although interactions between the effect of provincial environment and the effect of ownership form are plausible theoretically, the attendant loss of parsimony did not warrant the specification of interaction terms.

[103] The fact that the maximum tax rate on profits was higher for collective than for private firms reinforces the significance of the negative coefficient.

Table 5.3. *The Impact of Ownership Form and Provincial Environment on the Tax Ratio*

Independent Variables	Coefficients (SE)	Beta
Agricultural output value as share of total output value	-0.104^a (0.014)	-0.56
Output value of collectively owned township-, village-, and team-run industrial enterprises as share of total industrial output value	-0.62^a (0.011)	-0.32
Shanghai	0.108^a (0.006)	0.77
Zhejiang	0.019^a (0.003)	0.27
Constant	0.133 (0.01)	

$N = 138$
Adjusted R-squared = 0.81
Standard error of the estimate = 0.15

Notes: The variables, using county-level data, are defined as follows:
Tax ratio = *gongshang shuishou/guomin shouru*. *Gongshang shuishou* includes product, business, and value-added taxes, the industrial-commercial unified tax, profits taxes on collective, private, individual, and joint venture enterprises, and the individual adjustment tax (Informant 111). While *guomin shengchan zongzhi* (gross domestic product) would be a preferable measure of total output, comparable 1991 data were not available for all counties. Based on tests using *guomin shengchan zongzhi* for all counties for which it was available, it was determined that the choice between *guomin shouru* and *guomin shengchan zongzhi* did not affect the outcome in any meaningful way.
Agricultural share of total output = *nongye zongchanzhi/nongcun shehui zongchanzhi*.
Collective share of industrial output = (*xiangban gongye zongchanzhi + cun ji cun yi xia ban gongye zongchanzhi*)/*quanbu gongye zongchanzhi*. (It appears that the village-and-below figure includes only the output of village- and team-run enterprises.)
Shanghai = 1; Jiangsu and Zhejiang = 0.
Zhejiang = 1; Jiangsu and Shanghai = 0.
$^a p < 0.001$.
Sources: 1991 county-level data are drawn from: *Jiangsu shixian jingji 1992*; *Zhejiang tongji nianjian 1992*; *Shanghai xian guomin jingji tongji ziliao 1991*.

decrease in the tax ratio.[104] The impact of the Shanghai environment is positive and significant. The effect of being located in Shanghai as opposed to Jiangsu, *ceteris paribus*, is a 0.108 percentage point *increase* in the tax ratio. However, the effect of being in Zhejiang as opposed to Jiangsu is a

[104] An alternative model was specified using the private share of industrial output in place of the collective share of industrial output for counties for which comparable data were

0.019 percentage point increase in the tax ratio, suggesting that tax effort in Zhejiang is only slightly better than in Jiangsu.

Analysis of the outliers is also consistent with the findings of the case studies. The regression procedure identified the Wenzhou counties of Yueqing and Cangnan, both of which successfully developed on the basis of private ownership, as outliers. Since Yueqing was also a case study site, it is possible to provide a more nuanced account of the regression results in this case. Yueqing's status as an outlier is based on the fact that the actual tax ratio was twice that predicted by the regression model. Since the majority of privately owned firms in Yueqing were granted *collective* licenses as shareholding cooperative enterprises, their output was reported by the local statistical bureau in the collective category.[105] Nevertheless, these privately invested firms were taxed under private as opposed to collective institutional arrangements. Had the industrial output statistics for Yueqing been accurately reported as produced by privately owned firms, Yueqing would not have appeared as an outlier in the regression analysis, since the results indicate that the higher the private share of industrial output, the higher the tax ratio.[106]

The quantitative results must be interpreted with some caution, however. While they are consistent with the findings of the case studies, they may also reflect possible biases in the original data. Measurement of taxable resources in the private sector presents serious difficulties to local officials; therefore, total output may be disproportionately underreported in counties in which private industry dominates. In these circumstances, the denominator of the tax ratio (total output) may be consistently smaller, rendering the ratio as a whole larger.[107] However, times series data collected during field work show that between 1978 and 1991, total output increased at roughly comparable rates in the case study areas: it increased

available (Jiangsu and Zhejiang only). See Table 5.3a. As hypothesized, the relationship between the private share of industrial output and the tax ratio was positive and significant, indicating that the results of the model reported in Table 5.3 are relatively robust.

[105] When the township and village shares of industrial output are examined separately, it is clear that in the case of Yueqing, privately produced output is recorded under the village category.

[106] This was confirmed by estimating the correct private share of industrial output based on case study data and then reexamining the regression results.

[107] The possible direction of bias with respect to collective firms is more ambiguous. As indicated earlier in the chapter, output was underreported by some collective firms. On the other hand, although Chapter 3 indicates a move away from output value as a key performance indicator for township officials and collective enterprise managers, some enterprises may have overreported output value in order to meet performance targets.

Table 5.3. *The Impact of Ownership Form and Provincial Environment on the Tax Ratio*

Independent Variables	Coefficients (SE)	Beta
Agricultural output value as share of total output value	-0.07^a (0.009)	-0.53
Output value of privately owned industrial enterprises as share of total industrial output value	0.04^b (0.017)	0.15
Zhejiang	0.02^a (0.003)	0.45
Constant	0.08 (0.004)	
$N = 131$		
Adjusted R-squared = 0.5		
Standard error of the estimate = 0.02		

$^a p < 0.01.$
$^b p < 0.05.$

at an average annual rate of 21 percent in Wuxi County, 15 percent in Shanghai County, and 16 percent in Yueqing County. In addition, during the period under study, Yueqing – a county in which private investment was predominant – ranked among the top 2 percent to 3 percent of counties nationwide in terms of absolute level of fiscal income – a position not inconsistent with its relatively high tax ratio (*Zhongguo baiming caizheng da xian* 1991). Moreover, Hualing Town, the research site in Yueqing County, exceeded its 1991 tax quota of 13.3 million yuan by more than 3 million yuan – again, a finding consistent with a relatively high tax ratio (Informants 160 and 167). Nevertheless, given the data presently available, it is not possible to estimate with greater certainty what the degree of underreporting might be.

CONCLUSION: PROPERTY RIGHTS, REGULATORY
ENVIRONMENTS, AND REVENUE MOBILIZATION

To return to the question posed at the outset, how effective were local institutional arrangements in mobilizing revenue into budgetary channels?

Perpetuation of the collective model in which political and economic power were fused in the hands of local state officials hindered the mobilization of revenue into the budgetary system. While overall extraction remained high, local officials colluded with the collective firms in their jurisdictions to evade and avoid central tax levies. These practices allowed local officials to shift revenue from budgetary channels, which were shared with higher levels, to nonbudgetary channels, which were controlled locally. Thus, local officials were poor agents of the center in the taxation of collective firms.

In devising new institutional arrangements to extract revenue from private firms, local officials were responding to the same set of incentives. The institutional innovations benefited local governments by providing information about the resources of private firms. Although the approach adopted in Hualing represented an accommodation to private firms, it nevertheless brought additional revenue into budgetary channels. At the same time, the approach benefited the central government by revealing greater fiscal capacity in the local economy. Local officials in Songyang, who adopted a more adversarial approach to taxing the private sector, were even better agents of central interests with respect to the private firms within their jurisdiction. As in Hualing, the institutions designed to cope with the challenges of taxing private firms at the local level in Songyang also revealed fiscal capacity to higher levels.

All local institutions operated in broader provincial regulatory environments, and the particular provincial context had an independent impact on the effectiveness of these local institutional arrangements in mobilizing revenue into budgetary channels. The central state elicited different levels of political effort in revenue extraction across provinces. The disparity in political effort is illustrated by the contrast between Jiangsu, where monitoring was lax, and Shanghai, where it was strict. By relaxing or intensifying monitoring of local behavior, officials at the provincial level influenced policy implementation at lower levels. Thus, the approach to revenue extraction at the township level was shaped by the provincial regulatory environment and local institutional arrangements.

Joel Migdal (1988:279) criticizes studies that measure "'extraction' much more than 'regulation of social relationships'. . . ." This chapter has attempted to do both. The quantitative measures of extraction derived from the tax ratio model are consistent with the conclusions drawn from case studies designed to capture the complex institutional incentives and constraints that shaped the behavior of the officials populating the local arm of the state. This chapter has illustrated how the structure of property rights influenced the evolution of local institutions of revenue extraction and how the development of state and market institutions were closely linked.

6

Credit Allocation and Collective Organizational Structures

T HIS chapter shifts the focus from revenue extraction to credit allocation. As in the case of tax policy, township governments also had clear incentives to intervene in the implementation of credit policy. The rapid development of collective firms and their ability to undertake direct and indirect provision of public goods was supported by access to credit from the state banking system. Like revenue extraction, credit allocation for collective enterprises functioned as part of the larger collective organizational structure. This political backing allowed collectives in areas such as Wuxi and Songjiang to take on high levels of debt relative to equity, and it contributed to softness in the budget constraints of many collective firms. By contrast, private firms were not deeply embedded in this collective structure and were largely shut out of the state banking system through the early to mid-1990s.

Local institutional arrangements involving credit allocation had implications for the ability of the central state to realize its goals at the local level. Among the goals of financial reform in China have been for the central state to shift from direct, administrative means to indirect, economic means of controlling the banking system and for banks to enjoy greater autonomy in decisions regarding the allocation of credit. Yet these goals do not translate simply into a reduction of the state's role. Rather, the central state must play a different but equally important role in establishing banking institutions that can function free of day-to-day political interference. An underlying theme of this study is that the shift from a direct to an indirect role for the state in the economy is not a process of "state shrinking" but rather state building.[1] However, such a fundamental transformation in the role of the state is an intensely polit-

---

[1] For the term "state shrinking," see Schamis (n.d.).

ical process, since, as this chapter will demonstrate, it challenges vested interests throughout the state apparatus – particularly those of local governments.

The first section of this chapter provides an overview of the structure of the banking system and the goals of the major financial reforms. The second and third sections examine the allocation of credit to the collective and private sectors, respectively. The last section is a discussion of the state-building requirements of financial reform.

BANKING SYSTEM REFORMS: SYSTEM STRUCTURE AND POLICY GOALS

In reviewing the structure of the system and the policy goals for both the central bank and the state-run commercial banks, two broad categories of reforms are of particular interest: (1) the transformation of the People's Bank of China (PBOC) into a central bank designed to exercise indirect monetary control and (2) the creation of more autonomous state-owned commercial banks intended to behave like enterprises responsible for their own profits and losses.[2] However, as of the mid-1990s, the reformed banking system had failed to perform as intended; state-owned commercial banks were not sufficiently responsive to profit criteria in issuing bank loans, and the People's Bank of China was unsuccessful in its use of the tools of monetary policy to regulate the economy.

System Structure

The current structure of the Chinese banking system began to take shape with a major reorganization implemented in 1984.[3] The People's Bank of China, which until 1978 had been part of the Ministry of Finance, was designated as China's central bank in September 1983. As of January 1984, the PBOC ceased making loans directly to enterprises, and that function was taken over by the four state-owned commercial banks (Industrial and Commercial Bank, Agriculture Bank, Construction Bank, and Bank of China) referred to as specialized banks.[4]

---

[2] Other major initiatives of financial reform include the development of nonbank financial institutions and the development of money and capital markets. See Yi (1994).

[3] A good review is providing in Bowles and White (1993).

[4] Beginning in 1979, reformers gradually instituted the practice of issuing bank loans instead of budgetary grants for both working capital and investment capital.

The Industrial and Commercial Bank (ICB) was primarily responsible for working capital loans, technical renovation loans, and loans for new equipment purchases. In addition to its traditional role in lending to urban enterprises, the ICB also began to lend to rural enterprises, making it a player in the expansion of township and village industry. Most urban industrial and commercial enterprises held their deposits at the Industrial and Commercial Bank, and the bank made loans mainly on the basis of these deposits. The Agriculture Bank (AB), in addition to making loans to the state commercial system for the purchase of agricultural products, also handled loans for the development of rural enterprises, which it granted on the basis of deposits.[5] The Construction Bank (CB) handled loans for capital construction, used for building new plants and expanding plant capacity. The Construction Bank made loans primarily from budgetary funds allocated to it by the Ministry of Finance, although in order to increase its lending capacity, it also made loans from deposits. The Bank of China (BOC) handled foreign exchange transactions.

Although the banking system implemented significant reforms allowing competition among lenders with previously distinct bailiwicks,[6] as of the 1990s, the majority of banking transactions in the rural sector were still conducted through the Agriculture Bank or the Rural Credit Cooperatives (RCCs). This chapter focuses on the lending activity of these two institutions, referring to the lending activity of other commercial banks as required. Often the only bank represented by an office at the township level was the Agriculture Bank; however, the township-level office was not an independent accounting unit but rather was under the direction of the county-level branch office. The Rural Credit Cooperatives, by contrast, had nominal autonomy. They were created in the 1950s using the combined assets of township residents; they were independent accounting units; and they had the status of independent legal entities (*faren*). In reality, however, the Rural Credit Cooperatives often shared the same staff and leadership as the township Agriculture Bank office. In practice, the funds of the Agriculture Bank and Rural Credit Co-

---

[5] At times during the Maoist period, the functions of the Agriculture Bank were subsumed under the People's Bank of China; this was the case from 1965 through 1978. The Agriculture Bank was reestablished beginning in 1979.

[6] Competition would presumably induce banks to make fewer unprofitable loans. However, the subsequent discussion of loan criteria will show how enterprises and the local officials who oversaw them exploited loopholes in this partially reformed system to increase their access to loan capital.

operatives were combined, although the Rural Credit Cooperatives maintained separate account books.[7] Indeed, RCCs were described as "subordinates of state banks with little autonomy" (Wong 1996:155).

The Agriculture Bank and the Rural Credit Cooperatives depended heavily on local deposits for loan funds (*duocun duodai*). The growing supply of capital available for loans to township- and village-run collectives derived from rapid increases in savings fueled by rising rural incomes (Table 6.1). Household savings deposits in the Agriculture Bank increased dramatically from the late 1970s through the mid-1990s. Similarly, household deposits in the Rural Credit Cooperatives increased rapidly from an even larger base (Table 6.2). Together the Agriculture Bank and Rural Credit Cooperatives provided more than 380 billion yuan in loans to township- and village-run enterprises as of 1995, with 70 percent of the loans provided by RCCs.

Policy Goals

In establishing the People's Bank as the central bank, the central government's goal was to shift from direct to indirect monetary control. There were a number of instruments by which the central bank could, in theory, exercise indirect monetary control beginning in the 1980s, including (1) increasing the discount rate – the interest rate on central bank lending to the Agriculture Bank and the other commercial banks – (2) restricting central bank lending to the commercial banks, and (3) increasing the reserve requirements for the commercial banks (Zhou and Zhu 1987:401). Nevertheless, these indirect controls proved ineffective in maintaining macroeconomic balance during bouts of inflation in 1988 and again in 1993, forcing the central bank to intervene directly in the operation of the commercial banks by using administrative measures such as loan ceilings to bring about monetary control. By the mid-1990s, however, there was renewed emphasis on indirect monetary control. As Nicholas Lardy (1998:138) indicates, "the Central Bank Law of 1995 anticipates a shift to reliance on indirect instruments of monetary policy. Credit quotas are not even listed as a specific monetary policy tool. Movement in this direction was evident in 1997 when the scope of credit quotas was limited to the four largest banks and in 1998 when mandatory credit quotas for even the largest banks were eliminated."

The main policy goal with respect to the specialized banks, such as the

---

[7] Informants 57, 99, 177, and 198.

Table 6.1. *Agriculture Bank and Rural Credit Cooperative Assets and Liabilities, 1987–95*

Agriculture Bank

	1987	1988	1989	1990	1991	1992	1993	1994	1995
Liabilities (billion current yuan)									
Total	273.70	314.30	373.20	473.60	578.60	706.18	915.00	1,224.39	1,111.92
Deposits	148.70	171.40	205.50	192.11	245.28	313.82	384.27	518.56	693.94
Enterprise	30.50	35.10	36.90	43.80	54.60	76.52	109.83	141.44	190.93
Household	42.60	59.40	84.90	121.20	157.70	197.24	253.30	356.46	481.34
Other	75.60	76.90	83.70	27.11	32.98	40.05	21.14	20.66	21.68
Central bank loans to Agriculture Bank	83.50	99.40	118.30	143.90	175.00	208.11	271.88	355.46	86.12
Interbank loans to Agriculture Bank	5.50	8.80	16.00	99.53	116.80	145.02	149.29	193.46	211.61
Other liabilities	36.00	34.70	33.40	38.06	41.52	39.23	109.56	156.91	120.25
Assets (billion current yuan)									
Total	273.70	314.30	373.20	473.60	578.60	706.18	915.00	1,224.39	1,111.92
Loans		263.20	305.80	377.40	457.80	546.81	656.50	552.46	656.05
State industry		15.40	18.90	24.95	30.80	40.23	53.21	62.25	68.59
State commerce		156.90	187.40	235.90	286.90	331.53	339.75	211.38	258.73
Rural industry		40.80	42.10	46.20	49.80	58.25	77.46	93.84	110.55
Fixed-asset loans		5.80	6.60	7.60	9.90	13.92	15.31	19.48	24.04
Other		44.30	50.80	62.75	80.40	102.88	170.76	165.51	194.14
Required reserves		20.20	25.90	34.00	43.10	51.81	71.12	93.37	116.82
Deposits with central bank		13.30	25.00	38.80	42.80	34.06	53.62	57.34	58.12
Interbank loans		12.70	10.50	16.80	27.80	57.81	29.69	68.17	67.04
Other assets		4.90	6.00	6.60	7.10	15.70	104.07	453.05	213.89

Rural Credit Cooperatives

	1987	1988	1989	1990	1991	1992	1993	1994	1995
Liabilities (billion current yuan)									
Total	161.90	191.10	231.00	299.90	368.90	487.48	604.49	795.23	986.85
Deposits	122.50	140.00	166.30	214.50	270.90	347.77	429.06	566.97	717.29
Collective	21.90	25.70	25.70	30.30	39.30	61.04	71.91	86.06	97.66
Household	100.60	114.20	140.70	184.20	231.60	286.73	357.15	480.91	619.63
Interbank loans to Cooperatives	3.80	3.60	3.80	4.20	5.10	6.06	6.06	6.90	16.66
Other liabilities	35.60	47.50	60.90	81.30	92.90	133.65	169.37	221.37	252.90
Assets (billion current yuan)									
Total	161.90	191.10	231.00	299.90	368.90	487.48	604.49	795.23	986.85
Loans	77.10	90.90	109.10	141.30	180.80	245.39	326.16	415.95	517.58
Rural enterprises	35.90	44.00	54.00	70.10	91.00	129.43	178.25	227.70	277.96
Other[a]	41.20	46.90	55.10	71.20	89.80	115.97	147.91	188.24	239.62
Deposits with Agriculture Bank	55.20	58.00	65.60	77.20	91.60	108.05	136.84	167.74	190.82
Deposits with central bank[b]	4.70	4.90	3.70	5.30	9.10	3.04	1.57	8.82	18.73
Other assets	24.90	37.30	52.60	76.10	87.40	131.00	139.92	202.73	259.71

Note: Data for 1990 and after reflect definitional changes in total deposits and in interbank loans.
[a] Includes loans to collective agriculture, rural households, and other borrowers.
[b] Special reserve requirements.

Sources: *Zhongguo nongcun jinrong tongji 1979–1989. Zhongguo nongcun tongji nianjian.*

Table 6.2. Loans to Township- and Village-run Enterprises and Rural Household Savings Deposits, 1978–95

	Agriculture Bank Loans to TVEs		Agriculture Bank Rural Household Savings Deposits		
Year	Total Loans (Billion Current Yuan)	Total Loans (Percentage Increase)	Year	Household Deposits (Billion Current Yuan)	Household Deposits (Percentage Increase)
1979	2.99		1979	2.12	
1980	5.30	77.3	1980	3.22	51.9
1981	6.21	17.2	1981	4.26	32.3
1982	7.34	18.2	1982	5.38	26.3
1983	8.00	9.0	1983	6.70	24.5
1984	15.77	97.1	1984	10.05	50.0
1985	18.80	19.2	1985	15.53	54.5
1986	28.79	53.1	1986	25.77	65.9
1987	35.01	21.6	1987	42.62	65.4
1988	40.77	16.5	1988	59.37	39.3
1989	42.06	3.2	1989	84.85	42.9
1990	46.22	9.9	1990	121.21	42.9
1991	49.80	7.7	1991	157.76	30.2
1992	58.25	17.0	1992	197.24	25.0
1993	77.46	33.0	1993	253.30	28.4
1994	93.84	21.1	1994	356.46	40.7
1995	110.55	17.8	1995	481.34	35.0

Credit Cooperative
Loans to TVEs

Credit Cooperative
Rural Household Savings Deposits

Year	Total Loans (Billion Current Yuan)	Total Loans (Percentage Increase)	Year	Household Deposits (Billion Current Yuan)	Household Deposits (Percentage Increase)
1978	1.21		1978	5.57	
1979	1.41	16.5	1979	7.85	40.9
1980	2.74	94.6	1980	11.69	49.0
1981	3.55	28.9	1981	16.94	44.9
1982	4.23	19.3	1982	22.79	34.5
1983	6.00	42.0	1983	31.96	40.3
1984	13.50	124.8	1984	43.79	37.0
1985	16.44	21.8	1985	56.48	29.0
1986	26.50	61.7	1986	76.61	35.6
1987	35.93	35.6	1987	100.57	31.3
1988	44.61	24.2	1988	114.23	13.6
1989	54.19	21.5	1989	140.68	23.2
1990	70.07	29.3	1990	184.16	30.9
1991	91.03	29.9	1991	231.67	25.8
1992	129.43	42.2	1992	286.73	23.8
1993	178.25	37.7	1993	357.62	24.7
1994	227.70	27.7	1994	481.60	34.7
1995	277.96	22.1	1995	619.56	28.6

Sources: Zhongguo nongcun jinrong tongji 1979–1989. Zhongguo nongcun jinrong tongji nianjian.

Agriculture Bank, was to transform them into enterprises responsible for their own profits and losses. In January 1986, the State Council promulgated the Interim Regulations on Bank Management, stressing "the responsibility of banks to allocate credit efficiently" (Bowles and White 1989). In 1988, two years after the promulgation of the interim regulations, articles in the official *People's Daily* were still trying to establish that "loans should be granted on a priority basis to those enterprises that manufacture marketable products, that have good credit, and that can turn out better economic results. Credit will be tightened for those enterprises that are poorly managed, that manufacture unmarketable products, and that have bad credit" (Li 1988:5). Thus, in theory, banks, operating as profit-oriented firms, were to discipline enterprise borrowing, thereby increasing enterprise efficiency. However, writing a decade later, Lardy notes "the central problem that plagued China in the pre-reform era – inefficient allocation of capital – persists."

IMPLEMENTATION OF CREDIT POLICY IN THE COLLECTIVE SECTOR

Township leaders had powerful incentives to use their political influence over local lenders to induce them to make loans that promoted local party and government goals. These goals – reflecting the criteria by which township officials were evaluated and promoted – included the expansion of rural industry to meet rapidly increasing targets, the provision of public goods, and the maintenance of employment opportunities for local residents, among others. Bank loans to collective firms furthered these goals both directly and indirectly. In practice, however, township goals were often at odds with the goals of reforms in the financial sector.

Political interference in bank operations was facilitated by institutionalized relationships (Lardy 1998:90–1). Although township bank officials were appointed within the Agriculture Bank system by their county-level superiors, the leaders of the township party committee approved the appointments. Moreover, the party affairs of township bank officials were governed at the township level. Thus, township leaders exercised some authority over township bank officials via party channels. Interviews confirmed the institutional potential for and actual exercise of local party authority over banks.[8] Institutionalized control

---

[8] Informants 57, 63, 136, 159, 177, and 198. The same was true at the county level (Informant 163). As Lardy (1998:85) finds, "Chinese banks also extend loans at the 'request' of

extended even beyond party channels in some cases. In Dongtan Town, Wuxi County, a bank official reported that "the vice-general manager of the [town government's] industrial corporation is concurrently the manager of the credit cooperative; so the interests of the industrial corporation are attended to and borrowing money is convenient" (Informant 198).[9] Political interference might not have undermined financial discipline if local political officials had evaluated enterprise performance based on efficiency criteria, but efficiency considerations had low priority among local officials' goals, and, as a result, enterprise financial discipline was not enforced.

The Resort to Administrative Controls

The inability of the central government to maintain macroeconomic balance was reflected in the repeated boom–bust cycles experienced by the Chinese economy during the 1980s and early 1990s. The economy exhibited episodes of severe overheating in 1984 to 1985, 1987 to 1988, and again in 1992 to 1993. As many analysts have argued, uncontrolled bank lending contributed significantly to these episodes of overheating (Y. Huang 1990; Lardy 1998; Naughton 1990; 1991; 1992b). The expansionary environment of 1984 was followed by a contractionary phase in 1985: the People's Bank set lending ceilings for the specialized banks in order to bring the overheated economy back into balance (Tam 1986:435). However, as Barry Naughton (1992b) points out, "In the 1984–85 expansion, local political leaders [were] able to compel local bank branches to expand lending beyond their quotas." As a result, the expansionary atmosphere

> could be altered only by the adoption by the central political leadership of contractionary policies as a major point of the current *political* line. In a party plenum of October 1985, 'contraction' was indeed adopted as official party policy. Only in this atmosphere could a contractionary monetary policy be carried out. In order to make

local party and government officials to support their favorite projects." Indeed, the evidence presented in this section challenges the assertion of Che and Qian (1998) that township officials were effectively constrained from interfering in the allocation of credit to rural enterprises during the first fifteen years of reform.

[9] Moreover, as Christine Wong (1996:179) notes, banks were susceptible to pressure from local officials in part because they had "a good deal of control over the nonpecuniary benefits of bank staff, including the availability and conditions of housing, schooling, and job prospects for staff offspring."

credit quotas truly binding, it was necessary to elevate contractionary policy to the status of party policy: the contraction had to be "strict," in order for it to have any effect at all (Naughton 1991:66).

When the economy overheated in 1987 to 1988, the People's Bank attempted to regain macroeconomic balance by using the indirect monetary controls at its disposal. For example, it increased the reserve requirement from 10 to 12 percent (30 percent for the Construction Bank) and increased the discount rate on loans to the specialized banks (Xinhua, January 14, 1988). While these policies had some impact, credit was not effectively brought under control until the central bank set strict quotas on bank lending beginning in September 1988 (Naughton 1992b). Once again, quotas were employed in the context of a major politically driven austerity program focused on "rectifying the economic environment."

During the austerity program the scale of the township-level Agriculture Bank's total loans outstanding was controlled by binding targets (also described as mandatory plans – *zhilingxing jihua*) sent down by the county bank branch. Bank officials reported that, in principle, the targets were strict ceilings that the township-level office could not exceed by so much as one *fen*,[10] even though these ceilings often represented only a fraction of deposits in any given branch office. Indeed, in the townships where interviews were conducted, the bank office did not technically exceed these targets (Informants 159 and 198).[11] Central policy stipulated that total loans to rural enterprises would not increase at all during 1989.[12] This rather draconian policy was relaxed only slightly for the

---

[10] A fen is one hundredth of a yuan, or "a Chinese penny."

[11] This was not the case everywhere. As Brandt and Zhu (1995:11) point out, the central government "has not been able to commit credibly to controlling the supply of total credits within the quota of the credit plan. Thus, the specialized banks are able to lend outside the credit plan and to obtain resources from the monetary authorities for supplying [directed credits]." They cite as an example the interactions between the PBOC and the AB in 1988. The PBOC initially refused to provide additional credits to the AB when the latter exceeded its credit plan. However, after farmers were paid 2 to 3 billion yuan in "IOUs" instead of cash for procurement of agricultural products, the PBOC came through with additional credits. During the same year, loans by the AB to township- and village-run enterprises increased by 5.8 billion yuan or 16.5 percent (Table 6.1).

[12] See Agriculture Bank President Ma Yongwei's speech to the meeting of Agriculture Bank branch presidents on January 21, 1989 abstracted in Ma (1989). The reference is to the Third Plenum of the Thirteenth Central Committee, the party meeting at which the rectification campaign was initiated.

remainder of the rectification campaign.[13] The central office of the Agriculture Bank attempted to guarantee implementation by stipulating that adherence to the binding targets would be an important element of the performance evaluations of local bank branch executives (Ma Yongwei 1988). Loans for fixed-asset investment were even more tightly controlled during the period of rectification. Township-level offices did not have the authority to approve any loans in this category; rather, decisions regarding fixed-asset loans were made by the county branch. National statistics on loans to rural enterprises by the Agriculture Bank show that loan growth did contract sharply in 1989 and remain below average throughout the remainder of the austerity program, although it was not held to zero (Table 6.2).

In contrast to the local offices of the Agriculture Bank, credit cooperatives were more flexible, because, although the county-level branch of the Agriculture Bank also issued targets for loans outstanding to the cooperatives, these targets were guidance targets (*zhidaoxing*) and were thus nonbinding.[14] Rural Credit Cooperatives made loans based on the level of deposits, limited in part by the special reserve requirements set for cooperatives by the central bank (Table 6.1). However, loans made by RCCs increased rapidly even during the austerity program. Table 6.2 shows that, from the beginning of 1988 through the end of 1991, Rural Credit Cooperative loans increased by 153 percent, while Agriculture Bank loans increased by only 42 percent, even though household savings deposits in the Agriculture Bank were growing much more rapidly (increasing by 270 percent compared to 130 percent for RCCs during the same period). Operating under fewer constraints, the Rural Credit Cooperatives could lend more aggressively to township- and village-run collective enterprises.

Control by targets imparted a campaign mentality to local bank offi-

---

[13] The relaxation of the loan policy in 1990 and 1991 was in part a result of its severe impact on rural enterprises, many of which closed, at least temporarily, throwing rural residents out of work. Rural unemployment heightened concerns about political stability in the countryside. One bank official commented that at that time loans were intended to guarantee employment and that therefore the evaluation of loan guarantors existed in form only. The bank official's implication was that the evaluation has since become more rigorous (Informant 158). On general policy at that time, see Ma (1990).

[14] One article in the journal *Shanghai Jinrong* refers to 1988 binding targets to control the scale of loans made by credit cooperatives "in some places." See Jin (1990:38). Nevertheless, bank officials interviewed for this study emphasized the flexibility of credit cooperatives with respect to loans (Informant 198).

cials to the extent that compliance with targets was a key part of the political line. The Agriculture Bank office in Songyang Town, Songjiang County, reportedly did not fund a single new project during the entire three-year course of economic rectification (Informant 96). As a result, local officials were anxious to take advantage of the relaxed policies initiated by Deng's southern tour in February 1992 by making up for lost time (Informant 97). One local official commented that the town government was planning ten new projects funded by bank loans and that he would consider it a success even if several failed, because the important point was to acquire as many fixed assets as possible while credit policy was loose (Informant 84). Sharp increases in cadre performance targets (*kaohe zhibiao*) in 1991 and 1992 encouraged this mentality. The official noted that it was easier to meet rapid increases in the target for output value by building new enterprises than by improving the performance of existing ones. Similarly, in order to meet the target for the number of foreign joint venture contracts signed, the town's industrial corporation served as the guarantor for the foreign partners to secure bank loans locally even in the absence of adequate information about the partners' creditworthiness. When the ventures fell through, the bank, and the town as guarantor, were left with the burden of debt. In response to these types of behavior by town leaders, a bank official at the county level was already, as of April 1992, anticipating the need for yet another austerity program to counterbalance the fast-growth campaign initiated by Deng Xiaoping in February 1992. As he put it, "We have lost control over credit (*xindai shikong*)" (Informant 84).

Indeed, by mid-1993, yet another retrenchment had already been initiated by the central government – once again governed by binding targets (Lardy 1998:138; Perkins 1994:42–3). However, the contraction of credit was not readily apparent in the lending of the Agriculture Bank or the Rural Credit Cooperatives (Table 6.1) in 1993, and lending exhibited only a mild contraction in 1994.

The Implementation of Loan Criteria

While rural savings fueled the growth of loans to collective enterprises in the rural industrial sector, political interference on the part of the township government often shaped the ways in which loans were allocated. Township officials exercised influence over the implementation of loan criteria, including the use of enterprise credit ratings, the practice of requiring the borrower to provide loan matching funds from the borrower's own resources (*ziyou zijin*), and the practice of requiring a loan guarantor or collateral.[15]

Credit Ratings. The practice of rating enterprises (*xinyong pinggu*) represented a potentially important source of enterprise discipline; however, political interference distorted the intended principles of credit allocation. The exact criteria by which an enterprise was rated and the precise weighting of those criteria are unclear, but they included an enterprise's economic results (*jingji xiaoyi*), development trajectory (*fazhan qushi*), and potential sales performance (*chanpin xiaolu*) (Shen 1990:40). Specifically, township-level bank offices focused on an enterprise's output value, sales, and profits, and ratings were reviewed biannually (Informant 57).

The records of the Dongtan Town Agriculture Bank in Wuxi County show that in 1992, top-rated enterprises did indeed receive the lion's share of loan capital (68 percent), while second-rate enterprises received 11 percent, third-rate enterprises 5 percent, and unrated enterprises 16 percent.[16] (Unrated enterprises were typically those enterprises for which official criteria were considered "unrepresentative" of their development potential.) Loans to third-rate enterprises in Dongtan were slated to decrease by 70 thousand yuan in 1992, but the change was negligible – equivalent to less than 1 percent of total loans. In Songyang Town, Songjiang County, bank officials reported that third-rate enterprises could count on receiving at least the same amount in loans each year – even if they were losing money (Informant 96). Furthermore, a bank official from the neighboring township of Daqiao in Songjiang County reported that in 1991 nearly half the township- and village-run enterprises there were losing money and that the local office of the Agriculture Bank had granted them loans to pay wages at year-end (Infor-

---

[15] The following discussion of these loan criteria will treat the Agriculture Bank and the Rural Credit Cooperatives together, because their funds were often combined in practice. Other loan criteria included the stipulation that credit allocation must reflect national industrial development priorities, with, for example, no new loans going to firms in overcrowded processing industries.

[16] Other townships' bank/credit cooperative accounts revealed similar breakdowns (Informant 99). In the text "top-rated" is used as a shorthand to represent three categories – special-rate (*teji*), high-rate (*youji*), and first-rate (*yiji*). Few townships boasted any special-rate enterprises. Township bank officials combined high-rate and first-rate categories in reporting loan percentages, and it appears that these two categories of enterprises received similar treatment from the banks.

mant 101).[17] Nevertheless, low-rated enterprises did forfeit certain benefits; in Hualing Town, Yueqing County, top-rated enterprises enjoyed preferential interest rates, for example (Informant 159). Nevertheless, these data suggest that low-rated enterprises faced minimal discipline in the capital market; to the contrary, the continuation of loans to low-rated firms suggests a political concern for the maintenance of employment levels and employee welfare.

Moreover, credit ratings themselves were distorted. According to a commentator in the journal *Shanghai Jinrong*, in the process of rating enterprises, banks "are unable to avoid inappropriate local administrative interference. Some local governments and bureaus, in order to ensure that the enterprises under their jurisdiction receive a high rating, have no qualms about intervening personally" (Shen 1990:40). Interference was even more common in bank decision making regarding new projects. According to a township government official (Informant 196a) in Dongtan Town,

> There is government interference in the allocation of bank loans. Successful enterprises can get loans directly – and this is most enterprises. But especially for new enterprises, if the bank doesn't want to support them, the party secretary will go in person with the enterprise manager and accountant to the bank – but this is the minority. Of course, for less-developed townships, government interference is even greater. Still, the bank is already gradually beginning to operate by economic laws; it already considers its own economic results (*jingji xiaoyi*).

Similar interference is well documented for state enterprises (Y. Huang 1990; Lardy 1998; Walder 1992; White and Bowles 1987).

Matching Funds. Banks attempted to restrict the availability of credit to poor loan risks by requiring that borrowers demonstrate the existence of a certain percentage of matching funds from the borrowers' own resources (*ziyou zijin*). According to Agriculture Bank regulations, working-capital loans required matching funds (*ziyou zijin*) equivalent to 30 percent of the loan amount, while fixed-asset loans required 50 percent (Informant 96). In principle, *ziyou zijin* derived from an enterprise's retained profits as well as from certain officially mandated funds set aside from pretax profits and other sources of

---

[17] See also Li, Shi, and Zhu (1990:57), who discuss the use of loans to pay wages.

nondebt investment funds. For a variety of reasons, however, loan recipients often lacked sufficient matching funds to meet bank requirements.

In some cases, township bank officials simply waived the requirement in response to political pressure. In other cases, enterprises, acting with the support of the township government, evaded matching fund requirements by taking advantage of loopholes in the banking system. While reforms in the banking system allowed commercial banks to compete for accounts, disclosure practices were still based on the assumption that enterprises had accounts at only one bank. An enterprise could exploit the loophole by using funds from an undisclosed loan at one bank for *ziyou zijin* at another.[18] In this way, enterprises could reach high levels of indebtedness without the lenders' knowledge. In some cases, enterprises employed this strategy in open defiance of local Agriculture Bank officials – when they needed more credit but were unable to secure new loans or to pay back old loans at home banks (Bi and Yan 1990:56; Bowles and White 1993:119). In other cases, local representatives of the Agriculture Bank colluded in this practice – whether as a result of political pressure, shared local interests, or personal connections (Informant 96). For example, in Luhang Town, Shanghai County, a new enterprise was established in 1991 with a total investment of 1.59 million yuan, including 0.5 million yuan in loans from the town office of the Agriculture Bank, 0.49 million yuan in loans from the Construction Bank (located outside the town), 0.5 million yuan in loans from the Bank of China (also located outside the town), and 0.1 million yuan in old equipment transferred from another factory. With backing from the township industrial corporation, the new venture borrowed money from the local Agriculture Bank and, with the bank's knowledge, used these funds as matching funds to secure loans at the other banks (Informant 48). Thus, bank credits financed fully 94 percent of the assets of the new venture. This phenomenon highlights the ways in which township governments and their enterprises exploited incomplete reforms in the transitional banking system.

In response to this problem, only one locale, Yueqing County, Wenzhou, passed regulations requiring that each enterprise license state

---

[18] This phenomenon, referred to as *duotou kaihu*, has received extensive coverage in Chinese journals. See, for example, Bi and Yan (1990:56), Cai (1990:35–7), Luo, Deng, and Liu (1991:28–9), Mao (1991:21–2), and Shu, Wei, and Wang (1990:41–2).

the name of the home bank at which the enterprise held its accounts (*kaihu yinhang*). According to an official of the Industrial and Commercial Bank there,[19] the regulation was motivated by the severity of indebtedness (*fuzhai jingying*) in collective enterprises (Informant 158). The action suggests that a more complete regulatory framework would contribute significantly to greater financial discipline (Mao 1991:21; Shu, Wei, and Wang 1990:42).

Guarantors and Collateral. In principle, another element of financial discipline was the requirement that borrowers provide either guarantors or collateral for loans; however, in this case as in others, the disciplinary function of the requirement was undermined in practice.[20] According to regulations, the guarantor was required to be an "economic entity" (*jingji shiti*) with its own independent source of income. In addition, it had to be recognized as a legal entity (*faren*), and it could not be a government organ (*guojia jiguan*) (Xu 1992:42). These rules, of course, were intended to ensure that loans would actually be repaid – whether by the borrower or by the guarantor. Although the township industrial corporation (*gongye gongsi*) was a government office with official functions, it was simultaneously an economic and legal entity (Informant 46). Thus, in most cases, the township industrial corporation served as guarantor for township-run enterprises, while the village industrial and commercial corporation (*shiye gongsi*) – the economic arm of the village governance structure – served as guarantor for village-run enterprises (Informants 57 and 198). When enterprises defaulted on their loans, the corporation in some cases placed levies on the retained profits of the successful enterprises under its jurisdiction to repay delinquent loans of weaker

---

[19] Hualing Town, Wenzhou, is the only township investigated with an Industrial and Commercial Bank office at the township level.

[20] This requirement did not apply to working-capital loans within the quota (*ding'e*) planned for each township-run enterprise by the township office of the Agriculture Bank. Any loan funds above the planned amount or loan funds for new projects, however, would be subject to this requirement. (Top-ranked enterprises were exempt in many cases.) Only the township Agriculture Bank, which was the "home bank" for most township-run enterprises, had a plan quota for loans to these enterprises. The home bank did not need to rely on loan guarantors for planned loans because it handled accounts-receivable for township-run enterprises; therefore, the bank could deduct loan payments directly from payments received from the enterprise's clients (Informant 56). The ability to deduct loan payments directly from enterprise accounts, when used, was a powerful constraint on enterprise reliance on soft credit. However, this constraint depended jointly on the political will of the lender and on the existence of paying clients.

enterprises *(tongshou huandai).*[21] In other cases, however, it simply requested that the bank repeatedly extend the loan period (in some cases with the industrial corporation making the interest payments) or borrowed money from another source to cover the loan (Informants 68, 83, and 198). For example, a factory in Meilin Town (Shanghai) was unable to repay a 100 thousand yuan loan from the township Agriculture Bank because of its inability to collect accounts-receivable. The industrial corporation took out loans at interest from a number of diverse sources – including the YMCA of China (headquartered in Shanghai) – to repay the bank. The factory remained in debt to the industrial corporation, which, in turn, was in debt to a number of sources (Informant 68). Finally, in still other cases, the industrial corporation was considered an "empty" guarantor *(kong danbao),* because it failed to provide the necessary funds to back up the loans it guaranteed, and the loans simply remained on the bank books unpaid (Informants 96 and 177).[22]

When the township industrial corporation or the village company was unwilling to serve as the guarantor on a loan, the township public finance office *(caizhengsuo)* frequently served as guarantor, although informants acknowledged that the practice was a violation of the regulations (Informants 56, 68, and 70). Moreover, when a firm defaulted on a loan guaranteed by the public finance office, paying off the loan from finance office funds was a last resort. The public finance office would encourage the bank to roll over the loan account, or it would borrow money from other cash-flush government bureaus to pay off the loan (Informants 56 and 70). Typically, the bank was willing to roll over the loan account as long as the enterprise was still paying interest (Informant 127). In some locales, the public finance office also assisted weaker enterprises by making the interest payments for them (Informants 97 and 135).

The local government – whether via the industrial corporation or the public finance bureau – performed an important function in guaranteeing enterprise loans. It ostensibly reduced the risk borne by the banks, thereby encouraging them to make loans to relatively small-scale rural enterprises that otherwise faced formidable obstacles to development. At the same time, by reducing the risk to the enterprise, it encouraged the firm to undertake ambitious projects and fostered firm development.

---

[21] Informants 53, 83, 106, 177, and 198.

[22] This is also referred to as a guarantor in form but not substance *(xingshi danbao).* See Xu (1992:42–3).

However, in many cases the agencies of the township government, by serving as loan guarantors, contributed to the availability of soft credit for marginal enterprises, rather than increasing pressure on enterprises to perform.

Loans backed up by collateral (*diya danbao*) were also difficult to collect once they went into default, because the burden of collection fell directly to the bank. Banks came under pressure not to collect because the practice of repossessing and auctioning property was not well established in either social or legal terms (Zhou and Hu 1987:312). Representatives of the Agriculture Bank in Yueqing County reported that, as of the early 1990s, they had attempted and failed to collect several delinquent loans guaranteed by collateral (usually buildings or equipment). The property had not been auctioned because the courts were unwilling to pursue the cases vigorously (Informants 159 and 163). In other cases problems occurred because, although the value of the loan collateral had, at least nominally, been verified by a notary (*gongzheng*), when the enterprise defaulted on the loan and the Agriculture Bank attempted to collect, the collateral was found to be essentially worthless (Informant 177). Like the weakness of the regulatory framework described with regard to disclosure practices, the unwillingness of the courts to enforce loan contracts undermined the discipline imposed by the banking system.

Bad Debts

The record of banks in pursuing delinquent loans was mixed. The absence of effective legal recourse hindered the efforts of banks to collect loans. In light of this constraint, two approaches were common. First, banks would grant additional loans to an enterprise that was delinquent in its loan payments – even if the firm was losing money – in the hope that the firm would "turn things around" by developing some kind of marketable product (Informants 96, 101, and 158). Second, bank officials would rely on the township industrial corporation to repay the loan through the practice of *tongshou huandai* (that is, by placing a levy on the profits of a successful enterprise to pay off the debts of a weaker enterprise). However, many loans nominally guaranteed by township government agencies simply remained on the books.

As of the early 1990s, the officially reported share of nonperforming and unrecoverable (*daizhi/daizhang*) loans by the Agriculture Bank ranged from 1.4 percent of total loans outstanding in Dongtan Town,

Wuxi, to 4.4 percent in Hualing Town, Wenzhou, to 4.8 percent in Songyang Town, Shanghai.[23] However, as Lardy (1998:115) indicates, such figures were unreliable, because the central bank set *ceilings* on the proportion of loans that were *allowed to be classified* as nonperforming (5 percent) or unrecoverable (2 percent). As Wong (1996:159) reports, the true proportion of nonperforming and unrecoverable loans by the Agriculture Bank may have been as high 33 percent as of the early 1990s.

As Table 6.2 shows, lending by Rural Credit Cooperatives to township- and village-run collectives exceeded that of the Agriculture Bank, and the quality of the loan portfolio of the RCCs was reportedly even worse than that of the Agriculture Bank. According to one study, "measured by the share of loans that are 'past due,' the quality of township and village enterprise borrowing, most from rural credit cooperatives, is the lowest of any single category of loans" (Lardy 1998:277).[24] This finding is consistent with reports that loan guarantees offered by township and village corporations were often "empty (*kong*)."

Township Government Practices and Enterprise Dependence on Credit

Heavy reliance on bank loans was not only facilitated by, but also in part caused by, the practices of the township government. Collective enterprises retained only a fraction of their gross profits. In general, these firms paid, in addition to taxes, a variety of legally mandated fees and illegal exactions before paying a sizable share of the remaining profits to the local government. Indeed, managers of both township- and village-run collectives complained that local leaders took money from enterprises as they pleased, and bank officials complained that local governments treated enterprises like "money trees," undermining firms' financial health (Cai 1990:35–7).[25] According to a Songyang Town

---

[23] These figures do not include overdue loans (*yuqi daikuan*) in arrears for less than two years.

[24] See also Xu Yuyan, "Earnestly Resolve the New Problems in the Management of Credit to Township and Village Enterprises," *Jinrong shibao*, November 26, 1998, as cited in Lardy (1998:277).

[25] In Luhang Town, Shanghai, as of 1991, the town industrial corporation was still engaged in a *tongshou tongzhi* relationship with its enterprises. *Tongshou tongzhi* refers to a situation in which enterprises hand over all profits to the local government and look to the government for all major expenditures. This issue is discussed at greater length in Whiting (1993).

official, enterprises retained only about 12 percent of gross profits on average as of the early 1990s (Informant 97),[26] which limited the ability of enterprises to repay loans and provide for their own capital needs. The situation was exacerbated by the practice of exacting levies on profitable enterprises to pay off the debts of weaker enterprises for which the township industrial corporation served as loan guarantor. It was also exacerbated by the less common practice of forfeiting enterprise depreciation funds to the local government for other uses (Informants 70 and 121).

As the World Bank study on rural industry (Wang 1990:229) shows, the share of profits remitted by collectively owned enterprises to the township government that were used to finance productive investment in enterprises declined through the 1980s. Rather, remitted profits were increasingly spent on township and village construction, on educational and welfare-related projects, and on the salaries of the growing number of local cadres who were not on the official state payroll. As one contributor to the World Bank study points out, "The declining proportion of reinvestment in industry is making [township- and village-run collectives] increasingly dependent on credit financing" (Ibid). Not only were new enterprises more highly leveraged, but also with reinvestment from the township government not forthcoming and with bank loans for fixed-asset investment tightly restricted, existing enterprises commonly used working-capital funds (including working-capital loans) for fixed-asset investment.[27] These enterprises then turned once again to the banking system, anticipating easy access to additional working-capital loans.

A 1997 report by the Ministry of Agriculture identifies high levels of indebtedness as one of the most pressing problems facing TVEs.[28] The experiences of Songyang and Dongtan Towns in Songjiang and Wuxi Counties, respectively, demonstrate the extent of reliance on bank loans. According to the report of a Songyang Town government official, during the late 1980s and early 1990s, debt increased an average of 25 percent per year even as the net profits of town-run industrial enterprises

---

[26] It is not clear whether this estimate includes unsanctioned levies on firms by local government agencies.

[27] Informants 48, 59, 177, and 198. See also Li, Shi, and Zhu (1990:57).

[28] Nongyebu, "Guanyu woguo xiangzhen qiye qingkuang he jinhou gaige yu fazhan yijian de baogao (Report on the Situation of Township and Village Enterprises and Opinions on Future Reform and Development)," *Renmin ribao*, April 24, 1997.

declined (Informant 97).[29] Interest payments alone were becoming a burden, and by the late 1980s, interest payments equaled net profits on average. Debt as a share of total assets increased from 15 percent in 1980 to 40 percent in 1989, and by 1989, it was commonly 80 percent or more for *new* enterprises. The problem of severe indebtedness (*fuzhai jing-ying*) continued to worsen during the 1990s (Informant 208). As of 1996, debt as a share of total assets averaged 72 percent for *all* township- and village-run collectives in Songjiang County (Informant 214). Similarly, in Dongtan Town as of 1996, debt as a share of total assets for township- and village-run collectives was approximately 80 percent, while in Wuxi County as a whole it had reached 56 percent (Informant 222).

The ability of enterprises to repay their debts was further reduced by the declining profitability of investments. The first panel of Table 6.3 illustrates the national trend in profitability calculated as profits as a share of fixed and working capital. The second panel of the table provides the data available on Songjiang County for 1987 to 1989 and for 1993. Finally, interview data on Songyang Town's town-run industrial enterprises indicate that the profits produced by 100 yuan of fixed assets declined from 37 yuan in 1980 to 21 yuan in 1989 to 11 yuan in 1995 (Informants 97 and 208). A town government official attributed the decline to excessive investments in nonproductive assets, failed investment decisions, increasing costs for raw material and wages, unsalable products accumulating in inventory, mounting unpaid accounts-receivable, high interest payments, and burdensome taxes and fees (Informant 97; Wang and Li 1992:18–19). Others pointed to the growing competition confronting TVEs (Byrd and Zhu 1990; Naughton 1995; Informant 222).

From the perspective of the banks, not only did loan officers face political pressure in making loan decisions, but they also faced substantial information problems. Because of a shortage of well-trained personnel, banks often relied on self-reporting of production levels and profitability by enterprises without independent verification (Shen 1990:40). Furthermore, bank managers complained that they lacked both the personnel and the skills to evaluate new loan requests. The manager of the

---

[29] This trend appears to be widely felt across economic indicators. According to a survey of 200 large-scale rural industrial enterprises, from 1975 to 1985, the output value produced by each 10 thousand yuan of investment decreased 6.5 percent per year on average. Income from sales decreased 5.6 percent per year on average; gross profits decreased 8.3 percent; net profits decreased 8.8 percent; and enterprise retained profits decreased 9.4 percent (Zhou and Hu 1987:318).

Table 6.3. *Losses of Township- and Village-run Enterprises, 1985–97*

National-level Data

Year	Total Number of Firms (Million)	Loss-making Firms (Million)	Total Amount of Losses (Billion Yuan)	Share of Loss-making Firms (Percentage)	Losses as a Share of Net Profits (Percentage)	Profitability (Profit/Total Capital)
1985	1.850	0.065	0.849	3.5	5.0	22.8
1986	1.728	0.076	1.449	4.4	9.0	17.0
1987	1.583	0.074	1.834	4.7	9.7	7.9
1988	1.590	0.063	1.850	4.0	7.1	8.3
1989	1.536	0.079	3.790	5.1	15.8	6.3
1990	1.454	0.086	4.740	5.9	20.6	5.2
1991	1.442	0.067	4.270	4.6	15.0	5.1
1992	1.166	0.048	3.232	4.1	6.7	6.3
1993	1.294	0.053	4.934	4.1	6.9	6.2
1994	1.641					
1995	1.618	0.081	16.800	5.0	11.2	7.4
1996	1.550	0.088	21.205	5.7	12.3	8.1
1997	1.292	0.088	21.488	6.8	12.4	6.7

248

County-level Data, Songjiang County, Shanghai

Year	Total Number of Firms (Million)	Loss-making Firms (Million)	Total Amount of Losses (Billion Yuan)	Share of Loss-making Firms (Percentage)	Losses as a Share of Net Profits (Percentage)	Profitability (Profit/Total Capital)
1987	1,913	144	3.82	7.5	4.0	8.8
1988	2,142	155	5.74	7.2	5.1	9.2
1989	2,251	206	12.65	9.2	15.9	5.9
1990	2,278	234	15.18	10.3	17.5	
1991	2,332	209	12.98	9	10.9	
1992	2,322	227	30.62	9.8	20.4	
1993	2,390	250	21.35	10.5	7.2	6.1
1994	2,197	240	40.98	10.9	7.1	
1995	2,240	218	35.79	9.7	5.6	

Township-level Data, Songyang Town, Songjiang County

Year	Total Number of Firms (Million)	Loss-making Firms (Million)	Total Amount of Losses (Billion Yuan)	Share of Loss-making Firms (Percentage)	Losses as a Share of Net Profits (Percentage)
1989	199	8	0.48	4	5.3
1990	207	11	0.59	5.3	6.2
1991	218	8	0.29	3.7	3.1
1992	210	25	1.47	11.9	7.2
1993	222	24	2.29	10.8	7.1
1994	173	27	3.02	15.6	6.6
1995	172	22	2.98	12.8	10.4

Sources: National level: *Zhongguo xiangzhen qiye nianjian* (1989:638; 1990:107; 1991:186; 1992 [1990 data]:194; 1992 [1991 data]:200; 1993:232; 1994:364; 1996:99; 250; 1997:121; 248; 1998:108; 200; 214. County level: *Songjiang xian tongji nianjian* (1987:161; 1988:182; 1989:142; 1991:87; 1992:86; 1993:91; 1994:95; 1995:84; 1996:92). Township level: *S. zhen tongji nianjian* (1991:28; 1992:30; 1993:36; 1994:36; 1995:35; 1996:37).

Agriculture Bank in Songyang Town commented that it was impossible for his staff to conduct a feasibility study to assess the market potential of a proposed project. Instead, the staff relied on the opinions of the town's political leaders and the enterprise manager. As a result, the bank repeatedly granted loans for products that ultimately were unsalable. In many of these cases, firms in the same metropolitan area (in this example, greater Shanghai) producing the same products had already saturated the market (Informant 96).

Some local governments were successful in arranging loans from outside the home locale. In Dongtan Town, Wuxi County, as of the early 1990s, only about 25 percent of total loans outstanding of township- and village-run collectives came from banks located within the county itself (Informant 191). The county party committee assisted the town in securing loans from both banks and other institutions outside the area (Informant 198).[30] Although some governments in less developed regions tried to use administrative measures to prohibit the outward flow of capital, Dongtan Town could attract loans from banks in less developed areas as nearby as Anhui Province and as far away as Xinjiang Province (Informant 196). This practice suggests that, despite political barriers, capital had begun to flow toward more profitable – if not necessarily the most profitable – uses.

Despite the challenges facing transitional banking institutions, capital market discipline was gradually beginning to have some bite. Most loans went to highly rated enterprises. However, there remained a significant undisciplined element in bank lending to TVEs. Weak firms were supported through bank loans because such support was consistent with the desire of local government officials to increase output and maintain employment. These goals were defined by the incentive structure under which local government officials operated, and officials acted on these goals through their positions as (a) de facto owners of local enterprises, and (b) holders of political power over banks in a highly politicized economic system.

Other Sources of Capital for Rural Collectives

Even in light of continued political interference and an underdeveloped legal framework that hindered the ability of banks to recover delinquent

---

[30] One government official noted that the interest rate charged by the outside banks depended on the quality of the personal connections (Informant 191).

loans, access to easy credit through the banking system was gradually beginning to diminish as of the 1990s. As a result, townships and their enterprises turned increasingly to sources of capital outside the banking system. The first panel of Table 6.4 shows that the officially reported share of bank loans in fixed-asset investment by township- and village-run collectives nationwide declined from nearly 50 percent in 1987 to about 25 percent in 1996.[31] Moreover, by the mid-1990s, the rate of increase in the absolute amount of fixed-asset loans had slowed to single-digit rates. The second panel of Table 6.4 provides data on Songjiang County. There, bank loans as a share of total fixed-asset investment fell from a high of 53 percent in 1989 to a low of 5 percent in 1995, before recovering to 14 percent in 1997. However, the figures reflect only those loans made by the Agriculture Bank and the Rural Credit Cooperatives; loans made by other banks such as the Industrial and Commercial Bank are not included. Moreover, the proportion of bank loans is likely understated due to the widespread practice of using working-capital loans to invest in fixed assets. Indeed, the category of "own funds (*ziyou zijin*)" – masking significant working-capital loans – had become the single largest source of fixed-asset investment nationwide by 1994.

Much of the remaining capital for fixed-asset investment came from nonbank sources. These sources included government bureaus, other firms, and local residents. Among government bureaus, the largest provider of loans to rural collectives appeared to be the public finance bureau, although no official data are available to confirm this. In

---

[31] The table probably understates the actual proportion of loans. Item 2, *ziyou zijin*, most likely contains a large component of loans – whether through the exploitation of loopholes in bank disclosure rules or through loans from other sources. Outside capital (item 3) refers to funds from domestic or foreign joint ventures. This form of capital was becoming increasingly important as townships rushed to sign agreements with both state (and other domestic) enterprises and foreign firms to bring in additional capital and to meet performance targets. Item 4, grants from the bureau in charge – usually the township industrial corporation – were in many cases themselves bank loans taken out in the name of the industrial corporation (Informant 46). Funds collected from local residents (item 5) often took the form of loans with interest rates higher than those offered by banks in order to encourage residents to contribute to local industrial development (Informant 126). Finally, item 6, the "national support fund" (*guojia fuchi jijin*) was a preferential tax policy. Enterprises that exceeded their tax quotas received a certain percentage of the above-quota tax payment as a refund, which became the "support fund." According to one public finance official, one rationale for this policy was to help viable enterprises that were nevertheless faced with chronic indebtedness to repay their loans (Informant 135). Overall, while the table shows declining reliance on bank loans for fixed-asset investment, the data probably hide a sizable proportion of bank loans in other categories.

Table 6.4. Sources of Fixed-asset Investment for Township- and Village-run Enterprises, 1987–97

National Level Item	1987	1988	1989	1990	1991	1992	1993	1994	1995	1996	1997
(billion current yuan)											
Total	24.32	n/a	25.15	23.05	37.55	108.17	217.63	254.28	293.67	312.69	295.20
Bank loans	11.77		9.41	7.96	15.20	42.03	67.10	71.76	74.87	76.80	63.04
Own funds (ziyou zijin)	5.30		5.89	5.66	11.13	29.87	62.54	80.24	102.78	113.95	102.06
Imported capital	1.65		3.06	4.74	3.74	14.93	35.83	44.21	58.81	65.88	65.36
Foreign capital	0.30		0.79	2.23	1.61	6.40	18.03	22.96	30.60	32.25	31.82
Other outside capital	1.35		2.27	2.50	2.13	8.53	17.80	21.25	28.20	33.63	33.55
Bureau grants	1.72		1.99	1.53	2.09	4.58	8.47	7.35	6.01	5.72	4.17
Residents' funds	1.14		1.20	0.66	1.27	5.91	17.63	24.04	21.55	20.64	16.76
National support fund	0.87		0.97	0.72	1.05	1.92	2.37	2.20	2.03	1.80	1.95
Other	1.87		2.64	1.79	3.07	8.93	23.69	24.48	27.62	27.89	41.86
(percentage share)											
Total	100.0	n/a	100.0	100.0	100.0	100.0	100.0	100.0	100.0	100.0	100.0
Bank loans	48.4		37.4	34.5	40.5	38.9	30.8	28.2	25.5	24.6	21.4
Own funds (ziyou zijin)	21.8		23.4	24.5	29.6	27.6	28.7	31.6	35.0	36.4	34.6
Imported capital	6.8		12.1	20.6	10.0	13.8	16.5	17.4	20.0	21.1	22.1
Foreign capital	1.2		3.1	9.7	4.3	5.9	8.3	9.0	10.4	10.3	10.8
Other outside capital	5.6		9.0	10.9	5.7	7.9	8.2	8.4	9.6	10.8	11.4
Bureau grants	7.1		7.9	6.6	5.6	4.2	3.9	2.9	2.0	1.8	1.4
Residents' funds	4.7		4.8	2.9	3.4	5.5	8.1	9.5	7.3	6.6	5.7
National support fund	3.6		3.8	3.1	2.8	1.8	1.1	0.9	0.7	0.6	0.7
Other	7.7		10.5	7.7	8.2	8.3	10.9	9.6	9.4	8.9	14.2

Songjiang County

Item	1987	1988	1989	1990	1991	1992	1993	1994	1995	1996	1997
(million current yuan)											
Total	107.27	170.65	166.32	190.47	221.01	422.19	742.41	1,404.69	2,265.92	1,763.77	2,228.42
Bank loans	52.51	88.34	88.55	85.57			171.79	68.39	179.99	117.39	311.75
Own funds (ziyou zijin)	20.01	31.80	32.70	31.25			247.84	270.77	373.57	433.55	669.88
Foreign capital	5.12	21.39	10.39	35.56			212.18	823.40	1,391.78	934.68	975.71
Bureau grants	19.26	18.38	13.15	24.43			3.82	17.11	59.90	21.67	25.73
National support fund	2.30	3.01	4.30								
Other	8.07	7.73	17.23	13.66			106.78	225.02	260.68	256.48	245.35
(percentage share)											
Total	100.0	100.0	100.0	100.0	100.0	100.0	100.0	100.0	100.0	100.0	100.0
Bank loans	49.0	51.8	53.2	44.9			23.1	4.9	7.9	6.7	14.0
Own funds (ziyou zijin)	18.7	18.6	19.7	16.4			33.4	19.3	16.5	24.6	30.1
Foreign capital	4.8	12.5	6.2	18.7			28.6	58.6	61.4	53.0	43.8
Bureau grants	18.0	10.8	7.9	12.8			0.5	1.2	2.6	1.2	1.2
National support fund	2.1	1.8	2.6								
Other	7.5	4.5	10.4	7.2			14.4	16.0	11.5	14.5	11.0

Sources: Zhongguo xiangzhen qiye nianjian (1989:61; 1991a:180; 1991b:188; 1992:194; 1993:226; 1994:336; 1995:226; 1996:246; 1997:232; 1998:173). Songjiang tongji nianjian.

addition to serving as loan guarantors for some enterprises, public finance bureaus at both the township and county levels also made loans at interest from their circulating funds (*zhouzhuanjin*) directly to enterprises.[32] These loans were used primarily for loss-making or troubled enterprises that were denied bank loans (Informants 112 and 181). Not only did public finance office loan practices undermine the principle of allocating loans based on credit ratings, but also they undermined the implementation of industrial policy priorities. One enterprise in Luhang Town (Shanghai), for example, was denied a loan to develop a metal processing workshop because of a bank regulation prohibiting new loans to processing industries. It was granted a loan for the same project by the county public finance bureau (Informant 49).

It appears that virtually any government bureau that had funds at its disposal used them to make loans to enterprises either directly or indirectly through the public finance office. Indeed, in some places, government bureaus were assigned to assist specific enterprises by the local government. The legal fees received by legal services offices and the trademark fees received by industrial and commercial bureaus, for example, were periodically used to provide loan funds to local collectives (Informant 112). According to one tax official, it was also common for the tax bureau to allow rural collectives to be in arrears in paying their taxes. Enterprises then used these funds to supplement their working capital (Informant 194).

When enterprises needed funds, the local government often "built bridges" to other enterprises for short-term loans.[33] One enterprise in Nantang Township, Jiading County, for example, had 8.4 million yuan in bank loans outstanding as of 1991, while profits had fallen from a high of 2.3 million yuan in 1989 to 100 thousand yuan in 1991. As a result, the enterprise borrowed 500 thousand yuan from other rural enterprises in 1991 to keep up with loan payments (Informant 125). At least within a given locality, interenterprise loans were often made at the direction of the township government.

An even more prevalent form of interenterprise debt – one that crossed

---

[32] Informants 53, 70, 112, 125, and 181. Public finance officials did not use the terms "loan" or "interest" in order to distinguish these concepts from those used in the banking domain. Rather, loans were referred to as "credits" (*caizheng xinyong*) and interest charges were referred to as "use-fees" (*caizheng zijin zhanyong fei*). The circulating funds used for loans to TVEs apparently derived from nonbudgetary sources of fiscal revenue (Informant 70).

[33] Informants 46, 83, 125, and 198.

territorial boundaries and ownership categories – was the problem of mounting accounts-payable and accounts-receivable. The seriousness of the problem was reflected in the fact that austerity programs were regularly followed by efforts to eliminate so-called "triangular debts" (*sanjiaozhai*), that is, unpaid accounts among enterprises. According to a survey of 200 large-scale rural industrial enterprises as of 1985, accounts-payable was second only to bank loans in its share of total enterprise liabilities. In 1985, bank loans (including both working-capital and fixed-asset loans) accounted for 43 percent of total liabilities, while accounts-payable made up 32 percent (Zhou and Hu 1987:300). The same study shows that the share of accounts-payable in total liabilities was growing rapidly during the mid-1980s, increasing 10 percentage points between December 1984 and June 1986. As one factory manager on the receiving end of the problem in the 1990s put it, "Contracts here don't mean anything. Other units owe us a lot of money" (Informant 123). Moreover, enterprises had little recourse when clients failed to pay. Localism was so pervasive that when one county or township government sent court, police, or enterprise representatives to another locality to collect payment, the resident court and police personnel were often unwilling to act against the interests of the offending local enterprise.[34] Although enterprises may have been concerned about declining reputations in the long run, mounting accounts-payable was a short-term means of softening the budget constraint for a growing number of enterprises.

Like other capital sources, contributions from local residents also took many forms. As discussed in Chapter 4, the conversion of township- and village-run collectives to shareholding cooperatives in which the local government was the majority shareholder was promoted as a means of mobilizing idle capital held by rural residents outside the state-run banking system into local government-run firms. As a 1997 report by the Ministry of Agriculture stated, "The conversion of township- and village-run collective enterprises to the shareholding cooperative system, adopting the method of increasing the total number of enterprise shares, is beneficial to increasing the capital available to the enterprise."[35] In some

---

[34] Zhang Weiguo (formerly of the *Shanghai World Economic Herald*), lecture, University of Michigan Center for Chinese Studies, Ann Arbor, April 13, 1993.

[35] "*Xiangcun jiti qiye gaizu wei gufen hezuo zhi qiye, caiqu zengliang kuogu de zuofa, you li yu zengjia qiye zibenjin.*" Nongyebu, "Guanyu woguo xiangzhen qiye qingkuang he jinhou gaige yu fazhan yijian de baogao (Report on the Situation of Township and Village Enterprises and Opinions on Future Reform and Development)," *Renmin ribao*, April 24, 1997.

cases, the purchase of shares by workers was compulsory rather than voluntary. In other cases, workers who purchased shares in government-run shareholding cooperatives were lured into investing by promises of exorbitantly high returns. In Songjiang County, for example, workers were often promised *both* interest payments (equivalent to *lending* rates charged by banks) and dividend payments.[36] However, the township officials who orchestrated such shareholding conversions soon discovered that payments of both interest and dividends were unsustainable.[37] In some respects, however, this form of cooperative shareholding was simply a formalization and expansion of long-standing methods of mobilizing capital.

During the 1980s and 1990s, some local governments coordinated interest-bearing loans from residents for enterprise expansion. These loans often paid higher interest rates than banks, thereby adding to the burdensome interest payments owed by debt-laden rural collectives. One enterprise in Nantang Town, Shanghai, borrowed 125 thousand yuan from workers for use as working-capital funds at nearly twice the interest rate charged by the credit cooperative (Informants 126 and 134). In addition, the township as a whole collected approximately 4 million yuan from local workers and farmers at twice the interest rate offered on savings accounts by the bank. In the latter instance, government cadres were assigned quotas governing the amounts each was to collect from various target groups within the township. It was not clear how or when interest payments were to be made or whether local residents could withdraw their funds. Thus, this source of capital imposed little discipline on managerial behavior.

A more formal means of soliciting funds from local residents was through the issue of enterprise bonds. In Dongtan Town, nine enterprises had issued bonds as of mid-1992, six publicly and three internally. According to a township government official, one-, two-, and three-year bonds were available with annual interest rates ranging from 9.1 to 10 percent (Informant 198). These bond issues, approved by the county branch of the People's Bank of China, likely imposed greater discipline

---

[36] Payment of both interest and dividends was prohibited in the private variant of shareholding cooperatives.

[37] In Songyang Town in 1996, the rates promised to workers were 11 percent in interest and 25 percent in dividends. Once workers had purchased shares, however, they often found that enterprises were unable to make payment of either interest or dividends (Informant 214).

on the enterprise than the less formal and more compulsory approaches to collecting funds from the local population.

Finally, in coastal provinces, foreign investment has become an increasingly important source of capital for counties in peri-urban areas. Songjiang County in suburban Shanghai, for instance, began to attract a growing amount of foreign capital during the 1990s, and by 1994, foreign investment had overtaken domestic bank loans as the single largest source of capital for fixed-asset investment, providing fully 60 percent of fixed-asset investment by 1995. However, as Table 6.4 illustrates, foreign investment accounted for only 11 percent of fixed-asset investment in rural collectives nationwide as of 1997, and in Songjiang it accounted for only 44 percent of fixed-asset investment in the same year.

The Hard Budget Constraint at the Township Level

The data suggest that easy credit in a variety forms contributed to soft budget constraints for rural collective firms. However, even if enterprises had softened budget constraints, the township as a whole ostensibly had a hard budget constraint, since township governments could not in principle run budget deficits. What do the available data suggest about constraints on the economic behavior of the township as a whole?

Townships in some cases engaged in cross-subsidization of enterprise losses through the practice of *tongshou huandai*, but what was the extent of losses, and how persistent were they? As Lardy (1998:36) points out, "Loss-making is not confined to state-owned industrial firms." Indeed, he finds that while nonstate firms accounted for only about one-fifth of the financial losses of industrial enterprises as of 1985, their share had doubled to two-fifths by 1997.

Data available for Songyang Town from 1989 through 1995 show that in the rural collective sector, loss-making firms as a share of the total and losses as a share of total net profits both increased during the 1990s (Table 6.3). Data available for the larger county of Songjiang from 1987 through 1995 show that the county consistently tolerated losses among 10 to 11 percent of township- and village-run collectives during the 1990s. The amount of total losses increased fairly steadily, and losses as a share of net profits reached a high of more than 20 percent in 1992. National-level data show that the rural collective sector as a whole also maintained a fairly steady proportion of loss-making firms, while the amount of losses grew over time. The national-level data also suggest that losses as a share

257

of net profits coincided to some extent with campaign cycles in the economy, with the greatest increases in losses occurring following the onset of contractionary policies. Overall, townships tended to maintain a stable or slightly increasing share of loss-making enterprises, while the amount of losses also tended to increase. The ability of townships to sustain loss-making enterprises was a likely indication of softened budget constraints.

IMPLEMENTATION OF CREDIT POLICY IN
THE PRIVATE SECTOR

The relationship between private firms and the state banking system was very different from the one between collective enterprises and state banks described in the preceding section. As a matter of policy, private firms received relatively little support from state banks. As one prominent private entrepreneur lamented, "It's much more difficult getting bank lending if you're a privately owned company. . . ."[38] Discrimination against private firms in the allocation of credit through the state banking system encouraged the adoption of "fake collective" status by some private firms and the use of bribes by others. In general, however, the kinds of manipulation of credit policy that undermined capital market discipline and contributed to soft budget constraints in the collective sector were not evident in the private sector. Private sector investment derived primarily from informal sources, although new formal, nonstate financial institutions have begun to provide credit to private firms.

A Policy of Nonsupport

In principle, banks and Rural Credit Cooperatives at the township level did not support private enterprise during the period under study. Representatives of local banks and credit cooperatives expressed this principle in a variety of ways: "In general, we don't make loans [to private enterprises] (*yiban bu daikuan*)"; "Control is pretty tight (*kongzhi bijiao jin*)"; "We don't support [private enterprises] (*bu zhichi*)"; "[Loans to private enterprises] have nothing to recommend them (*meiyou haochu*)"; "We have no loans to private firms (*meiyou daikuan*)"; "We don't make loans to private enterprises because funds are tight (*zijin jinzhang*)."[39] In practice, however, lending policies for private firms were

---

[38] "Banking One Day on That Entrepreneurial Spirit," *South China Morning Post*, January 22, 1999.

[39] Informants 111, 136, 99/159, 57, 198, and 177, respectively.

not quite so clear-cut. Indeed, some banks and credit cooperatives (particularly those in the Wuxi area) reported that they did not grant any loans to private firms,[40] and fixed-asset loans were virtually unheard-of in any of the research sites.[41] Nevertheless, some township lenders chose not to refuse loans to private firms but rather to severely limit the scale of loans, while imposing much stricter loan requirements than those faced by collective firms.

The scale of loans available through local banks and, more commonly, Rural Credit Cooperatives, varied somewhat by locale within the context of overall limitations. Consistent with their relative importance in the local economy, private firms in the Wenzhou area received greater support from local lenders than did those in the Shanghai area.[42] The Agriculture Bank in Hualing Town, Wenzhou, while professing that it did "not actively support private or individual enterprises," nevertheless expressed willingness to grants loans of up to 30 thousand yuan – and in special cases as much as 50 thousand yuan – to private firms as of the early 1990s (Informant 159). The Hualing Industrial and Commercial Bank also described setting limits on loans to private firms. According to a bank representative, loans to private and individual firms represented only about 5 percent of approximately 18 million yuan in total loans to industry (Informant 158). The Industrial and Commercial Bank was willing to make larger loans, however – up to 100 thousand yuan, according to the bank representative, but as much as 250 thousand yuan, according to one private entrepreneur (Informant 149). Among the private entrepreneurs in Hualing who reported borrowing from state banks, several had received top credit ratings and had obtained six-month working-capital loans ranging from 190 to 250 thousand yuan at a monthly interest rate of 0.72 percent (Informants 149, 150, and 152). Other, lower-rated private firms had received six-month working-capital loans ranging from 50 to 60 thousand yuan at monthly interest rates of 1.15 to 1.2 percent (Informants 155 and 156).

In the Shanghai area access to credit for private firms was much more restricted. Even as of 1996, state-run commercial banks in Shanghai lacked any internal guidelines for lending to private industrial enter-

---

[40] Informants 177, 198, and 224.   [41] Informants 114, 136, 137, 149, 156, and 157.

[42] Here, "private" refers to enterprises holding a private (*siying*) license. As noted in Chapter 4, firms with private investment and registered as a shareholding cooperative enterprise (*gufen hezuo qiye*) were regarded as legitimate collectives in Wenzhou and were treated as such by local banks.

prises (Informant 215). In Songyang Town as of the early 1990s, only the Rural Credit Cooperative reported making loans to private firms; none exceeded 10 thousand yuan.[43] Total loans to private firms accounted for only 0.2 percent of the Rural Credit Cooperative's total loans outstanding in 1991 (Informant 99). In Luhang Town, one private entrepreneur reported that the maximum amount he could borrow was 3 thousand yuan, an amount so small that he declined the loan (Informant 55). Finally, while the Agriculture Bank in Nantang Township did not make loans to private firms, the Rural Credit Cooperative extended the first loans to private firms in 1991, by making three working-capital loans to private enterprises in amounts ranging from 30 to 200 thousand yuan (Informants 136 and 137).

In contrast to the phenomenon of "empty guarantors (*kong danbao*)" characteristic of collective enterprises, the requirements for guarantors of private enterprise loans were comparatively strict. Ironically, according to one private entrepreneur, "Banks have the old mentality that it is safe to lend to state-owned companies. Even if what they lend cannot be returned, it doesn't matter, because everything still belongs to the state. However, if they lend to a private firm and even if only some of the money is not repaid, or repaid a little late, they have to get involved."[44] Banks and credit cooperatives insisted that guarantors be profit-making enterprises and not government bureaus that might never make good on a delinquent loan.[45] Moreover, banks and credit cooperatives required that loan matching funds (*ziyou zijin*) be in the form of cash. As an official of the Agriculture Bank in Songjiang County who oversaw the local offices of Rural Credit Cooperatives stated, "requirements for *ziyou zijin* are relatively strict for private enterprises; they must be in the form of cash. [In contrast], the bank is pretty flexible with collective enterprises" (Informant 106). As one private entrepreneur noted in this context, "there is no special help [from the local government or the bank] as there is for collectives" (Informant 89). Moreover, even as of 1996, state-run banks in Shanghai had not yet instituted a policy governing the use of

---

[43] Informants 86, 89, 96, and 99.

[44] "Banking One Day on That Entrepreneurial Spirit," *South China Morning Post*, January 22, 1999.

[45] Informants 57, 86, 111, 149, and 155. Two exceptions were found among informants. In one case in Nantang Town, Shanghai, the village where the firm was located served as guarantor. In the other case, the industry office (*gongban*) in Hualing Town, Wenzhou, served as guarantor. Informants 137 and 152.

collateral by private enterprises to secure larger loans. According to a local official in Songjiang, other provinces had had such policies in place for some time (Informant 215).

"Fake Collectives" and Bribes

Discrimination against private firms by state banks prompted some private investors to register falsely as individually contracted collectives (*geren chengbao jiti qiye*).[46] In such cases the portion of profit turned over to the local government often secured not only a collective license but also the willingness of the local government to serve as loan guarantor. However, since local banks were aware of this practice, these firms were still denied bank credit in some cases. The local office of the Agriculture Bank in Dongtan Town, Wuxi, refused to grant loans to individually contracted collectives (Informant 198). In a more equivocal case, an entrepreneur in Luhang Town, Shanghai, reported that individually contracted firms were the first to be cutoff when the local bank reached its lending quota. His application to borrow 50 thousand yuan was denied for this reason.[47]

Other outlets stymied, some private entrepreneurs resorted to bribery. The fact that some private entrepreneurs in Luhang had given gifts to bank officers to obtain loans was revealed when several bank officers were disciplined (Informant 57). While practices such as false registration and bribery facilitated access to bank loans in some cases, in general they failed to prevent creditworthy private investors from being frozen out of the state banking system.

Reliance on Informal and Nonstate Capital Sources

Indeed, private enterprises obtained most of their capital from informal sources. Many private entrepreneurs borrowed money from friends and relatives for start-up capital and relied on reinvesting profits for expansion.[48] Other private investors used personal connections to arrange

---

[46] Informants 5 and 189. Similarly, private investors who acquired legitimate collective licenses as shareholding cooperatives reported that it was easier for them than for private firms to get loans. Informants 151 and 155.

[47] Note, however, that the amount requested was larger than what a private entrepreneur would likely be granted by the Agriculture Bank in the Shanghai area (Informant 113).

[48] Informants 86, 115, 149, and 150.

informal loans from government units, often at interest rates several times higher than those charged by banks.[49]

Private banks have a varied history of official tolerance and repression, particularly in Wenzhou.[50] Unauthorized private banks were shut down repeatedly in Wenzhou during the 1980s and 1990s (Lardy 1998:126). Some private banks were legitimized through conversion to urban credit cooperatives, but they were not immune from persecution either (Informants 144a and 158). In the Shanghai area, private entrepreneurs established mutual assistance funds (*huzhu jijin*), in some cases under the guise of the private entrepreneurs association. Reminiscent of traditional practices, in the case of one mutual assistance fund, each owner contributed a certain amount of capital to the pool and received interest on his share of the pool, which was used by members in turn (Informant 54). The private entrepreneurs association also made funds available to private enterprises that had little or no access to credit through the state banking system (Informants 89, 111, and 115). This kind of cooperative effort was formalized at the national level in 1995 with the establishment of the Minsheng Bank (Xinhua, December 3, 1994). The creation of Minsheng as a private shareholding bank was spearheaded by the All-China Federation of Industry and Commerce to fill the lacuna left by the unwillingness of state-run banks to lend to private enterprises. By 1996, at the end of the first full year of operation, total assets had reach 8 billion yuan (Lardy 1998:69).

Nevertheless, surveys of private entrepreneurs consistently found that access to capital was a major obstacle to private development. A 1989 survey reported that access to capital was the biggest problem facing 63 percent of private entrepreneurs during the start-up period and that it continued to be the biggest problem facing 56 percent of entrepreneurs even after they had become established.[51] Similarly, the findings of a

---

[49] Informants 55 and 114. One private entrepreneur reported borrowing funds directly from a collective enterprise at monthly interest rates that reached as high as 3 percent.

[50] This chapter focuses primarily on the allocation of credit through the state banking system; a complete discussion of alternative sources of credit is beyond the scope of the chapter. On the experience in Wenzhou, see Yuan (1987:98–122); and Zhang and Li (1990b:128–45). On nonstate financial institutions, see Lardy (1998); Manoharan (1991); and Tam (1991; 1992).

[51] Zhonggong zhongyang nongcun zhengce yanjiushi and Guowuyuan nongcun fazhan yanjiu zhongxin nongcun diaocha bangongshi. "Dui baijia nongcun siying qiye diaocha de chubu fenxi (An Initial Analysis of a Survey of One Hundred Rural Private Enterprises)," *Nongye jingji wenti* No. 2 (1989), pp. 18–23.

survey commissioned by the All-China Federation of Industry and Commerce found that difficulties in acquiring loans through the state banking system ranked among the most intractable problems encountered by private entrepreneurs.[52]

CONCLUSION: STATE BUILDING AND FINANCIAL REFORM

The high degree of politicization of credit allocation at the local level undermined the achievement of central policy goals in the banking sector. While discipline in the capital market improved during the 1990s, township officials were still capable of intervening to pursue their goals at the expense of responsible credit policy. As a result, banks continued to support weak collective firms with loans. At the same time, creditworthy private firms were largely excluded from access to credit through the state-run banking system. Finally, without adequate autonomy from the local government, neither banks nor collective firms responded with sufficient alacrity to the indirect levers of macroeconomic control.

Some observers argue that the high degree to which collective firms were leveraged was not problematic in light of the similar characteristics of successful firms in other East Asian countries. However, the Chinese case differs in certain key respects. Township- and village-run firms were not "national champions" – that is, elite firms cultivated by the national state to compete successfully in world markets – but rather "township champions." Because township officials were overwhelmingly oriented toward the development and welfare of their own townships, they pursued policies that, viewed from a national perspective, unnecessarily duplicated productive capacity and wasted scarce capital resources. Because of the power of local officials stemming from their multiple roles as de facto enterprise owners, tax collectors, and bank overseers, township- and village-run collectives were inadequately regulated by central fiscal and monetary policies. Neither the market nor the state consistently disciplined the use of capital. Weak capital market discipline was further exacerbated by other problems such as the lack of adequate information and the absence of a complete legal and regulatory framework with full disclosure requirements and contract enforcement. These problems highlight the state-building aspects of financial reform. To be

---

[52] Agence France Presse, October 21, 1994, reprinted in *China News Digest*, October 23–25, 1994.

effective, local state banks require an adequately trained staff, insulated from local political interference and capable of evaluating loan requests, monitoring and assessing enterprise performance, and withholding credit from poor performers.

7

The Political Economy of
Institutional Change

THIS study has analyzed how the actions of local state officials shaped institutions of property rights in rural industry and how the structure of property rights, in turn, influenced the extractive institutions and allocative practices of the state in each of three locales. This local story is set in the context of a larger constellation of national-level institutions and policies. The policies and actions of the central state, refracted through the prism of intervening levels of administrative hierarchy, created incentives and constraints that shaped the behavior of local state officials. In this way, national institutions have been taken as exogenous to the dynamics examined in the study thus far. This stance was appropriate both because the study has focused on incentives and constraints at the local level and because national institutions were relatively unchanging in their fundamentals over the period covered by the core of the study.

This concluding chapter broadens the scope of the analysis by examining interactions between the dynamics of the system at the local level and at the central level. Specifically, the actions of local officials have created pressure for change at the central level. Indeed, since 1994, fundamental changes have occurred in the national institutional environment. This chapter addresses the occurrence of major changes in central state institutions and analyzes their effects on the evolution of property rights at the local level.

Changes at the national level – in particular those beginning in 1994 – can be understood to a large extent as a reaction to the strategic maneuvering of local officials. As we have seen in the preceding chapters, local officials were poor agents of the center in the administration of taxation and credit allocation, particularly when dealing with local collective firms. Their actions contributed both to the steady decline of budgetary revenue as a share of GDP and to the concomitant increase in off-budget revenue; they also exacerbated inflationary cycles that wreaked havoc with the domestic political economy. These problems contributed directly to the articulation of a major national reform agenda at the Third Plenum of the Fourteenth Central Committee in November 1993, which, in turn, led to the initiation of far-reaching fiscal reforms in 1994 and 1996.

The establishment of new state fiscal institutions, along with changes in the national political and market environments, are fundamentally reshaping the incentives and constraints facing local officials. These changes have gone some distance toward hardening the budget constraints of township governments. As a result, local officials are making dramatic changes in the types of property rights they are willing to support. Indeed, it was only in the mid-1990s, when the incentives and constraints faced by local state officials changed substantially, that townships began privatizing collectively owned TVEs in significant numbers.[1] It is difficult to explain the first wave of privatization in the mid-1990s if we assume, following Oi (1998), that budget constraints at the township level had been hardened more than a decade earlier. Rather, such dramatic change at the local level can be explained most clearly by looking at equally fundamental changes in national-level institutions. Only as budget constraints began to harden in the mid-1990s as a result of changes in national institutions was the real cost of carrying many marginal collective firms driven home to township officials. At the same time, gradual improvements in the legal and constitutional framework and increasingly complete markets for factors and products have begun to improve the climate for private ownership of industrial enterprises on a nationwide scale.

Like the asteroid and resulting dust cloud that changed the climate in which the dinosaurs lived, a combination of fundamental changes in China's national institutions is transforming the environment for local officials and the rural enterprises they govern.[2] China's emergent private sector is relatively well adapted to the new climate, while the collective sector, which has been so actively promoted by local officials through-

---

[1] Privatization of publicly owned firms should be distinguished from new entry by private investors.
[2] Thus, the analogy introduced here may be extended to encompass "man-made" factors that change the environment.

out the reform era, is less well so. Whether the national climatic changes will constitute an "extinction-level event" for collectives remains to be seen.

However, as stark a departure from the previous policy environment as the post-1994 reforms appear to be, and as dramatic a repudiation of the past as the privatization of collectives appears to be, these developments can be readily understood in the context of the theoretical framework developed in this study. Examined from an evolutionary perspective, the same theoretical framework that explained the emergence of distinctive regional patterns of collective and private ownership explains the dramatic move toward privatization of rural collectives in the mid-1990s. Within a given configuration of national institutions, the evolution of local institutions appears to be path dependent. However, when substantial change occurs in the larger institutional environment, dramatic and seemingly disjunct change can occur in the paths of local institutional development. The theoretical purchase afforded by examining bounded rational choice within an empirically grounded framework of incentives and constraints is no less useful in explaining behavior across institutional "macroclimates" than within them.

This chapter begins by reviewing the nature of local institutional variation and apparently path-dependent change that occurred within the context of central state institutions prior to 1994. Subsequent sections highlight how the behavior of local officials precipitated far-reaching changes in national-level institutions circa 1994 and how these changes, in turn, transformed the environment for local officials with important implications for property rights and extractive institutions in the rural sector during the post-1994 period. The chapter concludes with some reflections on the study of institutional change.

CHANGE IN LOCAL INSTITUTIONS BEFORE 1994

The Economic and Political Incentive Structure

The importance of the economic and political incentives crafted by the upper levels of the state apparatus in shaping local institutions is undeniable (Chapter 3). The post-1980 revenue-sharing fiscal system made local governments essentially self-financing and intensified economic incentives for officials in Shanghai, Wuxi, and Wenzhou to develop the local tax base in ways consistent with the "industry-centered tax structure."[3] Local governments vigorously pursued the development of industrial enterprises as the most lucrative source of both budgetary and nonbudgetary revenues.

The political incentives created by the cadre evaluation system also had an effect on the behavior of local cadres by both reinforcing and balancing economic incentives to promote industry. On the one hand, industrial performance was consistently used as the main basis for determining a township official's bonus. During the mid-1980s, the gross value of industrial output was the key indicator used to assess economic performance; however, basing bonuses on industrial output encouraged production without regard to either the efficiency of the production process or the marketability of the products. The county-level officials who set specific performance targets demonstrated sensitivity to this moral-hazard problem by shifting the emphasis to industrial sales or profits as the proxy measure for overall industrial performance. As a result, the interests of township officials were even more closely linked to the performance of industrial assets in the local community.

On the other hand, political incentives also served to balance the weight given to economic incentives. They fostered the provision of public goods by requiring local officials to perform up to minimum standards on other indicators (covering areas such as education, family planning, infrastructural development, and public order) or face penalties. These requirements often took the form of "unfunded mandates," since they were significantly underfunded in the formal budget (Whiting 1999a). The effect of these requirements is evident in the fiscal accounts of townships. In Shanghai's Nantang Township, for example, 40 percent of budgetary expenditures and about 10 percent of nonbudgetary expenditures (accounting for nearly 25 percent of total expenditures) were dedicated to education and health during the early 1990s (Table 3.1). It is noteworthy that even 10 percent of highly discretionary nonbudgetary funds were spent on education and public health. Approximately 25 percent of budgetary expenditures and more than 55 percent of nonbudgetary expenditures (accounting for 40 percent of total expenditures) went to other purposes, including salaries for the growing number of employees in the township government bureaucracy and to township

---

[3] The term is Christine Wong's. See Wong (1997:175). Only with the 1994 tax reforms does the creation of a new business tax on services and the assignment of this revenue source to local governments create a stronger incentive for local governments to promote commercial as opposed to industrial development.

construction. To be sure, political incentives did not eliminate the use of township funds for more self-serving ends; quite visibly, township construction included the financing of plush office buildings and cars for township officials in addition to more basic infrastructural development. At the same time, township officials felt obligated to justify their more extravagant expenditures in terms of the overall benefit to the local community – as necessary to attract foreign buyers and investors, for example. In sum, local officials were political actors whose decision-making calculus and responsibilities extended well beyond industrial performance.

These political incentives may apply more consistently to township leaders than to village leaders. Township leaders are more tightly integrated into the state system: they are state cadres and receive a base salary from the state, while village leaders are collective cadres and receive no fixed salary from the state. In addition, village leaders have an even greater measure of discretionary control over the resources of village-run collective enterprises than township leaders have over township-run collectives, and there is even less separation between the enterprise and the local budget at the village level. Control over village resources gives village leaders some independence vis-à-vis township officials, and highly successful rural industrialization may make promotion less attractive to village leaders. However, control over village resources also reinforces the desire on the part of village leaders to maintain their positions of authority within the village, and, through the 1990s in the sites investigated for this study, the appointment of village officials was controlled by township leaders, suggesting that higher levels retained the ability to shape the incentives of village as well as township leaders.[4]

Finally, the cadre evaluation system provided a relatively objective basis and specified relatively simple and readily measurable criteria for evaluating the performance of officials across locales. The system injected an element of political competition among local officials. Not only were the officials aware of how they ranked on the most important performance indicators compared to the leaders of other townships or villages, but they were rewarded or penalized accordingly. In this way,

---

[4] The true democratization of the selection process for village leaders would likely reduce the influence of higher levels on the behavior of village leaders. While village leaders are nominally elected, the selection of nominees is usually controlled by the township via party channels.

the system could reduce the significance of personal ties and nepotism in the evaluation and promotion process to some degree.[5] More importantly, the system provided the concrete means by which officials at the next higher level could monitor the behavior of local officials on a few key indicators. The system also allowed bureaucratic superiors to adjust their priorities, changing performance indicators (or the relative emphasis they received) as needed. In this way, it conveyed information to local cadres about which policies should receive their attention and which they could disregard in their quest to advance within the political system. While the political incentives contained in the cadre evaluation system evidently had some effect through the 1990s, we can expect that, to the extent that a career in the state apparatus ceases to offer professional rewards in some way commensurate with rewards in the private sector, township officials may increasingly give priority to personal goals over officially defined goals.

Apparent Path Dependence in the Evolution of Property Rights

Local officials in Wuxi, Shanghai, and Wenzhou clearly took the development of local industry to be a priority. However, they did not approach this task in the same ways. Political and economic resources inherited from the commune era had a decisive impact on local officials' choices about the forms of property rights they would actively support, and local state involvement played a critical role in the further development of industry in each case (Chapters 2 and 4). Dependence on local resource endowments on the one hand, and complementarities between the nature of market and legal institutions and ownership forms on the other, combined to create apparent path dependence in the trajectories of rural industrial development during the first decade and a half of reform.

Officials in Wuxi, and to a lesser extent in Shanghai, controlled surplus investment capital derived from commune and brigade enterprises dating back to the 1960s. Not only was the commune-era collective economy a source of capital for subsequent local government investment in township- and village-run enterprises, but TVEs themselves in Wuxi and Shanghai were part of a collective organizational structure that per-

---

[5] As noted in Chapter 3, it was not uncommon for township leaders to face transfers, promotions, or demotions across townships within the same county. Thus, they were not tied to their township of origin.

sisted into the reform era. Despite the nominal shift from communes and brigades to townships and villages that was intended to separate political from economic functions, political and economic power remained fused to a significant degree in the collective industrial sector. The local state played a crucial role in channeling credit from the state-run banking system, particularly the Agriculture Bank and its affiliated rural credit cooperatives, to investment-hungry collectives (Chapter 6). Reliance by collective enterprises on bank loans, especially for fixed-asset investment, was at its height from the mid-1980s to the mid-1990s. Local officials used their political authority over the officers of the local bank branches to direct loans to particular projects and to provide local loan "guarantees." As discussed in Chapter 6, such "guarantees" were empty, and many loans have gone unpaid. Indeed, the record of township- and village-run collectives in repaying loans "is the lowest of any single category of loans" in the state-run banking system as measured by the share of loans that are past due.[6]

Furthermore, local officials in the Wuxi research site forthrightly sought to protect local collectives and refused to license private firms, while local officials in the Shanghai research sites did not actively support private firms but tolerated them as long as they did not compete directly with local collectives. As a result, collectively owned firms continued to dominate the landscape in these areas.

By contrast, local officials in Wenzhou entered the reform era with little surplus investment capital at their disposal. Instead of perpetuating a weak collective economy, they sought to develop local industry by encouraging private investment, thereby drawing on the local tradition of petty commerce and the capital available in society. Their main task, therefore, was to reduce the risk faced by private investors. Local cadres, acting in a larger political–legal climate that was overtly hostile to the interests of private capital, fostered the evolution of property rights in ways that provided increasingly explicit and secure claims by private entrepreneurs to their assets. Local practice evolved from illicit affiliation of private firms with existing collective firms or village organizations, to formation of shareholding companies in which the contributions of private investors were relatively well specified, to establishment of outright private ownership.

An essential part of these efforts was devising property rights forms that elicited credible commitment from both the local and central state.

---

[6] *Jinrong shibao*, as cited in Lardy (1998:277).

The early approach of allowing informal affiliation with existing collectives was inadequate because private claims to assets were often not explicitly recognized or honored. To the extent that property claims were based on personal ties, the security of the investor was threatened by changes in official personnel. This study suggests that the shareholding cooperative form of ownership gained prominence because it provided the most credible commitment to private investment by both the local and central levels given the political and economic conditions existing at the time. It made explicit each investor's claim to his share of the assets, and, at the same time, it afforded private investors a collective license that was recognized as legitimate beyond the local community. As a result of these local government efforts to support the claims of private investors, privately invested firms in the form of shareholding cooperatives came to account for the majority of firms in the Wenzhou research site.

The partnership between the local state and private capital reflects their mutual dependence. Local officials in Wenzhou were dependent upon private industry for revenue. In the Wenzhou research site, fully 60 percent of tax receipts from rural industry came from privately invested firms in the early 1990s. This dependence extended to the county level where more than 90 percent of revenue came from rural enterprise – mainly rural industry. Although private entrepreneurs enjoyed greater autonomy from the local state than did collective managers in their day-to-day operations, they were ultimately dependent upon local state officials for the security of the claim on their assets and for support in interactions with the state bureaucracy. The low degree of legal recognition and ideological support for outright private ownership nationwide clearly influenced the efforts of officials in Wenzhou to devise secure property rights for private investors. Furthermore, in the context of incomplete markets for both factors and products, private investors required the intercession of local officials to gain access to inputs such as land for factory buildings and production permits for entry into restricted product markets, which were controlled by state agencies at higher levels. Such problems suggest that full autonomy may be unattainable in the absence of relatively complete markets and an effective legal system.

The extent to which the law can become a tool to guarantee enterprise autonomy against transgressions by the state in China remains an open question, and yet establishing generally applicable rules of the game is an important aspect of the transition from a planned to a market economy. This study raises some intriguing possibilities. The greatest areas of weakness for private firms identified by this study are also areas addressed by a growing number of laws, including the Civil Procedure Law and the Administrative Litigation Law. The latter includes within its scope complaints against administrative organs regarding denial or revocation of licenses, failure to protect property rights, and infringement of lawful business autonomy, among others.[7] Much of the political research to date focuses on legal actions against official organs by individuals or households rather than private firms, although a growing number of references to legal actions by private firms appear in Chinese sources.[8] However, Western legal experts express skepticism about the willingness or ability of courts to enforce rulings against the interests of local state officials.[9] Local leaders continue to exert influence over courts as they do over other state agencies within their jurisdiction. Thus, the forces shaping the interests of local governments continue to be important in assessing the potential for enterprise autonomy.[10]

The Evolution of Local Extractive Institutions

The varied structures of property rights in Wuxi, Shanghai, and Wenzhou were associated with different levels of transaction costs and different distributions of bargaining power within the community. These factors shaped the ways in which the state institutions responsible for extraction of revenue and financing of public goods evolved in each community (Chapter 5).

Where privately invested firms emerged as an important part of the local economy, local officials had an incentive to adopt innovative revenue collection mechanisms, because the information costs associated with revenue extraction were high. Private firms enjoyed greater operational autonomy from the local state than did collective firms, and existing tax organs were ill equipped to measure sales, costs, or other

---

[7] See "Zhonghua renmin gongheguo xingzheng susong fa (Administrative Litigation Law of the PRC)," translated in *Chinese Law and Government* Vol. 24, No. 3 (Fall 1991), pp. 22–34, esp. p. 23. See also Potter (1994a; 1994b).

[8] Further research is required in this area. On individual actions, see Li and O'Brien (1996). On actions by firms, see Lubman (1999), Lyons (1994), and Potter (1994a:350; 1994b:288).

[9] See the special issue of *China Quarterly* on "China's Legal Reforms," esp. Clarke (1995).

[10] Indeed, "rights" are not upheld as such but rather are underpinned by the interests of local state officials.

attributes of firms that operated outside the collective organizational framework. Because of these obstacles, the higher the share of private firms in the tax base, the higher the overall transaction costs of revenue extraction were likely to be. Yet, the ongoing need for revenue on the part of local state officials meant that it was desirable to have an objective basis for its extraction. Subjective guesses at the revenue potential of the private sector risked either grossly undertaxing it, and therefore unnecessarily reducing the resources available to state officials, or severely overtaxing it, and driving an important part of the tax base out of business.

At the same time, however, revenue dependence conferred on the private sector a degree of bargaining power, commensurate with its weight in the local economy. In the Wenzhou site, where the private sector accounted for a large portion of the economy, it implicitly exercised some bargaining power in interactions with the local government.[11] By contrast, in the Shanghai sites, where private firms were tolerated but accounted for only a small portion of the economy, the private sector exercised little bargaining power. The institutions that began to emerge in Wenzhou and Shanghai in the 1980s and early 1990s to deal with the challenges of taxing this new and growing part of the economy reflected the influence of both transaction costs and bargaining power.

The institution of *daizhengshui* – a simple procedure for estimating and collecting enterprise taxes – represented an accommodation between the local state and private capital in Wenzhou. On the one hand, it provided an objective basis for tax assessment. On the other hand, by keeping accounting requirements simple, it reduced the information costs associated with revenue extraction to both the local state and private firms, and it afforded private firms greater predictability than did the more subjective methods of revenue extraction employed toward private firms elsewhere. Local officials in Wenzhou had an interest in the long-term health of the private sector, and since private firms – in contrast to collective firms – received relatively little

---

[11] The implicit bargaining power that encourages local officials to take the interests of private firms into account does not depend on organized bargaining activity on the part of private entrepreneurs as long as most private firms are likely to respond to official actions in similar ways. Moreover, this kind of bargaining power is likely to become even more apparent as capital mobility increases. If private entrepreneurs can easily move their businesses to other locales, they then have the ability to "shop around" for the most favorable regulatory environment.

support from state-run banks, they had a limited ability to absorb unpredictable and predatory claims. Extralegal levies on private firms over and above their tax obligations were likely to take on the nature of an exchange relationship where additional contributions brought added policy supports.

By contrast, the approach to revenue extraction adopted by local officials in Songyang Town, Shanghai, did not represent an accommodation. The private enterprise accounting station set up by tax officials was intended to tax private firms according to the letter of the rather Byzantine tax code. Private entrepreneurs had little bargaining power, reflecting their minor position in the local economy, and they were made to bear much of the cost of measurement and enforcement. Moreover, since private firms had little bargaining power, extralegal levies were more likely to take the form of outright predation. Through the early 1990s, local officials in Songyang were not dependent on the long-term health of the private economy and were therefore less concerned with private firms' ability to reinvest.[12]

In both Wenzhou and Shanghai, local officials dealt with the challenges of taxing the reemerging private sector by adapting various practices used to tax private firms before the "socialist transformation" eliminated the private sector in the mid-1950s. Given the wide range of possible responses, the fact that the shape of local institutional arrangements closely resembled earlier practices suggests a boundedly rational approach to revenue extraction. As Paul Pierson (1993:613) notes, "Overwhelmed by the complexity of the problems they confront, decision makers lean heavily on preexisting policy frameworks, adjusting only at the margins to accommodate distinctive features of new situations." The particular institutional adaptations in Wenzhou and Shanghai not only had distinct historical antecedents but also differed in ways that reflected the different levels of transaction costs and distributions of bargaining power in each community.

With respect to township- and village-run collectives in Wuxi and Shanghai, local officials had a vested interest in maintaining the status quo that allowed them to manipulate revenue extraction to conform with local goals. The close integration of township- and village-run enterprises

---

[12] This argument operates at the institutional level of analysis. Institutions pattern behavior in consistent ways, but their impact is not deterministic. While the argument focuses on formal institutional change, it does not preclude a role for individual accommodations between local state officials and private entrepreneurs.

into the existing collective organizational structure meant that collective enterprise managers enjoyed relatively little autonomy from the local state.[13] Managers were subordinates in a hierarchical relationship with local state officials. The separation between the finances of the township or village and its collective enterprises was highly imperfect. As a result, the information costs faced by local officials in extracting revenue from these firms were relatively low. Indeed, public ownership often entails lower costs of revenue extraction to the local state, because it provides institutional arrangements that internalize transactions, creating "enforceable norms for the transmission of information" (Evans 1995:26). Thus, local officials had both the incentive and the opportunity to shift revenue from budgetary channels, on which the central government had a claim, into nonbudgetary channels, controlled completely at the local level.

Local officials' collusion with collective firms in avoiding and evading central taxes created softness in tax obligations that contributed to their ability to support a larger number of economically marginal collective enterprises. Moreover, collective firms directly performed many sociopolitical functions at the behest of the local state.[14] The requirement that collectives directly finance local infrastructure projects or provide employment for local residents without regard to the needs of the firm can be interpreted in this light. Local officials regarded employment provision, for example, as a core part of their effort to maintain public order and improve the welfare of local residents. Furthermore, the high degree of total revenue extraction from and direct provision of public and welfare goods by collective firms was supported by access to soft credit from the state banking system, over which local officials exercised some political influence. Revenue extraction from collective enterprises was therefore part and parcel of the larger collective organizational structure that harnessed the resources of the community to the political purposes pursued by local state officials. In sum, the ownership structure of firms in the local economy, itself shaped by the local state, had a marked effect on local extractive institutions.

---

[13] Collective managers had some bargaining power vis-à-vis township officials due to the greater intimacy of their knowledge about their firms, but they were still dependent for their positions as managers upon the continued support of township officials.

[14] Similarly, Christine Wong finds that significant differences in the provision of public goods at the grass roots can be attributed to the presence or absence of collective enterprises (Wong 1997).

REFORM AT THE NATIONAL LEVEL: "ENDOGENIZING"
CENTRAL STATE INSTITUTIONS

Declining Budgetary Revenue: The Impetus for the 1994 Reforms

Local governments were poor agents of the center in the administration of taxation and credit allocation, particularly when dealing with local collective firms (Chapters 5 and 6). Nevertheless, central state officials have continued to face a strong revenue imperative – an imperative that the center has regarded as threatened by the strategic maneuvering of local governments.

From the perspective of the central state, an important question was how effective local institutional arrangements were in mobilizing revenue into budgetary channels. In one sense the central state had an indirect interest in the generation and extraction of revenue even outside budgetary channels, since the expenditure of nonbudgetary revenue was influenced by the political incentives structured by higher levels. Nonbudgetary funds contributed to the ability of local cadres to respond to the "unfunded mandates" foisted upon them by the center. Nevertheless, the central state also sought more direct control over revenue through the budget.

Perpetuation of the collective model in which political and economic power were fused in the hands of local state officials hindered the mobilization of revenue into the budgetary system. While overall extraction remained high, local officials distorted the accounts of collective firms by underreporting output and sales, inflating costs, and manipulating records so that firms would "qualify" for centrally mandated tax reductions and exemptions. In other words, local officials colluded with the collective firms in their jurisdictions to evade and avoid central tax levies. Such practices allowed local officials to shift revenue from budgetary channels, which were shared with higher levels, to nonbudgetary channels, which were controlled locally. Thus, nonbudgetary revenues accounted for between 40 and 60 percent of total revenues in the collective sites for which data were available (Tables 3.3 and 3.4).

In devising new institutional arrangements to extract revenue from private firms, local officials were responding to the same set of incentives to control as much revenue as possible at the local level. The institutional innovations accrued to the benefit of local governments first and foremost by providing information about the resources of private firms. This information could be used in a variety of ways. It is noteworthy that the accommodation struck between the local state and private firms in Hualing Town, Wenzhou, allowed at least 30 percent of total revenues to enter local coffers via nonbudgetary channels (Table 3.4). But to the extent that new institutional arrangements brought additional revenue into budgetary channels, they also accrued to the benefit of the central government. Thus, it is also noteworthy that Hualing exceeded its 1991 tax quota by close to 25 percent, revealing significant revenue capacity to higher levels. Local officials in Songyang Town, Shanghai, who adopted a more adversarial approach to the private sector, were even better agents of central interests with respect to the private firms within their jurisdiction. In both Hualing and Songyang, the institutions designed to cope with the challenges of taxing private firms at the local level also revealed fiscal capacity to higher levels.

All local institutions operated in broader provincial regulatory environments, and the particular provincial context had an independent impact on the effectiveness of the local institutional arrangements in mobilizing revenue into budgetary channels. The central state elicited very different levels of political effort in revenue extraction across provinces. The disparity in political effort is illustrated by the contrast between Jiangsu and Shanghai. Despite roughly similar levels of tax capacity, Shanghai's fiscal contract required it to remit more revenue to the center than did Jiangsu's. Consistent with this requirement, Shanghai extracted significantly more revenue via budgetary channels than did Jiangsu. The contrast was clear all the way down to the township level, where the implementation of tax policy in Shanghai's rural industrial sector was subject to more aggressive monitoring efforts by higher levels.[15] Fiscal pressure elicited greater political effort, but this begs the question of why some provinces faced greater fiscal pressure than others. Although the literature on central–provincial relations suggests a

---

[15] Lin Zhimin (1994) argues that, at least until the late 1980s, the large size of Shanghai's fiscal contributions to the center resulted in tighter central control, and Shanghai had less freedom in its fiscal relations with lower levels than did other provincial-level units. Certainly, the weaker performance of urban, state industry in Shanghai as compared to Jiangsu made Shanghai's tax burden seem even more onerous. The belief on the part of some officials in Shanghai Municipality that competition from rural, nonstate industry was in part to blame for the poor performance of state industry likely contributed to the more aggressive monitoring of taxation in Shanghai's rural industrial sector. However, such monitoring did not completely preclude collusive behavior between local officials and their collective enterprises, which allowed officials to shift revenues from budgetary to nonbudgetary channels – even in Shanghai. The costs of monitoring necessary to ensure perfect compliance would likely outweigh the benefits.

number of hypotheses, there is, as yet, no comprehensive theory that allows one to specify completely the nature and sources of bargaining in the central–provincial relationship.[16] More important for the purposes of this local study, however, is that, whatever motivated the actions of officials at the provincial level, they could strongly influence policy implementation at lower levels by relaxing or intensifying their monitoring of local behavior. Thus, the approach to revenue extraction at the township level was shaped both by the provincial regulatory environment and by the local institutional arrangements.

The implementation of tax policy, specifically the mobilization of revenue into budgetary channels, had a direct bearing on the achievement of a wide range of central state goals. First, the growing reliance on off-budget revenue reduced the ability of the state to address the problem of inequality across locales, since only budgetary revenues were subject to revenue sharing. Second, the explosion of off-budget revenue contributed to inflationary pressures in the economy, since local officials exercised greater discretion over these funds and tended to use them for investments that fueled demand for scarce building materials and industrial inputs. Weak implementation of tax policy undermined the ability of the center to use this policy tool to influence the scale and direction of investment in the context of a national industrial policy. Third, poor implementation undermined the ability of higher levels to mobilize revenue for priority projects (such as large infrastructure projects) that exceeded the fiscal capacity of lower-level units.

Budgetary revenue as a share of GDP declined steadily from the late 1970s through the mid-1990s, while the center's share of budgetary revenue declined over much of the same period. As Barry Naughton (1992a) points out, an important factor contributing to overall fiscal decline was the declining profitability of the state-owned industrial sector in the face of growing competition from entry by both collective and private firms. Fiscal incentives, however, were also a crucial factor. Indeed, budgetary revenue as a share of GDP fell from 34 percent in 1978 to 12.7 percent in 1994, while officially reported extrabudgetary

---

[16] Yasheng Huang (1996:282) suggests that "the Center seeks to integrate more closely those provinces that are more economically developed by dispatching [officials with close ties to the Center] to run them." As a major center of urban industry, Shanghai historically has been a main contributor of fiscal revenue to the central government, and its leaders have typically had close ties to the Center. Central–provincial relations are, of course, also affected by other factors, such as personal politics. See Bo (1998), Chung (1995b), Jia and Lin (1994), and Lieberthal and Oksenberg (1988).

revenue as a share of GDP climbed from 2.6 percent to 4 percent in 1994.[17]

Reform at the Central Level: The 1994 Reforms

The fiscal reforms of 1994 and 1996 can be understood in light of the center's fiscal dilemma. These reforms were, at root, centralizing initiatives designed to give the central government greater control over fiscal resources. In forcing through these initiatives, the center resorted to its political hold over the vestiges of the Leninist system. As Yasheng Huang's (1996) work shows, the central state can use its control over the personnel appointment system to implement policies that reshape the incentives and constraints facing local state officials. The 1994 reforms in the assignment of fiscal revenue and the 1996 reforms in the management of off-budget funds were intended to change the previously existing incentives for weak tax enforcement in local publicly owned firms.[18] The changes in central institutions documented here also provide evidence of significant institutional adaptability within the state apparatus, in contrast to those scholars who find only secular institutional decay.

The introduction of the new tax assignment system in 1994 changed the fiscal landscape for local state officials in important ways. In November 1993, the CCP Central Committee announced the replacement of the existing fiscal contract system (*caizheng baoganzhi*) with the tax assignment system (*fenshuizhi*). This reform was explicitly intended to arrest the decline in the "two ratios," that is, budgetary revenue as a share of GDP and central government revenue as a share of total budgetary revenue. The new system separated tax types into central, local, and shared taxes.[19] Among the major revenue-generating taxes, the new value-added tax is shared, with the center claiming the largest portion (75 percent); in addition, the center claims the new consumption tax as a central tax, leaving the new business tax on services, enterprise income taxes, individual income taxes, the agriculture tax, and other minor

---

[17] The figure for extrabudgetary funds is the official national figure. See Whiting (1999a).

[18] It is important to note that these reforms are neither inevitable nor guaranteed of success. The mere existence of a revenue imperative does not guarantee that it can be successfully met. Indeed, successful implementation of these reforms requires substantial political capital and bureaucratic capacity on the part of the central state apparatus.

[19] However, China retained its unitary structure in which only the central government has the authority to authorize taxes.

taxes to be controlled at the local level.[20] To implement this division of revenue, the central government for the first time established central tax offices (*guoshuiju*) at provincial, municipal, and county levels, as well as in some townships.[21] The new central tax offices were made responsible for collecting both central and shared taxes, while local tax offices (*dishuiju*) were made responsible for collecting local taxes.[22] Thus, major revenue sources were reassigned to central control, and new organs were put in place to collect these revenues.

The immediate result of the centralizing initiatives was to put a squeeze on local governments across the country (Figure 7.1).[23] In Songjiang County, for example, consolidated budgetary revenue following the 1994 reforms fell from 271 million yuan in 1993 to 177 million yuan in 1994 – a decline of 35 percent.[24] By 1995, it had recovered to only 247 million yuan.[25]

Furthermore, the 1994 reforms formally abolished the practice of repaying bank loans from pretax profits, a practice employed by collectively owned firms that had effectively shifted much of the debt burden from enterprises to the fiscal system and had permitted the accumulation of high debt-to-equity ratios for many rural collectives. The reforms

---

[20] To gain local government acquiescence in this centralizing initiative, the center guaranteed that local revenues would not fall below 1993 levels. It further agreed to rebate 30 percent of the annual increase in the local portion of the VAT and 30 percent of the increase in the consumption tax to local governments for a limited period of time. The division of local revenues among provincial, municipal, county, and township governments was left to local governments to decide among themselves. As a result, there is substantial variation in the assignment of local revenue sources among different levels of local government.

[21] For example, the township-level research site in Wuxi County established separate state and local tax offices, while the township-level site in Songjiang County did not.

[22] The new central tax offices are under the vertical management of the State General Administration of Taxation (SGAT), with each level supervising the one immediately below it. By contrast, local tax offices function under the dual leadership of the local government and the SGAT, with the local government playing the primary role. One local tax, the agriculture tax, is typically collected by the public finance office rather than by the local tax bureau. Gan (1994) and Huang and Mao (1994).

[23] Fiscal reform was slower to reach the township level; however, the new tax assignment system was not fully implemented in all township-level research sites until 1996.

[24] The tax rebate made this decline less acute but no less real. For a more detailed discussion of a broader range of cases see Whiting (1999a).

[25] Consolidated budgetary revenue in 1992 was 228 million yuan in Songjiang County. The inclusion of the 1992 figure as a basis for comparison is useful because the 1993 figure was inflated by many local governments since, as part of the 1994 reforms, the central government guaranteed that local revenues would not fall below the 1993 level. In the case of Songjiang, 1994 revenue represented a decline even compared to the 1992 level.

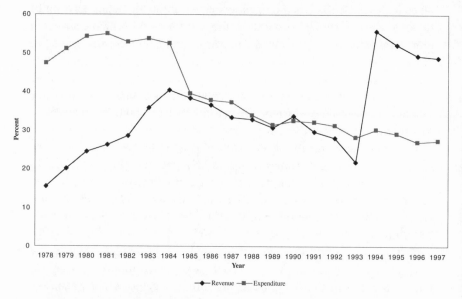

Figure 7.1. Central government share of total budgetary revenue and expenditure, 1978–97.

also revoked the formal authority of local governments to approve tax exemptions and reductions for collective firms – the main avenues for tax avoidance in the pre-1994 system (Z. Wang 1994).[26] The elimination of these tax breaks contributed to the hardening of tax obligations of collective firms.

Another intent of the 1994 reform was to eliminate the incentives contained in the pre-1994 fiscal system for local officials to behave strategically by interfering in the collection of formal tax revenues and directing their efforts toward the collection of off-budget revenues. Central tax offices operating at local levels should, in principle, be more faithful agents of the center. However, not surprisingly, the newly established central tax offices were not immediately independent of influence by local governments. In many cases new central and local tax offices were

[26] In a partial reversal, however, the new township and village enterprise law passed in 1996 recognized preferential tax treatment for enterprises in four new categories: (1) newly established enterprises facing financial difficulties, (2) enterprises in minority or impoverished areas, (3) enterprises in selected food-processing industries, and (4) enterprises conforming to state industrial policy guidelines for tax exemptions or reductions. Nevertheless, approval for such preferential treatment was, in principle, centralized.

created simply by dividing personnel from existing local tax bureaus between the two new organs while they continued to work in the same old office space and operate according to the same old procedures.[27] According to one report, central and local tax organs at the city and county levels were established by "splitting the tax organs first and improving them later" (Jiang 1994:1). That improvement was clearly needed was suggested by the assessment of another observer that "local sentiment was so opposed to the tax reform that some officials refused to be transferred to the new state tax bureaux."[28] There is indirect evidence to suggest that at least some of those staffing central tax offices at the lower levels continue to regard themselves as agents of the local, not the central, government. Local policy analysts note that implementation of tax policy under the new system has been undermined by the "biased actions" and "discriminatory attitudes" of local governments.[29] According to Lu Fengquan (1994:18–21),

The relevant authorities report that difficulties in collecting taxes owed by enterprises are much greater than in the past. Since they now have separate financial resources and sources of taxation, local governments do not concern themselves with financial resources for the central government. Whenever conflict occurs between building their own and the central government's financial resources, local governments always act to protect their own financial resources. Therefore, local government departmentalism will weaken the national government's ability to regulate the industrial structure.[30]

---

[27] "Guangdong State and Local Taxation Bureaus Open for Business Today," Jiang (1994:1); Ju (1994:1); *Nanfang ribao*, July 28, 1994, p. 1; "Tianjin Divides Functions of State, Local Tax Bureaus," *Tianjin ribao*, August 4, 1994, p. 1.

[28] *China News Analysis* No. 1508 (April 15, 1994), p. 8. Similarly, in Wuxi County local tax collectors resisted splitting the tax bureau. The bureau was reportedly among the last to split in Jiangsu Province (Informant 229).

[29] Huang and Mao (1994) and Sun and Wang (1994). See also "Jiangsu's Yu Xingde on Tax Collection Problems," Nanjing Jiangsu People's Radio Network, November 24, 1994, translated in *Foreign Broadcast Information Service (FBIS) – China Report*, December 1, 1994, pp. 45–6; and "Tax Loopholes Must Be Closed," *China Daily*, August 17, 1994, p. 4.

[30] Indeed, the change in fiscal system has generated a major shift in the performance criteria set for township executives by their superiors at the county level in Songjiang County, for example. While, before 1994, taxes were not included as a line-item performance criterion in Songjiang since such a practice might encourage local officials to reveal too much fiscal capacity to higher levels, after 1994, the collection of *local* tax types was introduced as a specific performance criterion for the first time (Informant 214).

Moreover, enterprises are now required to pay taxes to not one but two agencies. Thus, as one analyst concludes, "the difficulty of central tax offices in collecting taxes at the grass roots is great" (Ruan 1994:56).

Indeed, central tax offices at the county and township levels continued to rely on quantitative targets set within the state tax administration hierarchy to ensure minimally adequate tax collection of newly centralized tax types.[31] For example, the central tax office in Wuxi's Dongtan Town received a target for 1995 of 40 million yuan for all central tax types, a target that, not coincidentally, was met precisely but not exceeded.[32] At the same time, enterprises in Dongtan accumulated nearly two million yuan in arrears on central taxes.[33] Local officials and collective enterprise managers suggested that – once the tax target was met – accumulating arrears allowed financial resources to be retained locally. Most of the tax arrears were incurred by town-run collectives that benefited from the additional working capital (Informants 220 and 227). In these cases, arrears were paid in the next fiscal year, when they would be applied to the new year's revenue targets.[34] Nationwide, tax arrears of township- and village-run collectives reached a high of 61 billion yuan in 1996, equivalent to 43 percent of their recorded tax liability (*Zhongguo xiangzhen qiye nianjian* 1997:248).

---

[31] The results of a pilot enterprise survey conducted by the author in Hebei Province in 1997 show that 40 percent of all enterprises surveyed reported being governed by tax targets in 1996 (Whiting 1999a).

[32] Without a truly independent central tax office, incentives to collect the VAT are particularly weak in Dongtan because of the way *local* revenues are divided. Of the 25 percent of VAT revenue that is assigned to subnational governments, the province assigned 12.5 percent to Wuxi County, while the county assigned none (0 percent) to the town (Informants 231 and 232). It should be noted that the 25 percent of VAT revenue assigned to local governments is deposited directly into local treasury accounts, while the 75 percent of the VAT assigned to the central government is deposited directly into central treasury accounts. Caizhengbu, Zhongguo renmin yinhang, and guojia shuiwuju, "Shixing 'fenshuizhi' caizheng tizhi hou youguan yusuan guanli wenti de zanxing guiding (Provisional Regulations on Relevant Questions on Budgetary Management after Implementation of the 'Taxation Assignment' Fiscal System)," in *Caizheng shuishou falü shouce, diyibian* (1998:127–35).

[33] On tax arrears, see "Shuishou dafu zengjia, qianshui shu'e buxiao (Tax Receipts Increase on a Large Scale, Amount of Tax Arrears Are Sizable)," *Liaowang* No. 4 (1997), pp. 21–2, and "Qieshi caiqu youxiao cuoshi quebao wancheng he chao'e wancheng quannian shuishou renwu (Resolutely Take Effective Measures to Ensure Meeting and Exceeding Year-end Tax Targets)," *Zhongguo shuiwu* No. 6 (1998), p. 1.

[34] These practices depended on the weak enforcement of late penalties and interest payments on tax arrears.

Two points emerge from this discussion of the 1994 reforms. First, the challenges of building institutions to mobilize revenue from rich collective economies were not instantaneously met by the establishment of central tax offices; indeed, the development of new institutional capacity is a slow and, at times, tortuous process. Second, the difficulties the center faced in institutionalizing the new reforms notwithstanding, local governments faced a very real revenue squeeze beginning in 1994 that reduced budgetary revenues, thereby undermining their ability and willingness to support a large number of economically marginal collective enterprises.

Reining in "Off-budget" Revenues: The 1996 Reforms

Given the "hit" to budgetary revenues suffered by local governments beginning in 1994, off-budget revenues continued to increase in size and importance. However, off-budget funds themselves became the target of comprehensive reform beginning in 1996. As noted in Chapter 2, the profits remitted and fees paid by collective enterprises were classified as "self-raised funds" of townships prior to 1996. These funds typically accounted for close to one-half the total revenue available to townships in areas of collective dominance such as Shanghai and Wuxi, and townships had exercised significant de facto autonomy over the collection and use of these off-budget funds. A major reform initiative promulgated by the State Council in 1996 redefined these funds as official "extrabudgetary revenue."[35] At the same time, the State Council asserted unprecedented central authority over all such extrabudgetary revenue: it decreed that all extrabudgetary funds are public fiscal revenues subject to state control and are not proprietary resources to be used at the discretion of local governments or agencies. Furthermore, the State Council limited the ability of township governments to draw freely on the resources of "their" enterprises by declaring all extrabudgetary levies not approved by the central or provincial government to be illegal. This measure was a direct attack on the use of collective enterprises as "money trees" or "second trea-

---

[35] Guowuyuan, "Guanyu jiaqiang yusuanwai zijin guanli de jueding (Decision regarding Strengthening Management of Extrabudgetary Funds)," *Guowuyuan gongbao* No. 21 (August 1, 1996), pp. 819–24. See also Caizhengbu, "Guanyu jiaqiang xiangzhen yusuanwai zijin guanli de tongzhi (Notice regarding Strengthening Management of Extrabudgetary Funds in Towns and Townships)," in *Caizheng shuishou falü shouce, diyibian* (1998:86–91).

suries" for the revenue demands of local officials.[36] Enforcement of this measure was buttressed by including the elimination of unsanctioned levies in the performance criteria of county and township officials.[37] A joint report issued by the State Council and the CCP Central Committee emphasized that such reform was necessary to end the fusion of the government and the enterprise, to force publicly owned firms to sharpen their market orientation, and to create a level playing field on which all firms could compete.[38] While the 1996 reforms, like the 1994 reforms, face major hurdles in implementation, they weaken the incentive and opportunity for local governments to collude with enterprises to evade tax obligations only to tap the same revenue through off-budget levies.[39]

[36] As noted in Chapter 2, endless demands on collective enterprises for revenue to support the activities of local government officials led them to be referred to as "money trees." Such revenue demands by local officials were indirectly subsidized by easy access to credit via the state-run banking system.

[37] Zhonggong zhongyang bangongting guowuyuan bangongting, "Guanyu zhuanfa caizhengbu 'Guanyu zhili luan shoufei de guiding de tongzhi' (Notice regarding Transmission of Ministry of Finance 'Regulations on Controlling the Chaotic Levying of Fees')," in Ding (1996:8); and Zhonggong zhongyang guowuyuan, "Guanyu qieshi zuohao jianqing nongmin fudan gongzuo de jueding (Decision regarding Conscientiously Doing Well the Work to Reduce Farmers' Burdens)," *Guowuyuan gongbao* No. 12 (April 21, 1997), pp. 563–8. Because township and village enterprises (TVEs) are governed by the Ministry of Agriculture, TVE burdens were addressed in this document regarding farmers' burdens.

[38] Zhonggong zhongyang bangongting guowuyuan bangongting, "Zhuanfa quanguo zhili sanluan lingdao xiaozu 'guanyu zhili sanluan gongzuo de zongjie baogao' de tongzhi (Notice on Transmission of 'Summary Report regarding Work on Controlling the Three Types of Chaotic [Fees] Issued by the National Leadership Small Group for Controlling the Three Types of Chaotic [Fees]')," in Ding (1996:11–19).

[39] Reforms currently under discussion in China suggest that ongoing changes in the management of extrabudgetary revenue may further exacerbate the tensions between central and local governments. The Ministry of Finance and State Development and Planning Commission have proposed abolishing many official extrabudgetary levies and replacing them with formal taxes (*feigaishui*). The most prominent example of this initiative is the proposed amendment to the highway law, which would replace with a national gasoline tax many of the fees typically collected by local transportation bureaus and shared with local governments. The proposed fuel tax would be a central tax type to be collected by the central, not local, tax bureau. At issue is the share of fuel tax revenue that would be returned to local coffers. Fearing that the fuel tax would represent another major redistribution of control over revenue to the center, local governments have expressed their opposition to such a reform initiative through the National People's Congress, which must pass the amendment to the highway law in order for the proposed reform measure to go forward. See "Yunniang bannian de 'feigaishui' fang'an yijing wancheng: woguo shoufei nian jian sanqianyi (The Program for 'Replacing Fees with Taxes' that Has Been Brewing for a Half Year Is Already Complete)," *Guangzhou ribao* (Internet edition), November 15, 1998; and "State Hopes to Levy Fuel Tax from April," *China Daily* (Internet edition), January 7, 1999.

Reforming the State-run Banking System

Although banking reform has proceeded more slowly than fiscal reform, events in the financial sector contributed to the squeeze on townships and their enterprises during the mid-1990s. Renewed economic retrenchment from 1993 to 1994 restricted credit to TVEs from the state-run banking system, as financial resources were redirected to bail out failing SOEs (Brandt and Zhu 1995:11). Indeed, in Songjiang County, bank loans to TVEs for fixed-asset investment were cut in half from 1993 to 1994, and loans as a share of total fixed-asset investment fell to a ten-year low of 5 percent, after reaching highs of more than 50 percent during the mid- to late-1980s (Table 6.4). While bank loans recovered somewhat in 1995, the retrenchment signaled the beginning of the end of reliance on soft bank credits for collectively owned TVEs.

This transition, albeit gradual, was reinforced by the announcement at the Third Plenum of the Fourteenth Central Committee in November 1993 of plans for comprehensive financial sector reforms, including further commercialization of state-run commercial banks such as the Agriculture Bank, one of the main lenders serving TVEs.[40] The commercial banking law was explicitly intended to "insulate banks at the local level from political interference in lending decisions" (Lardy 1998:181). Indeed, by early 1998, Premier Zhu Rongji announced that the power of local state officials "to command local bank presidents" had been abolished.[41] As with fiscal reform, serious challenges remain in the course of implementation. Nevertheless, declining access to soft credit through the state-run banking system contributed to hardening budget constraints for rural collectives beginning in the mid-1990s.

---

[40] This decision was reflected in a specific document promulgated the following month: "Decision on Reform of the Financial System," *Guowuyuan gongbao* No. 31 (January 29, 1994), pp. 1488–96.

[41] "Central Authorities Forbid Local Governments to Interfere in Banks' Loan-Granting Power," *Ming Pao*, January 11, 1998, p. A8, as cited in Lardy (1998:207). Further measures are being instituted to increase the autonomy of the state-run banking system from interference by local political leaders. Provincial branches of the People's Bank of China will be eliminated and replaced with regional branches that do not coincide with any given political jurisdiction. "Dang zhongyang guowuyuan jueding dui Zhongguo renmin yinhang guanli tizhi shixing gaige (CCP Central Committee and State Council Decide to Implement Reform in the Management System of the People's Bank of China)," *Renmin ribao* (Internet edition), November 16, 1998.

Increasing Marketization

Other forces also contributed to the financial pressures faced by collective enterprises. Market allocation of factors of production increased in importance. As Barry Naughton (1995:290) notes, "The most fundamental achievement of the renewal of reform in 1992–93 was rapid progress toward market prices. . . . For the first time, the government moved decisively . . . to cut back the plan in order to move toward full market pricing." Indeed, as of 1997, fully 70 percent of labor allocation and 62 percent of product pricing and distribution were governed by market forces. Even for other factors, such as land and capital for which market penetration was more limited, 23 percent of land transfers and 17 percent of capital distribution were already allocated by the market as of 1997.[42] To the extent that collective firms had been able to acquire bureaucratically allocated goods at below-market prices, moves toward strictly market allocation increased their costs significantly.

At the same time, steadily increasing competition in product markets eroded the profits of rural collectives in many sectors.[43] In Wuxi and Songjiang collective enterprise managers and township leaders alike reported that, as of 1996, increasing competition (particularly from private enterprises across the border in Zhejiang) was negatively affecting their sales and profitability. Indeed, a Ministry of Agriculture report published in 1997 identified product market competition as the biggest challenge facing TVEs during the mid-1990s.[44] Subsequent reports highlighted the increasing difficulties facing these firms, including a slowing growth rate, declining profitability, growing losses, and an impaired ability to absorb surplus labor.[45] At the same time, county officials in both Wuxi and Songjiang lamented that, at least until the mid-1990s, townships and their collective enterprises had faced little or no risk in making industrial investments and that they consistently took responsibility for profits but not losses (Informants 204 and 222). Rather, taxes and debts owed to the central state and state-run banks had gone unpaid.

---

[42] These estimates were produced by scholars affiliated with the State Planning and Development Commission and Beijing University (Chang and Gao 1998:50–1).

[43] For a more detailed discussion of product market discipline, see Whiting (1996).

[44] Ministry of Agriculture "Report on the Situation of Township and Village Enterprises and Opinions on Future Reform and Development," *Renmin ribao*, April 24, 1997.

[45] *Renmin ribao*, September 17, 1998, p. 2. Lardy (1998:36) reports that as of 1997 the nonstate industrial sector (dominated by TVEs) accounted for 45 percent of the financial losses of all industrial enterprises.

CHANGE IN LOCAL INSTITUTIONS AFTER 1994

As the theoretical framework developed in this study would lead us to expect, changes in the institutionally defined incentives and constraints confronting local officials are driving changes in the types of property rights that they are willing to support.

Leaving the Path: Privatizing Rural Collectives

Collective enterprises, which for decades had been tightly integrated into the collective organizational structure of the townships in Wuxi and Shanghai, enjoyed an advantage over private enterprises in the context of (1) a tax system readily manipulated by local officials, (2) bureaucratic allocation of capital, land, and other inputs, (3) highly restricted product markets, and (4) an ideological and legal climate hostile to private ownership. Indeed, we have seen how difficult it was for highly motivated officials in Wenzhou to promote private ownership under such conditions. However, by 1996, with hardening tax obligations, declining access to soft credit through the state-run banking system, and increasingly competitive markets for other factors and products, local officials in both Wuxi and Songjiang Counties began for the first time to push townships and their collective enterprises toward outright privatization (Informants 204 and 222). According to official policy statements, property rights reform in Songjiang had entered a new phase as of late 1996. Local leaders adopted the slogan – now echoing across China – of "*zhuada fangxiao* (holding on to the large and letting go of the small)," indicating their goal of maintaining control and income rights over a select group of large enterprises, while transferring property rights over the remaining enterprises to private entities through a variety of means. These means included auctions and leases of enterprises to private owners, both domestic and foreign. In Songjiang as of late 1996, 110 collective enterprises with 120 million yuan in assets had been auctioned to private owners, while 119 collective enterprises had been taken over by foreign joint ventures (Informant 213). Thus, in the first few months of implementation, nearly 15 percent of collectively owned industrial enterprises in the county had been privatized through these procedures. Privatization also occurred through the creation of new shareholding cooperatives. In these enterprises the local government ceased to hold a controlling stake (*kong gu*) in the enterprise, and control was actually turned over to the shareholders and the board of directors, and, through them, to the enterprise manager. While these practices had been around since the mid-1980s, they had been expressly "experimental" before 1996 and had been implemented on a very limited scale. Moreover, the way shareholding cooperatives had been established in Songjiang prior to 1996, income and control rights had *not* effectively been transferred away from township governments.[46] The privatization of TVEs in such "bastions of collectivism" as Songjiang and Wuxi marks a dramatic change in the disposition of local officials toward property rights in their jurisdictions.[47] Officials in those locales had nurtured and protected collective ownership, which had roots in the Maoist era, through nearly two decades of reform. The transition, still in the early stages in Songjiang and Wuxi, reflects the major changes in the national institutional environment. Figure 7.2 illustrates the transformation of property rights in Yueqing, Songjiang, and Wuxi through 1997. The status of property rights as of this date, particularly in Songjiang and Wuxi, presents a dramatic contrast with the status as of 1994, illustrated in Figure 4.2. In turn, the decisions of local officials in areas such as Songjiang and Wuxi to privatize part of the tax base and to uphold private property rights in a variety of forms helps to create credible commitment to private property rights throughout the Chinese state as a whole.

Changes in the Political-Legal Environment

The Fifteenth Party Congress, held in the fall of 1997, ratified changes already in motion. While public ownership was still upheld as the dominant form of ownership, "nonpublic" ownership was explicitly acknowledged as an important component part of the socialist market economy. CCP General Secretary Jiang Zemin (1997) recognized that "it is necessary to improve the legal system concerning property and to protect the legitimate rights and interests of and fair competition among all types of enterprises and at the same time exercise supervision over them according to law." By the end of the decade, legal protection of the private sector was enshrined in an amendment to the constitution, and landmark court rulings signaled a change in the legal status of the private

---

[46] See Whiting (1999b) for evidence on this point.

[47] On the transformation of property rights in Wuxi, see Zhonggong Xishan shiwei Xishan shi renmin zhengfu, "Guanyu jinyibu tuijin zhen, cun jiti qiye gaige de yijian (Opinion on Advancing the Reform to Town- and Village-run Collective Enterprises)," in *Xishan shi nianjian* (1997:227–31).

Yueqing County, Wenzhou

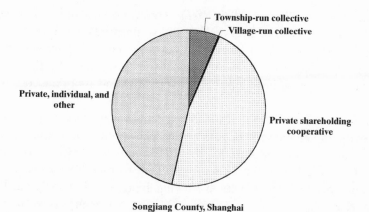

Township-run collective
Village-run collective

Private, individual, and other

Private shareholding cooperative

Songjiang County, Shanghai

Private, individual, and other

Village-run collective

Township-run collective

Wuxi County, Wuxi

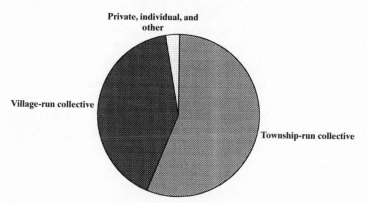

Private, individual, and other

Village-run collective

Township-run collective

Figure 7.2. Gross value of industrial output by ownership, 1997. *Note*: The figure for Wuxi County represents 1996 data. *Sources*: See Table 4.1.

sector.[48] More strikingly, Jiang (1997) called for "quickening the pace" in relinquishing control over small public enterprises and invigorating them through reorganization, merger, leasing, contracting, shareholding conversion, or auction. The Ministry of Agriculture subsequently reiterated the message, adding bankruptcy to privatization as options for rural collectives.[49]

These changes in the political and market environments are gradually improving the climate for private enterprise – not just in Wenzhou but nationwide – making it more feasible for private enterprise to compete with the collective sector and for further privatization to occur. As Christine Wong (1996:243) states, "taking Jiangsu and Shanghai as the bastions of the collectivist Jiangnan Model, one [can] correlate the declining share of their rural enterprises in total rural industrial output with a loosening of the hold of collective enterprises on the rural enterprise sector . . . this would be consistent with the overall growth of openly private enterprise in the rural sector." The 1994 tax reforms explicitly leveled the playing field for firms of all ownership types not only by eliminating special tax exemptions and reductions available only to rural collectives but also by establishing a single, uniform income tax rate for all firms. Increasingly complete markets for factors and products also facilitated private firms' ability to compete.[50] Finally, changes in the party platform and in the constitution are gradually creating a more hos-

---

[48] Article 11 was amended to read: "The nonpublic sector, including self-employed and private businesses, within the domain stipulated by law, is an important component of the country's socialist market economy. . . . The country should protect the legitimate rights and interests of the self-employed and private enterprises, and the country should also exercise guidance, supervision, and management over them, according to law." Zhongguo gongchandang zhongyang weiyuanhui, "Guanyu xiugai xianfa bufen neirong de jianyi (Opinion regarding Revising Part of the Content of the Constitution)," *Renmin ribao*, January 31, 1999, p. 1. Such legal protection was demonstrated in a well-publicized court case in Northeast China in 1999. The legitimacy of the claim of a private investor to assets he had registered under collective ownership was upheld by an intermediate court. See "Businessman Has Triumphal Day in Court," *China Daily* (Internet edition), February 15, 1999. As noted in Chapter 4, such claims had not received explicit legal recognition before the late 1990s.

[49] See Nongyebu, "Guanyu dangqian shenhua xiangzhen qiye gaige you guan wenti de tongzhi (Notice regarding Questions on the Current Deepening of Rural Enterprise Reform)," cited in *Renmin ribao*, July 17, 1998, p. 2. This document also attempted to stem the tide of abuse accompanying privatization, including the transfer of assets to local "insiders" at fire sale prices, etc.

[50] This issue also received attention at the Fifteenth Party Congress. Jiang (1997) called for continued development of "all kinds of markets with emphasis on markets for capital, labor, technology, and other factors of production."

pitable political climate for private ownership of industry. Of course, in the contemporary Chinese context, the actions of local officials still remain important to guaranteeing property rights on the ground. Thus, the changes in the incentives and constraints facing local officials in areas in which collective enterprises have been dominant up to now are equally – if not more – significant than constitutional and legal guarantees.

For privately invested firms in Wenzhou and elsewhere, the changes have improved their ability to compete in the national and international marketplaces.[51] With the passage of a national company law (*gongsi fa*) that allows qualifying firms to register simply as corporations, a firm's status as "private" or "collective" may ultimately become virtually irrelevant.[52] Private investors in places such as Wenzhou are well poised to capitalize on changes in the political and economic environments that are gradually putting public and private firms on a level playing field.

CONCLUSION: THE POLITICS OF MARKET TRANSITION

Complementarities among local public ownership, local bureaucratic influence over factor allocation and product distribution, and local administration of state fiscal policy contributed to the apparently path-dependent development of township- and village-run collectives in places such as Shanghai and Wuxi through the mid-1990s. However, the collective organizational structure, of which these firms were a part, hindered the mobilization of revenue into central state coffers and contributed to the fiscal crisis that precipitated the new national reform agenda set out in late 1993. The major central state initiatives announced in 1993 have begun to change key elements of the political economy in which rural industry operates. This central–local feedback loop is depicted in Figure 7.3. The fiscal reforms, banking reforms, and expanded market competition of the mid-1990s are beginning to harden the budget constraints of local state officials and weaken their ability and willingness to support a large number of collective enterprises within their jurisdictions. As a result, the first wave of privatization swept through Shanghai and Wuxi in the mid-1990s. In this new environment, the ability

---

[51] Private enterprises have gained the right to export products directly without going through state-run trade corporations. *Jingji ribao*, February 9, 1999.

[52] "Zhonghua renmin gongheguo gongsi fa (Company Law of the PRC)," in *Gongsi falu quanshu* (1994:2–17).

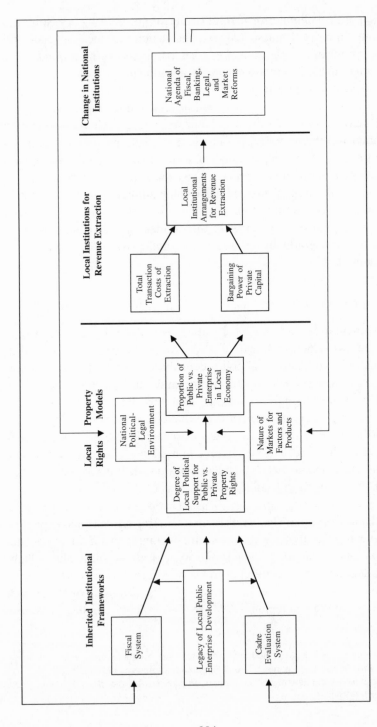

Figure 7.3. Explaining local and national institutional change.

294

of firms to compete in the national and international marketplace will become more critical to their survival. The economic reforms of the mid-1990s, along with changes to the political–legal infrastructure, are also improving the environment for private firms in Wenzhou and nationwide; thus, the reforms both facilitate the expansion of private enterprise and intensify the market competition faced by the collective enterprises that remain.

However, this concluding chapter is not intended to offer support for some teleology of the market: the notion that the Chinese economy is necessarily evolving toward some "natural" and "correct" free-market end state is inconsistent with both the theoretical underpinnings and the empirical findings of this study. To the contrary, this study highlights the embeddedness of both local state officials and the firms they govern in a complex political economy.[53]

During the first decade and a half of reform, collective enterprises, promoted by local cadres, were able to draw on the political and economic resources of their communities to generate both jobs and revenue. The fact that they were buttressed by access to soft bank credits and cushioned by softness in their tax obligations through the mid-1990s meant that these firms were not perfectly efficient, "first-best" alternatives to the large, state-owned enterprises that had dominated the planned economy.[54] Nevertheless, they contributed significantly to China's economic growth, its transformation from agriculture to industry, and its transition from plan to market.

Full privatization in China is not yet set in stone, and it is not yet clear whether the changes in national institutions reviewed here will ultimately constitute an "extinction-level event" for collective enterprises. Even the strategies adopted in Songjiang and Wuxi Counties entail the retention of a core of collectively owned enterprises that continue to receive preferential treatment and are still expected to generate jobs and revenue for township governments. Some of these enterprises may learn to adapt to a more competitive market environment, while others may not.

---

[53] The notion of embeddedness is closely associated with Granovetter's (1985) analysis of social networks, but my use of the term here gives more weight to state and market institutions following Polanyi (1957). See also Hollingsworth and Boyer (1997) and Evans (1995).

[54] The relative "success" of TVEs in the 1980s led some analysts to assume that market conditions and hard budget constraints obtained in the rural industrial sector, despite evidence to the contrary. See, for example, Lewis (1997) and Steinfeld (1998:255).

At the same time, concerns about the maintenance of political order stemming from increasing layoffs by public enterprises – including both SOEs and TVEs – are slowing the full implementation of many of the new reform initiatives. As Polanyi's (1957 [1944]) work would suggest, the state is likely to intervene to stem the political threat posed by the ravages of an untamed market. For example, central state officials loosened criteria for bank lending as layoffs began to threaten social stability in the late 1990s.[55] In addition, they expressed concern at the pace of privatization in light of growing labor unrest.[56] Their concerns are particularly acute, since the full set of institutions that are desirable in governing a functioning market economy, such as social security, unemployment, and health insurance programs, are not yet in place in most urban – not to mention rural – communities.[57]

Thus, this chapter espouses the notion that markets do not exist in the "state of nature" but rather must be regulated by the state. As we have seen in Russia, Poland, and elsewhere in Eastern Europe, the radical, "big bang" approach to socialist transition, involving the rapid and simultaneous liberalization of prices and privatization of public enterprises, in many cases destroyed the very state institutions needed to govern the economy during the process of transition (Murrell 1992; Poznanski 1996). This problem highlights the essential political and social foundations of market institutions so vividly evoked by Polanyi's analysis of England's "great transformation" two centuries ago.

Political institutions remain important even in the face of more pervasive market competition. The changes in local political economies are already driving changes in the performance criteria by which local cadres are evaluated by their superiors. While performance criteria do create pressure to compete economically, they also hold local cadres responsible for the provision of public goods and services and the maintenance of public order in their communities. In this way, political institutions are, paradoxically, both reinforcing and tempering market-oriented changes in the economy.

The Chinese state faces additional challenges in the course of reform,

---

[55] "State-owned Commerical Banks Pledge to Increase Lending This Year," *South China Morning Post* (Internet edition), January 23, 1999.

[56] "China Tells Officials to Stop 'Blindly Selling' State Enterprises," Agence France Presse, as reported in Clarnet News Service, August 5, 1998. Another important concern involves corruption in the valuation of state assets.

[57] On the development of these programs in rural areas, see Ogborn, Ramachandran, and West (1997).

as this study demonstrates. The ownership structure of firms in the local economy continues to shape extractive institutions at the grass roots. To the extent that collective enterprise managers are no longer appointed by local state officials and firm management is increasingly independent from the local state, the costs of revenue extraction – that is, the costs of gathering information, negotiating agreements, measuring resources, monitoring behavior, and enforcing performance – are likely to increase. These costs are rising at a time when the demand for state revenue is growing as well, as reflected in the need for expanded educational programs, welfare, social security, recapitalization of a weakened banking system, and so on. Such demands create renewed pressure for extractive agencies to innovate in developing new institutional arrangements. However, the new central and local tax offices are embedded in the state apparatus in distinct ways: they face different incentives and draw on distinct types of bureaucratic resources in their efforts to tax local firms. Thus, they are likely to develop at different rates and in different directions, and neither agency is guaranteed of success. Indeed, the bargaining power of firms in each local community is also in flux, and this, too, will continue to shape the development of extractive institutions. Thus, revenue mobilization remains an ongoing struggle in the transition from a planned to a market economy.

As institutional approaches to political economy have been confronted with the challenge of explaining dramatic change, they have adopted more characteristics of evolutionary theorizing (North 1990; Poznanski 1996).[58] Evolutionary theories

> place processes of change at the very center of inquiry. . . . An evolutionary view of economic processes holds that the relative success of different [communities] is largely a function of their effectiveness in reacting to exogenous events and in generating productive social change. For economic systems, innovation and adaptability are the crucial ingredients for success. (Murrell 1992:85)

In political economy, evolutionary processes are characterized by the existence of actors embedded in state and market institutions who continuously search for "strategies of survival." A search is necessary because decision makers, while intentionally rational, are not always confronted with a single or obvious "rational choice"; rather, they are often

---

[58] On the theoretical underpinnings of evolutionary approaches to political economy, see Nelson (1995) and Nelson and Winter (1982).

confronted with uncertainty and a lack of information about what the best choice might be. When the choice is unclear they may resort to habit, custom, imitation, or experimentation to inform their strategies. Which strategies ultimately "succeed" are determined by the selection mechanisms created by the institutional environment.

Some of the best work on institutional change in the Chinese case has implicitly relied on evolutionary notions without making the approach explicit (Naughton 1995; Oi 1998). In drawing out the underlying evolutionary framework, it is essential to identify the selection mechanisms that determine which strategies are successful.

In the Chinese political economy, selection is occurring on multiple levels simultaneously. One set of mechanisms determines which firms "survive" in the economic system, while another set determines which local leaders "survive" within the political system. As this study has demonstrated, even the selection mechanisms operating on firms are not purely economic.[59] At the outset of the reform process, political criteria clearly had primacy. However, the national reform agenda articulated in 1993 is changing the institutional environment for enterprises. Markets will increasingly determine their survival, but local political officials will still have some authority to influence the outcome. Indeed, we have seen how the selection criteria contained in the cadre evaluation system reward certain behavior on the part of local political leaders, creating incentives for them to intervene in the economy in particular ways. We have also seen how the specific content of the cadre evaluation system has changed over time. Yet local officials continue to be selected and promoted based on criteria that include not only economic performance but also provision of public goods and maintenance of social control, and they retain the ability to intervene in the economy to further these goals.

Both before and after 1994, the incentives and constraints contained in the fiscal system, the cadre evaluation system, and the national political and market environments influenced the forms of property rights that local officials were willing to support. As the national institutional environment changed, so did the disposition of local officials toward particular forms of property rights. Property rights, themselves engendered by the state, in turn, shaped the nature of extractive institutions. This evo-

---

[59] As Richard Nelson points out, evolutionary theory is particularly useful (as compared to neoliberal economic theory) "where market selection is strongly mixed with political . . . influences" (Nelson 1995:85).

lutionary framework helps to explain the dominance of collective ownership in Wuxi and Shanghai from the Maoist period through the first decade and a half of reform as well as the dramatic move toward privatization of collectives in these locales beginning in the mid-1990s. It also helps to explain the expanding presence of private capital in the Chinese economy more generally.

Within a given configuration of national institutions, the evolution of local institutions appears to be path dependent. However, when substantial change occurs in the larger institutional environment, dramatic change can occur at the local level as well. Viewed from an evolutionary perspective, even sweeping change can be explained by examining the complex interactions of individuals, institutions, and the larger environment in which those individuals and institutions exist. At the same time, the state institutions that govern the economy are sufficiently complex and the capacities of those who staff the state apparatus and participate in the economy are sufficiently bounded that instantaneous change is virtually impossible. Thus, even dramatic change occurs incrementally.[60] The presence of complementarities among institutions and policies means that singular changes interact to bring about more fundamental changes in the incentives and constraints in the institutional environment. Yet, even in the new environment, most existing entities will be replaced gradually, while a few may adapt successfully to the new conditions. This approach sheds new light on the process of change without predetermining its endpoint.

---

[60] This position is in contrast to that of Yang (1996) who argues that institutional change in China is abrupt and discontinuous. For a detailed analysis of his argument, see Whiting (1997).

Appendix

Informants

No.	Position	Unit
1	assistant manager	state–collective joint venture enterprise
2	assistant manager	state–collective joint venture enterprise
3	manager	state–collective joint venture enterprise
4	manager	state–collective joint venture enterprise
5	manager	individually contracted collective enterprise
5b	owner/manager	private enterprise
6	director	industrial corporation
7	manager	individually contracted collective enterprise
8	owner/manager	private enterprise
9	manager	individually contracted collective enterprise
10	manager	collective enterprise
11	researcher	Fudan University
12	owner/manager	private enterprise
13	researcher	Shanghai Academy of Social Sciences
14	staff representative	rural enterprise management bureau
15	manager	individually contracted collective enterprise
16	manager	collective enterprise
17	manager	collective enterprise
18	staff representative	tax and public finance bureau
19	manager	state–collective joint venture enterprise
20	assistant manager	foreign joint venture enterprise
21	manager	collective enterprise
22	director	industry office
23	party secretary	party committee
24	manager	shareholding cooperative enterprise
25	director	industrial corporation
26	manager	state–collective joint venture enterprise
27	village head	village committee
28	manager	individually contracted collective enterprise

Level	Location	Date
township	Songjiang County, Shanghai	9/91
township	Songjiang County, Shanghai	9/91
township	Songjiang County, Shanghai	9/91
township	Songjiang County, Shanghai	9/91
township	Yongjia County, Zhejiang	9/91
township	Yongjia County, Zhejiang	9/91
district	Wenzhou City, Zhejiang	9/91
district	Wenzhou City, Zhejiang	9/91
district	Huangyan City, Zhejiang	9/91
township	Yin County, Zhejiang	9/91
township	Yin County, Zhejiang	9/91
	Shanghai	10/91
village	Yueqing County, Zhejiang	10/91
	Shanghai	10/91
county	Yin County, Zhejiang	11/91
township	Yin County, Zhejiang	11/91
district	Ningbo City, Zhejiang	11/91
village	Ningbo City, Zhejiang	11/91
district	Ningbo City, Zhejiang	11/91
township	Yin County, Zhejiang	11/91
township	Yin County, Zhejiang	11/91
township	Yin County, Zhejiang	11/91
township	Yin County, Zhejiang	12/91
township	Chuansha County, Shanghai	12/91
township	Chuansha County, Shanghai	12/91
township	Chuansha County, Shanghai	12/91
township	Chuansha County, Shanghai	12/91
village	Chuansha County, Shanghai	12/91
village	Chuansha County, Shanghai	12/91

(*continued*)

No.	Position	Unit
29	village head, accountant	village committee
30	manager/team head	collective enterprise
31	manager	collective enterprise
32	manager, accountant	state–collective joint venture enterprise
33	manager	state–collective joint venture enterprise
34	director	public finance bureau
35	government executive	township government
36	director	rural enterprise management bureau
37	director	rural enterprise management department
38	staff representative	committee for science and technology
39	deputy director	party agriculture committee
40	researcher	Shanghai Agricultural College
41	researcher	Huadong Institute
42	staff representative	party committee rural research section
43	director	office of management and administration
44	staff representative	Agriculture Bank
45	director	rural enterprise management bureau
46	director	industrial corporation
47	manager	collective enterprise
48	accountant	collective enterprise
49	manager	collective enterprise
50	accountant	state–collective joint venture enterprise
51	assistant manager	collective enterprise
52	deputy director	party committee policy research office
53	deputy director	public finance bureau
54	director	industrial and commerical bureau
55	owner/manager	private enterprise
56	director	public finance bureau
57	staff representatives	Agriculture Bank and Rural Credit Cooperative
58	manager	foreign joint venture enterprise
59	manager	state–collective joint venture enterprise
60	government executive	township government
61	director	industrial corporation
62	village head	village committee
63	director	tax bureau
64	government executive	town government
65	director	office of management and administration
66	government executive	town government
67	manager	collective enterprise
68	director	industrial corporation
69	accountant	collective enterprise
70	director	public finance bureau
71	deputy village head	village committee

Level	Location	Date
village	Chuansha County, Shanghai	12/91
team	Chuansha County, Shanghai	12/91
township	Chuansha County, Shanghai	12/91
township	Chuansha County, Shanghai	12/91
township	Chuansha County, Shanghai	12/91
township	Chuansha County, Shanghai	12/91
township	Chuansha County, Shanghai	12/91
county	Chuansha County, Shanghai	12/91
province	Shanghai	2/92
province	Shanghai	2/92
province	Shanghai	2/92
	Shanghai	2/92
	Shanghai	2/92
province	Shanghai	2/92
county	Shanghai County, Shanghai	2/92
county	Shanghai County, Shanghai	2/92
county	Shanghai County, Shanghai	2/92
township	Shanghai County, Shanghai	2/92
township	Shanghai County, Shanghai	2/92
township	Shanghai County, Shanghai	2/92
township	Shanghai County, Shanghai	2/92
township	Shanghai County, Shanghai	2/92
township	Shanghai County, Shanghai	3/92
county	Shanghai County, Shanghai	3/92
county	Shanghai County, Shanghai	3/92
township	Shanghai County, Shanghai	3/92
township	Shanghai County, Shanghai	3/92
township	Shanghai County, Shanghai	3/92
township	Shanghai County, Shanghai	3/92
township	Shanghai County, Shanghai	3/92
township	Shanghai County, Shanghai	3/92
township	Shanghai County, Shanghai	3/92
township	Shanghai County, Shanghai	3/92
village	Shanghai County, Shanghai	3/92
township	Shanghai County, Shanghai	3/92
township	Shanghai County, Shanghai	3/92
township	Shanghai County, Shanghai	3/92
township	Shanghai County, Shanghai	3/92
township	Shanghai County, Shanghai	3/92
township	Shanghai County, Shanghai	3/92
township	Shanghai County, Shanghai	3/92
village	Shanghai County, Shanghai	3/92

(continued)

No.	Position	Unit
72	manager	state–collective joint venture enterprise
73	manager	collective enterprise
74	party secretary	party committee/village corporation
75	team head	team committee
76	government executive	county government
77	manager	collective enterprise
78	deputy director	industrial corporation
79	manager	state–collective joint venture enterprise
80	manager	state–collective joint venture enterprise
81	party secretary	collective enterprise
82	deputy director	industrial corporation
83	director	industrial corporation
84	staff representative	Bank of China
85	manager	collective enterprise
86	director	industrial and commercial bureau
87	village head, accountant	village committee
88	manager	state–collective joint venture enterprise
89	owner/manager	private enterprise
90	assistant manager	collective enterprise
91	manager	collective enterprise
92	staff representative	private enterprise accounting station
93	director	tax bureau
94	owner/manager	private enterprise
95	manager	individually contracted collective
96	deputy director	Agriculture Bank
97	government executive	town government
98	director	office of management and administration
99	director	Rural Credit Cooperative
100	staff representative	tax bureau
101	staff representative	Agriculture Bank
102	deputy director	rural enterprise management bureau
103	government executive	county government
104	manager	collective enterprise
105	deputy director	rural enterprise management bureau
106	staff representative	Agriculture Bank
107	staff representative	foreign economic committee
108	staff representative	statistical bureau
109	staff representative	planning committee
110	staff representative	tax bureau
111	deputy director	industrial and commercial bureau
112	staff representative	public finance bureau
113	manager	individually contracted collective enterprise
114	owner/manager	private enterprise
115	owner/manager	private enterprise

Level	Location	Date
village	Shanghai County, Shanghai	3/92
team	Shanghai County, Shanghai	3/92
village	Shanghai County, Shanghai	3/92
team	Shanghai County, Shanghai	3/92
county	Shanghai County, Shanghai	3/92
township	Songjiang County, Shanghai	4/92
township	Songjiang County, Shanghai	4/92
township	Songjiang County, Shanghai	4/92
township	Songjiang County, Shanghai	4/92
township	Songjiang County, Shanghai	4/92
township	Songjiang County, Shanghai	4/92
township	Songjiang County, Shanghai	4/92
county	Songjiang County, Shanghai	4/92
village	Songjiang County, Shanghai	4/92
township	Songjiang County, Shanghai	4/92
village	Songjiang County, Shanghai	4/92
village	Songjiang County, Shanghai	4/92
township	Songjiang County, Shanghai	4/92
team	Songjiang County, Shanghai	4/92
village	Songjiang County, Shanghai	4/92
township	Songjiang County, Shanghai	4/92
township	Songjiang County, Shanghai	4/92
township	Songjiang County, Shanghai	4/92
team	Songjiang County, Shanghai	4/92
township	Songjiang County, Shanghai	4/92
township	Songjiang County, Shanghai	4/92
township	Songjiang County, Shanghai	4/92
township	Songjiang County, Shanghai	4/92
township	Songjiang County, Shanghai	4/92
township	Songjiang County, Shanghai	4/92
county	Songjiang County, Shanghai	4/92
county	Songjiang County, Shanghai	4/92
township	Songjiang County, Shanghai	4/92
county	Songjiang County, Shanghai	4/92
county	Songjiang County, Shanghai	4/92
county	Songjiang County, Shanghai	4/92
county	Songjiang County, Shanghai	4/92
county	Songjiang County, Shanghai	4/92
county	Songjiang County, Shanghai	4/92
county	Songjiang County, Shanghai	4/92
county	Songjiang County, Shanghai	4/92
team	Shanghai County, Shanghai	5/92
team	Shanghai County, Shanghai	5/92
team	Shanghai County, Shanghai	5/92

(*continued*)

No.	Position	Unit
116	party secretary	village committee
117	manager	individually contracted collective enterprise
118	staff representative	statistical bureau
119	staff representative	township government
120	manager	state–collective joint venture enterprise
121	director	industrial corporation
122	village head	village committee
123	manager, party secretary	state–collective joint venture enterprise
124	manager	state–collective joint venture enterprise
125	manager, party secretary	state–collective joint venture enterprise
126	manager/village head	collective enterprise
127	manager, accountant	collective enterprise
128	manager	foreign joint venture enterprise
129	manager	state–collective joint venture enterprise
130	manager	individually contracted collective enterprise
131	village head	village committee
132	owner/manager	private enterprise
133	staff representative	tax bureau
134	party secretary	party committee
135	director	public finance bureau
136	director	Agriculture Bank
137	director	Rural Credit Cooperative
138	director	office of management and administration
139	director	tax bureau
140	researcher	China Comprehensive Development Institute
141	staff representative	statistical bureau
142	deputy director	rural enterprise management bureau
143	government executive	township government
144	government executive	township government
145	director	industry bureau
146	assistant manager	collective enterprise
147	manager	collective enterprise
148	owner/manager	shareholding cooperative enterprise
149	owner/manager	private enterprise
150	assistant manager	private enterprise
151	owner/manager	shareholding cooperative enterprise
152	owner/manager	private enterprise
153	manager	collective enterprise
154	manager	shareholding cooperative enterprise
155	owner/manager	shareholding cooperative enterprise
156	owner/manager	private enterprise
157	director	industrial and commercial bureau
158	staff representative	Industrial and Commercial Bank

Level	Location	Date
village	Shanghai County, Shanghai	5/92
team	Shanghai County, Shanghai	5/92
county	Shanghai County, Shanghai	5/92
township	Jiading County, Shanghai	5/92
township	Jiading County, Shanghai	5/92
township	Jiading County, Shanghai	5/92
village	Jiading County, Shanghai	5/92
township	Jiading County, Shanghai	5/92
village	Jiading County, Shanghai	5/92
township	Jiading County, Shanghai	5/92
village	Jiading County, Shanghai	5/92
village	Jiading County, Shanghai	5/92
township	Jiading County, Shanghai	5/92
township	Jiading County, Shanghai	5/92
team	Jiading County, Shanghai	6/92
village	Jiading County, Shanghai	6/92
village	Jiading County, Shanghai	6/92
township	Jiading County, Shanghai	6/92
township	Jiading County, Shanghai	6/92
township	Jiading County, Shanghai	6/92
township	Jiading County, Shanghai	6/92
township	Jiading County, Shanghai	6/92
township	Jiading County, Shanghai	6/92
township	Jiading County, Shanghai	6/92
	Shanghai	6/92
county	Jiading County, Shanghai	6/92
county	Jiading County, Shanghai	6/92
county	Jiading County, Shanghai	6/92
township	Yueqing County, Zhejiang	6/92
township	Yueqing County, Zhejiang	6/92
township	Yueqing County, Zhejiang	6/92
village	Yueqing County, Zhejiang	6/92
village	Yueqing County, Zhejiang	6/92
township	Yueqing County, Zhejiang	6/92
township	Yueqing County, Zhejiang	6/92
township	Yueqing County, Zhejiang	6/92
township	Yueqing County, Zhejiang	6/92
township	Yueqing County, Zhejiang	6/92
township	Yueqing County, Zhejiang	6/92
township	Yueqing County, Zhejiang	6/92
township	Yueqing County, Zhejiang	6/92
township	Yueqing County, Zhejiang	6/92
township	Yueqing County, Zhejiang	6/92

(continued)

No.	Position	Unit
159	staff representative	Agriculture Bank
160	director	tax and public finance bureau
161	assistant manager	private enterprise
162	staff representative	tax and public finance bureau
163	staff representative	Agriculture Bank
164	deputy director	rural enterprise management bureau
165	staff representative	party committee research section
166	staff representative	industrial and commercial bureau
167	deputy director	tax and public finance bureau
168	staff representative	industrial and commercial bureau
169	staff representative	party committee agriculture committee
170	staff representative	bureau
171	staff representative	system reform commission
172	staff representative	statistical bureau
173	manager	shareholding cooperative enterprise
174	researcher	Zhejiang Academy of Social Sciences
175	staff representative	party committee
176	director	township foreign trade company
177	staff representative	Agriculture Bank
178	party secretary	party committee
179	party secretary	village committee
180	manager	collective enterprise
181	staff representative	public finance bureau
182	staff representative	tax bureau
183	staff representative	industrial and commercial bureau
184	manager	foreign joint venture enterprise
184a	staff representative	party committee agriculture committee
185	researcher	Chinese Academy of Social Sciences
186	researcher	World Bank
187	deputy director	Ministry of Agriculture, Rural Enterprise Section
188	deputy director	Ministry of Agriculture, Policy Reform Section
189	researcher	State Council Development Research Center
190	deputy director	Ministry of Agriculture, Rural Economy Center
191	deputy director	economic committee
192	deputy director	industrial corporation
193	deputy director	industrial and commercial bureau
194	staff representative	tax bureau
195	manager	collective enterprise
196	deputy director	office of management and administration
197	manager	collective enterprise

Level	Location	Date
township	Yueqing County, Zhejiang	6/92
township	Yueqing County, Zhejiang	6/92
village	Yueqing County, Zhejiang	6/92
county	Yueqing County, Zhejiang	6/92
county	Yueqing County, Zhejiang	6/92
county	Yueqing County, Zhejiang	6/92
county	Yueqing County, Zhejiang	6/92
county	Yueqing County, Zhejiang	6/92
county	Yueqing County, Zhejiang	6/92
prefecture	Wenzhou City, Zhejiang	6/92
prefecture	Wenzhou City, Zhejiang	6/92
district	Wenzhou City, Zhejiang	6/92
prefecture	Wenzhou City, Zhejiang	6/92
prefecture	Wenzhou City, Zhejiang	6/92
district	Wenzhou City, Zhejiang	6/92
	Zhejiang	6/92
township	Changshu City, Jiangsu	7/92
township	Changshu City, Jiangsu	7/92
township	Changshu City, Jiangsu	7/92
township	Changshu City, Jiangsu	7/92
village	Changshu City, Jiangsu	7/92
village	Changshu City, Jiangsu	7/92
township	Changshu City, Jiangsu	7/92
township	Changshu City, Jiangsu	7/92
township	Changshu City, Jiangsu	7/92
township	Changshu City, Jiangsu	7/92
prefecture	Suzhou City, Jiangsu	7/92
	Beijing	7/92
	Beijing	7/92
	Beijing	7/92
	Beijing	7/92
	Beijing	8/92
	Beijing	8/92
county	Wuxi County, Jiangsu	8/92
township	Wuxi County, Jiangsu	8/92
township	Wuxi County, Jiangsu	8/92
township	Wuxi County, Jiangsu	8/92
township	Wuxi County, Jiangsu	8/92
township	Wuxi County, Jiangsu	8/92
village	Wuxi County, Jiangsu	8/92

(continued)

No.	Position	Unit
198	staff representative	Agriculture Bank
199	manager	collective enterprise
200	manager	collective enterprise
201	assistant manager	foreign joint venture enterprise
202	village head	village committee
203	director	party committee rural policy research office
204	deputy director	party committee policy research office
205	deputy director	rural enterprise management bureau
206	deputy director	economic conglomerate
207	manager	shareholding cooperative enterprise
208	director	office of management and administration
209	accountant	shareholding cooperative enterprise
210	manager	shareholding cooperative enterprise
211	director	central tax bureau
212	director	public finance bureau
213	government executive	county government
214	deputy director	office of management and administration
215	deputy director	industrial corporation
216	director	industrial corporation
217	manager	shareholding cooperative enterprise
218	director	office of management and administration
219	party secretary	tax bureau
220	director	central tax bureau
221	director	local tax bureau
222	director	office of management and administration
223	director	industrial and commercial bureau
224	director	Agriculture Bank
225	manager	shareholding cooperative enterprise
226	manager	collective enterprise
227	assistant manager	shareholding cooperative enterprise
228	assistant manager	shareholding cooperative enterprise
229	staff representative	public finance bureau
230	staff representative	public finance bureau
231	staff representative	central tax bureau
232	staff representative	local tax bureau
233	staff representative	party committee agriculture committee
234	party secretary	party committee
235	owner/manager	shareholding cooperative enterprise
236	owner/manager	shareholding company
237	owner/manager	shareholding cooperative enterprise
238	director	tax bureau
239	owner/manager	private enterprise
240	owner/manager	shareholding cooperative enterprise

Appendix

Level	Location	Date
township	Wuxi County, Jiangsu	8/92
township	Wuxi County, Jiangsu	8/92
village	Wuxi County, Jiangsu	8/92
township	Wuxi County, Jiangsu	8/92
village	Wuxi County, Jiangsu	8/92
province	Shanghai	8/96
county	Songjiang County, Shanghai	8/96
county	Songjiang County, Shanghai	8/96
township	Songjiang County, Shanghai	8/96
township	Songjiang County, Shanghai	8/96
township	Songjiang County, Shanghai	8/96
township	Songjiang County, Shanghai	8/96
township	Songjiang County, Shanghai	8/96
county	Songjiang County, Shanghai	8/96
county	Songjiang County, Shanghai	8/96
county	Songjiang County, Shanghai	8/96
county	Songjiang County, Shanghai	8/96
township	Songjiang County, Shanghai	8/96
township	Songjiang County, Shanghai	8/96
township	Songjiang County, Shanghai	8/96
township	Songjiang County, Shanghai	8/96
township	Songjiang County, Shanghai	8/96
township	Xishan City, Jiangsu	8/96
township	Xishan City, Jiangsu	8/96
township	Xishan City, Jiangsu	8/96
township	Xishan City, Jiangsu	8/96
township	Xishan City, Jiangsu	8/96
township	Xishan City, Jiangsu	8/96
township	Xishan City, Jiangsu	8/96
township	Xishan City, Jiangsu	8/96
township	Xishan City, Jiangsu	8/96
township	Xishan City, Jiangsu	8/96
township	Xishan City, Jiangsu	8/96
county	Xishan City, Jiangsu	8/96
county	Xishan City, Jiangsu	8/96
county	Xishan City, Jiangsu	8/96
township	Yueqing City, Zhejiang	8/96
township	Yueqing City, Zhejiang	8/96
township	Yueqing City, Zhejiang	8/96
township	Yueqing City, Zhejiang	8/96
township	Yueqing City, Zhejiang	8/96
township	Yueqing City, Zhejiang	8/96
township	Yueqing City, Zhejiang	8/96

(*continued*)

No.	Position	Unit
241	director	public finance bureau
242	owner/manager	shareholding cooperative enterprise
243	government executive	town government
244	director	industrial and commerical bureau
245	manager	shareholding cooperative enterprise
246	staff representative	central tax bureau
247	staff representative	economic system reform commission
248	government executive	city government
249	staff representative	public finance bureau
250	staff representative	city government
251	staff representative	city government
252	staff representative	statistical bureau

Level	Location	Date
township	Yueqing City, Zhejiang	8/96
township	Yueqing City, Zhejiang	8/96
township	Yueqing City, Zhejiang	8/96
township	Yueqing City, Zhejiang	8/96
township	Yueqing City, Zhejiang	8/96
county	Yueqing City, Zhejiang	8/96
county	Yueqing City, Zhejiang	8/96
county	Yueqing City, Zhejiang	8/96
township	Songjiang County, Shanghai	8/96
county	Xishan City, Jiangsu	5/99
county	Yueqing City, Zhejiang	5/99
county	Songjiang County, Shanghai	5/99

Bibliography

Alchian, Armen A. 1977. *Economic Forces at Work*. Indianapolis: Liberty Press.
Alchian, Armen A., and Harold Demsetz. 1973. "The Property Right Paradigm." *Journal of Economic History* 33(1).
Alston, Lee J., Thrainn Eggertsson, and Douglass C. North. 1996. *Empirical Studies of Institutional Change*. New York: Cambridge University Press.
Amsden, Alice. 1989. *Asia's Next Giant: South Korea and Late Industrialization*. New York: Oxford University Press.
Ardant, Gabriel. 1975. "Financial Policy and Economic Infrastructure of Modern States and Nations." In *The Formation of National States in Western Europe*, ed. Charles Tilly. Princeton: Princeton University Press.
Arthur, W. Brian. 1989. "Competing Technologies, Increasing Returns, and Lock-in by Historical Events." *Economic Journal* 99 (March): 116–31.
Bachman, David. 1987. "Implementing Chinese Tax Policy." In *Policy Implementation in Post-Mao China*, ed. David M. Lampton, 119–53. Berkeley: University of California Press.
——— 1991. *Bureaucracy, Economy, and Leadership in China: The Institutional Origins of the Great Leap Forward*. New York: Cambridge University Press.
Bahl, Roy W. 1971. "A Regression Approach to Tax Effort and Tax Ratio Analysis." *International Monetary Fund Staff Papers* 18(3): 570–608 (November).
Balassa, Bela. 1988. "The Lessons of East Asian Development: An Overview." *Economic Development and Cultural Change* 36(3): S273–S290 (April).
Bates, Robert. 1989. *Beyond the Miracle of the Market: The Political Economy of Agrarian Development in Kenya*. New York: Cambridge University Press.
——— 1981. *Markets and States in Tropical Africa: The Political Basis of Agricultural Policies*. Berkeley: University of California Press.
Bell, Lynda S. 1985. "Merchants, Peasants, and the State: The Organization and Politics of Chinese Silk Production, Wuxi County, 1870–1937." Ph.D. diss., University of California, Los Angeles.
Bernhardt, Kathryn. 1992. *Rents, Taxes, and Peasant Resistance: The Lower Yangzi Region 1840–1950*. Stanford: Stanford University Press.

Bibliography

Bi Honglin and Yan Xiu. 1990. "Duotou kaihu duotou daikuan de biduan ji duice (The harmful practice of multiple accounts and multiple loans and countermeasures)." *Zhongguo nongcun jinrong* (China's rural finance) 8.

Biewuxuanze: Xiangzhen qiye yu guomin jingji de xietiao fazhan (No other choice: Coordinating the development of rural enterprise and the national economy). 1990. Beijing: Gaige chubanshe.

Bird, Richard M. 1978. "Assessing Tax Performance in Developing Countries: A Critical Review of the Literature." In *Taxation and Economic Development*, ed. J. F. J. Toye, 33–61. London: F. Cass.

Blecher, Marc, and Vivienne Shue. 1996. *Tethered Deer: Government and Economy in a Chinese County*. Stanford: Stanford University Press.

Bo, Zhiyue. 1998. "Managing Political Elites in Post-Deng China." Paper presented at the Workshop on Cadre Monitoring and Reward, June 6–7, San Diego.

Boone, Catherine. 1992. *Merchant Capital and the Roots of State Power in Senegal 1930–1985*. New York: Cambridge University Press.

Bowles, Paul, and Gordon White. 1989. "Contradictions in China's Financial Reforms: The Relationship between Banks and Enterprises." *Cambridge Journal of Economics* 13 (December): 481–95.

——— 1993. *The Political Economy of China's Financial Reforms: Finance in Late Development*. Boulder: Westview Press.

Brandt, Loren, and Xiaodong Zhu. 1995. "Soft Budget Constraints and Inflation Cycles: A Positive Model of the Post-Reform Chinese Economy." Unpublished manuscript, University of Toronto.

Brean, Donald J. S., ed. 1998. *Taxation in Modern China*. New York: Routledge.

Bruun, Ole. 1993. *Business and Bureaucracy in a Chinese City: An Ethnography of Private Business Households in Contemporary China*. Berkeley: University of California Institute of East Asian Studies.

Buchanan, James M. 1980. "Rent Seeking and Profit Seeking." In *Toward a Theory of the Rent-Seeking Society*, ed. Robert D. Buchanan, Robert D. Tollison, and Gordon Tullock, 3–15. College Station: Texas A&M University Press.

Buchanan, James M., Robert D. Tollison, and Gordon Tullock, eds. 1980. *Toward a Theory of the Rent-Seeking Society*. College Station: Texas A&M University Press.

Byrd, William A., and Alan Gelb. 1990. "Why Industrialize? The Incentives for Rural Community Governments." In *China's Rural Industry: Structure, Development, and Reform*, ed. William A. Byrd and Lin Qingsong, 358–88. New York: Oxford University Press.

Byrd, William A., and Lin Qingsong. 1990a. "China's Rural Industry: An Introduction." In *China's Rural Industry: Structure, Development, and Reform*, ed. William A. Byrd and Lin Qingsong, 3–18. New York: Oxford University Press.

Byrd, William A., and Lin Qingsong, eds. 1990b. *China's Rural Industry: Structure, Development, and Reform*. New York: Oxford University Press.

Byrd, William A., and N. Zhu. 1990. "Market Interactions and Industrial Structure." In *China's Rural Industry: Structure, Development, and Reform*, ed. William A. Byrd and Lin Qingsong, 85–111. New York: Oxford University Press.

Cai Xiongwei. 1990. "Xiangzhen qiye de 'zhaiwulian' weihe nanyi jiekai (Why the township and village enterprise 'debt chain' is hard to break)." *Shanghai jinrong* (Shanghai finance) 12: 35–7.

Caijing yanjiu (Fiscal and economic research). Periodical.

Caishui gaige shinian (Ten years of fiscal reform). 1989. Beijing: Zhongguo caizheng jingji chubanshe.

Caizheng (Public finance). Periodical.

Caizheng shuishou falü shouce, diyibian (Handbook of fiscal and tax laws, vol. 1). 1998. Beijing: Renmin fayuan chubanshe.

Cangnan juan: Zhongguo guoqing congshu – Bai xian shi jingji shehui diaocha (Cangnan volume: China national conditions series – An economic and social survey of one hundred counties and cities). 1996. Beijing: Zhongguo dabaike quanshu chubanshe.

Cassel, Dieter, and Gunter Heiduk, eds. 1990. *China's Contemporary Economic Reforms as a Development Strategy*. Baden-Baden: Nomos Verlagsgesellschaft.

Chan, Anita, Richard Madsen, and Jonathan Unger. 1992. *Chen Village under Mao and Deng*. Berkeley: University of California Press.

Chan, Kam Wing. 1994. *Cities with Invisible Walls: Reinterpreting Urbanization in Post-1949 China*. New York: Oxford University Press.

Chang Xiuze and Gao Minghua. 1998. "Zhongguo guomin jingji shichanghua de tuijin chengdu ji fazhan silu (The extent of marketization of the Chinese national economy and thoughts on development)." *Jingji yanjiu* (Economic research) 11: 48–55.

Chaudhry, Kiren Aziz. 1993. "The Myths of the Market and the Common History of Late Developers." *Politics and Society* 21(3): 245–74 (September).

1989. "The Price of Wealth: Business and State in Labor Remittance and Oil Economies." *International Organization* 43(1): 101–45 (Winter).

1997. *The Price of Wealth: Economies and Institutions in the Middle East*. Ithaca: Cornell University Press.

Che, Jiahua, and Yingyi Qian. 1998. "Institutional Environment, Community Government, and Corporate Governance: Understanding China's Township–Village Enterprises." *Journal of Law Economics and Organization* 14(1): 1–23.

Chelliah, Raja J. 1971. "Trends in Taxation in Developing Countries." *International Monetary Fund Staff Papers* 18(2): 327–54 (July).

Chelliah, Raja J., Hessel J. Bass, and Margaret R. Kelly. 1975. "Tax Ratios and Tax Effort in Developing Countries, 1969–71." *International Monetary Fund Staff Papers* 22(1): 187–205 (March).

Chen Jianguang. 1994. "Xiangzhen qiye gufen hezuozhi zhuyao moshi (Major models of shareholding cooperative forms in the rural enterprise sector)." In *Zhongguo xiangzhen qiye nianjian*, 406–8.

1995. "Xiangzhen qiye gufen hezuozhi wenti tansuo (An exploration of questions on the cooperative shareholding system in rural enterprises)." In *Zhongguo xiangzhen qiye nianjian*, 342–44.

317

Chen Jiyuan and Xia Defang, eds. 1988. *Xiangzhen qiye moshi yanjiu* (Research on rural enterprise models). Beijing: Zhongguo shehui kexue chubanshe.

Chen Zuolü. 1991. "Jianqing qiye fudan zengqiang qiye houjin (Lighten enterprise burdens and increase enterprise momentum)." *Jiangsu xiangzhen qiye* (Jiangsu rural enterprise) 7: 28–9.

Cheng, Tun-jen. 1990. "Political Regimes and Development Strategies: South Korea and Taiwan." In *Manufacturing Miracles: Paths of Industrialization in Latin America and East Asia*, ed. Gary Gereffi and Donald L. Wyman. Princeton: Princeton University Press.

Cheng Xiangqing, Li Po, and Xu Huafei. 1989. "Siying qiye fazhan xianzhuang yu mianlin de wenti (The current situation for private enterprise development and problems ahead)." *Zhongguo nongcun jingji* (China's rural economy) 2: 24–31.

China Daily. Periodical.

"China's Legal Reforms." 1995. *China Quarterly* 141 (March).

China Quarterly. Periodical.

Chinese Law and Government. Periodical.

Chuansha diaoyan (Chuansha investigation and research). Periodical.

Chung, Jae Ho. 1995a. "Beijing Confronting the Provinces: The 1994 Tax-Sharing Reform and Its Implications for Central–Provincial Relations in China." *China Information* 9(2–3): 1–23 (Winter).

1995b. "Studies in Central–Provincial Relations in the People's Republic of China: A Mid-Term Appraisal." *China Quarterly* 142 (June): 487–508.

Clarke, Donald C. 1992. "Regulation and Its Discontents: Understanding Economic Law in China." *Stanford Journal of International Law* 28(2).

1995. "The Execution of Civil Judgments in China." *China Quarterly* 141 (March): 65–81.

1996. "The Creation of a Legal Structure for Market Institutions in China." In *Reforming Asian Socialism: The Growth of Market Institutions*, ed. John McMillan and Barry Naughton, 39–59. Ann Arbor: University of Michigan Press.

Coase, J. H. 1937. "The Nature of the Firm." *Economica* 4 (November): 386–405.

Coleman, James S. 1990. *Foundations of Social Theory.* Cambridge: Harvard Belknap Press.

Cook, Karen Schweers, and Margaret Levi, eds. 1990. *The Limits of Rationality.* Chicago: University of Chicago Press.

Cortell, Andrew P., and Susan Peterson. 1999. "Altered States: Explaining Domestic Institutional Change." *British Journal of Political Science* 29(1).

Cumings, Bruce. 1981. "The Origins and Development of the Northeast Asian Political Economy: Industrial Sectors, Product Cycles, and Political Consequences." *International Organization* 38(1): 1–40 (Winter).

Dangdai Zhongguo de jingji tizhi gaige (Economic system reform in contemporary China). 1984. Beijing: Zhongguo shehui kexue chubanshe.

Dangdai Zhongguo de xiangzhen qiye (Township and village enterprises in contemporary China). 1991. Beijing: Dangdai zhongguo Chubanshe.

Denzau, Arthur T., and Douglass C. North. 1994. "Shared Mental Models: Ideologies and Institutions." *Kyklos* 47(1): 3–31.

Deyo, Frederic C., ed. 1987. *The Political Economy of the New Asian Industrialism*. Ithaca: Cornell University Press.

Diao, Richard K. 1969. *Zhonggong shuishou zhidu* (Taxation system of communist China). Hong Kong: Union Research Institute.

Ding Xianjue et al., eds. 1996. *Shoufei jijin guanli shouce* (Handbook on management of fees and funds). Hangzhou: Zhejiang renmin chubanshe.

Dong Chaocai. 1989. "Qiye gufenhua – Wenzhou jingji fazhan de xin taishi (Enterprise shareholding conversions – A new phase in Wenzhou's economic development)." In *Wenzhou zhi lu congshu: Kaituozhe de guiji – Wenzhou shi difang fagui jianbian* (The Wenzhou path series: The reformers' course – A concise collection of local laws and regulations from Wenzhou Municipality). Shanghai: Tongji daxue chubanshe.

Du Haiyan. 1992. *Zhongguo nongcun gongyehua yanjiu* (Research on rural industrialization in China). Hubei: Zhongguo wujia chubanshe.

Du Yan. 1987. "Xiangzhen gongye qiye jingying de shichang huanjing (The market environment in which rural industrial enterprises operate)." *Fazhan yanjiu* (Development research) 49 (February): 272–3.

Du Yan et al. 1989. "Zhongguo nongcun gaige shiyan qu 1989 nian bannian gongzuo baogao (1989 mid-year work report on China's rural reform experimental zones)." *Fazhan yanjiu* (Development research) 125 (October): 1015–44.

Ecklund, George N. 1966. *Financing the Chinese Government Budget: Mainland China, 1950–1959*. Chicago: Aldine.

Eggertsson, Thrainn. 1990. *Economic Behavior and Institutions*. New York: Cambridge University Press.

Ellickson, Robert C. 1991. *Order without Law: How Neighbors Settle Disputes*. Cambridge: Harvard University Press.

Evans, Peter. 1979. *Dependent Development: The Alliance of Multinational, State, and Local Capital in Brazil*. Princeton: Princeton University Press.

1995. *Embedded Autonomy: States and Industrial Transformation*. Princeton: Princeton University Press.

Evans, Peter B., Dietrich Rueschemeyer, and Theda Skocpol, eds. 1985. *Bringing the State Back In*. New York: Cambridge University Press.

Fan, Gang. 1998. "Market-Oriented Economic Reform and the Growth of Off-Budget Local Public Finance." In *Taxation in Modern China*, ed. Donald J. S. Brean, 209–27. New York: Routledge.

Fang Weizhong et al., eds. 1984. *Zhonghua renmin gongheguo jiugji dashiji, 1949–1980* (People's Republic of China chronology of major economic events, 1949–1980). Beijing: Zhongguo shehui kexue chubanshe.

Fazhi ribao (Legal daily). Periodical.

Fei Hsiao T'ung et al. 1986. *Small Towns in China – Functions, Problems and Prospects*. Beijing: New World Press.

Fei Xiaotong and Luo Hanxian, eds. 1988. *Xiangzhen jingji bijiao moshi* (Comparative rural economic models). Chongqing: Chongqing chubanshe.

Bibliography

Feng Jiqun. 1988a. "Gao yige you tese de Shanghai xiangzhen qiye tiaoli (Produce a Shanghai statute on township and village enterprises with special characteristics)." *Shanghai gongye jingji bao* (Shanghai industrial economy), January 21.

1988b. "Jinshui loutai nan de yue (The waterfront pavilion rarely gets the moonlight)." *Shanghai gongye jingji bao* (Shanghai industrial economy), March 10.

1988c. "Xiangzhen qiye houjin buzu ling ren danyou (The insufficient momentum of township and village enterprises worries many)." *Shanghai gongye jingji bao* (Shanghai industrial economy), February 15.

Finifter, Ada, ed. 1982. *Political Science: The State of the Discipline.* Washington, D.C.: American Political Science Association.

Furubotn, Eirik G., and Svetozar Pejovich. 1974. "Introduction: The New Property Rights Literature." In *The Economics of Property Rights*, ed. Eirik G. Furubotn and Svetozar Pejovich. Cambridge: Ballinger.

Gan Darong. 1994. "Fenshuizhi gaige dui xianji caizheng de yingxiang qianxi (A elementary analysis of the influence of the tax assignment system reform on county finances)." *Caijing yanjiu* (Public finance research) 4: 38–9.

Gao Kuanzhong. 1991. "Wending he fazhan nongcun geti, siying jingji de ruogan wenti tantao (An inquiry into several questions on stabilizing and developing the rural individual and private economies)." In *Zhongguo nongcun: Zhengce yanjiu beiwanglu* (China's countryside: Policy research memorandum), vol. 2, 310–20. Beijing: Nongye chubanshe.

Gao Zhongxun. 1991. "Zai 'dali tuijin gufen hezuo jingji fazhan' huiyishang de zongjie jianghua (Concluding speech at the conference on 'vigorously advancing the development of the cooperative shareholding economy')." In *Gufen hezuo jingji wenjian huibian* (A collection of documents on the cooperative shareholding economy), ed. Yueqingxian tizhi gaige weiyuanhui, 12–16. N.p.

Geddes, Barbara. 1994. *Politician's Dilemma: Building State Capacity in Latin America.* Berkeley: University of California Press.

George, Alexander L. 1979. "Case Studies and Theory Development: The Method of Structured, Focused Comparison." In *Diplomacy: New Approaches in History, Theory, and Policy*, ed. Paul Gordon Lauren, 43–68. New York: Free Press.

Gereffi, Gary, and Donald L. Wyman, eds. 1990. *Manufacturing Miracles: Paths of Industrialization in Latin America and East Asia.* Princeton: Princeton University Press.

Gerschenkron, Alexander. 1962. *Economic Backwardness in Historical Perspective: A Book of Essays.* Cambridge: Harvard University Press.

Gerth, H. H., and C. Wright Mills, eds. and trans. 1946. *From Max Weber: Essays in Sociology.* New York: Oxford University Press.

Granick, David. 1990. *Chinese State Enterprises: A Regional Property Rights Analysis.* Chicago: University of Chicago Press.

Granovetter, Mark. 1985. "Economic Action and Social Structures: The Problem of Embeddedness." *American Journal of Sociology* 91: 481–510.

Groves, Theodore, Yongmiao Hong, John McMillan, and Barry Naughton. 1994.

"Autonomy and Incentives in Chinese State Enterprises." *Quarterly Journal of Economics* 109(1) (February).

Guan Hong. 1996. "1995 nian quanguo xiangzhen caizheng qingkuang (The 1995 fiscal situation of townships nationwide)." *Difang caizheng* (Local public finance).

Guan Shan and Jiang Hong, eds. 1990. *Kuaikuai jingjixue: Zhongguo difang zhengfu jingji xingwei fenxi* (Territorial economics: An analysis of the economic behavior of local governments in China). Beijing: Haiyang chubanshe.

"Guangdong State and Local Taxation Bureaus Open for Business Today." 1994. *Nanfang ribao* (Southern daily), July 28. Translated in *Foreign Broadcast Information Service – China*, July 29, 1994, pp. 45–6.

Gufen hezuo jingji wenjian huibian. 1991. (A collection of documents on the cooperative shareholding economy). N.p.

Guo Shutian and Liu Chunbin. 1991. *Shiheng de Zhongguo: Chengshihua de guoqu, xianzai yu weilai* (China out-of-balance: The past, present, and future of urbanization). Shijiazhuang: Hebei renmin chubanshe.

Guowuyuan fazhan yanjiu zhongxin. 1989. "Woguo geti siying jingji diaocha baogao (Report on the survey of China's individual and private economy)." *Jingji gongzuozhe xuexi ziliao* (Study materials for economic administrators) 58. Reprinted in *Fuyin baokan ziliao – Jingji tizhi gaige* (Reprints of periodical materials – Economic system reform) 3 (1990): 60–79.

Guowuyuan gongbao (State council bulletin). Periodical.

H. zhenzhi (H. town gazetteer). 1993. Beijing: Zhongguo guoji guangbo chubanshe.

Haggard, Stephan. 1990. *Pathways from the Periphery: The Politics of Growth in Newly Industrializing Countries*. Ithaca: Cornell University Press.

Hamilton, Gary. C., and Nicole Woolsey Biggart. 1988. "Market, Culture, and Authority: A Comparative Analysis of Management and Organization in the Far East." *American Journal of Sociology* 94(Suppl.): 552–94.

Han Guojian. 1993. "China to Unify Tax System." *Beijing Review*, June 21–27, pp. 19–22.

Han Qing and Yue Furong, eds. 1987. *Laodong renshi zhidu gaige wenxuan* (Selected essays on reform of the labor and personnel system). Changsha: Hunan renmin chubanshe.

He Baoshan et al., eds. 1991. *Jiangsu nongcun feinonghua fazhan yanjiu* (Research on the nonagricultural development of rural Jiangsu). Shanghai: Shanghai renmin chubanshe.

He Jizhi, Wei Shixiang, and Lin Luolun, eds. 1991. *Xiangzhen gongzuo renyuan gangwei guifan* (Norms for the positions of township staff members). Beijing: Zhongguo renshi chubanshe.

He Rongfei et al. 1987. *Wenzhou jingji geju – Women de zuofa he tansuoxing yijian* (The structure of the Wenzhou economy: Our methods and ideas). Wenzhou: Zhejiang renmin chubanshe.

1989. *Wenzhou minjian shichang kaocha* (An investigation into Wenzhou's private marketplace). Beijing: Renmin chubanshe.

Bibliography

Held, David. 1989. *Political Theory and the Modern State: Essays on State, Power, and Democracy*. Cambridge: Polity Press.

Hirschman, Albert O. 1979. *Exit, Voice, and Loyalty*. Cambridge: Harvard University Press.

Hollingsworth, J. Rogers, and Robert Boyer, eds. 1997. *Contemporary Capitalism: The Embeddedness of Institutions*. New York: Cambridge University Press.

Hongqi (Red flag). Periodical.

Huang, Philip C. C. 1990. *The Peasant Family and Rural Development in the Yangzi Delta, 1350–1988*. Stanford: Stanford University Press.

———. 1991. "A Response to Ramon Myers." *Journal of Asian Studies* 50(3): 629–33.

Huang Shiqiu and Mao Xunliang. 1994. "Guanyu xianyu jingji yu xin caishui tizhi jiegui de sikao (Thoughts on integrating the new tax and fiscal system and the county economy." *Jingji tizhi gaige* (Economic system reform) 1: 57–60.

Huang, Yasheng. 1990. "Web of Interests and Patterns of Behavior of Chinese Local Economic Bureaucracies and Enterprises during Reforms." *China Quarterly* 123 (September): 431–58.

———. 1994. "Information, Bureaucracy, and Economic Reforms in China and the Soviet Union." *World Politics* 47(1): 102–34 (October).

———. 1996. *Inflation and Investment Controls in China: The Political Economy of Central–Local Relations during the Reform Era*. New York: Cambridge University Press.

Huntington, Samuel P. 1971. "The Change to Change: Modernization, Development, and Politics." *Comparative Politics* 3(3): 283–322 (April).

Hussain, Athar, and Nicholas Stern. 1991. "The Role of the State, Ownership, and Taxation in Transitional Economies." Working paper, London School of Economics, Institute for Policy Reform.

Jacka, Tamara. 1997. *Women's Work in Rural China*. New York: Cambridge University Press.

Jia Hao, and Lin Zhimin, eds. 1994. *Changing Central–Local Relations in China: Reform and State Capacity*. Boulder: Westview Press.

Jiading nianjian 1989–1990 (Jiading yearbook 1989–1990). 1991. Shanghai: Tongji daxue chubanshe.

Jiading xian tongji ziliao huibian (Jiading County compendium of statistical materials). Annual. Jiading: Jiading xian tongjiju.

Jiang Daming. 1991. "Guojia yu xiangzhen qiye zai caizheng fenpei guanxi shang de xin wenti (New issues surrounding the relationship between the state and township- and village-run enterprises in the distribution of fiscal resources)." *Caizheng* (Public finance) 2: 63–4.

Jiang Jinghe. 1994. "Heilongjiang Successfully Completed Building Two Tax Organs." *Heilongjiang ribao* (Heilongjiang daily), September 19. Translated in *Foreign Broadcast Information Service – China*, October 4, 1994, p. 87.

Jiang Runzhou et al., eds. 1990. *Zhongguo shuiwu daquan* (Complete Chinese taxes). Shenyang: Liaoning renmin chubanshe.

Jiang Yonghua. 1996. "Jiaqiang xiangzhen caizheng jianshe nuli zhenxing xiangzhen caizheng (Strengthen construction of township public finance

[and] make efforts to vigorously develop township public finance)." *Difang caizheng* (Local public finance).

Jiang Zemin. 1997. "Full Text of Speech to the Fifteenth Party Congress." *China Daily*, September 30.

Jiangsu jingji nianjian (Jiangsu economic yearbook). Annual.

Jiangsu sheng dashiji, 1949–1985 (Jiangsu Province chronology of major events, 1949–1985). 1988. Nanjing: Jiangsu renmin chubanshe.

Jiangsu shixian jingji (Economies of cities and counties in Jiangsu). Annual. Beijing: Zhongguo tongji chubanshe.

"Jiangsu's Yu Xingde on Tax Collection Problems." 1994. Nanjing Jiangsu People's Radio Network, November 24. Translated in *Foreign Broadcast Information Service – China*, December 1, 1994, pp. 45–6.

Jiefang ribao (Liberation daily). Periodical.

Jin Chunpin. 1990. "Nongcun xinyong de kuisun xianxiang zhide zhongshi (It is worth taking seriously the phenomenon of losses on the part of rural credit cooperatives)." *Shanghai jinrong* (Shanghai finance) 2.

Jin Xin, Liu Zhicheng, and Wang Shaofei, eds. 1991. *Zhongguo shuiwu baike quanshu* (Chinese encyclopedia of taxation). Beijing: Jingji guanli chubanshe.

Jingji gongzuozhe xuexi ziliao (Study materials for economic administrators). Periodical. Reprinted in *Fuyin baokan ziliao – Jingji tizhi gaige* (Reprints of periodical materials – Economic system reform).

Jingji ribao (Economic daily). Periodical.

Jingji yanjiu (Economic research). Periodical.

Johnson, Chalmers. 1987. "Political Institutions and Economic Performance: The Government–Business Relationship in Japan, South Korea, and Taiwan." In *The Political Economy of the New Asian Industrialism*, ed. Frederic C. Deyo, 136–64. Ithaca: Cornell University Press.

Jones, Bryan. 1999. "Bounded Rationality." *Annual Review of Political Science* 2: 297–321.

Joseph, William A., Christine Wong, and David Zweig, eds. 1991. *New Perspectives on the Cultural Revolution*. Cambridge: Harvard University Press.

Ju Jingde. 1994. "Establishment of Separate Tax Organs Fully Under Way in Ningxia." *Ningxia ribao* (Ningxia daily), August 1. Translated in *Foreign Broadcast Information Service – China*, August 19, 1994, p. 58.

Katzenstein, Peter, ed. 1978. *Between Power and Plenty: Foreign Economic Policies of Advanced Industrial States*. Madison: University of Wisconsin Press.

Kelliher, Daniel. 1992. *Peasant Power in China: The Era of Rural Reform, 1979–1989*. New Haven: Yale University Press.

Kiser, Edgar. 1994. "Markets and Hierarchies in Early Modern Tax Systems: A Principal–Agent Analysis." *Politics and Society* 22(3): 284–315 (September).

Kiser, Edgar, and Xiaoxi Tong. 1992. "Determinants of the Amount and Type of Corruption in State Fiscal Bureaucracies." *Comparative Political Studies* 25(3): 300–31 (October).

Kohli, Atul. 1990. *Democracy and Discontent: India's Growing Crisis of Governability*. New York: Cambridge University Press.

Bibliography

Kohli, Atul, and Vivienne Shue. 1994. "State Power and Social Forces: On Political Contention and Accommodation in the Third World." In *State Power and Social Forces: Domination and Transformation in the Third World*, ed. Joel S. Migdal, Atul Kohli, and Vivienne Shue, 293–326. New York: Cambridge University Press.

Kornai, Janos. 1979. "Resource-Constrained Versus Demand-Constrained Systems." *Econometrica* 47(4): 801–19 (July).

——— 1980. *The Economics of Shortage*. Amsterdam: North-Holland Publishing Company.

——— 1986. "The Hungarian Reform Process: Visions, Hopes, and Reality." *Journal of Economic Literature* 24 (December): 1687–737.

——— 1992. *The Socialist System: The Political Economy of Socialism*. Princeton: Princeton University Press.

Krasner, Stephen D. 1978. *Defending the National Interest: Raw Materials Investments and U.S. Foreign Policy*. Princeton: Princeton University Press.

Lampton, David M., ed. 1987. *Policy Implementation in Post-Mao China*. Berkeley: University of California Press.

Lardy, Nicholas R. 1998. *China's Unfinished Economic Revolution*. Washington, D.C.: Brookings Institution Press.

Lauren, Paul Gordon, ed. 1979. *Diplomacy: New Approaches in History, Theory, and Policy*. New York: Free Press.

Lee, Hong Yung. 1991. *From Revolutionary Cadres to Party Technocrats in Socialist China*. Berkeley: University of California Press.

Levi, Margaret. 1988. *Of Rule and Revenue*. Berkeley: University of California Press.

——— 1990. "A Logic of Institutional Change." In *The Limits of Rationality*, ed. Karen Schweers Cook and Margaret Levi, 402–18. Chicago: University of Chicago Press.

Lewis, Steven. 1997. "Marketization and Government Credibility in Shanghai: Federalist and Local Corporatist Explanations." In *The Political Economy of Property Rights: Institutional Change and Credibility in the Reform of Centrally Planned Economies*, ed. David L. Weimer, 259–87. New York: Cambridge University Press.

Li Bingkun. 1990. "Xiangzhen qiye yunxing de hongguan tiaokong jizhi (Macroeconomic control mechanisms for rural enterprise)." In *Biewuxuanze: Xiangzhen qiye yu guomin jingji de xietiao fazhan* (No other choice: Coordinating the development of rural enterprise and the national economy). Beijing: Gaige chubanshe.

Li Chu'en, Shi Shoujiang, and Zhu Lifiang. 1990. "Xiangzhen qiye yuqi daizhi daikuan xintan (A new discussion of township and village enterprises' delinquent and unrecoverable loans)" *Zhongguo nongcun jinrong* (China's rural finance) 5.

Li Lianjiang and Kevin O'Brien. 1996. "Chinese Villagers and Popular Resistance." *Modern China* 22 (January): 28–61.

Li Shourong. 1988. "A Brief Discussion on Credit Restrictions." *Renmin ribao* (People's daily), March 3. Translated in *Foreign Broadcast Information Service Daily Report – China*, March 22, 1988, p. 32.

Bibliography

Li Wenjin. 1994. "Meiguo fenshuizhi dui woguo shenhua caishui gaige de qishi (Insights from the American tax system for deepening our tax and fiscal reforms)." *Neimenggu caijing xueyuan xuebao* 1: 21–6. Reprinted *in Fuyin baokan ziliao – Caizheng yu shuiwu* (Reprints of periodical materials – Public finance and tax) 5 (1994): 91–6.

Liaoning jingji bao (Liaoning economic news). Periodical.

Lieberthal, Kenneth G. 1980. *Revolution and Tradition in Tientsin, 1949–1952*. Stanford: Stanford University Press.

Lieberthal, Kenneth G., and David M. Lampton, eds. 1992. *Bureaucracy, Politics, and Decision Making in Post-Mao China*. Berkeley: University of California Press.

Lieberthal, Kenneth, and Michel Oksenberg. 1988. *Policy Making in China: Leaders, Structures, and Processes*. Princeton: Princeton University Press.

Liebowitz, S. J., and Stephen E. Margolis. 1995. "Path Dependence, Lock-In, and History." *Journal of Law, Economics, and Organization* 11(1): 205–26 (April).

Lin Bai et al., eds. 1987. *Wenzhou moshi de lilun tansuo* (A theoretical exploration of the Wenzhou model). Nanning: Guangxi renmin chubanshe.

Lin Nan, and Chih-jou Chen. 1994. "Local Initiatives in Institutional Transformation: The Nature and Emergence of Local Market Socialism in Jiangsu." Paper presented to the Annual Meeting of the Association for Asian Studies, March 24–7, Boston.

Lin Zhimin. 1994. "Reform and Shanghai: Changing Central–Local Fiscal Relations." In *Changing Central–Local Relations in China: Reform and State Capacity*, ed. Jia Hao and Lin Zhimin, 239–60. Boulder: Westview Press.

Ling Yaochu. 1992. "Zhengqi fenkai shi xiangzhen qiye shenhua gaige de toudeng dashi (The separation of the government and the enterprise is a matter of primary importance in deepening reform)." *Shanghai jiaoxian gongye* (Shanghai suburban industry) 2 (April): 7–8.

Litwack, John M. 1991. "Legality and Market Reform in Soviet-Type Economies." *Journal of Economic Perspectives* 5(4) (Fall).

Liu, Alan P. L. 1992. "The 'Wenzhou Model' of Development and China's Modernization." *Asian Survey* 32(8): 696–711 (August).

Liu Qinghuan. 1990. "Jiangsu xiangzhen gongye fazhan jianshi (A brief history of township and village industry in Jiangsu)." In *Jiangsu xiangzhen qiye guanli jingyan qian liexuan*, ed. Wu Xiangjun. Beijing: Zhonggong zhongyang dangxiao chubanshe.

Liu Wenpu, Zhang Houyi, and Qin Shaoxiang. 1989. "Guanyu nongcun siying jingji fazhan de lilun fenxi (A theoretical analysis of rural private economic development)." *Zhongguo shehui kexue* (Social science in China) 6: 63–75.

Liu Xirong. 1991. "Guanyu fazhan gufen hezuo jingji de jige wenti (Several questions regarding the development of the cooperative shareholding economy)." In *Gufen hezuo jingji wenjian huibian* (A collection of documents on the cooperative shareholding economy), 1–11. N.p.

Liu, Yia-Ling. 1992. "Reform from Below: The Private Economy and Local Politics in the Rural Industrialization of Wenzhou." *China Quarterly* 130 (June): 292–316.

Lotz, Jorgen R., and Elliot R. Morss. 1967. "Measuring 'Tax Effort' in Developing Countries." *International Monetary Fund Staff Papers* 14(3): 478–97 (November).

Lu Fengquan. 1994. "Effect on the Economy of 1994 Fiscal and Taxation System Reform." *Caijing yanjiu* 8 (August): 18–21.

Lu Lan and Li Guowen. 1996. "Xiangzhen qiye pan jian fu (Township and village enterprises hope for a reduction in burden)." *Zhongguo xiangzhen qiye bao* (China township and village enterprise news), February 13.

Lu Xizong. 1990. "Guanyu minghou liangnian xian dui xiangzhen caizheng baogan de yixie shexiang (Some thoughts on county–township fiscal contracts for the next two years)." *Shanghai nongcun jingji* (Shanghai rural economy) 6.

Lubman, Stanley. 1999. *Bird in a Cage: Legal Reform in China after Mao*. Stanford: Stanford University Press.

Luo Xianfu, Deng Heren, and Liu Zhonglong. 1991. "Qingli zhengdun qiye duotou kaihu (Sort out and rectify multiple enterprise accounts)." *Zhongguo jinrong* (China's finance) 4: 28–9.

Luo Xiaopeng. 1990. "Ownership and Status Stratification." In *China's Rural Industry: Structure, Development, and Reform*, ed. William A. Byrd and Lin Qingsong, 134–71. Oxford: Oxford University Press.

Luo Yousheng, Quan Maohui, and Gao Kuanzhong. 1989. "Nongcun siren qiye lifa tansuo (An exploration of rural private enterprise legislation)." In *Zhongguo nongcun: Zhengce yanjiu beiwanglu* (China's countryside: Policy research memorandum), vol. 1, 371–85. Beijing: Nongye chubanshe.

Lyons, Thomas P. 1994. "Economic Reform in Fujian: Another View from the Villages." In *The Economic Transformation of South China: Reform and Development in the Post-Mao Era*, ed. Thomas P. Lyons and Victor Nee, 141–68. Ithaca: Cornell University East Asia Program.

Lyons, Thomas P., and Victor Nee, eds. 1994. *The Economic Transformation of South China: Reform and Development in the Post-Mao Era*. Ithaca: Cornell University East Asia Program.

Ma Jisen. 1988. "A General Survey of the Resurgence of the Private Sector of China's Economy." *Social Sciences in China* 9(3) (September).

Ma Junlei, and Luo Liqin. 1994. "Important Reforms in China's Tax System." *JETRO China Newsletter* 110 (May–June): 12–21.

Ma Rong, Wang Hansheng, and Liu Shiding. 1994. *Zhongguo xiangzhen qiye de fazhan lishi yu yunxing jizhi* (The development history and operating mechanism of China's rural enterprises). Beijing: Beijing daxue chubanshe.

Ma Yongwei. 1988. "Ma Yongwei tongzhi zai Zhongguo nongye yinhang fenhang hangzhang huiyishang de jianghua (Comrade Ma Yongwei's speech to the meeting of branch presidents of the Agriculture Bank of China)." *Zhongguo nongcun jinrong* (China's rural finance) 23: 4–7.

———. 1989. "Jianchi guanche sanzhong quanhui de zhidao fangzhen nuli zuohao jinnian de nongcun jinrong gongzuo (Persist in implementing the guiding principles of the third plenum, conscientiously pursue this year's rural financial work)." *Zhongguo nongcun jinrong* (China's rural finance) 3: 8–12.

1990. "Jianchi guanche zhili zhengdun shenhua gaige de fangzhen zhichi nongcun jingji chixu wending xietiao de fazhan (Persist in implementing the principles of rectification and deepening reform, support the continued stable and coordinated development of the rural economy)." *Zhongguo nongcun jinrong* (China's rural finance) 3: 9–15.

Manion, Melanie. 1985. "The Cadre Management System, Post-Mao: The Appointment, Promotion, Transfer, and Removal of Party and State Leaders." *China Quarterly* 102: 203–33.

1993. *Retirement of Revolutionaries in China: Public Policies, Social Norms, Private Interests.* Princeton: Princeton University Press.

1994. "Survey Research in the Study of Contemporary China: Learning from Local Samples." *China Quarterly* 139: 741–66.

Mann, Susan. 1987. *Local Merchants and the Chinese Bureaucracy, 1750–1950.* Stanford: Stanford University Press.

Manoharan, Thiagarajan. 1991. "Credit and Financial Institutions at the Rural Level in China – Between Plan and Market." In *From Peasant to Entrepreneur: Growth and Change in Rural China*, ed. E. B. Vermeer, 183–216. Wageningen: Pudoc.

Mao Rongfang. 1991. "Qiye duotou kaihu de biduan yu guanli duice (The harmful practice of multiple enterprise accounts and managerial counter-measures)." *Shanghai jinrong* (Shanghai finance) 5: 21–2.

March, James G. 1978. "Bounded Rationality, Ambiguity, and the Engineering of Choice." *Bell Journal of Economics* 9(2): 587–608 (Autumn).

Martin, Michael F. 1992. "Defining China's Rural Population." *China Quarterly* 130: 392–402.

Meng Xin. 1990. "The Rural Labor Market." In *China's Rural Industry: Structure, Development, and Reform*, ed. William A. Byrd and Lin Qingsong, 299–322. Oxford: Oxford University Press.

Migdal, Joel S. 1983. "Studying the Politics of Development and Change: The State of the Art." In *Political Science: The State of the Discipline*, ed. Ada Finifter. Washington, D.C.: American Political Science Association.

1988. *Strong Societies and Weak States: State–Society Relations and State Capabilities in the Third World.* Princeton: Princeton University Press.

Migdal, Joel, Atul Kohli, and Vivienne Shue, eds. 1994. *State Power and Social Forces: Domination and Transformation in the Third World.* New York: Cambridge University Press.

Moe, Terry M. 1984. "The New Economics of Organization." *American Journal of Political Science* 28(4): 739–77.

Moore, Mick. 1997. "Societies, Polities, and Capitalists in Developing Countries: A Literature Survey." *Journal of Development Studies* 33(3): 287–363 (February).

Murrell, Peter. 1992. "Evolutionary and Radical Approaches to Economic Reform." *Economics of Planning* 25: 79–95.

Musgrave, Richard A., and Peggy B. Musgrave. 1984. *Public Finance in Theory and Practice.* New York: McGraw-Hill.

Myers, Ramon H. 1991. "How Did the Modern Chinese Economy Develop? – A Review Article." *Journal of Asian Studies* 50(3): 604–28.

Bibliography

Nan Fang. 1991. "Jianmian shui guanlizhong cunzai de wenti ji qi duice (Facing existing problems in the management of tax exemptions and reductions and their countermeasures)." *Caizheng* (Public finance) 4: 51–3.

Nashui zixun shouce (Consultation manual on paying taxes). 1986. Beijing: Beijing chubanshe.

Naughton, Barry. 1990. "Monetary Implications of Balanced Growth and the Current Macroeconomic Disturbances in China." In *China's Contemporary Economic Reforms as a Development Strategy*, ed. Dieter Cassel and Gunter Heiduk. Baden-Baden: Nomos Verlagsgesellschaft.

——— 1991. "Macroeconomic Management and System Reform in China." In *The Chinese State in the Era of Economic Reform: The Road to Crisis*, ed. Gordon White. Armonk: M. E. Sharpe.

——— 1992a. "Implications of the State Monopoly over Industry and Its Relaxation." *Modern China* 18(1): 14–41 (January).

——— 1992b. "Inflation: Patterns, Causes, and Cures." In *China's Economic Dilemmas in the 1990s: The Problems of Reforms, Modernization, and Interdependence*, U.S. Congress, Joint Economic Committee. Armonk: M. E. Sharpe.

——— 1995. *Growing Out of the Plan: Chinese Economic Reform, 1978–1993*. New York: Cambridge University Press.

Nee, Victor. 1989. "A Theory of Market Transition: From Redistribution to Markets in State Socialism." *American Sociological Review* 54 (October): 663–81.

——— 1992. "Organizational Dynamics of Market Transition: Hybrid Forms, Property Rights, and Mixed Economy in China." *Administrative Science Quarterly* 32: 1–27.

——— 1996. "The Emergence of Market Society: Changing Mechanisms of Stratification in China." *American Journal of Sociology* 101(4) (January).

Nee, Victor, and Paul Ingram. 1998. "Embeddedness and Beyond: Institutions, Exchange, and Social Structure." In *The New Institutionalism in Sociology*, ed. Mary C. Brinton and Victor Nee, 19–45. New York: Russell Sage Foundation.

Nee, Victor, and Sijin Su. 1996. "Local Corporatism and Informal Privatization in China's Market Transition." In *Reforming Asian Socialism: The Growth of Market Institutions*, ed. John McMillan and Barry Naughton, 111–34. Ann Arbor: University of Michigan Press.

Nelson, Richard R. 1995. "Recent Evolutionary Theorizing about Economic Change." *Journal of Economic Literature* 33 (March): 48–90.

Nelson, Richard R., and Sidney G. Winter. 1982. *An Evolutionary Theory of Economic Change*. Cambridge: Harvard University Press.

Newlyn, W. T. 1985. "Measuring Tax Effort in Developing Countries." *Journal of Development Studies* 21(3): 390–405 (April).

Niu Licheng, ed. 1990. *Zhongguo shuiwu zhinan* (Guide to Chinese taxes). Beijing: Zhongguo renmin daxue chubanshe.

Nolan, Peter, and Dong Fureng, eds. 1990. *Market Forces in China: Competition and Small Business – The Wenzhou Debate*. London: Zed Books.

Nongcun jiceng dang zuzhi diaocha yanjiu ketizu. 1992. "Guanyu Wenzhou gufen hezuo qiye dang zuzhi jianshe de kaocha baogao (Regarding the report on the investigation into the establishment of party organizations in Wenzhou's cooperative shareholding enterprises)." *Zhejiang shehui kexue* (Zhejiang social science) 4.

Nongcun shiyong fagui shouce (Handbook of commonly used rural laws and regulations). 1987. Beijing: Falü chubanshe.

Nongye jingji wenti (Problems of agricultural economy). Periodical.

Nongye jitihua zhongyao wenjian huibian (Collection of important documents on the collectivization of agriculture). 1982. Beijing: Zhonggong zhongyang dangxiao chubanshe.

North, Douglass C. 1981. *Structure and Change in Economic History*. New York: W. W. Norton.

    1984. "Government and the Cost of Exchange in History." *Journal of Economic History* 44(2): 255–64 (June).

    1990. *Institutions, Institutional Change, and Economic Performance*. New York: Cambridge University Press.

O'Brien, Kevin J. 1994. "Chinese People's Congresses and Legislative Embeddedness: Understanding Early Organizational Development." *Comparative Political Studies* 27(1) (April).

Ogborn, Keith, C. Ramachandran, and Loraine West. 1997. "Fiscal and Regulatory Framework for Social Security System Reform." Asian Development Bank, T. A. No. 2383-PRC.

Oi, Jean C. 1989. *State and Peasant in Contemporary China: The Political Economy of Village Government*. Berkeley: University of California Press.

    1992. "Fiscal Reform and the Economic Foundations of Local State Corporatism in China." *World Politics* 45(1): 99–126 (October).

    1995. "The Role of the Local State in China's Transitional Economy." *China Quarterly* 144 (December): 1132–50.

    1998. "The Evolution of Local State Corporatism." In *Zouping in Transition: The Process of Reform in Rural North China*, ed. Andrew G. Walder, 35–61. Cambridge: Harvard University Press.

    1999. *Rural China Takes Off*. Berkeley: University of California Press.

Oksenberg, Michel, and James Tong. 1991. "The Evolution of Central–Provincial Fiscal Relations in China, 1971–1984: The Formal System." *China Quarterly* 125 (March): 1–32.

Organski, A. F. K., and Jacek Kugler. 1980. *The War Ledger*. Chicago: University of Chicago Press.

Organski, A. F. K., Jacek Kugler, J. Timothy Johnson, and Youseff Cohen. 1994. *Births, Deaths, and Taxes: The Demographic and Political Transitions*. Chicago: University of Chicago Press.

Pan Shangeng, ed. 1988. *Wenzhou shiyanqu* (The Wenzhou experimental zone). Beijing: Zhongguo zhanwang chubanshe.

Parris, Kristen. 1993. "Local Initiative and National Reform: The Wenzhou Model of Development." *China Quarterly* 134 (June).

Pei, Minxin. 1994. *From Reform to Revolution: The Demise of Communism in China and the Soviet Union*. Cambridge: Harvard University Press.

    1997. "Racing against Time: Institutional Decay and Renewal in China." In *China Briefing 1995–96*, ed. William A. Joseph. Armonk: M. E. Sharpe.

Peng Guangrong. 1992. "Fangzhi xiangzhen qiye jingying jizhi de tuihua (Prevent the degeneration of the operating mechanism of rural enterprises)." *Jiangsu xiangzhen qiye* (Jiangsu rural enterprise) 2: 31–2.

Perkins, Dwight. 1977. *Rural Small-scale Industry in the People's Republic of China*. Berkeley: University of California Press.

——— 1994. "Completing China's Move to the Market." *Journal of Economic Perspectives* 8(2): 42–3 (Spring).

Perry, Elizabeth J. 1980. *Rebels and Revolutionaries in North China, 1845–1945*. Stanford: Stanford University Press.

——— 1994. "Trends in the Study of Chinese Politics: State–Society Relations." *China Quarterly* 139 (September): 704–13.

Pierson, Paul. 1993. "When Effect Becomes Cause: Policy Feedback and Political Change." *World Politics* 45(4): 595–628 (July).

Polanyi, Karl. 1957 [1944]. *The Great Transformation: The Political and Economic Origins of Our Time*. Boston: Beacon Press.

Potter, Pitman B. 1994a. "The Administrative Litigation Law of the PRC: Judicial Review and Bureaucratic Reform." In *Domestic Law Reforms in Post-Mao China*, ed. Pitman B. Potter, 270–304. Armonk: M. E. Sharpe.

——— 1994b. *Domestic Law Reforms in Post-Mao China*. Armonk: M. E. Sharpe.

——— 1994c. "Riding the Tiger: Legitimacy and Legal Culture in Post-Mao China." *China Quarterly* 138 (June): 325–58.

Poznanski, Kazimierz Z. 1996. *Poland's Protracted Transition: Institutional Change and Economic Growth, 1970–1994*. New York: Cambridge University Press.

"The Price of Economic Reforms: Central–Local Tensions." 1994. *China News Analysis* 1508 (April 15): 1–9.

"The Privately-Run Enterprises." 1989. *China News Analysis* 1382 (April 1): 5.

"Qieshi jiaqiang shuishou baozhang caizheng shouru (Conscientiously increase tax revenues, guarantee fiscal revenues)." *Jiefang ribao* (Liberation daily), May 16, 1988.

Qin Baowen. 1991a. "Guanyu xiangzhen gongye fazhan houjin wenti de tansuo (An exploration of the problem of momentum in the development of rural industry)." In *Jiading nianjian 1988–1990* (Jiading yearbook 1988–1990), 189–91. Shanghai: Tongji daxue chubanshe.

——— 1991b. "Jingti xiangzhen qiye jingying jizhi de tuihua (Be on guard against the degeneration of the operating mechanism of rural enterprises). *Jiading jingji* (Jiading economy) 21 (November): 1–3.

Qiu Jicheng. 1988. "Xiangzhen qiye – Shequ (zhengfu) guanli moshi de jiben xiansuo (Township and village enterprises – The basic threads of the community [government] management model)." *Fazhan yanjiu tongxun* (Development research) 104 (December): 748–59.

Rawski, Thomas G. 1989. *Economic Growth in Prewar China*. Berkeley: University of California Press.

Remmer, Karen L. 1997. "Theoretical Decay and Theoretical Development: The Resurgence of Institutional Analysis." *World Politics* 50(1): 34–62.

Renmin ribao (People's daily). Periodical.

330

Renshi gongzuo wenjian xuanbian – Ganbu guanli bufen (Selected documents on personnel work – Cadre management section). 1987. Beijing: Laodong renshi chubanshe.

Reynolds, Bruce, ed. 1988. *Chinese Economic Reform: How Far, How Fast?* Boston: Academic Press.

Riskin, Carl. 1971. "Small Industry and the Chinese Model of Development." *China Quarterly* 46 (April–June): 245–73.

———. 1978. "China's Rural Industries: Self-reliant Systems or Independent Kingdoms?" *China Quarterly* 73 (March): 77–98.

Rong Linfei. 1989. "Siying jingjizhong de yinbi xingwei (Hidden behaviors in the private economy)." In *Zhongguo de siying jingji – Xianzhuang, wenti, qianjing* (China's private economy – Current status, problems, and prospects), 262–75. Beijing: Zhongguo shehui kexue chubanshe.

Root, Hilton. 1989. "Tying the King's Hand: Credible Commitments and Royal Fiscal Policy during the Old Regime." *Rationality and Society* 1(2): 240–58 (October).

Rowe, William T. 1984. *Hankow: Commerce and Society in a Chinese City, 1796–1889*. Stanford: Stanford University Press.

Rozelle, Scott. 1994. "Decision-Making in China's Rural Economy: The Linkages between Village Leaders and Farm Households." *China Quarterly* 137 (March): 99–124.

Ruan Yisheng. 1994. "Lun fenshuizhi caizheng guanli tizhi (On the fiscal management system of the tax assignment system)." *Caimao yanjiu* 3: 44–8. Reprinted in *Fuyin baokan ziliao – Caizheng yu shuiwu* (Reprints of periodical materials – Public finance and tax) 7: 52–6.

Rueschemeyer, Dietrich, and Peter B. Evans. 1985. "The State and Economic Transformation: Toward an Analysis of the Conditions Underlying Effective Intervention." In *Bringing the State Back In*, ed. Peter B. Evans, Dietrich Rueschemeyer, and Theda Skocpol, 44–77. New York: Cambridge University Press.

"Rural Enterprises and the Private Economy: Rectification." 1990. *China News Analysis* 1405 (March 1).

S. zhen qiye guanli bangongshi. 1991. "Qiye guanli qingkuang jiaoliu (Exchange on the situation in enterprise management)." Unpublished report, No. 7 (July 27).

S. zhen renmin zhengfu. 1990. "Guanyu yijiujiuyi niandu gongye shengchan zerenzhi de yijian (Opinion regarding the 1991 production responsibility system)." Town government document No. 103.

Sang Jingshan and Wu Zhenxing. 1991. "Jianqing jiaoqu xiangzhen qiye fudan keburonghuan (Reducing the burdens of suburban township- and village-run enterprises can brook no delay)." *Shanghai nongcun jingji* (Shanghai's rural economy) 2: 27–9.

Schamis, Hector E. N.d. "Market Reform as State Crafting: The Case of Chile and Some Comparisons." Unpublished manuscript, Brown University.

Schmitter, Philippe C. 1979. "Still the Century of Corporatism?" In *Trends toward Corporatist Intermediation*, ed. Philippe C. Schmitter and Gerhard Lehmbruch, 7–48. London: Sage Publications.

Schmitter, Philippe, and Gerhard Lehmbruch, eds. 1979. *Trends toward Corporatist Intermediation*. London: Sage Publications.

"Separation of State, Local Tax Systems Nearly Complete." 1994. *Xinhua tongxun-she* (New China News Agency), August 15. Translated in *Foreign Broadcast Information Service – China*, August 18, 1994, p. 27.

Shanghai gongye jingji bao (Shanghai industrial economy). Periodical.

Shanghai guomin jingji tongji ziliao (Statistical materials on the Shanghai economy). Annual. N.p.

Shanghai jingji nianjian (Shanghai economic yearbook). Annual. Shanghai: Shanghai sanlian shudian.

Shanghai shi fagui guizhang huibian, 1986–1987 (Compilation of Shanghai Municipality law and regulations, 1986–1987). 1988. Shanghai: Shanghai renmin chubanshe.

Shanghai shi jingji tizhi gaige wenjian huibian (Shanghai Municipality compendium of documents on economic system reform). N.d. Shanghai: Shanghai shi qiye guanli xiehui chuban.

Shanghai shi shiyong shuilu shouce (Shanghai Municipality handbook of commonly used tax rates). 1991. N.p.

Shanghai xian guomin jingji tongji ziliao (Shanghai County economy statistical materials). Annual. Shanghai: Shanghai xian tongjiju.

Shao Xinfu et al. 1991. "Jiadingxian xiangzhen qiye chengbaozhi de shijian (The experience with Jiading County's township and village enterprise contracting system)." In *Jiading nianjian 1988–1990* (Jiading yearbook 1988–1990), 185–7. Shanghai: Tongji daxue chubanshe.

Shao Xinfu and Zhu Yixing. 1991. "Dui wanshan caizheng baogan tizhi de sikao (Reflections on improving the fiscal contract system)." In *Jiading nianjian 1988–1990* (Jiading yearbook 1988–1990), 142–3. Shanghai: Tongji daxue chubanshe.

Shen Keqiao. 1992. "Jingying changdi wu zhuoluo shuishou tanpai fudan zhong youshizhishi jianyi caiqu cuoshi cushi siying jingji jiankang fazhan (No place to conduct business and heavy burdens of taxes and fees: Experts recommend taking measures to promote the healthy development of the private economy)." *Jiefang ribao* (Liberation daily), August 13.

Shen Sandu. 1990. "Dui xinyong pinggu gongzuo de jidian sikao (Several thoughts on credit rating work)." *Shanghai jinrong* (Shanghai finance) 2.

Shen Yongquan and You Zhengting. 1991. "Dui xiangcun qiye houjin buzu zhuangkuang de fenxi ji gaijin jianyi (Analysis and suggestions about the lack of long-run momentum in TVEs)." In *Jiading nianjian 1988–1990* (Jiading yearbook 1988–1990), 187–8. Shanghai: Tongji daxue chubanshe.

"Shijiao sifenzhisan rujiao shoutao shengchanxian tingchan (Three quarters of the production lines for latex rubber gloves in suburban Shanghai cease production)." 1989. *Shanghai gongye jingji bao* (Shanghai industrial economy), June 15.

Shirk, Susan L. 1993. *The Political Logic of Economic Reform in China*. Berkeley: University of California Press.

Shiyijie sanzhong quanhui yilai jingji tizhi gaige zhongyao wenjian huibian (A compendium of important documents on economic system reform since the

Third Plenum of the Eleventh Central Committee). 1990. Beijing: Gaige chubanshe.

Shleifer, Andrei, and Robert W. Vishny. 1993. "Corruption." *Quarterly Journal of Economics* (1993): 599–617.

Shu Hengchang, Wei Deyong, and Wang Canwen. 1990. "Qingli duotou kaihu jiaqiang zhanghu guanli (Clear up multiple accounts, strengthen account management)." *Shanghai jinrong* (Shanghai finance) 12: 41–2.

Shue, Vivienne. 1980. *Peasant China in Transition: The Dynamics of Development toward Socialism, 1949–1956*. Berkeley: University of California Press.

1984. "Beyond the Budget: Finance Organization and Reform in a Chinese County." *Modern China* 10(2): 147–86 (April).

1988. *The Reach of the State: Sketches of the Chinese Body Politic*. Stanford: Stanford University Press.

Sigurdson, Jon. 1977. *Rural Industrialization in China*. Cambridge: Harvard University Press.

Simon, Herbert A. 1957. *Models of Man – Social and Rational*. New York: John Wiley.

1995. "Rationality in Political Behavior." *Political Psychology* 16(1): 45–61.

Siu, Helen F. 1989a. *Agents and Victims in South China: Accomplices in Rural Revolution*. New Haven: Yale University Press.

1989b. "Socialist Peddlars and Princes in a Chinese Market Town." *American Ethnologist* 16(2): 195–212 (May).

Skocpol, Theda. 1985. "Bringing the State Back In: Strategies of Analysis in Current Research." In *Bringing the State Back In*, ed. Peter B. Evans, Dietrich Rueschemeyer, and Theda Skocpol, 3–37. New York: Cambridge University Press.

1979. *States and Social Revolutions: A Comparative Analysis of France, Russia, and China*. New York: Cambridge University Press.

Smith, Adam. 1965 [1776]. *An Inquiry into the Nature and Causes of the Wealth of Nations*. New York: The Modern Library.

Smith, Tony. 1985. "Requiem or New Agenda for Third World Studies?" *World Politics* 37(4): 532–61 (July).

1979. "The Underdevelopment of Development Literature: The Case of Dependency Theory." *World Politics* 31(2): 247–88 (January).

Song Lina, and Du He. 1990. "The Role of Township Governments in Rural Industrialization." In *China's Rural Industry: Structure, Development, and Reform*, ed. William A. Byrd and Lin Qingsong, 342–57. New York: Oxford University Press.

Song Wenguang and Huang Dekang. N.d. "Guanyu woshi gufen hezuo qiye ruogan wenti de shuoming (An explanation of several questions regarding [Wenzhou's] cooperative shareholding enterprises)." Unpublished manuscript.

Songjiang caishui jianbao (Songjiang public finance and tax bulletin). Periodical.

Songjiang juan: Zhongguo guoqing congshu – Bai xian shi jingji shehui diaocha (Songjiang volume: China national conditions series – An economic and social survey of one hundred counties and cities). 1993. Beijing: Zhongguo dabaike quanshu chubanshe.

Songjiang tongji nianjian (Songjiang statistical yearbook). Annual. N.p.

Songjiang xianzhi (Gazetteer of Songjiang County). 1991. Shanghai: Shanghai renmin chubanshe.

Stallings, Barbara, ed. 1995. *Global Change, Regional Response: The New International Context of Development.* New York: Cambridge University Press.

Stark, David. 1996. "Recombinant Property in East European Capitalism." *American Journal of Sociology* 101(4): 993–1027 (January).

Steinfeld, Edward S. 1998. *Forging Reform in China: The Fate of State-owned Industry.* New York: Cambridge University Press.

Steinmo, Sven, Kathleen Thelen, and Frank Longstreth, eds. 1992. *Structuring Politics: Historical Institutionalism in Comparative Analysis.* New York: Cambridge University Press.

Stepan, Alfred. 1978. *The State and Society: Peru in Comparative Perspective.* Princeton: Princeton University Press.

S. tongji nianjian (S. statistical yearbook). Annual. N.p.

Sun Tanzhen, Zhu Gang, and Hu Bin. 1993. "Shichang jingji fazhan yu xian xiang(zhen) caizheng yunxing – Zhiduwai caizheng de shizheng fenxi (The development of a market economy and the operation of county and township public finance: A case study analysis of extrasystemic public finance)." Unpublished manuscript, Zhongguo shehui kexueyuan nongcun fazhan yanjiusuo, March.

Sun Wenxue and Wang Yuwu. 1994. "A Discussion on Obstacles to All-around Implementation of the Tax-assignment System and Their Solutions." *Caijing wenti yanjiu* (Research on financial and economic problems) 10 (October): 43–6. Translated in *Foreign Broadcast Information Service – China,* January 4, 1995, pp. 52–6.

Svejnar, Jan, and Josephine Woo. 1990. "Development Patterns in Four Counties." In *China's Rural Industry: Structure, Development, and Reform,* ed. William A. Byrd and Lin Qingsong, 63–84. New York: Oxford University Press.

Tam, On-kit. 1986. "Reform of China's Banking System." *World Economy* 9(4) (December).

1991. "Capital Market Development in China." *World Development* 19(5): 511–32.

1992. "A Private Bank in China: Hui Tong Urban Co-operative Bank." *China Quarterly* 131 (September): 766–77.

Tao Youzhi, ed. 1988. *Sunan moshi yu zhifu zhi dao* (The Sunan model and path to prosperity). Shanghai: Shanghai shehui kexueyuan chubanshe.

"Tax Loopholes Must Be Closed." 1994. *China Daily,* August 17. Reprinted in *Foreign Broadcast Information Service – China,* August 18, 1994, pp. 27–8.

"Tax Reform."1993. *China News Analysis* 1493 (September 15): 1–9.

Thelen, Kathleen, and Sven Steinmo. 1992. "Historical Institutionalism in Comparative Politics." In *Structuring Politics: Historical Institutionalism in Comparative Analysis,* ed. Sven Steinmo, Kathleen Thelen, and Frank Longstreth, 1–32. New York: Cambridge University Press.

"Tianjin Divides Functions of State, Local Tax Bureaus." 1994. *Tianjin ribao* (Tianjin daily), August 4. Translated in *Foreign Broadcast Information Service – China*, August 17, 1994, p. 61.

Tilly, Charles, ed. 1975. *The Formation of National States in Western Europe*. Princeton: Princeton University Press.

——— 1975. "Reflections on the History of European State-Making." In *The Formation of National States in Western Europe*, ed. Charles Tilly. Princeton: Princeton University Press.

——— 1985. "War Making and State Making as Organized Crime." In *Bringing the State Back In*, ed. Peter B. Evans, Dietrich Rueschemeyer, and Theda Skocpol, 161–91. New York: Cambridge University Press.

——— 1990. *Coercion, Capital, and European States, AD 990–1990*. Cambridge: Basil Blackwell.

Tong Wei. 1993. "Zengzhishui de guoji bijiao (An international comparison of value-added tax)." *Zhongyang caizheng jinrong xueyuan xuebao* (Bulletin of the central finance institute) 11: 31–6. Reprinted in *Fuyin baokan ziliao – Caizheng yu shuiwu* (Reprints of periodical materials – Public finance and tax) 1 (1994): 91–6.

Toye, J. F. J., ed. 1978. *Taxation and Economic Development*. London: F. Cass.

Trimberger, Ellen Kay. 1978. *Revolution from Above: Military Bureaucrats and Development in Japan, Turkey, Egypt, and Peru*. New Brunswick: Transactions Books.

Tsang Shu-ki, and Cheng Yuk-shing. 1994. "China's Tax Reforms of 1994: Breakthrough or Compromise?" *Asian Survey* 34(9): 769–88 (September).

Tversky, Amos, and Daniel Kahneman. 1974. "Judgment under Uncertainty: Heuristics and Biases." *Science* 185: 1124–31.

——— 1981. "The Framing of Decisions and the Psychology of Choice." *Science* 211: 453–8.

U.S. Congress, Joint Economic Committee. 1992. *China's Economic Dilemmas in the 1990s: The Problems of Reforms, Modernization, and Interdependence*. Armonk: M. E. Sharpe.

Valenzuela, J. Samuel, and Arturo Valenzuela. 1978. "Modernization and Dependency: Alternative Perspectives in the Study of Latin American Underdevelopment." *Comparative Politics* 10(4): 535–57 (July).

Van de Walle, Nicholas. 1989. "Privatization in Developing Countries: A Review of the Issues." *World Development* 17(5): 601–15.

Vermeer, E. B., ed. 1991. *From Peasant to Entrepreneur: Growth and Change in Rural China*. Wageningen: Pudoc.

Wade, Robert. 1990. *Governing the Market: Economic Theory and the Role of Government in East Asian Industrialization*. Princeton: Princeton University Press.

Walder, Andrew. 1992. "Local Bargaining Relationships and Urban Industrial Finance." In *Bureaucracy, Politics, and Decision Making in Post-Mao China*, ed. Kenneth Lieberthal and David Lampton, 308–33. Berkeley: University of California Press.

——— 1995. "The Quiet Revolution from Within: Economic Reform as a Source of Political Decline." In *The Waning of the Communist State: Economic Origins of Political Decline in China and Hungary*, ed. Andrew G. Walder, 1–24. Berkeley: University of California Press.

1998. "Zouping in Perspective." In *Zouping in Transition: The Process of Reform in Rural North China*, ed. Andrew G. Walder, 1–31. Berkeley: University of California Press.

Wang Guangyi and Li Jingbai. 1992. "Jingti: xindai zijin yingyunzhong de 'heidong' (Warning: The 'black hole' in which credit funds operate)." *Shanghai jinrong* (Shanghai finance) 11: 18–19.

Wang, Shaoguang. 1993. "The (Re-)Construction of Extractive Capacity of the State: The Case of Wuhan, 1949–1953." Unpublished manuscript, Yale University, Department of Political Science, May 20.

1995. "The Rise of the Regions: Fiscal Reform and the Decline of Central State Capacity in China." In *The Waning of the Communist State: Economic Origins of Political Decline in China and Hungary*, ed. Andrew G. Walder, 87–113. Berkeley: University of California Press.

Wang Xiaolu. 1990. "Capital Formation and Utilization." In *China's Rural Industry: Structure, Development, and Reform*, ed. William A. Byrd and Lin Qingsong, 222–42. New York: Oxford University Press.

Wang Xiaoyi, and Zhu Chengbao, eds. 1996. *Zhongguo xiangcun de minying qiye yu jiazu jingji: Zhejiang sheng Cangnan xian Xiangdong cun diaocha* (Nonstate enterprises and the family economy in rural China: A survey of Xiangdong Village, Cangnan County, Zhejiang Province). Taiyuan: Shanxi jingji chubanshe.

Wang Zhuo. 1994. "Ping caishui gaige de chengxiao yu yinyou (An assessment of the results and hidden fears regarding the tax and fiscal reforms)." *Jingji tizhi gaige* (Economic system reform) 4: 17–21.

Wank, David L. 1995. "Private Business, Bureaucracy, and Political Alliance in a Chinese City." *Australian Journal of Chinese Affairs* 33 (January): 55–71.

1996. "The Institutional Process of Market Clientelism: *Guanxi* and Private Business in a South China City." *China Quarterly* 147 (September): 820–38.

Waterbury, John. 1993. *Exposed to Innumerable Delusions: Public Enterprise and State Power in Egypt, India, Mexico, and Turkey*. New York: Cambridge University Press.

Weber, Max. 1946. "Politics as a Vocation." In *From Max Weber: Essays in Sociology*, ed. and trans. H. H. Gerth and C. Wright Mills, 77–128. New York: Oxford University Press.

Weimer, David L., ed. 1997. *The Political Economy of Property Rights: Institutional Change and Credibility in the Reform of Centrally Planned Economies*. New York: Cambridge University Press.

Weingast, Barry R. 1990. "The Role of Credible Commitments in State Finance." *Public Choice* 86: 89–97.

1993. "The Economic Role of Political Institutions." Unpublished manuscript, Stanford University.

1995. "The Economic Role of Political Institutions: Market Preserving Federalism and Economic Development." *Journal of Law, Economics, and Organization* 11(1): 1–31.

"Wenzhou shi mingxi chanquan shidian gongzuo huibaohui jiyao (Minutes of the follow-up meeting on the experiment to clarify property rights in Wenzhou Municipality)." 1989. Unpublished report, June 15.

Wenzhou zhi lu congshu: Kaituozhe de guiji – Wenzhou shi difang fagui jianbian (The Wenzhou path series: The reformers' course – A concise collection of local laws and regulations from Wenzhou Municipality). 1989. Shanghai: Tongji daxue chubanshe.

White, Gordon. 1993. *Riding the Tiger: The Politics of Economic Reform in Post-Mao China.* Stanford: Stanford University Press.

White, Gordon, ed. 1991. *The Chinese State in the Era of Economic Reform: The Road to Crisis.* Armonk: M. E. Sharpe.

White, Gordon, and Paul Bowles. 1987. *Towards a Capital Market? Reforms in the Chinese Banking System: Transcript of a Research Trip.* Research Report No. 6. Sussex: Institute of Development Studies China.

White, Lynn T., III. 1989. *Shanghai Shanghai'ed? Uneven Taxes in Reform China.* Occasional Papers and Monographs No. 84. Hong Kong: University of Hong Kong, Centre of Asian Studies.

Whiting, Susan H. 1993. "The Comfort of the Collective: The Political Economy of Rural Enterprise in Shanghai." Paper presented at the Annual Meeting of the Association for Asian Studies, March 25–28, Los Angeles.

1996a. "Contract Incentives and Market Discipline in China's Rural Industrial Sector." In *Reforming Asian Socialism: The Growth of Market Institutions,* ed. John McMillan and Barry Naughton, 63–110. Ann Arbor: University of Michigan Press.

1996b. Review of *From Reform to Revolution: The Demise of Communism in China and the Soviet Union,* by Minxin Pei. *Comparative Political Studies* 29(3): 357–63 (June).

1997. Review of *Tethered Deer: Government and Economy in a Chinese County,* by Marc Blecher and Vivienne Shue, and *Calamity and Reform in China: State, Rural Society, and Institutional Change since the Great Leap Famine,* by Dali L. Yang. *Comparative Political Studies* 30(6): 756–64 (December).

1998. "The Mobilization of Private Investment as a Problem of Trust in Local Governance Structures." In *Trust and Governance,* ed. Valerie Braithwaite and Margaret Levi, 167–93. New York: Russell Sage Foundation.

1999a. "Institutionalizing Fiscal Reform in China: The Problem of Extra-Budgetary Funds." Paper presented to the Annual Meeting of the Association for Asian Studies, March 11–14, Boston.

1999b. "Variation and Change in Ownership Forms in Rural Industry: The Role of Share-holding Cooperatives in Regional Development." In *Property Rights and Economic Reform in China,* ed. Jean C. Oi and Andrew G. Walder. Stanford: Stanford University Press.

Whyte, Martin King. 1995. "The Social Roots of China's Economic Development." *China Quarterly* 144: 999–1019.

Winckler, Edwin A., and Susan Greenhalgh, eds. 1988. *Contending Approaches to the Political Economy of Taiwan.* Armonk: M. E. Sharpe.

Wong, Christine P. W. 1979. "Rural Industrialization in China: Development of the 'Five Small Industries'." Ph.D. diss., University of California, Berkeley.

1985. "Material Allocation and Decentralization: Impact of the Local Sector on Industrial Reform." In *The Political Economy of Reform in Post-Mao China*, ed. Elizabeth Perry and Christine Wong, 253–78. Cambridge: Harvard University Press.

1988a. "Between Plan and Market: The Role of the Local Sector in Post-Mao China," In *Chinese Economic Reform: How Far, How Fast?* ed. Bruce Reynolds. Boston: Academic Press.

1988b. "Interpreting Rural Industrial Growth in the Post-Mao Period." *Modern China* 14(1): 3–30.

1991a. "The Maoist 'Model' Reconsidered: Local Self-Reliance and the Financing of Rural Industrialization." In *New Perspectives on the Cultural Revolution*, ed. William A. Joseph, Christine Wong, and David Zweig, 183–96. Cambridge: Harvard University Press.

1991b. "Central–Local Relations in an Era of Fiscal Decline: The Paradox of Fiscal Decentralization in Post-Mao China." *China Quarterly* 128 (December): 691–715.

1992. "Fiscal Reform and Local Industrialization: The Problematic Sequencing of Reform in Post-Mao China." *Modern China* 18(2): 197–227 (April).

1996. *People's Republic of China. From Centrally Planned to Market Economies: The Asian Approach*, vol. 2, part 1, ed. Pradumna Rana and Naved Hamid. Hong Kong: Oxford University Press.

1997. "Rural Public Finance." In *Financing Local Government in the People's Republic of China*, ed. Christine P. W. Wong, 167–212. Hong Kong: Oxford University Press.

1998. "Fiscal Dualism in China." In *Taxation in Modern China*, ed. Donald J. S. Brean, 187–208. New York: Routledge.

Wong, Christine P. W., Christopher Heady, and Wing Thye Woo. 1995. *Fiscal Management and Economic Reform in the People's Republic of China*. Hong Kong: Oxford University Press.

Wong, R. Bin. 1992. "A Note on the Myers-Huang Exchange." *Journal of Asian Studies* 51(3): 600–11.

1997. *China Transformed: Historical Change and the Limits of European Experience*. Ithaca: Cornell University Press.

Woo, Jung-en. 1991. *Race to the Swift: State and Finance in Korean Industrialization*. New York: Columbia University Press.

Woo-Cumings, Meredith. 1998. "Reforming Corporate Governance in Korea." Paper presented at the Conference on the Asian Economic Crisis, October 30–31, University of Washington, Seattle.

World Bank. 1990a. *China: Between Plan and Market*. Washington, D.C.

1990b. *China: Revenue Mobilization and Tax Policy: Issues and Options*. Washington, D.C.

Wu Dasheng and Ju Futian. 1994. "Sunan moshi (The Sunan model)." In *Zhongguo chengxiang xietiao fazhan yanjiu* (Research on China's coordinated urban–rural development), ed. Zhou Erliu and Zhang Yulin. Hong Kong: Oxford University Press.

Wu Honglin. 1989. "Wenzhou siren jingji mianmian guan (A look at every aspect of Wenzhou's private economy)." In *Zhongguo de siying jingji: xianzhuang, wenti, qianjing* (China's private economy: Present situation, problems, prospects), 135–50. Beijing: Zhongguo shehui kexue chubanshe.

Wu Xiangjun, ed. 1990. *Jiangsu xiangzhen qiye guanli jingyan qian liexuan.* Beijing: Zhonggong zhongyang dangxiao chubanshe.

Wu, Yu-shan. 1994. *Comparative Economic Transformations: Mainland China, Hungary, the Soviet Union, and Taiwan.* Stanford: Stanford University Press.

Wu Zhenxing and Gu A'er. 1988. "Jiaoxian xiangzhen qiye shehui fudan qingkuang diaocha (An investigation into the social burdens of suburban township- and village-run enterprises)." *Shanghai nongcun jingji* (Shanghai rural economy), supplement: 51–2.

Wuhan shi zhi: Shuiwu zhi (Wuhan City gazette: Tax annals). 1992. Wuhan: Wuhan daxue chubanshe.

Wuxi xian gongye zhi (Gazetteer of industry of Wuxi County). 1990. Shanghai: Shanghai renmin chubanshe.

Wuxi xian tongji nianjian (Wuxi County statistical yearbook). Annual. Wuxi: Wuxi xian tongjiju.

Xiangzhen caizheng shouce (Handbook on township finance). 1987. Chengdu: Sichuan kexue jishu chubanshe.

Xinhua (New China News Agency).

Xishan shi nianjian (Xishan City yearbook). Annual. Beijing: Fang zhi chubanshe.

Xu Baojian. 1996. "Jianqing xiangzhen qiye fudan ye shi jianqing nongmin fudan (Lightening the burdens on township and village enterprises is also lightening the burdens on farmers)." *Jingji ribao* (Economic daily), April 23.

Xu Heping. 1992. "Zhongshi danbao shencha que bao zhaiquan luoshi (Take seriously the investigation of guarantors, ensure the fulfillment of creditors' rights)." *Shanghai nongcun jinrong* (Shanghai rural finance) 1: 42–3.

Xu Rongan. 1994. "Guanyu ruogan guojia de shuizhi yu zhengguan wenti yanjiu (Research on the tax system and collection issues in several countries)." *Jingjixue dongtai* 1: 64–9. Reprinted in *Fuyin baokan ziliao – Caizheng yu shuiwu* 4 (1994): 92–6.

Xu Tangling. 1996. *Zhongguo nongcun jinrong shi lüe* (An outline history of China's rural finance). Beijing: Zhongguo jinrong chubanshe.

Yang Chungui. 1995. "Make an Effort to Grasp the Dialectics of Socialist Modernization – Studying Comrade Jiang Zemin's 'Correctly Handle Several Major Relationships in the Socialist Modernization Drive'." *Renmin ribao* (People's daily), November 6. Translated in *Foreign Broadcast Information Service Daily Report – China*, December 15, p. 17.

Yang, Dali L. *Calamity and Reform in China: State, Rural Society, and Institutional Change Since the Great Leap Famine.* Stanford: Stanford University Press.

Yang Xiong. 1988. "Chengjiaoxing xiangzhen qiye moshi – Hujiao moshi (Suburban rural enterprise models – The suburban Shanghai model)." In *Xiangzhen qiye moshi yanjiu* (Research on rural enterprise models), ed. Chen Jiyuan and Xia Defang, 236–55. Beijing: Zhongguo shehui kexue chubanshe.

Ye Jianping. 1996. "Xiangzhen qiye bei zhong fu ya wanyao (Rural enterprises are bent low by heavy burdens)." *Jingji cankao bao* (Economic reference newspaper), April 18.

Yi, Gang. 1994. *Money, Banking, and Financial Markets in China.* Boulder: Westview Press.

Young, Susan. 1989. "Policy, Practice and the Private Sector in China." *Australian Journal of Chinese Affairs* 21(June): 57–80.

———. 1995. *Private Business and Economic Reform in China.* Armonk: M. E. Sharpe.

Yu Guoyao and Li Yandong. 1989. "Dangqian xiangzhen qiye mianlin de zhuyao wenti – Jiangsusheng xiangzhen qiye de diaocha yu yanjiu (The main problems facing township- and village-run enterprises today)." *Nongye jingji wenti* (Problems of agricultural economics) 10: 22–6.

Yuan, Enzhen, ed. 1987. *Wenzhou moshi yu fuyu zhi lu* (The Wenzhou model and the road to affluence). Shanghai: Shanghai shehui kexueyuan chubanshe.

Yueqing sishi nian 1949–1989 (Forty years in Yueqing 1949–1989). 1989. Yueqing: Yueqing xian tongjiju.

"Yueqing shi gufenzhi shiqinian fazhan toushi (A perspective on seventeen years of development of the shareholding system in Yueqing)." 1996. Mimeo.

Yueqing tongji nianjian (Yueqing statistical yearbook). Annual. N.p.

"Zai woxian qiye gaizhi huiyishang de jianghua (Speech to the conference on reforming the enterprise system in my county)." 1995. Mimeo, June 16.

Zelin, Madeleine. 1991. "The Structure of the Chinese Economy During the Qing Period: Some Thoughts on the 150th Anniversary of the Opium War." In *Perspectives on Modern China: Four Anniversaries*, ed. Kenneth Lieberthal, Joyce Kallgren, Roderick MacFarquhar, and Frederic Wakeman. Armonk: M. E. Sharpe.

Zhang Gensheng et al. 1987. "Wenzhou moshi yu ruogan zhengce wenti (The Wenzhou model and several policy issues)." In *Wenzhou moshi de lilun tansuo* (A theoretical exploration of the Wenzhou model), ed. Lin Bai et al., 20–35. Nanning: Guangxi renmin chubanshe.

Zhang Houyi and Qin Shaoxiang. 1989. "Baiwan zichan siying qiye fazhan xianzhuang wenti ji qi duice (Present problems and Solutions in the development of million asset private enterprises)." *Jingji yanjiu cankao ziliao* 39. Reprinted in *Fuyin baokan ziliao – Jingji tizhi gaige* (Reprinted periodical materials – Economic system reform) 6 (1989): 59–67.

Zhang Jianhong. 1988. "Fada nongye diqu xiangzhen qiye moshi – Sunan moshi (Rural enterprise models in developed agricultural regions – The Sunan model)." In *Xiangzhen qiye moshi yanjiu* (Research on rural enterprise models), ed. Chen Jiyuan and Xia Defang. Beijing: Zhongguo shehui kexue chubanshe.

Zhang Liuzheng, ed. 1990. *Zhongguo nongcun jingji fazhan tansuo* (An exploration of China's rural economic development). Beijing: Zhongguo jingji chubanshe.

Zhang Renshou and Li Hong. 1990a. "Wenzhou moshi (The Wenzhou model)." In *Zhongguo nongcun jingji fazhan tansuo* (An exploration of China's rural economic development), ed. Zhang Liuzheng, 88–179. Beijing: Zhongguo jingji chubanshe.

1990b. *Wenzhou moshi yanjiu* (Research on the Wenzhou model). Beijing: Zhongguo shehui kexue chubanshe.

Zhang, Weiguo. 1993. Public lecture, University of Michigan, Center for Chinese Studies, Ann Arbor, April 13.

Zhao Ziyang. 1987. "Advance along the Road of Socialism with Chinese Characteristics." *Beijing Review* (November): 23–49.

Zhejiang tongji nianjian (Zhejiang statistical yearbook). Annual. Beijing: Zhongguo tongji chubanshe.

"Zhengque chuli sange guanxi shixian caizheng chixu zengshou (Correctly tackle the three relations and realize continued increases in fiscal income)." 1989. *Caizheng* (Public finance) 6: 21–23.

Zhili jingji huanjing zhengdun jingji shixu quanmian shenhua gaige dang zhongyang guowuyuan youguan zhengce fagui, diyiji (CCP Central Committee and State Council policies and regulations regarding bringing the economic environment under control, rectifying the economic order, and comprehensively deepening reform, vol. 1). 1990. Beijing: Dadi chubanshe.

Zhili zhengdun shenhua gaige zhengce fagui xuanbian (Selected policies and laws on rectification and deepening of reform). 1990. Beijing: Zhongguo caizheng jingji chubanshe.

Zhongguo baiming caizheng da xian (China's top one hundred revenue-generating counties). 1991. Beijing: Zhongguo tongji chubanshe.

Zhongguo de siying jingji – Xianzhuang, wenti, qianjing (China's private economy – Current status, problems, and prospects). 1989. Beijing: Zhongguo shehui kexue chubanshe.

Zhongguo nongcun: Zhengce yanjiu beiwanglu (China's countryside: Policy research memorandum), vol. 1. 1989. Beijing: Nongye chubanshe.

Zhongguo nongcun: Zhengce yanjiu beiwanglu (China's countryside: Policy research memorandum), vol. 2. 1991. Beijing: Nongye chubanshe.

Zhongguo nongcun jinrong tongji, 1979–1989 (China's rural financial statistics, 1979–1989). 1991. Beijing: Zhongguo tongji chubanshe.

Zhongguo nongcun tongji nianjian (China's rural statistical yearbook). Annual. Beijing: Zhongguo tongji chubanshe.

Zhongguo nongye nianjian (China's agricultural yearbook). Annual. Beijing: Nongye chubanshe.

Zhongguo renshi nianjian (China personnel yearbook). Annual. Beijing: Zhongguo renshi chubanshe.

Zhongguo tongji nianjian (China statistical yearbook). Annual. Beijing: Zhongguo tongji chubanshe.

Zhongguo xiangzhen qiye nianjian (China's rural enterprise yearbook). Annual. Beijing: Nongye chubanshe.

Zhongguo xiangzhen qiye tongji zhaiyao (China's rural enterprise statistical abstract). Annual. Beijing: Nongye chubanshe.

"*Zhonghua renmin gongheguo xiangcun jiti suoyouzhi qiye tiaoli*" *xuexi zhidao* ("People's Republic of China regulations on township and village collectively-owned enterprises" study guide). 1991. Beijing: Renmin chubanshe.

Bibliography

Zhou Erliu, and Zhang Yulin, eds. 1994. *Zhongguo chengxiang xietiao fazhan yanjiu* (Research on China's coordinated urban–rural development). Hong Kong: Oxford University Press.

Zhou Lufang. 1990. "Jiaqiang geti shuishou zhengguan gongzuo de jidian sikao (Several thoughts on strengthening tax collection work in the private sector)." *Shuiwu yanjiu* (Tax research) 1: 43–4.

Zhou Qiren and Hu Zhuangjun. 1987. " 'Fuzhai jingying' de hongguan xiaoying (The macro effects of 'chronic indebtedness')." *Fazhan yanjiu tongxun* (Development research news) 54 (May).

Zhou Xiaochuan and Zhu Li. 1987. "China's Banking System: Current Status, Perspective on Reform." *Journal of Comparative Economics* 11.

Zhu Longming and Yin Hua. 1992. "Xiangzhen qiye 'gufen hezuo zhi' de shijian he xiaoguo – Dui sanjia qiye de diaocha (The practice and results of the 'cooperative shareholding system' in rural enterprises – An investigation of three firms)." *Jiading jingji* (Jiading economy) 4 (April): 7–9.

Zweig, David. 1989. *Agrarian Radicalism in China, 1968–1981.* Cambridge: Harvard University Press.

——— 1992. "Urbanizing Rural China." In *Bureaucracy, Politics, and Decision Making in Post-Mao China*, ed. Kenneth G. Lieberthal and David M. Lampton. Berkeley: University of California Press.

——— 1997. *Freeing China's Farmers: Rural Restructuring in the Reform Era.* Armonk: M. E. Sharpe.

Zysman, John. 1977. *Political Strategies for Industrial Order: State, Market, and Industry in France.* Berkeley: University of California Press.

Index

Administrative Litigation Law, 273
Africa: and predatory state model, 7
agents *See* principal–agent relations.
agricultural producers cooperative,
    47–8
agriculture: and mechanization, 47; and
    rural industrial development, 42, 53; in
    Songjiang, 64; in Wuxi, 57–8, 61;
    Yueqing, 67
Agriculture Bank, 61, 144, 227–8; and
    attempts to limit credit, 236–8, 240;
    commercialization of, 287; and loans to
    private enterprises, 258–61. *See also*
    credit allocation.
Alchian, Armen, 124
All-China Federation of Industry and
    Commerce, 262–3
Asian financial crisis of 1997, 9
asset mobility, 37

Bank of China, 227–8. *See also* credit
    allocation.
bank loans: *See* credit allocation.
banking reforms: of 1993, 29, 287
bargaining power: of state and
    constituents, 20. *See also* private
    enterprise: bargaining power.
Bates, Robert, 16–17
Blecher, Mare, 13
Boone, Catherine, 11–12
bounded rationality, 18, 24, 183, 267, 297–9
budget constraints: softness in, 12, 120,
    226, 257–8, 295; hardness of, 266, 282,
    289, 293
budgetary revenue, 14, 23; 61, 144, 279;
    central government share of, 282;
    sources of, 79–84; and tax evasion, 198.
    See also nonbudgetary funds.

cadre evaluation system, 21, 25, 72, 73,
    100–18; and credit allocation, 234, 238;

and political and economic incentives,
    268–70, 296
cadres: collective, 83, 107; state, 83, 104
capital market, 240, 263. *See also* credit
    allocation.
capital mobility, 182
case study: design, 29, 121, 225; test of
    findings from, 220–4
chaebol, 8
Chaudhry, Kiren Aziz, 9, 196
Chen, Chih-jou, 150
Chengdu Conference, 47
Chenjiaqiao Township, 94
Chinese Academy of Social Sciences,
    199
Chuansha County, 30
Chuansha Printing and Dyeing Machinery
    Factory, 157–8
Civil Procedure Law, 273
cognitive psychology, xvi; and rational
    choice theory, 17, 183
collective enterprises, 23–4, 28; and
    nonbank sources of credit, 250–7; as
    dominant pattern of ownership in Wuxi
    and Shanghai, 123–4; fakes, 145–7;
    incentives for differential treatment of,
    96–9; political intervention in: 115–16,
    117, 118; and township as corporation
    model, 118–120. *See also* individually
    contracted collectives; township and
    village enterprises.
commune and brigade enterprises (CBEs):
    and credit allocation, 61–2, 63–4; during
    Cultural Revolution, 52; and links with
    urban industry, 59–61; and rural
    industrialization, 41–2, 47, 48–9; and ties
    with urban factories, 51; in Yueqing,
    70
complementarities, 3, 270, 293, 299
constitutional amendments. *See* political-
    legal environment.

Construction Bank of China, 227–8. *See also* credit allocation.
contracts, managerial, 108–9
cooperative shareholding enterprises, 121–2, 134–5, 136, 147
corporatism, 24, 190–1
corruption, 117; and bribes, 261
county-run enterprises: and rural industrialization, 53, 60–2, 65–6, 67
credible commitment: defined, 72; of state to fiscal contracts, 72, 74, 94, 217; of state to property rights, 122–3, 153–5, 163–5, 173, 271–2
credit: nonbank sources of, 250–7, 261–3; dependence on promoted by township government, 245–50; and fiscal reform, 281–2
credit allocation, 3, 4, 23, 28, 38, 44, 51, 58, 61, 100, 271, 296; and administrative controls, 235–8; and bad debts, 244–5; and commune and brigade enterprises, 62, 66; and credit ratings, 239–40; effect of cadre evaluation on, 110, 116, 117, 118, 234; and guarantors and collateral requirements, 90, 242–4; and intervention by local officials, 234, 263–4; and matching funds requirement, 240–2; and private enterprise, 144, 148, 149, 258–63; and shareholding cooperatives, 167–8
Cultural Revolution, 51, 52, 69

daizheng method: of taxation in Wenzhou, 185–8, 274; precursors, 188–9, 275
Dazhai Commune, 59
debt: of township and village enterprises, 246–7, 281
democratic appraisal: and taxation in Wenzhou, 189
Demsetz, Harold, 124
Deng Xiaoping, 40; impact of southern tour on private property legislation, 38, 168, 177
dependency theory, 5
depreciation funds, 52, 90, 246
developmental state: and statist theory, 7, 11; in theoretical debate, 13, 15
domestic state-collective joint ventures, 35
Dongtan Town, 205, 212, 239, 256–7: indebtedness of, 246–7; and noncollection of bad debts, 244–5; and political interference in loan decisions, 250; and private enterprise, 142, 261; and tax reform, 284

East Asian states: and state autonomy, 7
"eating in separate kitchens." *See* fiscal reforms.

economic committee: in Wuxi, 57
economic conglomerates, 76. *See also* township and village enterprises.
Economic Policy Research Center, 148–9
employment: in rural enterprises, 41, 56, 115–16, 202, 276; in shareholding cooperatives, 169
enterprise development: legacy of, 22, 42
Evans, Peter, 7–8
evolutionary economic theory, 20, 267, 297–9
exactions. *See* fees.
extrabudgetary revenue, 79, 84, 96, 279. *See also* nonbudgetary funds.

factor endowments, 46
factor markets, 22, 25, 288; and property rights, 125–6, 166–7, 266, 272, 292
fees: payment of by rural enterprises, 85, 92, 97; and reliance on bank loans, 245–6, 247; unsanctioned, 89, 92
Fei Hsiao T'ung, 53, 58, 60
Fifth Plenum of the Fourteenth Central Committee: and private enterprise, 139
Fifth Plenum of the Thirteenth Central Committee: and private enterprise, 138
First Five-Year Plan, 46–7
fiscal contracts, 25; impact on taxation of, 207, 213–19; lack of credible commitment to, 94–5; replaced by tax assignment system, 280–1
fiscal reforms, 38–9, 75–9, 177, 226, 293, 295, 296; and banking system; 287; impetus for, 277–80; and increasing marketization, 288–89, 198; at local level, 280–5; and "off-budget" revenues, 285–7; and privatization, 289–90; and tax reform, 284
"five small industries," 50, 51, 52
foreign capital, 257
Four Cleans Campaign, 50
Fourth Five-Year Plan, 52
Fourth Plenum of the Thirteenth Central Committee: and private enterprise, 137–8

ganbu. *See* cadres.
gentihu. *See* household firms.
Gerschenkron, Alexander, 7
grants: to rural enterprises, 44, 56, 61, 64, 66; to townships, 83
Great Leap Forward, 40, 46–9; and industrialization in Songjiang County, 63–4; in Wuxi County, 59; in Yueqing County, 68
guarantor: of bank loans, 90
gufen hezuo qiye. *See* shareholding cooperatives.

handicrafts: industry, 45; cooperatives, 47, 49; in Songjiang, 63; in Wuxi, 56; in Yueqing, 68–9
Hirschman, Albert, 154
historical institutionalism theory, 17
household firms, 36, 134, 147, 148; and taxation, 189; legal status, 152
Hualing Town, 240, 245: impact of Cultural Revolution, 69; nonbudgetary revenue, 86–7, 278; and shareholding cooperatives, 166, 169; and taxation of private sector, 182, 185–9
Huang, Yasheng, 13–14
Huang, Philip, 32, 45–6, 53, 56, 65
Huayang Commune, 65
Hussain, Athar, 23

ideological environment, 22. *See also* political-legal environment.
incentives, 16, 21, 72–3; dysfunctionality of, 110–15; to evade taxes, 93–6
India, 9
indirect taxes: evasion of, 207
individual household firms. See household firms.
individually contracted collectives: and institutional innovations, 36, 208–13
Industrial and Commercial Bank of China, 227–8. *See also* credit allocation.
industrial corporation, 90–1; as loan guarantor, 242–3, 244
industrial output: effect of cadre evaluation on, 111–15
industry bureau: in Wuxi, 57, 61, 139
information: asymmetric, 19; imperfect, 12, 20, 23–4, 115; and revenue extraction, 3–4, 273, 274; sources of, 51
information costs, 23: and taxation of private enterprise, 176, 183–5, 188, 195; and township and village enterprises, 176, 197. *See also* transaction costs.
institutional economics, 10, 18, 297
involution: state 13; and economic development, 46

Jiading County: and cadre evaluation, 105, 114; and tax evasion incentives, 95
Jiang Zemin, 290, 292
Jiangsu: fiscal contract compared to Shanghai, 213–19; and padded wage rolls, 203–4; and revenue extraction, 278

Kenya, 16
Kohli, Atul, 9
Korea, 7–9
Kornai, Janos, 12
Kunshan: and tax evasion incentives, 95, 96

land: access to, 167. *See also* factor markets.
legal environment, 22, 266. *See also* political-legal environment.
legal reforms, 29, 272–3
Levi, Margaret, 23
levies: *See* fees.
lianying qiye. See state-collective joint ventures.
Lin, Nan, 150
litergical tax management, 194, 195–6
Litwack, John, 125, 149, 151
Liu Xirong, 159
Liu, Yia-Ling, 132
loans. *See* credit allocation
local officials, 12: incentives for behavior of, 21
local state corporatism, 11–12, 118–20
Luhang Town: and cadre evaluation, 108; and credit for private enterprise, 261; and tax exemptions, 200

Malu Commune: Zhou Enlai's visit to, 50
Mann, Susan, 194
markets: completeness of as constraints on property rights, 139–42, 288–9, 292. *See also* factor markets; product markets
material supply bureau: in Wuxi, 48, 57, 61
Meilin Town, 94, 243
Migdal, Joel, 10, 15, 225
Ministry of Agriculture, 53, 216
Minsheng Bank: and credit for private enterprise, 262
modernization theory, 5
monitoring: of enterprise costs and income, 184, 187; through private entrepreneurs' association, 190–2; and provincial regulatory environments, 213, 214–15; of revenue extraction, 25, 28, 219, 225, 270. *See also* information costs; transaction costs.
moral hazard problem, 111

Nantang Township: and cadre evaluation, 107, 108, 114; and fiscal contracts, 208, 218; and nonbank sources of credit, 254; and private enterprise taxes, 98; and public goods, 268–9; and revenue sources, 80, 83, 86–7, 89, 90; and tax evasion, 94, 95, 200, 205.
National Work Conference on Finance and Banking, 51
Naughton, Barry, 13, 46, 279, 288
Nee, Victor, 125, 150
neoliberal theory, 5, 6; and property rights, 2, 295

new institutionalism, 10, 18
Ningbo: compared to Wenzhou, 68
nonbudetary funds, 14, 75; and fiscal
   reforms, 277, 278; sources of, 84–90; and
   tax evasion, 198, 200. *See also* budgetary
   revenue; off-budget revenues.
North China Agricultural Conference
   (1970), 51–2, 58
North, Douglass, 19, 115, 124, 149, 151, 153

off-budget revenues, 14, 23, 285–7; and
   state–local relations, 279, 280, 285–6

party committee: in Wuxi, 57
party membership: for private investors,
   165
path dependence, 3, 267, 270, 299
Pei, Minxin, 11
People's Bank of China, 227; and indirect
   monetary controls, 229, 236
Perkins, Dwight, 33–4
Pierson, Paul, 275
planned economy: legacy of, 178–82
Polanyi, Karl, 296
political-legal environment, 125, 133–9,
   271, 290–3
predatory state: and revenue extraction,
   14; and statist theory, 7, 11; in
   theoretical debate, 13, 15
principal–agent relations, 19, 25, 225,
   265
private banks, 262
private enterprise: and access to bank
   loans, 258–63; bargaining power, 176–7,
   182, 185, 193, 274; and clientelist
   networks, 150–1; forms of, 145–8;
   incentives for differential treatment of,
   96–9; political and legal environment
   for, 133–9; and political-legal reform,
   290–293; and sanctity of contracts, 150;
   and state plans, 140–1; in Wenzhou,
   123–4, 144–50; in Wuxi and Songjiang,
   142–4
private enterprise accounting station: and
   individually contracted collectives, 211;
   and taxation in Shanghai, 189–93, 275;
   precursors, 193–6
private entrepreneurs' association, 24,
   190–1, 193, 195, 196, 262
private firms (*siying qiye*), 152; and access
   to credit, 168
privatization, 3, 5, 266, 289–90, 296
product markets, 22, 25, 288;
   competitiveness of, 219, 288; and
   property rights, 125–6, 165–6, 266, 272,
   292
production permits, 166
profit taxes: evasion, 207

property rights, 37, 145–50; defined, 19,
   124; forms of, 35–6; evolution of, 270–3;
   and privatization, 5; sociological
   approaches to, 122; spatial pattern of,
   123–4; theory of, 124–6. *See also*
   credible commitment.
province: regulatory environment of. *See*
   Jiangsu; Shanghai.
public finance bureau: establishment of at
   township level, 77; in Songjiang, 63; as
   lender, 254; as loan guarantor, 243, 254
public goods: defined, 72; provision of, 14,
   21, 72, 78, 89, 104, 116, 201, 202–3, 226,
   276, 296

Qing period: taxation policy in, 194–6

ratchet effect, 110
rational choice model, xvi, 17–18, 97, 297
Rawski, Thomas, 45
reform: *See* fiscal reforms; legal reforms.
regression analysis: *See* taxation, ratio.
regulatory environment: at provincial
   level, xvii, 213–219
resource endowments, 3, 121, 270
revenue extraction, 297; evolution of local
   institutions for, 273–7; and fiscal reform,
   277–80; imperative of, 18, 21, 72, 176;
   innovation in 182, 196, 198, 208, 274–5,
   277–8; monitoring of, 25, 28, 219, 225,
   270; and property rights, 2, 3, 19, 20–5,
   28–9, 35, 38, 177; and research plan, xvii.
   See also taxation; tax evasion; profit
   taxes.
revenue-sharing: contracts, 78, 79–80, 83;
   system, 72, 73, 74, 75–9. *See also* fiscal
   contracts.
Riskin, Carl, 40
Rural Credit Cooperatives, 228–9; and
   attempts to limit credit, 237, 238; and
   bad debts of township and village
   enterprises, 245; and loans to private
   enterprises, 258–60
rural industrialization: and cadre
   evaluation, 104, 107–10; incentives for
   promotion of, 79–93; and research
   design, 36; and rustication, 50–1; as
   source of township revenue, 99–100;
   state support of, 44–6, 50–1; and
   theoretical debate, 11; in Wuxi and
   Shanghai, 2, 33–5, 177
Russia: compared with China, 296
rustication: as resource for rural
   industrialization, 50–1, 59, 60, 65–6

sales: under reporting of as tax evasion,
   205
Saudi Arabia, 9, 10

savings deposits: and rural enterprise
development, 229, 230–3
school-run enterprises, 200–1
selection pressures, 20, 298
self-raised revenue, 79, 84, 85–9
self-reliance, 40, 42, 44, 50
self-sufficiency, 42, 62
Shanghai Conference, 48
Shanghai County, 30, 47
Shanghai Municipality: and collective
property, 33; dominance of public
ownership, 5; and fiscal contract, 25;
fiscal contract compared to Jiangsu,
213–19; and padded wage rolls, 203;
and private enterprise, 262, 274, 275;
and property rights, 22, 24, 271; and
revenue extraction, 91–2, 85–6, 278; and
township and village enterprises, 275–6.
See also Nantang Township; Jiading
County.
Shanghai Sea Transport Bureau, 61
shareholding cooperatives, 35–6, 152; and
access to factor inputs, 166–8; and access
to markets, 165–6; and creation of
credible committment, 163–5;
government-run, 155–9; predominance
of in Yueqing, 167–73; private, 159–63;
and privatization, 289–90; and property
rights, 272; as source of capital, 255–6
Shue, Vivienne: and localism, 12–13
Simon, Herbert, 17
siren qiye. See private enterprise.
siying qiye. See private enterprise.
Siu, Helen, 13
Sixth Plenum of the Eighth Central
Committee, 47
SOE: *See* state-owned enterprises
Songjiang County, 63–6, 70–1: and banking
reform, 287; and budget constraints, 257;
and cadre evaluation, 108, 114; and fiscal
contracts, 208; industrial output of
collective enterprises, 127; industrial
development compared with Wuxi and
Yueqing, 40–2, 44; and local
shareholding cooperatives, 36, 158, 173;
and privatization of township and
village enterprises, 289, 290
Songyang Town: and credit, 239, 245–7,
250; and collective enterprises, 210–11,
245–6; and mobilization of capital,
255–6; and private enterprise, 143, 182,
189–96, 278; and revenue extraction,
275; and tax evasion, 95, 199
state, 5: definition of, 1; economic model
of, 18
State Administration of Taxation, 183
state autonomy, 7; and state capacity, 8, 9,
10, 15

State Council Development Research
Center, 183
state-collective joint ventures, 36
state-owned enterprises (SOEs):
and political intervention, 12,
287
state penetration: and township and
villege enterprises, 12–14
state plans, 139–42
state-society theory, 10, 15–16, 17
statist theory, xvi, 5, 6–11
Steinfeld, Edward, 11, 42
Steinmo, Sven, 17
Stern, Nicholas, 23
Su, Sijin, 150
Svejnar, Jan, 127

Taiwan: impact on Wenzhou of proximity
to, 68
tax arrears, 201, 254
taxation, 95, 220–1; and fiscal contracts,
216; institutional shortcomings, 179–82,
211; ratio, 220–4; reform, 280–5, 292; of
rural industry, 79–80, 90; unitary system,
75, 78
tax capacity: defined, 220; operationalized,
220–1
tax effort: defined, 220; operationalized,
221–2
tax evasion, xvii, 4, 25, 28, 74, 197, 282; in
collective sector, 197–208; incentives,
93–6; by private entrepreneurs, 183, 191.
See also revenue extraction.
Tenth Plenum of the Eighth Central
Committee, 49
Thelen, Kathleen, 17
Third Plenum of the Thirteenth Central
Committee, 177
Third Plenum of the Fourteenth Central
Committee: and reform, 28–9, 177,
287
township and village enterprises (TVEs),
293, 295, 296; and credit, 238–58; and
fiscal reform, 285–6; integration into
state plans, 140–2; and links with urban
enterprises, 57, 59–60, 65; and local state
intervention, 11, 12; and marketization,
288; political and legal support for,
133–4; and privatization, 289–90; as
shareholding cooperatives, 156–9; as
source of township revenue, 14, 35, 75,
80, 84, 91–3; and tax avoidance, 198,
199–201; and tax evasion, 201–5; and
unity of economic and political power,
270–1, 276, 286
transaction costs: and property rights, 23,
124, 176; and revenue extraction, 19,
182, 274–6, 297

unfunded mandates, 268, 277
urban–rural linkages: absence of in
  Yueqing, 68; in Songjiang, 65, 66; in
  Wuxi, 57, 60

Van de Walle, Nicholas, 176

wages: and tax evasion, 203–4, 217–19; and
  bank loans, 239–40
Walder, Andrew, 14
"walking on two legs," 40, 47, 51–2
Wang, Shaoguang, 194
Wank, David, 150
Weber, Max, 194
Weingast, Barry, 154, 163–4
welfare enterprises, 200
Wenzhou: and private enterprise, 130–3,
  144–50, 264, 274, 275; and private
  shareholding cooperatives, 159–65; and
  property rights, 22, 24, 32, 33, 130–2, 271,
  272; and taxation, 185–8. *See also*
  Yueqing County.
Wong, Christine, 42, 52, 78, 292
Woo, Josephine, 127
World Bank, 28, 58, 115, 117, 120, 127–8,
  133, 143–4, 179, 246
Wuhan, 48, 70–1; cadre evaluation, 115;
  and collective enterprises, 32, 33, 127;
  impact of state plan, 140; and

industrialization, 40–2, 44, 53, 56–62; and
  private enterprise, 142–4; as research
  site, 30; and shareholding cooperatives,
  173; and tax avoidance, 200–1; and
  taxation under PRC, 194–5; and
  unsanctioned fees, 92
Wuhan Steel Factory, 61
Wuxi: and property rights, 126–30, 271;
  and township and village enterprises,
  275–6, 289, 290

Yemen, 9
Yueqing County, 30, 165, 166, 167–73;
  industrial development, 40–2, 44, 67–70,
  71; and loan collateral, 244; and output of
  collective enterprises, 127; and
  privatization, 290; and taxation, 185–8,
  223–4
Yueqing Sewing Machine Factory, 69

Zaire, 7
Zelin, Madeleine, 45
zili gengsheng. See self-reliance.
Zhejiang Academy of Social Sciences, 132,
  149
Zhejiang Province: regulatory
  environment, 221–4
Zhou Enlai, 50
Zhu Rongi, 287